Advanced Research in Asian Economic Studies – Vol. 3

International Economic Integration and Asia

Advanced Research in Asian Economic Studies **(ISSN: 1793-0944)**

Series Editor: Manoranjan DUTTA
(Rutgers, The State University of New Jersey, USA)

Published

Vol. 1 Asian Economic Cooperation in the New Millennium: China's Economic Presence
Edited by Calla WIEMER (East Asian Institute, National University of Singapore), Heping Cao (Peking University, China)

Vol. 2 China's Industrial Revolution and Economic Presence
by Manoranjan Dutta (Rutgers, The State University of New Jersey, USA)

Vol. 3 International Economic Integration and Asia
Edited by Michael G Plummer & Erik Jones (Johns Hopkins University SAIS-Bologna, Italy)

Advanced Research in Asian Economic Studies – Vol. 3

International Economic Integration and Asia

edited by

Michael G Plummer

Erik Jones

Johns Hopkins University
SAIS-Bologna, Italy

World Scientific

NEW JERSEY • LONDON • SINGAPORE • BEIJING • SHANGHAI • HONG KONG • TAIPEI • CHENNAI

Published by

World Scientific Publishing Co. Pte. Ltd.
5 Toh Tuck Link, Singapore 596224
USA office: 27 Warren Street, Suite 401-402, Hackensack, NJ 07601
UK office: 57 Shelton Street, Covent Garden, London WC2H 9HE

Library of Congress Cataloging-in-Publication Data
International economic integration and Asia / edited by Michael G. Plummer & Erik Jones.
p. cm. -- (Advanced research in Asian economic studies, 1793-0944 ; v. 3)
Includes bibliographical references and index.
ISBN 981-256-757-7
1. ASEAN. 2. International economic integration. 3. Asia--Economic integration. 4. Asia--Economic policy. I. Plummer, Michael G., 1959– II. Jones, Erik.

HC412.I5235 2006
337.1'5--dc22

2006050158

British Library Cataloguing-in-Publication Data
A catalogue record for this book is available from the British Library.

Printed in Singapore by World Scientific Printers (S) Pte Ltd

In memory of

Robert H. Evans
1937–2005

Director
SAIS Bologna Center
1992–2003

PREFACE

This project was born out of a desire to combine the study of politics and economics, Asia and Europe. Although the focus is on the economics of Asian regionalism, we have endeavored to make sure that the volume is as interdisciplinary and interregional as possible. In his role as director of the SAIS Bologna Center, Professor Robert H. Evans gave us the support we needed to get this project off the ground. It is only just, therefore, that we dedicate our efforts in his memory.

Our task in preparing this volume has been made all the easier by our contributors, who have been very generous in taking the time to respond to our suggestions and to address issues raised by one another. Without their support, this project would not have been possible. They have and deserve our deepest thanks.

We would also like to thank some of the many students from the SAIS Bologna Center who helped us at every stage in the development of these essays. Daniel Gould, Fiona Stewart, and Stefanie Weitz were particularly important at the start of our work in 2003. Sarah Bignami and Sara Giannozzi played critical roles at the end.

Finally, and most important, we would like to thank the editor of the *Journal of Asian Economics*, Professor Jan Dutta, for his support and encouragement. The usual disclaimer applies.

Erik Jones
Bologna

Michael G. Plummer
Honolulu

June 2006

CONTENTS

LIST OF FIGURES

LIST OF TABLES

LIST OF ABBREVIATIONS

ABB	Arellano, Bond and Bover's estimator
ABF	Asian Bond Fund
ABMI	Asian Bond Market Initiative
ACFTA	ASEAN-China Free Trade Area
ACU	Asian Currency Unit
ADB	Asian Development Bank
ADF	Augmented Dickey-Fuller
AEC	ASEAN Economic Community
AFTA	ASEAN Free-Trade Area
AIA	ASEAN Investment Area
AIC	Akaike Information Criterion
AIP	ASEAN Industrial Project
AMF	Asian Monetary Fund
AMU	Arab Maghreb Union
APEC	Asia Pacific Economic Cooperation
ASA	ASEAN Swap Arrangement
ASEAN	Association of South East Asian Nations
ASEAN+3	ASEAN plus China, Japan, and South Korea
ASEM	Asia-Europe Meeting
BORD	Bilateral Trade Cost—reflects border effects
BRCT	Acceding and Candidate Countries: Bulgaria, Romania, Croatia and Turkey
BSAs	Bilateral Swap Arrangements
CAP	Common Agricultural Policy
CEECs	Central and Eastern European countries
CEFTA	Central European Free Trade Area
CEPA	Closer Economic Partnership Agreement
CEPT	Common Effective Preferential Tariff
CER	Closer Economic Relations
CES	Constant Elasticity of Substitution
CET	Common External Tariffs
CET	Constant Elasticity of Transformation
CFA	Communauté Financière d'Afrique
CIS	Commonwealth of Independent States
CGE	Computable General Equilibrium
CLOB	International—Over-the-Counter Market
CMI	Chiang Mai Initiative
CPIs	Consumer Price Indices
DG	Directorate General

DGDP	Difference in Factor Endowment
EAEC	East Asian Economic Caucus
EAEG	East Asian Economic Grouping
EAFTA	East Asian Free Trade Area
EAI	Enterprise for ASEAN Initiative
ECB	European Central Bank
ECJ	European Court of Justice
ECSC	European Coal and Steel Community
EEC	European Economic Community
ECO	Economic Cooperation Organization
ECSC	European Coal and Steel Community
ECU	European Currency Unit
ELES	Extended Linear Expenditure System
EMEAP	Executives Meeting of East Asia-Pacific Central Banks
EMS	European Monetary System
EMU	European Monetary Union
EPA	Economic Partnership Agreement
ERM	Exchange Rate Mechanism
ERPD	Economic Review and Policy Dialogue
ERT	European Roundtable of Industrialists
EU	European Union
EV	Equivalent Variation
FDI	Foreign Direct Investment
FEM	Fixed Effects Model
FSAP	Financial Sector Assessment Program
FTAA	Free Trade Area of the Americas
GAFTA	Greater Arab Free Trade Area
GATT	General Agreement on Tariffs and Trade
GDDS	General Data Dissemination System
GDP	Gross Domestic Product
GMP	Global Mediterranean Policy
HDI	Human Development Index
HICP	Harmonized Index of Consumer Prices
HTM	Hausman and Taylor model
ICSEAD	International Center for the Study of the East Asian Development
IMF	International Monetary Fund
IT	Information Technology
KLSE	Kuala Lumpur Stock Exchange
JSEPA	Agreement between Japan and the Republic of Singapore for a New-Age Economic Partnership
LANG	Common Language Between Two Countries

MEFTA	Middle-East Free Trade Area
MERCOSUR	Southern Common Market
MFA	Multi-Fibre Arrangement
MFG	Manila Framework Group
NAFTA	North American Free Trade Agreement
NIEs	Newly Industrialized Economics
NMS	New EU Member Countries
NTBs	Non Tariff Barriers
NTT	New Trade Theory
OCA	Optimal Currency Area
ODA	Official Development Assistance
OECD	Organization for Economic Cooperation and Development
REG	Denotes the Regional Arrangements between the EU and Mediterranean Countries
REM	Random Effects Model
RTAs	Regional Trade Arrangements
ROSCs	Reports on the Observance of Standards and Codes
SAARC	South Asian Association for Regional Cooperation
SBC	Schwartz Bayesian Criterion
SEA	Single European Act
SES	Stock Exchange of Singapore
SDDS	Special Data Dissemination Standard
SGDP	Country Size
SGP	Stability and Growth Pact
SIMI	Similarity in Country Size
SPARTECA	South Pacific Regional Trade and Economic Cooperation Agreement
SMP	Single Market Program
TAC	Treaty of Amity and Cooperation
TIFAs	Trade and Investment Framework Agreements
UNCTAD	United Nations Conference on Trade and Development
UNDP	United Nations Development Program
VAR	Vector Autoregression
WTO	World Trade Organization

CONTRIBUTORS

James Angresano *Department of Economics, Albertson College of Idaho*

Maggi Brigham *Department of Sociology and Political Science, Norwegian University of Science and Technology*

Reid W. Click *Elliot School of International Affairs, George Washington University*

Mary Farrell *Centre d'Etudes et de Recherches Internationales, Sciences-Po*

Erik Jones *SAIS Bologna Center, Johns Hopkins University*

Masahiro Kawai *Institute of Social Science, University of Tokyo*

Hiro Lee *Osaka School of International Public Policy, Osaka University*

Jonathon W. Moses *Department of Sociology and Political Science, Norwegian University of Science and Technology*

Craig Parsons *Department of Political Science, University of Oregon*

Nicolas Péridy *Faculté des Sciences économiques et de Gestion, University of Nantes*

Michael G. Plummer *SAIS Bologna Center, Johns Hopkins University*

Richard Pomfret *School of Economics, University of Adelaide*

J. David Richardson *Maxwell School, Syracuse University*

Sergio Rossi *Department of Political Economy, University of Fribourg*

Dominique van der Mensbrugghe *The World Bank*

INTRODUCTION

INTERNATIONAL ECONOMIC INTEGRATION AND ASIA: AN OVERVIEW

Michael G. Plummer and Erik Jones

The trend towards regionalism in Asia is no longer particularly new. True, the ASEAN Free-Trade Area (AFTA), formed in 1992, was the only major formal economic integration accord in East Asia in the 1990s, and even AFTA has not been completely implemented yet, with the newer ASEAN Member Countries still having a long way to go. In fact, there have been only a few relatively small accords (such as the Japan-Singapore and Singapore-United States free-trade areas) that have actually been substantially in effect since 2002. But no doubt this was the calm before the storm. Now a plethora of regional accords have either been signed or are in the works. And these accords are no longer the minor bilateral agreements that have been much debated over the past few years; some are major arrangements indeed. The ASEAN-China agreement of November 2004 is one example. Others range from ambitious proposals coming out of Japan to ASEAN+3 (that is, ASEAN, China, Japan, and South Korea) initiatives to smaller free-trade areas such as the Thailand-Australia free-trade area.

Certainly, bilateral and regional accords, consistent with the letter of the WTO but denounced by many as being against its spirit, are reshaping the emerging commercial policy of East Asia and will constitute an important part of its future. Such accords are also moving beyond the traditional confines of real-sector integration to embrace financial cooperation as well. In fact, the link between trade and finance has become increasingly appreciated in the international economic literature. History has taught that the failure to allow sufficiently for financial aspects of trade integration can do much to undermine the sustainability of an agreement.

In this book, which is a compilation of works of some of the most influential scholars in the area of Asian economic integration and global economic cooperation, we have two major goals: (1) to consider the implications for Asia of global bilateral and plurilateral accords, both within and outside of Asia; and (2) to identify some of the key lessons that regionalism outside of Asia, particularly in Europe, may hold for the fledgling Asian economic integration trend. In approaching the topic of East Asian regionalism in this way, we attempt to augment our understanding of what the trend implies, suggest how it can best be directed, evaluate the economic costs and benefits of various agreements in the works, and draw lessons from the rest of the world in configuring the process.

In this introduction, we present a quick review of economic integration in East Asia (Section 1), followed in Section 2 by a brief review of lessons that might be gleaned from the oft-cited European experience, as well as a statistical overview of economic links between Europe and Asia. A synopsis of the chapters included in the volume is offered in Section 3.

An Overview of East Asian Integration[1]

There have been many excellent surveys of regional economic integration in Asia (e.g., Kawai in this volume, Naya 2002, Asian Development Bank 2002). ASEAN tends to stand at the core of Asian integration, at least from an institutional perspective. We provide in this section a brief contextual review of this evolution. As AFTA and free-trade areas (FTAs) between ASEAN Member Countries and outside partners dominate the trend towards regionalism in Asia, our focus is on ASEAN.

Briefly, we would first suggest several factors influencing the regionalism trend in East Asia that stem directly from the Asian Financial Crisis, including: (1) the obvious contagion relationships,

---

[1] This section borrows from Naya and Plummer (2005).

which demonstrated the policy externalities across countries in ASEAN and the Asian Newly Industrialized Economics (NIEs);[2] (2) major disappointment with respect to the US reaction to the Crisis, leaving the feeling of 'being in it alone together'; (3) the lack of progress in the Asia Pacific Economic Cooperation (APEC) organization in achieving closer trade and financial cooperation, as well as associated development assistance cooperation; (4) Japan's offer to create an Asian Monetary Fund during the Crisis — opposed by the IMF and the United States — gave the impression that Japan wanted to be pro-active in the region; (5) arguably, China's decision not to devalue during this period also created a sense of solidarity; (6) the 'New Miyazawa Plan,' launched in October 1998 which dedicated $30 billion to help spur recovery in East Asia (and deemed highly successful); [3] and (7) the policies promulgated by the IMF to solve the Crisis were deemed inappropriate, giving greater credibility to the 'Asian approach.'

Hence, the Crisis itself set the stage for serious and durable East Asian regionalism. There are many other internal and external forces at work that have expedited the process, such as the rise of regionalism globally and its potential negative effects on the region; the successful example of the Single Market Program in Europe and, eventually, monetary union; general pessimism regarding what can be achieved at the WTO in light of failure to move forward at the Seattle and Cancun WTO Ministerials; and the potential inherent benefits of FTAs.[4]

Table I.1 gives a chronology of the most significant Asian initiatives that have developed over time. Despite the many early agreements in ASEAN's history that were mainly political and token in nature, its first major initiative was AFTA (1992).[5] However, in true ASEAN fashion,

---

[2] The NIEs are composed of South Korea, Singapore, Taipei, China, and Hong Kong, China.

[3] Kawai, this volume.

[4] The WTO Ministerial meeting in Hong Kong in December 2005 prepared the framework for what seemed to be a possible accord under the Doha Development Agenda. However, the negotiators failed to meet their self-imposed deadline of April 2006 and at the time of this writing, no agreement is in sight.

[5] For example, the Preferential Trading Agreement (PTA), was a positive-list approach to trade liberalization with small margins of preference and limited product coverage, expanded somewhat during the 1980s but with no real impact on trade. Industrial cooperation, such as the ASEAN Industrial Project (AIP) system, never really got off the ground.

rather than commit to regional integration in sensitive areas, the specifics of AFTA were left somewhat ambiguous, with the agreement committing the ASEAN Member Countries to free trade in manufactures over a 15-year timeframe. Also, the definition of 'free trade' was loose, as it included tariffs in the range of 0-5 percent, rather than the traditional zero percent.[6] After the original agreement, ASEAN broadened the scope of goods covered by AFTA and the period of implementation has been shortened such that AFTA was technically in full effect for the original Member Countries (Indonesia, Malaysia, the Philippines, Singapore and Thailand) and Brunei Darussalam in 2004, though there continue to be transitional periods for products on the temporary exclusion lists (e.g., sensitive products such as rice and automobiles in some cases) and some country-specific implementation problems in certain areas. The original target for full implementation was 2006 for Vietnam, 2008 for Laos and Myanmar, and 2010 for Cambodia. Recently, ASEAN decided to speed up the process such that AFTA will be fully completed in 2007. ASEAN has also made important strides in the area of investment cooperation, e.g., in the form of ASEAN 'one-stop investment centers' and the ASEAN Investment Area (AIA). These efforts at industrial cooperation have been designed with essentially the same goal in mind as AFTA: reduce transactions costs associated with intra-regional economic interaction.

In November 2002 the ASEAN Heads of Government proposed that the region should consider the possibility of creating an 'ASEAN Economic Community' (AEC) by 2020, with even more recent proposals to move up the date to 2015. This explicitly put the European experience front and center in terms of design, even if the ASEAN leaders have in mind an Economic Community with ASEAN characteristics. The ASEAN leaders agreed, at the Bali ASEAN Summit in October 2003, to create a region in which goods, services, capital and skilled labor would flow freely, though the details remain to be worked out.

---

[6] In fact, this range of tariffs probably contradicts the requirements spelled out in Article XXIV of the GATT/WTO, but as was noted earlier ASEAN benefits from the Enabling Clause, which has always freed it from these constraints.

The reasons behind the decision to create the AEC are many, including: (1) the desire to create a post-AFTA agenda that would be comprehensive; (2) the perceived need to deepen economic integration in ASEAN in light of the new international commercial environment, especially the dominance of FTAs; (3) the possibility that bilateral FTAs could actually jeopardize ASEAN integration since all Member Countries were free to pursue their own commercial-policy agenda; and (4) the recognition since the Asian Crisis that cooperation in the real and financial sectors must be extended concomitantly, and that free flows of skilled labor will be necessary to do this.[7]

In addition to an ebb in progress related to the APEC 'Bogor Vision' of open trade and investment, there have been several events that have shifted the ASEAN focus to its East Asian neighbors. First, even with the successful APEC Summits at Blake Island and Bogor, the East Asian Economic Grouping (EAEG) concept never faded away. On the contrary, it began to grow in substance. Strangely, the initiative came from ASEAN's effort to expand economic cooperation with the EU, but the EU's desire to deal with all of East Asia led to ASEAN's asking China, South Korea, and Japan to participate. The first Asia-Europe Meeting (ASEM) was held in Bangkok in March 1996, and officials from ASEAN and the rest of East Asia met with EU representatives — a format which was regularized and continues to date. Even though the initial impetus for these meetings was economic cooperation with the EU, the significance for East Asian regionalism lies in that these meetings brought officials from ASEAN, China, South Korea, and Japan together, to discuss issues of economic cooperation. In 1997, these meetings culminated in an informal summit of the APT Heads of State in Kuala Lumpur.

The original 'Miyazawa Plan' was initiated by Japan during the Asian Crisis to create an Asian Monetary Fund to supplement the IMF. It was opposed by the IMF and the United States, but eventually led to the establishment of currency swap arrangements among East Asian countries (essentially bilateral swaps between Japan and individual

[7] The free flow of all labor, including unskilled labor, was deemed too politically difficult to consider in the AEC.

countries) during the annual meeting of the Asian Development Bank in May 2000 (the 'Chiang Mai Agreement').

However, financial integration in general is a complicated process. Usually it occurs well into the process of regional integration, as suggested by the experiences of the EU and the creation of the euro (discussed below), which was only possible after decades of a customs union and a common market. Because the benefits of monetary cooperation are less clear — particularly in the Asian case, since exchange rate stability among Asian countries is of limited value for the many countries that trade heavily outside the region — and the political benefits are far less obvious than in the EU case, countries have begun to focus more on FTAs, at least as a first step.

The lack of influence of APEC in the Asian Financial Crisis has served to solidify East Asia's move in favor of an APT approach. The current spate of agreements, however, have not been extended to the entire APT, but rather have come more from ASEAN to individual countries. For example, the completion of the China-ASEAN joint FTA study in the summer of 2001 prompted Japan to quickly initiate a study of its own with ASEAN. One month later, at the 2001 APT meeting in November, ASEAN and China announced their intention to negotiate a free trade area within 10 years (the agreement was formalized in a Framework Agreement in December 2004). At the end of 2005, the first East Asian Summit was held.

In short, regional economic cooperation accords in Asia have been booming; in addition to the FTAs cited above, many more are being currently negotiated. This has led to many concerns regarding the potential significance of this trend to the multilateral trade system and 'open regionalism' in the region. President Kuroda of the Asian Development Bank has expressed concern for an Asian 'noodle bowl' effect, that is, the possibility that these accords will evolve in such a way as to be incompatible and deleterious to trade and investment in the region. But regardless of whether or not the trend is positive for the regional and global Good, it has become a 'fact on the ground' meritorious of serious academic study. This book hopes to contribute to its analysis.

Table I.1. Chronology of Asian Integration: ASEAN and ASEAN+3

Main Points: ASEAN	ASEAN Summit	Year	APT Summits	Main Points: APT
PANEL A				
ASEAN Concord 1. Established ASEAN Secretariat 2. Treaty of Amity: Mutual Respect for independence, sovereignty, equality, territorial integrity and identity of nations, i.e. non inference 3.Establishment of Zone of Peace, freedom, and neutrality	1st-Bali	1976		
1. ASEAN Industrial Project agreed upon 2. Preferential Trading Agreement (PTA)	2nd-Kuala Lumpur	1977		
1. Accelerate PTA 2. Accelerate and make more flexible ASEAN Industrial Joint Venture (AIJV)	3rd-Manila	1987		
1. ASEAN Free Trade Area (AFTA) 2. Common Effective Preferential Tariff (CEPT)	4th-Singapore	1992		
	5th-Bangkok	1995		
1. Proposal for ASEAN Vision 2020	1st informal-Jakarta	1996		
2. ASEAN 2020 presented, a broad long term vision for ASEAN in 2020 (with ASEAN Economic Community in mind)	2nd informal-Kuala Lumpur	1997	1st-Kuala Lumpur	1st ASEAN+3 (China, Korea and Japan)
Hanoi Plan of Action adopted to move towards Vision 2020: 1. Advance AFTA to 2002, 90% intra-trade subject to 0-5% tariff 2. ASEAN Investment Area (AIA)-goal investment liberalization within by ASEAN 2010, outside ASEAN by 2020 3. ASEAN Surveillance 4. Eminent Persons Group (EPG) proposed to come up with plan for ASEAN Vision 2020	6th- Hanoi	1998	2nd-Hanoi	-East Asian Vision Group (EAVG) proposed by Kim Dae Jung, President of Korea to look into East Asian Integration

Table I.1 (*Continued*)

PANEL B				
EPG develops plan for Vision 2020: 1. Concern that ASEAN not effective in responding to Asian Crisis, so proposed financial cooperation. 2. Speed up AFTA 3. Accelerate AIA 4. To respond to surge of China, need to become more competitive, attract investment, faster integration, and promote IT	3rd informal-Manila	1999	3rd-Manila	
Adopted Initiative for ASEAN Integration (IAI): 1. Framework for more developed ASEAN members to assist those less-developed members in need 2. Focus on factors to enhance competitiveness for new economy: education, skills development, and work training	4th informal-Singapore	2000	4th-Singapore	-East Asian Study Group (EASG) to consider EAFTA and agree to hold East Asian Summit -Two big ideas: 1) Development of institutional link between Southeast Asia and East Asia 2) Study group for merit of an East Asian Free Trade Area (EAFTA) and investment area -Begin financial cooperation, ex. Chiang Mai Initiative May 2000 -Propose Expert Group Study on ASEAN-China FTA
-Challenges facing ASEAN: Declining FDI, erosion of competitiveness. -Road map for Integration for ASEAN to achieve 2020 -Go beyond AFTA and AIA by deepening market liberalization for both trade and investment	7th-Brunei	2001	5th-Brunei	-Endorse EAVG recommendation for EAFTA but overshadowed by China-ASEAN Free Trade Agreement proposal within 10 years, with the adoption Early Harvest Provision to speed up FTA -Prompted by China-ASEAN FTA proposal, Prime Minister Koizumi proposed Japan-ASEAN Economic Partnership in reaction to China-ASEAN proposal -Japan-Singapore Agreement for a New Age Partnership singed January 2002 and enforced Summer 2002
-AEC end goal of Vision 2020	8th-Phnom Penh	2002	6th-Phnom Penh	Adopt EASG recommendations of deepening and broadening of East Asian integration
	9th-Bali	2003	9th-Bali	
-Vientiane Action Plan -Australia attends for 1st time	10th-Vietianne	2004	10th-Vietianne	China speeds up FTA with ASEAN from 2015 to 2010

Notes: In 1998, 1999 and 2000 China speeches always contain idea of giving advice to ASEAN. Difficult to imagine this from leaders of other countries, like Japan and Korea.

Source: Adopted from Naya and Plummer (2005).

The EU and Asia: Lessons and Statistics

The EU is widely believed to be the most successful example of regional economic integration created in the post-World War II period. Given the rise in East Asian regionalism reviewed above, it seems natural to consider to what degree the EU experience might be applicable to 'widening' and 'deepening' of economic integration in Asia. Moreover, the sheer size of the EU in the global economy renders it extremely important to the export-oriented developing countries of East Asia. Hence the reason why many of the contributions to this volume consider both 'lessons and links' associated with the EU-Asian relationship.

To begin, we note that the East Asian *status quo* today is very different from the origins of integration in Europe. First, the contemporary global marketplace is much more open. The GATT/WTO rounds as well as unilateral liberalization have led to extensive reductions in trade barriers and to huge increases in international capital flows (including foreign direct investment [FDI]). In turn, this openness suggests that the costs of using regional integration as a form of 'fortress,' that is, to maximize trade diversion, are consequently much higher than they were in the past, as separating the regional economy from the global production chain has become too costly.

Second, regionalism *globally* has grown by leaps and bounds — particularly recently; trade groupings reported to the WTO come to well over 200, with a majority being established after 1995. East Asia has been negatively affected by economic integration in its largest markets (United States, EU) by recent integration schemes and, hence, is apprehensive regarding new initiatives, such as the enlargement of the EU to include Central and Eastern Europe and the Free Trade Area of the Americas (FTAA) proposal.[8] Thus, the recent decisions to engage in horizontal and vertical integration stems both from the EU example of success as well as a defensive reaction to integration elsewhere. It may also be an example of 'the flag following trade,' rather than 'trade following the flag' (as in the case of the EU).

---

[8] For example, the Single Market Program had a significantly negative impact on Asian exports and NAFTA seems to have hurt certain export sectors (see Kreinin and Plummer 2002).

The differences are not only evident in comparisons across time. They also show up in comparisons across countries and regions. The expansion of the EU to include the 10 Central and Eastern European countries in May 2004 is the first time that the EU embraced 'transitional' countries; prior to that date all 15 EU countries were developed countries. East Asia, on the other hand, features developed; 'dynamic Asian economies'; middle-income developing countries; and least-developed countries. The Asian Development Bank in its *Asian Development Outlook 2002* notes that the coefficient of variation (standard deviation divided by the mean) on income levels within ASEAN was 1.61 in 2000, whereas the corresponding figure for the EU was 0.6. Economic-integration initiatives are far more complicated and risky in such an environment.[9]

The EU is also more integrated than East Asia. As of 2004, intra-Asian trade came to slightly less than one-half of total trade (48 percent).[10] This is far less than the two-third share of intra-Western Europe trade, although somewhat higher than intra-NAFTA trade (40 percent) and significantly higher than intra-Latin American trade (17 percent). As intra-regional trade in Asia has evolved as part of a regionalization process and the EU has been pushed by a series of policy-driven discriminatory initiatives (beginning with the European Coal and Steel Community and the European Payments Union and continuing on to the Treaty of Rome, the Single Market Program, and Economic and Monetary Union), it is, perhaps, unfair to make a direct comparison of Western Europe and East Asia as 'natural' economic blocs. Indeed, double-density measures, in which intra-regional trade is normalized by shares in global trade, tend to be higher in the context of East Asia, ranging in 2000 from 1.4 to 2.2 in the case of EU countries and 2.6 to 5.5 in the original ASEAN countries.

Hence, at least at the level of intra-regional trade, the EU and the East Asian situations are arguably similar in terms of statistical indicators. But this is not true at the subregional context, where most economic-

[9] See, for example, ADB (2002) for a discussion of related issues.

[10] Trade data cited in this section derive from IMF, *Direction of Trade Statistics*, various issues.

integration initiatives are taking place. Intra-ASEAN trade came to only about one-fourth of total regional trade, and there is not an obvious trend in terms of changing shares: since 1990, intra-regional exports have fluctuated between one-fifth and one-fourth of total trade, and intra-regional imports have been slightly lower.[11] This underscores the fact that ASEAN could never presume to use an inward-looking regional approach in order to develop, as the EU did in the 1950s and 1960s: the region is just too small and dependent on the rest of the world. A 'Fortress ASEAN' would be a disaster, a reality that the ASEAN leaders appreciate as they have always stressed 'open regionalism' in their initiatives.[12]

Regarding the 'links' between the EU and East Asia, Western Europe is Asia's third most important trading partner, after Asia itself and North America. While trade with the United States is almost 50 percent higher than trade with the EU, at 17 percent the EU share in Asian trade is significant and constitutes a key market for Asian exports. In fact, from the perspective of the structure of trade, Asian exports to the EU tend to be in the region's most dynamic areas, especially electrical machinery, electronics, and transport equipment (SITC 7).[13] For all East Asian countries save Indonesia and Vietnam, SITC 7 is the largest sector for exports to the EU at the 1-digit level, and in most cases it constitutes greater than half of all exports, even in resource-abundant countries such as Malaysia and the Philippines. Moreover, in all cases save Singapore — where SITC 7 already constituted over three-fourths of total exports to the EU — the share of SITC has grown significantly since 1995, in some cases spectacularly (e.g., in the Philippines from 39 percent to 76 percent). In sum, the EU is a key market in terms of quantity and quality, even if it is not the largest.

The same can be said of FDI flows. Promoting FDI as a means of attracting (non-debt creating) long-term capital flows, foreign exchange, access to foreign markets, and technology transfer is a high priority for

[11] This discrepancy comes, inter alia, from much double-counting in intra-regional ASEAN trade, e.g., in the area of petroleum-related trade.

[12] 'Open regionalism' is a term developed in the context of APEC in which regional initiatives are all non-discriminatory vis-à-vis third parties.

[13] The data summarized in this section come from Plummer (2002).

all Asian countries from the least to the most developed, and in most cases is thought to have played a salient role in economic growth performance.[14] Regional economic integration accords such as AFTA can promote FDI inflows through reductions in transactions costs (be they border or non-border in origin). In doing so, they establish an attractive business environment within which multinationals can profit from a vertical division of labor, as well as facilitate the emergence of multinationals within the developing region itself. EU integration constitutes an excellent example of how this process can work.

The EU continues to be an important supplier of FDI to East Asia.[15] In the early-mid 1990s, the United States and Japan each exported more FDI to ASEAN than the combined EU-4, in some years signficantly more so. However, recent FDI data suggest an increasing European presence in ASEAN; EU-4 FDI outflows to ASEAN exceeded both Japanese and U.S. FDI outflows to the region in 1999, and exceeded U.S. FDI outflows in 2000.

In terms of FDI stocks, the major EU countries in 1999 had much smaller positions compared to the United States and Japan.[16] Among the EU countries, the United Kingdom had the largest FDI stock in ASEAN ($6.3 billion), followed by Germany ($6 billion) and France ($3.6 billion). This compares with U.S. and Japanese positions of $46 billion and $21 billion, respectively. However, over the 1990-1999 period, EU FDI stocks grew fairly impressively. In fact, in terms of US dollars, the growth in German outward FDI stock in ASEAN was, at 302 percent, the fastest of all these countries. The U.S. outward FDI stock grew by 293 percent and French FDI stocks by 109 percent, whereas the stock of the United Kingdom and Japan actually fell by 15 percent and 24 percent, respectively.

---

[14] Certain high-growth countries, especially Japan and South Korea, did not actively promote FDI during their respective high-growth phases. However, today they have placed an emphasis on promoting FDI inflows.

[15] This discussion is drawn from Plummer (2002).

[16] The data for this paragraph were taken from OECD, *International Direct Investment Statistics 2001* (CD-Rom, 1980-2000), with author's adjustments to convert to U.S. dollars in the case of the EU countries and Japan.

Overview of the Book

The starting point for our analysis is the burst of integration activity both within and involving the Asian region. In Chapter 1, Masahiro Kawai provides an unblinkered assessment of what has been accomplished and what remains to be achieved. He argues that much of Asian regionalism has been triggered both by competitive forces and by the examples of regionalism elsewhere. Kawai describes past milestones and then goes on to explain how existing impediments can be surmounted. Here he focuses not only on issues related to trade, finance, and exchanges, but also on the biggest questions of trust and leadership. He concludes that Asian regionalism will develop as Asian economic interdependence continues to deepen. Nevertheless, he cautions that Asian leaders must work hard to develop a shared vision of their regional future, and they must also be sure to ensure that this vision is shared by the public as well.

Any vision of Asian regionalism must rest on an understanding of the most appropriate sequencing for formal integration. The standard presumption is to start with trade. However, this presumption may not be best for Asia. In Chapter 2, Richard Pomfret examines the relative failure of Asian trade integration and contrasts that with the real potential for integration in the monetary domain. Although Pomfret is careful to note the difficulties that such monetary integration would entail, he is optimistic that progress in forming an Asian currency region would stimulate progress in trade integration as well. The biggest challenge, of course, will be the larger Asian countries — and particularly China, which remains committed to the use of capital controls. Nevertheless, Pomfret concludes that monetary integration would be more likely to lead trade integration in Asia than the other way around.

Both Kawai and Pomfret note the influence of the European example on the development of Asian Regionalism. In Chapter 3, James Angresano considers what lessons Europe may hold for Asia. His analysis focuses on the prospects for further deepening relations between ASEAN, China, Korea, and Japan (ASEAN+3). As with both Kawai and Pomfret, however, Angresano gives particular emphasis to China and Japan. He argues that while European experience reveals the importance of political commitment, it does not provide a clear institutional blueprint that the Asian countries should strive to adapt. Instead, Angresano cautions against transplanting institutions out of context and he stresses that Asian regionalism should emerge from the pattern of Asian development. This argument is not a hand-wave at cultural relativism. Rather it is an explanation of where institutions matter and why. In this sense, Angresano's analysis dovetails with Kawai and Pomfret: He reinforces the call for political vision and leadership and yet remains open to the eventuality that Asian regionalism will develop in its own fashion.

The next two chapters focus on particular aspects of Asian regionalism. In Chapter 4, Reid Click and Michael Plummer draw attention to the co-integration of stock market performance to ask whether further institutional integration is warranted. They focus on five stock markets — Indonesia, Malaysia, Philippines, Singapore, and Thailand — representing the original members of ASEAN. And they find that these markets are not completely segmented by national boundaries. Indeed, the level of co-integration is such, Click and Plummer argue, that further formal integration is not only feasible but also desirable because there is less diversification benefit from investing in separate national markets and a common regional market would offer greater liquidity.

The prospects for an Asian currency union is the subject of Chapter 5. Taking the example of European monetary integration and now eurozone enlargement, Sergio Rossi questions whether the institutions and processes used to create a single currency in Europe could be applied to Asia. Rossi is sceptical. Although he admits to the arbitrariness of some of the criteria used for convergence in the European case, he also notes the importance of dynamics related to relative levels of development and productivity growth — specifically the Balassa-Samuelson effect. His scepticism has been expressed by the European Council as well. At its June 2006 summit in Brussels, the European Council rejected Lithuania's bid to join the single currency, citing an expected acceleration of Lithuanian price inflation as justification. Although five of the Central and East European member states formally protested this decision, the underlying logic is widely accepted. As Lithuania catches up to EU productivity levels, it should be expected to experience relatively higher rates of domestic price inflation. This same logic applies to the Asian countries. As Rossi notes, the productivity differentials across Asia are even larger than across Europe, and so the obstacles to forming a stable monetary union are greater as well.

The next three papers look at relations between Europe and Asia. In Chapter 6, Hiro Lee and Dominique van der Mensbrugghe use a computable general equilibrium (CGE) model to analyze the impact of European Union enlargement both within Europe and on the Asian region. They find that while the Central and East European countries will benefit from joining the EU, the ASEAN region will face greater competition in those sectors where the new member states are competitive — 'processed food, textiles, apparel and transport equipment'. And while the effect will be small, it will also be concentrated on the 'low and lower-middle income countries of ASEAN and China'.

Chapter 7 looks away from the East Asian region to focus on the impact of Europe on the countries of South Asia. The South Asian region is often ignored in discussions of Asian regionalism because it has made so little progress in terms of formal regional integration. As Jonathon Moses and Maggi Brigham demonstrate, it may also be ignored because its economic relationship with Europe is so marginal. Through a careful review of the data for trade, investment, and migration, Moses and Brigham reveal how little the countries of South Asia interact with the countries of Europe. As a result, they suggest, the two regions not only lose the potential gains from their interaction, but also the potential stimulus this might have for South Asia economic and political development. Moses and Brigham place particular emphasis on the possibilities for increased migration as a source of developmental stimulus. However, they are careful to note that such migration would require a substantial change both in economic thinking about development and in political thinking about relations between Europe and the outside world.

The economic relationship between Europe and South Asia is weak. By contrast, the economic relationship between Europe and the South Mediterranean is very strong. If it is true, as Moses and Brigham argue, that a strong North-South economic relationship provides a useful engine for development, then the effects should be evident in the Mediterranean. The Mediterranean example could also offer important lessons as to how the countries of East Asia should structure their economic relations with the North — and with Europe. This is the logic behind Chapter 8, where Nicolas Péridy compares the external trade policies of the Mediterranean countries with those of ASEAN. Péridy finds that the preferential trading arrangements between the Mediterranean countries and Europe have added considerably to Mediterranean growth. Therefore he argues that the ASEAN countries will do well to strike similar deals with their wealthier major trading partners — specifically, Japan, Australia, and New Zealand.

Economic development is not guaranteed even with close relations between rich countries and poor. Moreover, this is true within geographic regions as well as between them. In Chapter 9, Mary Farrell examines the transfer mechanisms in the European Union in order to foster economic convergence and promote political cohesion. Her goal is to draw lessons from the experience of Ireland and Spain for consideration in the context of ASEAN — which, if anything, is even more economically diverse than the EU. She finds that while the amount of transfers made into both countries was considerable, the evidence does not show a large impact either on the reduction of unemployment or on the acceleration of economic growth. On the contrary, where there has been either success or failure, the determinants are more likely to be found in domestic politics than in international transfers or regional integration.

By implication, ASEAN would do well to focus more attention on the need for domestic structural adjustment than on the development of common redistributive institutions. That said, however, Farrell does note the success of EU transfer mechanisms in purely political terms. Although such instruments may not have fostered real changes in underlying economic performance, they did generate popular support for European integration in both Ireland and Spain by underscoring the solidarity of the region as a whole. This finding brings us back to the point made initially in the chapter by Kawai. Integration requires a common vision of the future, it requires leadership, and it requires political unity. Whatever their economic effectiveness, common transfer mechanisms provide one means of demonstrating that politics matters.

The primacy of politics is the subject of Chapter 10. J. David Richardson and Craig Parsons examine the history of market integration in Europe and North America in order to map the determinants for political success. Their findings mirror closely the issues raised by Kawai. However, they go farther to insist on the need for regional institutions, common regulatory authorities, and independent judicial enforcement. Such factors have been conspicuously absent in Asia, Richardson and Parsons note. However, they were absent in Europe before the start of European integration as well. And where Europe benefited from the example of the United States, Asia can learn from Europe. Hence there is more reason for optimism with regard to Asian regionalism than the history of regional integration in Asia might suggest. To be successful, however, the project will have to be political as well as economic, formal and institutional as well as indirect or market-driven.

In conclusion, these papers provide an overview of Asian regionalism that is dynamic and distinctive, innovative and yet still familiar. They also point to two challenges for the future. One is to ensure that Asia remains open to the world at large. The other is to guarantee that the fruits of Asian regionalism are evenly distributed among the participating countries themselves. Such challenges must be considered in any vision for the future of Asia. We hope that in some small way, these essays will help provoke the necessary consideration.

References

Asian Development Bank. 2002. *Asian Development Outlook 2002.* Manila: ADB.

Dutta, M. 2003. 'EU and The Euro Revolution: The Theory of Optimum Currency Area Revisited.' Working Paper, Johns Hopkins University SAIS-Bologna.

Kreinin, Mordechai E. and Michael G. Plummer. 2002. *Economic Integration and Development: Has Regionalism Delivered for Developing Countries?* London: Edward Elgar.

Naya, Seiji F. 2002. *The Asian Development Experience.* Manila: Asian Development Bank.

Naya, Seiji F., and Michael G. Plummer. 2005. *The Economics of the Enterprise for ASEAN Initiative.* Singapore, ISEAS.

Plummer, Michael G. 2002. 'The EU and ASEAN: Real Integration and Lessons in Financial Cooperation.' *World Economy* 25(10): 1469-1500.

CHAPTER 1

EAST ASIAN ECONOMIC REGIONALISM: PROGRESS AND CHALLENGES

Masahiro Kawai[1]

Over the last two decades, the East Asian economies have liberalized substantially foreign trade and direct investment (FDI) regimes within the frameworks of GATT/WTO and APEC. The resulting expansion of trade and FDI has become the engine of economic growth and development in East Asia. Since the early 1990s, emerging East Asia has also liberalized its financial system and capital accounts. The consequent financial openness has contributed to rapid economic growth by attracting both long-term and short-term capital and, together with trade and FDI openness, deepened market-driven economic interdependence in East Asia. But it added financial vulnerabilities, culminating in the form of a financial crisis in 1997–98.

Following the crisis, the East Asian economies have embarked on various initiatives for economic regionalism in the areas of trade/investment and money/finance. The crisis prompted the regional economies which were increasingly interdependent to realize the importance of economic cooperation among themselves and to make efforts to institutionalize such interdependence. For example, Japan and Singapore concluded an economic partnership agreement (EPA), and many official discussions and negotiations for bilateral and sub-regional free trade agreements (FTAs) — such as Japan–Korea EPA, China–ASEAN FTA and Japan–ASEAN EPA — are currently underway. In the financial area, the ASEAN+3 members — comprising ASEAN, China, Japan and Korea — began to undertake the Chiang Mai Initiative, economic surveillance and policy dialogue, and the Asian bond market development initiative.

---

[1] The author is grateful to Michael Plummer for advice on the paper and to Steven Green for editorial assistance. He also acknowledges financial support under Grant-in-Aid for Scientific Research (B-16330058) provided by the Japan Society for the Promotion of Science.

The organization of the paper is as follows. Section 1 discusses the logic of recent economic regionalism in East Asia, emphasizing the importance of increasing economic interdependence among the regional economies and the lack of regional institutions and mechanisms that match such interdependence. It emphasizes the surprising extent to which the regional economies are integrated through trade, FDI and finance and are interdependent in macroeconomic cycles. Section 2 considers (past and present) economic cooperation initiatives in Asia, followed in Section 3 by a closer analysis of the issues and challenges for closer economic regionalism — or greater institutionalization of regional economic integration in East Asia — that can potentially lead to the creation of an East Asian Economic Community. Section 4 provides concluding remarks, arguing that deeper economic integration in trade, investment and finance and further institutionalization of such integration can mutually reinforce each other. Trust building and political leadership are essential to transforming the current drive for economic regionalism into a much higher level of integration.

The Logic of Economic Regionalism in East Asia

The most fundamental rationale behind the emergence of recent economic regionalism is the deepening of regional economic interdependence in East Asia. Economic regionalism, through various types of policy coordination, can resolve the 'collective action' problem by internalizing externalities and spill-over effects that arise from interdependence.

The East Asia region has long enjoyed market-driven integration through trade and FDI, while embracing a multilateral liberalization framework under the GATT/WTO and, more recently, open regionalism through Asia–Pacific Economic Cooperation (APEC). The region has avoided discriminatory trade practices. FDI flows to the East Asian economies, driven initially by Japanese multinational corporations after the Plaza Accord in the mid–1980s, have generated intra-industry trade within the region and have contributed to deeper economic integration. More recently, NIEs and some middle-income ASEAN countries have become active as investors, particularly in China, whose rise as a large trading nation has also strengthened trade — particularly intra-industry trade — linkages among the East Asian economies, many of which are generated by multinationals.

The degree of regional economic integration through trade in East Asia has been rising fast over the last twenty-five years. Table 1.1a summarizes changes in the share of intra-regional trade for various groupings in the world over the period 1980 to 2004. The table demonstrates that intra-regional trade as a share of East Asia's total trade has risen from 22 percent in 1980 to 44 percent in 2004 (excluding Japan) or from 35 percent to 55 percent over the same period (including Japan). Now almost 55 percent of East Asia's trade is with itself. The recent share of intra-regional trade within East Asia is still lower than that in the European Union–15 (62 percent), but exceeds that of the North American Free Trade Area (46 percent) in 2004.

Table 1.1b summarizes changes in the intra-regional trade intensity indexes for the same groupings over the same period.[2] The table demonstrates that within East Asia, whether including Japan or not, the trade intensity indexes, at around 2.3, is higher than those for the EU (1.7), though it is lower than that for NAFTA (2.7) in 2004. This observation confirms that the degree of regional economic integration through trade in East Asia is quite high and comparable to levels seen in NAFTA or the EU. It must be emphasized that intra-East Asia trade has expanded rapidly but not at the expense of extra-regional trade. This suggests that East Asia continues to maintain export competitiveness *vis-à-vis* countries outside the region.

[2] The advantage of using trade intensity indexes over trade shares is that the former control for a region's relative size in world trade and, hence, present a better measure of closeness of the economies within a region. However, a small regional group tends to have a high trade intensity index.

Table 1.1a. Intra-Regional Trade Share[(a)] (in percentage)

Regions	*1980*	*1985*	*1990*	*1995*	*2000*	*2001*	*2002*	*2003*	*2004*
East Asia-15, including Japan[(c)]	34.6	37.1	43.1	52.0	52.2	51.7	53.7	54.7	55.2
Emerging East Asia-14[(c)]	22.1	27.5	32.9	39.2	40.7	40.9	43.2	43.9	44.2
NIEs-4	6.4	6.5	11.9	15.5	15.5	14.9	15.5	15.0	14.4
ASEAN-10[(c)]	18.0	20.3	18.9	24.1	24.7	24.1	24.4	23.9	23.9
NAFTA	33.8	38.7	37.9	43.2	48.8	49.1	48.4	47.3	46.4
MERCOSUR	11.1	7.2	10.9	19.2	20.3	17.9	13.6	14.7	15.2
Old European Union-15	60.7	59.8	66.2	64.2	62.3	62.2	62.5	63.0	62.1
New European Union-25	61.3	59.8	67.0	67.4	66.8	67.2	67.8	68.6	67.9

Note: (a) The intra-regional trade share is defined as: $X_{ii}/\{(X_{i.} + X_{.i})/2\}$ where X_{ii} represents exports of region i to region i, $X_{i.}$ represents total exports of region i to the world, and $X_{.i}$ represents total exports of the world to region i.

(b) The trade intensity index is defined as: $[X_{ii}/\{(X_{i.} + X_{.i})/2\}]/[\{(X_{i.} + X_{.i})/2\}/X_{..}]$ where $X_{..}$ represents total world exports

(c) East Asia-15 includes Emerging East Asia-14 and Japan. Emerging East Asia-14 includes the Asian NIEs (Hong Kong, Korea, Singapore and Taiwan), nine ASEAN members (Brunei, Cambodia, Indonesia, Laos, Malaysia, Myanmar, Philippines, Thailand and Vietnam) and China. ASEAN-10 includes Singapore.

(d) Computation is based on exporting countries' export data, except for Taiwan in 1980 where importers' import data are used when necessary.

Source: Computed from IMF, *Direction of Trade Statistics*; CEIC database.

Table 1.1b. Intra-Regional Trade Intensity Index[b]

Regions	*1980*	*1985*	*1990*	*1995*	*2000*	*2001*	*2002*	*2003*	*2004*
East Asia-15, including Japan[c]	2.6	2.3	2.2	2.1	2.2	2.3	2.3	2.3	2.3
Emerging East Asia-14[c]	3.2	3.3	2.7	2.3	2.3	2.4	2.4	2.4	2.3
NIEs-4	1.9	1.5	1.5	1.5	1.6	1.7	1.7	1.7	1.6
ASEAN-10[c]	4.8	5.7	4.4	3.7	4.0	4.1	4.2	4.2	4.2
NAFTA	2.1	2.0	2.1	2.4	2.2	2.3	2.4	2.6	2.7
MERCOSUR	6.6	4.9	9.7	13.2	14.8	13.0	11.6	12.7	12.0
Old European Union-15	1.5	1.6	1.5	1.7	1.7	1.7	1.7	1.7	1.7
New European Union-25	1.5	1.6	1.5	1.7	1.8	1.7	1.7	1.7	1.7

Note: (a) The intra-regional trade share is defined as: $X_{ii}/\{(X_{i\cdot} + X_{\cdot i})/2\}$ where X_{ii} represents exports of region i to region i, $X_{i\cdot}$ represents total exports of region i to the world, and $X_{\cdot i}$ represents total exports of the world to region i.

(b) The trade intensity index is defined as: $[X_{ii}/\{(X_{i\cdot} + X_{\cdot i})/2\}]/[\{(X_{i\cdot} + X_{\cdot i})/2\}/X_{\cdot\cdot}]$ where $X_{\cdot\cdot}$ represents total world exports

(c) East Asia-15 includes Emerging East Asia-14 and Japan. Emerging East Asia-14 includes the Asian NIEs (Hong Kong, Korea, Singapore and Taiwan), nine ASEAN members (Brunei, Cambodia, Indonesia, Laos, Malaysia, Myanmar, Philippines, Thailand and Vietnam) and China. ASEAN-10 includes Singapore.

(d) Computation is based on exporting countries' export data, except for Taiwan in 1980 where importers' import data are used when necessary.

Source: Computed from IMF, *Direction of Trade Statistics*; CEIC database.

The recent rise in Asian NIEs' investment contributes to the integration of the East Asian economies through FDI and FDI-driven trade. East Asia has seen the formation of an 'FDI-trade nexus' — mutual reinforcement between FDI and trade. An underlying determinant of the FDI-trade nexus is the establishment of regional production networks and supply chains by multinational corporations. These networks have promoted intra-regional division of labor in East Asia through fragmentation of the production process into different sub-processes located in different countries based on comparative advantage — relative factor proportions and technological capabilities. This strategy has stimulated vertical intra-industry trade in parts, components, semi-finished and finished products.[3] Its important implication is that large inflows of FDI to emerging East Asia have stimulated the region's engagement with trade, in a way that reflects the individual economies' stages of industrial development. More recently China has also begun to participate in such activities in an explosive way.

Market-driven financial integration has also been underway as a result of the increased deregulation of the financial system, opening of financial services to foreign institutions, and liberalization of the capital account in the East Asian economies. Commercial banks have extended cross-border loans to banks and corporations throughout the region, and such banks have contributed to a closely connected banking sector within East Asia. Opening of securities markets, particularly equity markets, has attracted foreign portfolio capital inflows. Active commercial bank loans and portfolio flows have linked the economies in the region financially, creating positive correlations of asset price movements within the region. At least part of the contagion of currency crises in the region in 1997 was a reflection of such financial linkages.

Macroeconomic interdependence within the region has recently become stronger, as evidenced by a simultaneous contraction of economic activity throughout East Asia in 1998 and a simultaneous expansion in 1999–2000. Though the regional economies may have been affected by some common global factors such as US economic cycles and informa-

[3] See Athukorala (2003), Kawai and Urata (2004) and Kawai (2004a).

tion technology (IT) stock price movements, many of the recent, synchronized economic activities in the region can be attributed to strong macroeconomic interdependence.

Cross-country correlation analyses of major macroeconomic variables — such as real GDP growth rates, real private consumption, real fixed investment, and price inflation rates — over the last twenty-five years indicate that macroeconomic activities of the East Asian economies are generally highly correlated with each other, with the exception of China. Table 1.2 is a summary of factor loadings obtained from the first principal components of East Asian economies' variables.[4] The table indicates that Japan's real activity variables are more highly correlated with those of emerging East Asia than are US activity variables. On the other hand, inflation rates of the United States and Japan are equally highly correlated with those of emerging East Asia. This suggests that the degree of emerging East Asia's real economic interdependence with Japan is greater than with the United States, while the degrees of its nominal interdependence with Japan and the United States are equally strong. An important reason for this is that the United States is subject to supply shocks that are different from those affecting East Asia, while it has traditionally provided a nominal anchor role for East Asia through the latter's currency pegging to the U.S. dollar. [5] In view of the rising trade and FDI integration in East Asia, there is a growing need for setting up more formal institutional mechanisms for trade and investment facilitation, harmonization of rules, standards and procedures, and dispute settlements. The deepening macroeconomic and financial interdependence also suggests a need for concerted efforts to internalize externalities and spillover effects, because macroeconomic/financial developments and policies of one country can easily affect other countries' performance and developments.

---

[4] See Kawai and Motonishi (2004) for details.

[5] Earlier studies by Eichengreen and Bayoumi (1999) found that, in terms of supply shocks, some East Asian nations were just as closely connected with one another as European countries were. In terms of demand shocks, ASEAN countries were also reasonably connected. See also Bayoumi and Eichengreen (1994) and Bayoumi, Eichengreen and Mauro (2000). Using more recent data, Kawai and Motonishi (2004) confirm that many East Asian economies are subject to largely symmetric supply shocks.

Table 1.2. Correlation Coefficients between the First Principal Component Scores for East Asia and the Individual Economy Data (1980-2002)

Panel A

Countries/ Regions	*Real GDP*	*Real Con.*	*Real Inv.*	*Real Mon. Supply*	*Real St. Price*	*Real Eff. Ex. Rate*	*GDP Def.*	*CPI*	*WPI*
China	0.07	-0.14	-0.26	-0.22	--	0.43	-0.40	0.15	--
Taiwan	0.51	0.28	0.28	0.28	0.71	0.72	0.35	0.85	0.50
Hong Kong	0.74	0.63	0.58	0.41	--	0.48	-0.06	0.80	--
Singapore	0.77	0.76	0.59	0.04	--	0.77	0.08	0.87	0.45
Malaysia	0.90	0.87	0.95	0.53	--	0.81	0.40	0.79	0.68
Thailand	0.89	0.92	0.88	0.69	--	0.80	0.54	0.87	0.70
Philippines	0.33	0.31	0.55	0.77	0.91	0.81	-0.06	0.57	0.27
Indonesia	0.89	0.65	0.89	0.61	--	0.86	0.99	0.21	0.92

Notes: (a) The figures are correlation coefficients between the first principal component scores for East Asia and the original, log first-differenced series of individual countries.

(b) In this analysis, East Asia includes Japan, Korea, China, Taiwan, Hong Kong, Singapore, Malaysia, Thailand, Philippines, and Indonesia.

Source: Table 5 from Kawai and Motonishi (2004).

Table 1.2 (*Continued*)

Panel B

Countries/ Regions	*Real GDP*	*Real Con.*	*Real Inv.*	*Real Mon. Supply*	*Real St. Price*	*Real Eff. Ex. Rate*	*GDP Def.*	*CPI*	*WPI*
China	0.07	-0.14	-0.26	-0.22	--	0.43	-0.40	0.15	--
Taiwan	0.51	0.28	0.28	0.28	0.71	0.72	0.35	0.85	0.50
Hong Kong	0.74	0.63	0.58	0.41	--	0.48	-0.06	0.80	--
Singapore	0.77	0.76	0.59	0.04	--	0.77	0.08	0.87	0.45
Malaysia	0.90	0.87	0.95	0.53	--	0.81	0.40	0.79	0.68
Thailand	0.89	0.92	0.88	0.69	--	0.80	0.54	0.87	0.70
Philippines	0.33	0.31	0.55	0.77	0.91	0.81	-0.06	0.57	0.27
Indonesia	0.89	0.65	0.89	0.61	--	0.86	0.99	0.21	0.92

Notes: (a) The figures are correlation coefficients between the first principal component scores for East Asia and the original, log first-differenced series of individual countries.
(b) In this analysis, East Asia includes Japan, Korea, China, Taiwan, Hong Kong, Singapore, Malaysia, Thailand, Philippines, and Indonesia.

Source: Table 5 from Kawai and Motonishi (2004).

It makes sense for such interdependent regional economies to institutionalize *de facto* integration through the establishment of regional frameworks for trade and investment liberalization and macroeconomic and financial management. Given that one country's turbulence, shocks and crises could be easily transmitted to other economies within the same region, it is critical to establish financial safety nets. Joint action among such economies would be easier because they are small in number — so the transactions cost for collective action is small — and tend to face similar shocks and similar policy challenges.

Response to Economic Regionalism in Europe and North America

The initiatives for economic regionalism represent the efforts of East Asian economies toward greater institutionalization of *de facto* economic integration — particularly through trade and FDI. They have made these efforts essentially for three reasons:

- As a defensive response to the proliferation of regional trade arrangements (RTAs) elsewhere — particularly in Europe and the Western Hemisphere — and due to their dissatisfaction with slow progress on trade/investment liberalization at the global and trans-regional levels;
- Due to their willingness to enhance productivity and international competitiveness through exploitation of scale economies and dynamic efficiency; and
- For promotion of deeper integration and institution building at the regional level.

Regionalism elsewhere — including the formation of an economic and monetary union in Europe and the European Union's expansion to the east as well as the success of NAFTA and its move to the Free Trade Area of the Americas (FTAA) in the Western Hemisphere — is the first factor that has motivated the East Asian economies to pursue regional trade arrangements. There had already been 184 RTAs reported to the WTO for the whole world by 2003. Governments in East Asia fear that unless they strengthen their own regional trade arrangements, they would be disadvantaged in global competition and multilateral negotiations. They have increasingly realized the importance of uniting themselves to gain bargaining power *vis-à-vis* the European Union, the United States and other groupings. The slow progress on the WTO/Doha liberalization process and the perceived ineffectiveness of the APEC process have stoked these fears.

Policymakers in East Asia are increasingly of the view that they need to secure a bigger market within their own region so that scale economies and dynamic efficiency gains can be exploited. They believe East Asia's RTAs can help raise both productivity and international competitiveness. In addition, these RTAs are perceived as facilitating trade and investment, promoting harmonization of rules-making, standard-setting and procedures, and providing dispute resolution mechanisms, particularly in the areas of services, labor mobility, investment, competition policy, intellectual property rights, contingency protection and rules of origin — areas in which it is difficult to make substantial progress in a multilateral framework (OECD 2003). This effort is basically one of institution building for further deepening of trade and investment integration.

Response to the Financial Crisis

While the most fundamental driving force behind the recent move to closer economic regionalism in the money/finance area is the deepening of economic interdependence in the region, the impact of the Asian financial crisis cannot be neglected. There are also several other reasons for recent financial cooperation in the region:

- The hard lesson learnt from the Asian financial crisis of 1997–98, i.e., the need to establish regional 'self-help' mechanisms for effective prevention, management and resolution of regional financial crises;
- Dissatisfaction with the existing global financial arrangement governed by the IMF; and
- Regional financial stability as a basis for global financial stability as well as the region's willingness to increase the Asian voice in, and for, global financial management.

The Asian financial crisis has taught an important lesson, which is that there is a clear need for effective prevention, management and resolution of financial crises and contagion. The global initiative for the new international financial architecture that intends to strengthen the international financial system in this regard has been unsatisfactory and disappointing. The national efforts to strengthen individual economic fundamentals, to reduce the likelihood of home-grown crises and to increase domestic resilience to crises and contagion — particularly through the ROSCs — take time to bear fruit.[6] In addition, the East Asian economies have been dissatisfied with the way the IMF handled the crisis, particularly in Thailand and Indonesia. Hence, the general sentiment in East Asia has been that the regional economies must establish their own 'self-help' mechanisms through systematic macroeconomic and financial cooperation for prevention and management of possible crises in the future. Such cooperation should include information exchange, policy dialogue, a regional liquidity support arrangement, and joint policymaking in certain critical areas, such as exchange rate policy coordination.

There are some proactive responses to the crisis. Since regional financial stability is a basis for global financial stability, effective regional financial cooperation is an obvious benefit not only for the regional economies but also for the global community. In this sense East Asian regional financial cooperation is consistent with, and even strengthens, the IMF's global role. At the same time, given the perceived imbalance and unfairness in the current distribution of IMF quotas, which is unreal-

---

[6] One of the principal tools for strengthening national policies and institutions has been the development of international best practices in macroeconomic policy areas, financial sector regulation and supervision, and capital market infrastructure. These best practices are presented by the Reports on the Observance of Standards and Codes (ROSCs), which cover twelve areas: Macroeconomic policy area — monetary and financial policy transparency, fiscal transparency, and special data dissemination standard (SDDS) in addition to the general data dissemination system (GDDS); Financial sector regulation and supervision — banking supervision, securities regulation, insurance supervision, payments systems, and anti-money laundering; and Capital market infrastructure — corporate governance, accounting standards, auditing standards, and insolvency and creditor rights. An important instrument is the Financial Sector Assessment Program (FSAP) supported jointly by the IMF and the World Bank.

istically skewed against East Asia, regional policymakers have a sincere desire to make their voice heard in global financial management. Indeed they believe they can play a greater role by joining their forces together.

Initiatives for Economic Regionalism

Following the unsatisfactory progress of the Uruguay Round Ministerial meeting in December 1990, Malaysian Prime Minister Mohamad Mahathir proposed the formation of a regional trade grouping — comprised of ASEAN countries, Japan, China, Korea and Hong Kong. This group of economies was called the 'East Asian Economic Group (EAEG).' Objectives behind his proposal were to establish a regional trade arrangement for the group in response to the emergence of preferential regional trade arrangements elsewhere, including in North America, and to exercise a global impact on trade issues, like the Cairns Group. In October 1991, ASEAN Economic Ministers considered Mahathir's proposal as useful and renamed the grouping as the 'East Asian Economic Caucus (EAEC)' which would facilitate discussions on regional economic issues.

However, the United States objected to the EAEG/EAEC proposal on the ground that it could divide the Asia–Pacific, by excluding the United States, and reduce the effectiveness of the trade/investment liberalization process within APEC. Japan showed hesitation in supporting the proposal because of its consideration of US opposition — Japan had trade conflicts with the United States and did not wish to make the bilateral relationship worse — as well as because of the strategic priority it placed on the APEC process. China also took a cautious approach. Interest in the EAEG/EAEC proposal waned eventually in the absence of support from key countries in Northeast Asia.[7] But when the leaders of Japan, China and Korea were invited to the informal ASEAN Leaders' meeting in December 1997, in the midst of the Asian financial crisis, the *de facto* ASEAN+3 process began. Hence, the EAEG/EAEC proposal can be considered a precursor to the ASEAN+3 process, because membership of

---

[7] Nonetheless, this proposal was not completely forgotten. When the Asia-Europe Meeting (ASEM) was created in 1996, the Asian participants were essentially EAEG/EAEC economies.

the latter overlaps that of the former.

Following the success of the August 1997 meeting in Tokyo to agree on a much-needed financial support package for crisis-affected Thailand, Japan, with support from South Korea and the ASEAN countries that participated in the Thai package, proposed in September to establish an Asian Monetary Fund (AMF) to supplement IMF resources for crisis prevention and resolution. Its idea was to pool foreign exchange reserves of the East Asian economies that can be mobilized to deter currency speculation or to contain a currency crisis in a member economy. It was said that as much as US$100 billion would be mobilized. The United States and the IMF opposed this proposition on grounds of moral hazard and duplication. They argued that an East Asian country hit by a currency crisis would bypass the tough conditionality of the IMF and receive easy money from the AMF, thereby creating potential for moral hazard; and that an AMF would be redundant in the presence of an effective global crisis manager, the IMF. Without China's support, the idea had to be aborted.[8]

Another example, which was highly successful, was the so-called 'New Miyazawa Initiative' which contributed to the resolution of the Asian financial crisis. In October 1998, Japan pledged US$30 billion to support the economic recovery of the crisis-affected countries. Half of the pledged amount was dedicated to short-term financial needs during the process of implementing economic restructuring and reform, while the rest was earmarked for medium- and long-term reforms. Part of short-term financial support was dedicated to currency swap arrange-

[8] In November 1997 the East Asian economies, together with the United States, Canada, Australia and New Zealand, agreed to establish the so-called 'Manila Framework Group.' Many, but not all, of the MFG member economies participated in the Thai financial package. Its objective was to develop a concerted framework for Asia-Pacific financial cooperation in order to restore and enhance the prospects for financial stability in the region. Its initiatives included the establishment of a new mechanism for regional surveillance to complement IMF surveillance; enhancement of economic and technical cooperation, particularly in strengthening domestic financial systems and regulatory capacities; strengthening the IMF's capacity to respond to financial crises; and development of a cooperative financing arrangement for the region to complement IMF resources. However, the MFG was dissolved in November 2004 after six years of meetings among finance ministry and central bank deputies.

ments with Korea (US$5.0 billion) and Malaysia (US$2.5 billion). The initiative provided major assistance for restructuring corporate debt, reforming financial sectors, strengthening social safety nets, generating employment, and addressing the credit crunch. A commitment to provide a large amount of resources helped stabilize the regional markets and economies, thereby facilitating the recovery process. It is important to mention that the short-term financial support provided to Korea and Malaysia became a model for bilateral currency swap arrangements under the Chiang Mai Initiative.

Trade and Investment Initiatives

Recently, many governments in East Asia have promoted bilateral and regional trade arrangements. Notably, Japan recently implemented a bilateral economic partnership agreement (EPA) with Singapore in November 2002,[9] and has concluded another one with Mexico. In response to the Japan–Singapore negotiation, China and ASEAN began official negotiations to complete a free trade agreement (FTA) by 2010 with advanced ASEAN members and by 2015 with less advanced members. They have already implemented the 'early harvest' measures since January 2004.[10] Japan and ASEAN agreed to begin negotiations in 2005 on an EPA with a view to achieve free trade by 2012. Korea has also agreed on a similar negotiation with ASEAN to be completed by 2009. Japan has begun bilateral negotiations for EPAs with Korea, Malaysia, Thailand, and the Philippines — it may also begin negotiations with Indonesia. In this sense, there have been domino and bandwagon effects among Japan, China and Korea in their drive for regional FTAs/EPAs with ASEAN.

---

[9] More precisely, the Japan-Singapore agreement is called the 'Agreement between Japan and the Republic of Singapore for a New-Age Economic Partnership (JSEPA)' and goes beyond a conventional free trade agreement.

[10] 'Early harvest' refers to provisions of the 'Framework Agreement on China-ASEAN Comprehensive Economic Cooperation,' intended to liberalize, before the full completion of the FTA, tariffs in priority sectors of interest and implement other trade and investment facilitation deemed to generate immediate benefits to ASEAN and China.

Table 1.3. FTA/EPA Initiatives in East Asia (as of April 2006)

Panel A

In Effect	Under Official Negotiation	Under Consultation/Study
Asia-Pacific Trade Agreement (1976)	Singapore-Mexico (July 2000)	Japan-Australia
Laos-Thailand (1991)	Singapore-Canada (Jan. 2002)	Japan-Chile
ASEAN FTA (1992)	Singapore-Chile	Japan-India
Singapore-New Zealand (Jan. 2001)	Singapore-P3 (CER, Chile)	Japan-Switzerland
Japan-Singapore (Nov. 2002)	Hong Kong-New Zealand (Nov. 2000)	Japan-China-Korea
Singapore-Australia (2003)	Japan-Philippines (a.c. Nov. 2004)	China-India
Singapore-EFTA (Jan. 2003)	Japan-Malaysia (signed Dec. 2005)	Korea-Australia
Singapore-USA (Jan. 2004)	Japan-Thailand (a.c. Aug. 2005)	Korea-New Zealand
Singapore-Jordan (2004)	Japan-Korea (Dec. 2003)	Korea-India
China-Hong Kong (Jan. 2004)	Japan-ASEAN (Nov. 2005)	Korea-USA
China-Macao (Jan. 2004)	Japan-Indonesia (July 2005)	Korea-MERCOSUR

Panel B

In Effect	Under Official Negotiation	Under Consultation/Study
Korea-Chile (April 2004)	China-New Zealand (Dec. 2004)	Korea-China
Thailand-India (Sep. 2004)	China-Australia (May 2005)	Singapore-Taiwan
Thailand-Australia (Jan. 2005)	Korea-Canada (July 2005)	ASEAN-EU
Japan-Mexico (April 2005)	Korea-Mexico (early 2006)	Malaysia-India
China-ASEAN (July 2005)	Korea-USA	Indonesia-India
Singapore-India (Aug. 2005)	Thailand-Bahrain (signed)	
Thailand-New Zealand (2005)	Thailand-Peru (agreed April 2004)	
Korea-Singapore (2006)	Thailand-USA (June 2004)	
Korea-EFTA (2006)	Malaysia-Australia (May 2005)	
China-Chile (2006)	Malaysia-New Zealand	
Singapore-Panama (2006)	Malaysia-USA	
Korea-ASEAN (July 2006)	ASEAN-India (Jan. 2004)	
	ASEAN-CER (Feb. 2005)	
	ASEAN-Australia-New Zealand	

Notes: The shaded arrangements are those within East Asia (ASEAN+3, Taiwan and Hong Kong).

Source: An updated version of Table 1.7 in Fukasaku, Kawai, Plummer and Trzeciak-Duval (2005).

China has also proposed an FTA among China, Japan and Korea. A region-wide FTA for ASEAN+3, including China, Japan and Korea, has also been proposed.[11] Table 1.3 summarizes the recent initiatives for FTAs and EPAs by the East Asian economies.

One of the interesting features of the East Asian drive toward regional and bilateral trade arrangements is that these economies have also concluded, or have been negotiating, FTAs/EPAs with countries or groups outside of East Asia. For example, Japan has concluded negotiations with Mexico. Korea has put into effect its FTA with Chile. Singapore has implemented a closer economic partnership agreement (CEPA) with New Zealand and Australia as well as FTAs with the European Free Trade Area (EFTA) and the United States. It is currently negotiating with Mexico and Canada. Thailand has put into effect an FTA with Australia and is negotiating one with the United States and with India. ASEAN as a group has begun negotiations with India and is also considering similar negotiations with the United States and the European Union. These attempts suggest that the economies in the region wish to maintain open trading relations with other parts of the world rather than become inward-looking.

East Asia's move to regional trade arrangements symbolizes a change in its long-standing policy of pursuing trade liberalization only in a global or trans-regional framework based on the WTO and APEC — apart from ASEAN which has formed the ASEAN Free Trade Area (AFTA). The region has decided to shift its trade policy to a three-track approach based on global (WTO–based) cum trans-regional (APEC–based), regional (within ASEAN+3), and bilateral liberalization. For East Asian economies, regional and bilateral liberalization is an attempt to achieve deeper integration with their trading partners on a formal basis, going beyond reductions in border restrictions — i.e., pursuing investment liberalization, promoting greater competition in the domestic market, and harmonizing standards and procedures.

---

[11] However, no timeframe is set for negotiations. Japan is indeed cautious about such an arrangement with China at this point. Its official view is that before negotiating on an FTA/EPA, It believes that China must clearly show its compliance with all the commitments made in WTO accession negotiations.

Three Pillars of Financial Regionalism

The East Asian economies have also embarked on initiatives for regional financial arrangements. Such initiatives are founded on three major pillars:

- Creation of a regional liquidity support facility through the Chiang Mai Initiative;
- Establishment of economic surveillance, particularly through the ASEAN+3 Economic Review and Policy Dialogue process; and
- Development of Asian bond markets.

The hallmark liquidity support facility in East Asia is the Chiang Mai Initiative (CMI), which is designed to reduce the risk of liquidity crises or manage regional currency attacks, contagion and crises once they occur. The Asian financial crisis highlighted the importance of establishing an effective financing facility so that the economies in the region can prevent currency crises or respond effectively to crises once they occur in a world of increased financial globalization. The finance ministers of ASEAN+3 who met in Chiang Mai in May 2000 agreed to establish a regional network of swap arrangements for its members, thus embarking on the so-called CMI.[12] The CMI is comprised of two elements — the expansion of the existing ASEAN Swap Arrangement (ASA), in both amounts and membership, and the creation of a new network of bilateral swap arrangements (BSAs) among ASEAN+3 members.[13] By March 2006, seventeen BSAs had been concluded in line with the main principles, amounting to a total of US$71.5 billion excluding the commitments

[12] ASEAN+3 was formed in April 1999. Stubbs (2002) takes the view that the ASEAN+3 will rise as a major regional and international player. See Kawai (2002a) and Kuroda and Kawai (2002).

[13] The ASEAN Swap Arrangement (ASA), established among the members of the original ASEAN-5 in August 1977 with a total facility of US$100 million, was augmented to a total of US$200 million in 1978. Under the CMI, ASA membership was extended to include all ASEAN members, and its facility was further augmented to US$1 billion.

made under the New Miyazawa Initiative, and US$79 billion including these commitments (Table 1.4).[14] This signified the conclusion of all conceivable BSAs at the time, and no further BSA negotiation is currently under way.

One of the important features of CMI BSA is that members requesting liquidity support can immediately obtain short-term financial assistance for the first 10 percent of the facility. The remaining 90 percent is provided to the requesting member under an IMF program. Linking CMI liquidity support to an IMF program — and hence its conditionality — is designed to address the concern that balance of payments difficulties may be due to fundamental problems, rather than a mere panic and herd behavior by investors, and that the potential moral hazard problem could be non-negligible in the absence of tough IMF conditionality. The general view is that, due to the region's limited capacity to produce and enforce effective adjustment policies, the CMI members will have to rely on the IMF, at least for the time being.[15]

Establishing processes for regional economic surveillance and policy dialogue is an obvious first step for meaningful financial cooperation. Economic surveillance involves not only analyses of macroeconomic and financial conditions and policies of member economies but also identification of vulnerable aspects of the economy and finance as well as appropriate policy responses. This process requires frank and candid exchanges of views and policy dialogue among other member economies, and will hopefully induce good policies through peer pressure.

[14] For calculation purposes, the amounts of two-way BSAs are doubled. The amount that Japan committed under the New Miyazawa Initiative totals US$7.5 billion — or US$5 billion with South Korea and US$2.5 billion with Malaysia. Note that Brunei, Cambodia, Laos, Myanmar and Vietnam are not part of BSAs, though they are ASA members.

[15] On the other hand, some ASEAN+3 members, such as Malaysia, believe that the CMI should not be linked to IMF programs.

Table 1.4. Progress on BSAs under the Chiang Mai Initiative (as of March 2006)

BSAs	*Currencies*	*Conclusion Dates*	*Size*
Japan-South Korea	USD/Won or USD/Yen	July 4, 2001/May 27, 2005	US$ 10.0 billion[(a,c)] (Jap-Kor) US$ 5.0 billion[(a,c)] (Kor-Jap)
Japan-Thailand	USD/Baht or USD/Yen	July 30, 2001/March 7, 2005	US$ 3.0 billion (2-way)
Japan-Philippines	USD/Peso	August 27, 2001	US$ 3.0 billion (1-way)
Japan-Malaysia	USD/Ringgit	October 5, 2001	US$ 1.0 billion[(b)] (1-way)
China-Thailand	USD/Baht	December 6, 2001	US$ 2.0 billion (1-way)
Japan-China	Yen/Renminbi or Renminib/Yen	March 28, 2002	US$ 3.0 billion[(c)] (2-way)
China-South Korea	Renminbi-Won or Won/Renminbi	June 24, 2002/May 27, 2005	US$ 4.0 billion[(c)] (2-way)
South Korea-Thailand	USD/Baht or USD/Won	June 25, 2002/Dec 12, 2005	US$ 1.0 billion (2-way)
South Korea-Malaysia	USD/Ringgit or USD/Won	July 26, 2002/Oct 14, 2005	US$ 1.5 billion (2-way)
South Korea-Philippines	USD/Peso or USD/Won	Aug 9, 2002/Oct 17, 2005	US$ 1.5 billion (2-way)
China-Malaysia	USD/Ringgit	October 9, 2002	US$ 1.5 billion (1-way)
Japan-Indonesia	USD/Rupiah	Feb 17, 2003/Aug 31, 2005	US$ 6.0 billion (1-way)
China-Philippines	Renminbi/Peso	August 29, 2003	US$ 1.0 billion[(c)] (1-way)
Japan-Singapore	USD/Singapore Dollar USD/Yen	Nov 10, 2003/Nov 8, 2005	US$ 3.0 billion (Jap-Sing) US$ 1.0 billion (Sing-Jap)
South Korea-Indonesia	USD/Rupiah or USD/Won	Dec 24, 2003	US$ 1.0 billion (2-way)
China-Indonesia	USD/Rupiah	Dec 30, 2003/Oct 17, 2005	US$ 2.0 billion (1-way)
Japan-South Korea	Yen/Won or Won/Yen	February 24, 2006	US$ 3.0 billion (2-way)

Notes: (a) The amount excludes US$5.0 billion committed (on June 17, 1999) under the New Miyazawa Initiative.
(b) The amount excludes US$2.5 billion committed (on August 18, 1999) under the New Miyazawa Initiative.
(c) The amounts are US dollar equivalents.

There are several mechanisms for regional information sharing, policy dialogue, and economic surveillance. ASEAN+3 finance ministers agreed in May 2000 to introduce an ASEAN+3 Economic Review and Policy Dialogue (ERPD) process, which turned out to be the most important mechanism of all.[16] Its first surveillance meeting was held in April 2002. The purpose of this process is to strengthen policy dialogue, coordination and collaboration on the financial, monetary and fiscal issues of common interest. Its primary focus is on global and regional economic monitoring, individual country monitoring, macroeconomic risk assessment and management, and banking and financial system conditions. Steps have been taken for cooperation in monitoring short-tem capital flows and developing a regional early-warning system to assess regional financial vulnerabilities, with a view to preventing financial crises in the future. However, this process has not yet been as effective as it should be. There is no clear linkage between surveillance and CMI. There is no independent, professional organization that prepares comprehensive analyses or assessments or identifies issues for discussion.[17]

Initiatives have been taken to develop Asian bond markets in view of the need to channel a vast pool of savings to long-term investment for growth and development within the region. This effort reflects the recognition that the financial system in East Asia has been too dependent on bank financing domestically and on foreign-currency financing externally and, hence, needs to be strengthened through the development of national and regional capital, in particular of bond, markets. Development of well-functioning, local-currency denominated bond markets is expected to reduce incentives for banks and corporations to rely on bank financing and/or external borrowing. It is expected to mitigate the 'double mismatch' problem of international capital markets — i.e., of currency and maturity mismatches.

The EMEAP–led central bank process established an Asian Bond

---

[16] Other major mechanisms include the ASEAN Surveillance Process, EMEAP (Executives Meeting of East Asia-Pacific Central Banks), and trans-regional forums such as Asia-Pacific Economic Cooperation (APEC) and Asia-Europe Meeting (ASEM).

[17] The Asian Development Bank provides some data on developing member economies. The IMF used to play the role of a secretariat for the MFG.

Fund (ABF) in June 2003 to facilitate bond issuance. The idea behind the process is to help expand the bond market through the demand side by purchasing sovereign or quasi-sovereign bonds using foreign exchange reserves. So far, only U.S. dollar-denominated bonds have been purchased. Given the recognition that local-currency denominated bonds need to be promoted in order to address the issue of the 'double mismatch,' the central bankers have introduced ABF–2 (December 2004), which involves purchases of Asian-currency denominated bonds. The ASEAN+3 Finance Minister process has undertaken the Asian Bond Market Initiative (ABMI) to develop local currency denominated bonds through the demand side since August 2003. One of its aims is to establish a market infrastructure for bond market development — including the establishment of a regional bond guarantee agency, the strengthening of regional rating agencies and the promotion of secondary markets — and to encourage bond issues denominated in a basket of Asian currencies.

East Asian Economic Community

One of the recent, most significant developments is the agreement by East Asian Leaders in Vientiane in November 2004 that they would make efforts to form an 'East Asian Community' and hold an East Asian Summit for this purpose. The idea of creating an 'East Asian Community' was proposed by East Asia Vision Group (2001). The Vision Group recommended: (a) economic cooperation; (b) financial cooperation; (c) political and security cooperation; (d) environmental cooperation; (e) social and cultural cooperation; and (f) institutional cooperation. A core component of these recommendations that is relevant to trade/investment integration and international financial management is (a) and (b).

Economic cooperation includes the following first four items and financial cooperation includes the last three items:

- Establishment of the East Asian Free Trade Area (EAFTA) and liberalization of trade well ahead of the APEC Bogor Goal;
- Expansion of the Framework Agreement on an ASEAN Investment Area to all of East Asia;

- Promotion of development and technological cooperation among regional countries, particularly to provide assistance to less developed countries;
- Realization of a knowledge-based economy and the establishment of future-oriented economic structure;
- Establishment of a self-help regional facility for financial cooperation;
- Adoption of a better exchange rate coordination mechanism consistent with both financial stability and economic development; and
- Strengthening of the regional monitoring and surveillance process within East Asia to supplement IMF global surveillance and Article IV consultation measures.

The Vision Group essentially envisions the progressive integration of the East Asian economies, ultimately leading to an East Asian economic community. Once a region-wide FTA is formed and institutions for international financial management and exchange rate coordination are established, the basic foundation of an East Asian economic community will have been provided. Thus the Vision Group has offered an important long-term vision of the economic future of East Asia.

The ASEAN+3 government officials responded to the Vision Group's recommendations by submitting their report to the ASEAN+3 Summit meeting (East Asia Study Group 2002). They have taken most of the recommendations and laid out some concrete implementable measures in the short run as well as some goals in the medium- and long-term. Their views are summarized by the following statements:

- East Asian cooperation is inevitable and necessary;
- Deeper integration of an East Asian community is beneficial and desirable; and
- Integration in East Asia will evolve over time as we consolidate the coherence, efficiency, and progress of the ASEAN+3 framework.

Challenges for Closer Economic Regionalism in East Asia

If an East Asian economic community is to be created, the region must become a single market. A starting point for this would be to establish a single East Asia-wide FTA, which should evolve to an East Asian customs union and a common market. Establishing a single East Asia-wide FTA, however, is no easy task once there is a proliferation of many different FTAs/EPAs in the region. Each FTA/EPA may have different rules of origin and external tariffs. One challenge is how to avoid the so-called 'spaghetti bowl' effect by ensuring consistency across different trade arrangements. To make the task easier, each FTA/EPA should have transparent, simple rules with regard to external tariffs, exclusion lists, rules of origin, and harmonization of standards, procedures and regulations. Convergence towards identical rules and common tariff rates, rules and standards is highly desirable.

A second area is financial regionalism. The ASEAN+3 countries have been reviewing the CMI since May 2004, including the amount, modality and IMF linkages. The total amount covered by the CMI is limited in view of the potential size of speculative capital flows and, hence, should be increased substantially perhaps by as much as ten times the current size. Over the medium term, its bilateral nature may be modified to become centralized and multilateral in order to make its joint activation effective and prompt in the event of a crisis.[18] Again over the medium term, the degree of the CMI's linkage to IMF programs may be reduced or even eliminated as the quality of economic surveillance is improved. In this sense, CMI and surveillance are inter-linked. Over the short term, the central issue is how to improve the effectiveness and quality of surveillance within ASEAN+3, along the line of the G–7 and OECD processes (Economic Policy Committee, Economic Development and Review Committee, and Working Party No. 3). One way to strengthen regional surveillance would be to set up a competent Secretariat, whose primary role would be to assist the ASEAN+3 surveillance process by providing high-quality and in-depth economic reviews and assessments, timely identification of emerging issues and vulnerabilities affecting the region,

[18] Rajan and Siregan (2004) go one step further and propose to establish a centralized reserve pooling system.

and effective policy advice. This secretariat must have adequate professional staff to monitor regional capital flows and financial and exchange market developments, update early warning indicators, and analyze regional and country economic conditions.

To develop Asian-currency denominated bond markets, sufficient incentives must be created on the part of both investors and issuers. Corporate governance of potential issuers needs to be enhanced, and well-designed national and regional market infrastructure needs to be developed, including disclosure requirements, accounting and auditing standards, rating agencies, depository and clearance systems and insolvency procedures for bond defaults. An important challenge will be how to strike the right balance between the efficient development of local-currency bond markets and the effective management of capital accounts. The reason for this is that well-functioning bond markets would require an open capital account, which can be an important source of financial instability.

A third area is exchange rate policy. A variety of exchange rate regimes exist in East Asia, but no concrete steps have been taken so far to initiate exchange rate policy coordination. Given a rising degree of economic interdependence among the East Asian economies through trade, investment and financial flows, it is increasingly important to maintain intra-regional exchange rate stability, which requires closer policy coordination among the financial and monetary authorities in the region. One country's exchange rate adjustment can have serious, competitive implications for neighboring economies — hence the need for coordination on exchange rate policies. Essentially, intra-regional exchange rate stability is a public good for regional growth and economic stability. Another reason for regional policy coordination is the fact that crisis contagion tends to be concentrated, and economic spill-overs tend to be significant, within a region.

East Asia's exchange rate policy coordination may evolve in three stages:[19]

[19] See Montiel (2004) for an excellent review.

- Loose policy coordination: information coordination, initial institutional coordination, and resource coordination;
- Tight policy coordination: macroeconomic and exchange rate policy coordination for intra-regional exchange rate stabilization; and
- Complete policy coordination: economic and monetary union with a single currency.

First, regional policymakers can strengthen information coordination, particularly on policy dialogue and surveillance. This dialogue should focus on exchange market developments, capital flows, foreign exchange reserves, and monetary, fiscal policy and exchange rate policies. In the current context, the regional authorities need to discuss such issues as foreign exchange reserve management, impact of a possible exit of the Chinese RMB from a U.S. dollar peg, and policies to facilitate smooth adjustments of trans-Pacific payments imbalances.

Policymakers should begin institutional coordination, including the creation of a regional common unit of account, or the Asian Currency Unit (ACU), and the adoption of a G–3 currency basket system. The ACU can be created by constructing a basket of regional currencies that include 13 currencies for ASEAN+3. Just like the European Currency Unit (ECU) under the EMS (1979–98), the weights of the regional currencies would reflect the relative importance of the countries in the region. The ACU could be used to denominate economic transactions (current and capital accounts) and asset stocks (foreign exchange reserves and cross-border bonds) and to measure the degree of each currency's exchange rate deviation from the regional average. In addition, the emerging economies in East Asia may adopt a common G–3 currency basket system. For them, because of their increasingly interdependent nature, a certain degree of intra-regional exchange rate stability is clearly desirable, while at the same time maintaining extra-regional exchange rate stability. This can be achieved by individual economy each using a common basket of G–3 currencies — the U.S. dollar, the euro and the Japanese yen — as a reference for exchange rate stabilization. The reason is that with diverse economic relationships with the United States,

Japan and the European Union, the region's economies would be able to achieve a reasonable degree of exchange rate stability, on an effective basis, by adopting a well-balanced G–3 currency basket which would provide a better buffer to an economy due to yen/dollar and yen/euro rate volatility.[20] The degree of exchange rate stabilization can be left to an economy's specific conditions and preferences. Adoption of a common currency basket within emerging East Asia — and loosely or tightly stabilizing each exchange rate to such a basket — would provide a benefit of maintaining relative stability of intra-regional as well as extra-regional exchange rates.[21]

Before moving to the second stage, region's policymakers may consider strengthening resource coordination. This involves expanding the CMI into a centralized, multilaterally administered arrangement with substantially larger stocks of resources than are presently available.[22] This expanded reserve pooling arrangement will be increasingly independent of IMF programs and, hence, require alternative conditionality to be developed for currency crises. With a centrally administered CMI with its own secretariat, the ASEAN+3 countries will have effectively

---

[20] In the post-crisis period, Korea and Thailand appear to be shifting to a *de facto* currency basket system, a la Singapore. See Kawai (2002b). McKinnon (2000, 2001), however, takes the view that the East Asian economies have resurrected the U.S. dollar standard system. See Kawai (2004a) who aruges for the adoption of a G-3 currency basket system.

[21] This approach is consistent with what Goldstein (2002) calls 'managed floating plus.' A 'managed float' is a system with occasional intervention to limit excessive short-term fluctuations in exchange rates without being accompanied by a publicly announced exchange rate target, and a 'plus' is inflation targeting and aggressive measures to reduce currency mismatches. Our approach is to adopt a G-3 currency basket as an exchange rate reference in the context of 'managed floating plus,' a la Williamson (1999, 2000, 2001). Even when a G-3 currency basket system is desirable for the region as a whole, however, it may not be easy for any single economy to move unilaterally away from the current, U.S. dollar-centered exchange rate arrangement to a new arrangement in which the relative weight of the dollar is smaller and that of the yen and euro larger. When neighboring countries stabilize their exchange rates primarily against the U.S. dollar, there may not be much incentive for any one country to unilaterally alter its exchange rate policy, which demonstrates a potential 'collective action' problem associated with a move to a G-3 currency basket arrangement (Ogawa and Ito 2002). Overcoming this problem requires a concerted move among the economies concerned.

[22] Rajan and Siregan (2004) propose to establish a centralized reserve pooling system.

established an Asian Monetary Fund (AMF). The region should be in a position to address the earlier concern that an AMF that could lend too generously with too little conditionality might create a moral hazard for the government at the receiving end as well as for investors with stakes in the countries in question.[23] It is therefore essential to improve economic surveillance, acquire capacity to formulate appropriate adjustment policy in the event of a liquidity crisis and, to the extent necessary, enforce effective private sector involvement.

Second, as the region becomes more integrated, it exhibits greater economic and political convergence, and hence is better prepared for a more permanent commitment to economic policy coordination, more formal institutions capable of supporting intra-regional exchange rate stability need to be built. In the second stage of exchange rate policy coordination, two approaches are possible. A realistic approach is a multi-track approach where several groups of economies in East Asia — like Japan and Korea, or Singapore, Malaysia and Brunei — that are close enough may initiate sub-regional currency stabilization schemes a la European Snake or ERM. This approach might be more realistic because economies that are ready can go ahead for closer monetary and exchange rate policy coordination, and latecomers will gradually catch up with the forerunners. To help sustain either approach, systematic macroeconomic policy coordination is essential — particularly monetary and fiscal policy rules — to make the stabilization system credible.

Finally, in the last stage the region may establish economic and monetary union with a common currency, like the euro regime. A common currency arrangement, however, cannot be expected in the very near future because of the lack of political commitments, political and economic convergence, and deeper complementary institutions.[24] Such an arrangement would require member economies' readiness to accept complete coordination of monetary policy — and closer coordination of other economic policies — long before its implementation.

---

[23] Nonetheless, Rapkin (2001) takes a pessimistic view of an AMF.

[24] See Wyploz (2004) for the importance of institutional integration for a currency union.

Overcoming Impediments to Closer Economic Regionalism

There are four possible impediments to deepening economic integration and advancing economic regionalism in East Asia:

- East Asia's global orientation in trade, FDI, money and finance — its openness to North America and Europe;
- Concern about possible conflict with global economic systems governed by the WTO and the IMF — fear of protectionism, discrimination, trade diversion and proliferation of financial crises;
- Diversity and heterogeneity in economic, financial and social developments within East Asia — differences in per capita incomes, industrial and financial structures, and domestic institutional and human capacities;
- Lack of political consensus for closer economic regionalism.

Sceptics might argue that East Asia is more closely integrated with the United States and Europe than with regional economies and that the region can gain more from further integration with the global market than with the regional market. Hence, forming an East Asia-wide RTA, with the United States and Europe excluded, is not a commendable idea because they are still important markets for the region's final products. The belief is that the expansion of intra-regional trade in East Asia, supported by FDI, has been made possible by open markets in the United States and Europe that have been absorbing East Asian finished products. In the money and finance area, the region's global orientation provides greater risk sharing for smooth consumption. The region's economies are also still highly dependent on the U.S. dollar for exchange rate stabilization, trade invoicing, external asset holding, foreign exchange reserve holding, and external liabilities.

The corollary of this view would be that global frameworks of trade/investment liberalization and of international financial management would be more important for East Asia than are regional frameworks. This implies that trade and investment liberalization within the WTO, or at least within APEC, would be more desirable than through regional FTAs. This argument tends to be supported by those who cast doubt about East Asian trade regionalism because it might undermine the WTO principle of maintaining a liberal, non-discriminatory, and multilateral trading system.[25] It also implies that international financial management under the IMF's umbrella, rather than under a regional financial arrangement, would be more beneficial to East Asia.

One of the most serious challenges is that the East Asian economies are quite diverse and varied in their economic systems and stages of financial and social developments — such as per capita income levels, industrial and financial structures, trade openness and patterns, scope and extent of exchange and capital controls, institutional and human capacities, and health and other social conditions.[26] Diversity and heterogeneity imply that low-income countries — where market infrastructure is insufficiently developed — will be slow in trade, investment and financial liberalization and market opening and, hence, it will be difficult to integrate themselves with the rest of East Asia at a fast pace. This constitutes an obvious impediment to economic regionalism for the whole of East Asia. In addition, given such economic diversity and heterogeneity, economies in the region have different policy objectives and priorities and desire to maintain national sovereignty over economic policies. In order for the economies to take joint action at the regional level, there must be substantial economic convergence.

Finally, one might argue that there is no political consensus for economic integration within East Asia due to differences in political systems, 'history' issues and the lack of mutual trust. No single economic power plays a dominant role in East Asia similar to that of the United States in the Western Hemisphere, nor does any bipolar relationship exist similar to the Franco–German alliance in Western Europe. Japan has been mired in economic stagnation over the last decade and China, while recently emerging as an economic power, has yet to achieve transition to a market economy and, more fundamentally, political transition.

---

[25] Lloyd (2002) argues that bilateralism/FTAs will likely lead toward, and not impede, multilateralism, while Brown, Deardorff and Stern (2003) continue to believe in superiority of multilateralism.

[26] Ravenhill (2001) argues that diversity of membership and conflicts of power and interest sharply limit potential for cooperation in East Asia, while Terada (2003) provides a constructive and relatively optimistic account of the regional grouping.

It is useful to point out that some of these impediments are real, but they are not insurmountable. There is no doubt that global frameworks for trade/investment liberalization (WTO) and international financial management (IMF) remain important. Yet there is room for regional frameworks to play complementary roles. In the trade and investment area, the United States is no longer the most dominant economic partner for many East Asian economies, and the regional markets for final products are expanding fast. Large part of inward FDI flows in the region now originates from within the region. In addition, East Asia is in no way inward looking as evidenced by the fact that many of them are negotiating on FTAs with countries outside of the region and are at the same time focusing on domestic structural reforms, higher productivity and economic growth, thus minimizing trade diversion effects. The East Asian approach is to regard the WTO principle — and APEC principles — as the basic infrastructure for international trade rules and achieve greater liberalization beyond the commitments of the WTO and APEC — called the 'WTO–plus' or 'APEC–plus' approach.

In the money and finance area, regional policymakers have found it absolutely necessary to manage financial globalization through various measures, including the strengthening of a regional financial architecture. They have also found the cost of excessive reliance on the U.S. dollar very high, so that they have embarked on measures to increase the use of regional currencies such as the Asian bond market development. These regional efforts are not a substitute for, but a complement of, global and national efforts for crisis prevention, management and resolution.

Diversity and heterogeneity are not the ultimate impediments to economic regionalism, but a lack of political will could be. One clear observation is that, despite heterogeneity and differences in economic and social systems among the countries in the region, they have increasingly come to realize that the economic logic for strengthening regional frameworks for trade/investment integration and international financial management is overriding. They have found the large benefit of economic integration and its institutionalization to outweigh the costs of not doing so. It is extremely important to raise the economic basis of poor members within East Asia to encourage them to grow. For the time being, a realistic approach would be a multi-track approach: Countries that are ready for deeper integration and closer cooperation may negotiate on RTAs and financial arrangements, while those countries not ready are advised to pursue structural, institutional and governance reforms — with assistance from Japan, Korea, advanced ASEAN members and multilateral development banks — to enable them to from further liberalization and integration. As these low-income countries catch up with their more advanced peers, they can start participating in closer economic regionalism.

Trust Building and Leadership

On the issue of political consensus, it is important to point out that the region's governments have initiated efforts to form an 'East Asian Community,' whose important component is an East Asian economic community. Though a unified ASEAN remains as an important key player in East Asia,[27] Japan and China are the most important drivers and they must form a solid bipolar alliance and joint leadership. For this purpose, they need to resolve the issues impeding deeper economic integration between them and to re-establish mutual trust.[28] Without this, the region cannot make meaningful progress on economic regionalism that may eventually lead to an East Asian economic community.

It is important to realize that China is changing rapidly in its approach to regional economic cooperation. The payoff of such a policy appears high for China because its economic growth depends on the favorable prospect of the regional economies, political stability, and peace and security. Its FTA initiative with ASEAN is one important sign of its willingness to deepen its economic, as well as political, relationship with its Southeast Asian neighbors. Its active engagement with the CMI and surveillance is another sign. China faces two big challenges. First, transition from a plan to a market must be achieved. In particular, further liberalization of trade, investment and capital accounts is crucial for its integration

---

[27] Ba (2003) argues that while important differences remain, the relationship between China and ASEAN has improved markedly over the past decade.

[28] Rozman (2002) argues that China continues to see Japan as a partner and a rival, struggling to balance between the two.

with the regional and global economy, which needs to be pursued in a cautious, well-sequenced way. Second, its political system transition must be achieved in an orderly way for the stability of not only China but also of East Asia and the World.

The absence of a solid, region-wide security arrangement with military functions may make it difficult for the region's economies to deepen economic cooperation, including initiatives for the creation of a region-wide FTA and formal financial institutions, and eventually an East Asian economic community. This absence may be partly attributed to the difference in political systems, the lack of common culture, religion, value, shared history, and mutual trust across East Asia. Many of these points are valid. However, a convergence toward similar political systems will inevitably take pace as China and other communist countries continue to pursue market-based structural reforms and achieve economic development and further integration with the global and regional economies, because these will encourage them to move toward more democratic societies.

It is essential that Japan and China, the two economic powers in the region, work together for closer economic regionalism. To some extent, healthy rivalry between the two major powers is desirable as long as it enhances market-driven competition and does not impede mutual trust and sense of community in East Asia. The two countries must jointly work hard on key issues:

- Japan and China must resolve the 'history' issue permanently so that the two countries can rebuild mutual trust for greater economic integration.
- Japan and China must cooperate as bipolar partners to nurture emerging economic regionalism in East Asia particularly on trade, investment, and financial issues. Such regionalism includes the formation of an East Asia-wide FTA, a zone of stable Asian currencies, and eventually an 'East Asia Economic Community.'
- Japan and China need to strengthen various types of economic policy dialogue including, for example, investment rules, protection

of intellectual property rights, macroeconomic policy management, food and energy security, etc.

This is entirely possible if both sides take bold and forward-looking political gestures.

Concluding Remarks

This paper has demonstrated that the East Asian economies have achieved strong economic interdependence, particularly through domestic structural reforms, external liberalization and market-driven integration with the global and regional economies. Expansion of foreign trade, direct investment and financial flows has created a 'naturally' integrated economic zone in East Asia. Reflecting the rising economic interdependence and in response to the traumatic financial crisis of 1997–98, East Asia has embarked on various initiatives for economic regionalism. Such initiatives include the formation of several bilateral FTAs, the beginning of negotiations for regional FTAs, the establishment of a regional surveillance mechanism, the introduction of a regional liquidity support system (CMI) and Asian bond market development. These essentially entail the formal institutionalization of *de facto* economic integration and interdependence in East Asia in a way that complements global frameworks of the WTO and the IMF.

There are several challenges for the region. First, the regional economies should accelerate negotiations on bilateral and regional FTAs — such as a Japan–Korea EPA, Japan–ASEAN EPA, China–ASEAN FTA and Korea–ASEAN FTA — which provide a critical basis for further integration and interdependence. Such regional trade agreements need to avoid the counterproductive 'spaghetti bowl' effect, by ensuring coherence of rules, standards and procedures across different FTAs in the region, and maintain WTO consistency — and even strengthen the WTO framework by pursuing an outward-oriented, 'WTO–plus' approach. This requires substantial structural reforms on the part of all economies, including in both manufacturing and agricultural sectors. This is particularly the case with ASEAN: Its middle-income member states must reform their economies to cope with greater international competition, particularly *vis-à-vis* China, while its low-income members must pursue institutional and governance reforms to enable them to benefit from trade and FDI openness.

Second, the regional economies need to make further progress in the money and finance area, by strengthening the liquidity provision mechanism (CMI), the policy dialogue and economic surveillance process, and Asian bond market development initiatives. It is crucial to enhance the functioning of the CMI on the occasion of its review starting in May 2004 through: the enlargement of its size by as much as ten times the current commitment; multilateralization and joint activation of the currency swap arrangements; reduction of its IMF linkages with enhanced economic surveillance; and greater use of Asian currencies for swap arrangements. For such reforms, however, the region must address the earlier concern that an AMF that could lend too generously with too little conditionality might create a moral hazard for the government at the receiving end as well as for investors with stakes in the countries in question. It is therefore essential to make the surveillance process effective, improve the regional capacity to formulate appropriate adjustment policy in the event of liquidity crisis and, to the extent necessary, enforce effective private sector involvement. Once these efforts are made, East Asia will have effectively established an Asian Monetary Fund that can contribute to regional financial stability without creating fears of moral hazard.

Third, it is time to initiate exchange rate policy coordination because there has not been much progress in this area. The first step would be for the regional economies to discuss exchange rate issues as part of an enhanced surveillance process. The next task is to introduce a G–3 currency basket arrangement based on the Japanese yen, the US dollar and the euro among the emerging East Asian economies. The third task is to introduce a regional common unit of account in East Asia — an Asian Currency Unit (ACU) — whose weights should reflect the relative importance of the regional economies. It would be useful for ASEAN+3 to discuss member countries' exchange rate deviations from the regional average in reference to the ACU. Once the region (or a group of countries in the region) becomes more integrated over time, exhibits greater economic and political convergence, and hence is better prepared for a more permanent commitment to economic policy coordination, more formal institutions capable of supporting intra-regional exchange rate stability — such as an 'Asian Snake' or an 'Asian ERM' — need to be built, perhaps on a multi-track basis.

Finally, it is important to overcome various impediments to closer economic regionalism. Some of the impediments will become less serious as economic interdependence deepens in the region, while others require fundamental efforts such as integrating ASEAN late-comers with the regional and global markets. The region must nurture the sense of mutual trust and community by developing a long-term vision for the political and economic future of East Asia and having such a vision shared by the general public in the region. One vision for a future East Asian economic community would be a full-fledged economic and monetary union with a single currency like the euro zone. Japan and China must assume joint leadership toward East Asian economic integration by permanently resolving, and putting behind, the 'history' issue.

References

Athukorala, Prema-chandra. 2003. 'Product Fragmentation and Trade Patterns in East Asia.' Working Paper No. 2003/21 (October), Division of Economics, Research School of Pacific and Asian Studies, Australian National University.

Baldwin, Richard E. 1997. 'The Causes of Regionalism.' *World Economy* 20(7): 865-888.

Bayoumi, Tamin and Barry Eichengreen. 1994. 'One Money or Many? Analyzing the Prospects for Monetary Unification in Various Parts of the World.' *Princeton Studies in International Finance*, No. 76, International Finance Section, Princeton University, Princeton.

Bayoumi, Tamin, Barry Eichengreen and Paolo Mauro. 2000. 'On Regional Monetary Arrangements for ASEAN.' *Journal of the Japanese and International Economies* 14 (June): 121-148.

Bird, Graham and Ramkishen S. Rajan. 2002. 'The Evolving Asian Financial Architecture.' *Essays in International Economics*, No. 226 (February), International Economics Section, Princeton University, Princeton.

Brainard, S. Lael. 1997. 'An Empirical Assessment of the Proximity-Concentration Trade-off between Multinational Sales and Trade.' *American Economic Review* 87(4): 520-544.

Brown, Drusilla K., Alan V. Deardorff and Robert M. Stern. 2003. 'Multilateral, Regional and Bilateral Trade-Policy Options for the United States and Japan.' *World Economy* 26(6): 803-828.

East Asia Study Group. 2002. 'Final Report of the East Asia Study Group.' ASEAN+3 Summit (November 4), Phnom Penh, Cambodia.

East Asia Vision Group. 2001. 'Toward an East Asian Community: Region of Peace, Prosperity and Progress.' East Asia Vision Group Report.

Eichengreen, Barry. 1999. *Toward a New International Financial Architecture: A Practical Post-Asia Agenda.* Washington, DC: Institute for International Economics.

Eichengreen, Barry. 2004a. 'Hanging Together? On Monetary and Financial Cooperation.' Shahid Yusuf, M. Anjun Altaf and Kaoru Nabeshima, eds., *Global Change and East Asian Policy Initiatives.* Washington, DC and New York: World Bank and Oxford University Press, pp. 25-62.

Eichengreen, Barry. 2004b. 'The Case for Floating Exchange Rates in Asia.' Asian Development Bank, ed., *Monetary and Financial Integration in East Asia: The Way Ahead*, Vol. 2. Houndmills and New York: Palgrave MacMillan, pp. 49-89.

Eichengreen, Barry and Tamim Bayoumi. 1999. 'Is Asia an Optimum Currency Area? Can It Become One? Regional, Global and Historical Perspectives on Asian Monetary Relations.' S. Collignon, J. Pisani-Ferry and Y.C. Park, eds., *Exchange Rate Policies in Emerging Asian Countries*. London: Routledge, pp. 347–366.

Feenstra, Robert C. 1998. 'Integration of Trade and Disintegration of Production in the Global Economy.' *Journal of Economic Perspectives* 12(4): 31-50.

Frankel, Jeffrey A. 1999. 'No Single Currency Regime Is Right for All Countries or at All Times.' *Essays in International Finance*, No. 215 (August), International Finance Section, Princeton University, Princeton.

Fukao, Kyoji, Hikari Ishido and Keiko Ito. 2003. 'Vertical Intra-industry Trade and Foreign Direct Investment in East Asia.' *Journal of the Japanese and International Economies* 17(4): 468-506.

Fukasaku, Kiichiro, Masahiro Kawai, Michael G Plummer and Alexandra Trzeciak-Duval. 2004. 'Overview: Miracle, Crisis and Beyond.' Chapter 1 of a Joint MOF/PRI-OECD Research Project, *The Impact and Coherence of OECD Country Policies on Asian Developing Economies.*

Girardin, Eric. 2004. 'Information Exchange, Surveillance Systems and Regional Institutions in East Asia.' Asian Development Bank, ed., *Monetary and Financial Integration in East Asia: The Way Ahead*, Vol. 1. Houndmills and New York: Palgrave MacMillan, pp. 53-95.

Goldstein, Morris. 2002. 'Managed Floating Plus.' *Policy Analyses in International Economics*, No. 66 (March), Institute for International Economics, Washington, DC.

Goto, Junichi and Koichi Hamada. 1994. 'Economic Preconditions for Asian Regional Integration.' Takatoshi Ito and Anne O. Krueger, eds., *Macroeconomic Linkage: Savings, Exchange Rates, and Capital Flows.* Chicago: University of Chicago Press, pp. 359-385.

Hernandez, Leonardo and Peter J. Montiel. 2003. 'Post-crisis Exchange Rate Policy in Five Asian Countries: Filling in the 'Hollow Middle'?' *Journal of the Japanese and International Economies* 17(3): 336-369.

Hew, Denis and Hadi Soesastro. 2003. 'Realizing the ASEAN Economic Community by 2020 — ISEAS and ASEAN-ISIS Approaches.' *ASEAN Economic Bulletin* 20(3): 292-296.

International Monetary Fund (IMF). 2003. 'The IMF and Recent Capital Account Crises: Indonesia, Korea, Brazil.' Evaluation Report, Independent Evaluation Office, Washington, DC.

Kawai, Masahiro. 1997. 'Japan's Trade and Investment in East Asia.' David Robertson, ed., *East Asian Trade after the Uruguay Round.* Cambridge: Cambridge University Press, pp. 209-226.

Kawai, Masahiro. 2002a. 'Global, Regional and National Approaches to the International Financial Architecture: Lessons from the East Asian Crisis.' *International Economy* 7: 65-108.

Kawai, Masahiro. 2002b. 'Exchange Rate Arrangements in East Asia: Lessons from the 1997-98 Currency Crisis.' *Monetary and Economic Studies, Special Edition* 20 (December): 167-204.

Kawai, Masahiro. 2004. 'The Case for a Tri-polar Currency Basket System for Emerging East Asia.' Gordon de Brouwer and Masahiro Kawai, eds., *Exchange Rate Regimes in East Asia.* London and New York: Routledge Curzon, pp. 360-384.

Kawai, Masahiro. 2005a. 'Trade and Investment Integration and Cooperation in East Asia: Empirical Evidence and Issues.' *ADB, Asian Economic Cooperation and Integration: Progress, Prospects, and Challenges.* Manila: ADB, pp. 161-193.

Kawai, Masahiro and Taizo Motonishi. 2005. 'Macroeconomic Interdependence in East Asia: Empirical Evidence and Issues.' *ADB, Asian Economic Cooperation and Integration: Progress, Prospects, and Challenges.* Manila: ADB, pp. 213-268.

Kawai, Masahiro, Richard Newfarmer and Sergio Schmukler. 2003. 'Crisis and Contagion in East Asia: Nine Lessons.' *Eastern Economic Journal* 31(2): 185-207.

Kawai, Masahiro and Shinji Takagi. 2000. 'Proposed Strategy for a Regional Exchange Rate Arrangement in Post-Crisis East Asia.' *Policy Research Working Paper*, No. 2502 (December), World Bank, Washington, DC.

Kawai, Masahiro and Shujiro Urata. 1998. 'Are Trade and Direct Investment Substitutes or Complements? An Empirical Analysis of Japanese Manufacturing Industries.' Hiro Lee and David W. Roland-Holst, eds., *Economic Development and Cooperation in the Pacific Basin: Trade, Investment, and Environmental Issues.* Cambridge, UK: Cambridge University Press, pp. 251-293.

Kawai, Masahiro and Shujiro Urata. 2004. 'Trade and Foreign Direct Investment in East Asia.' Gordon de Brouwer and Masahiro Kawai, eds., *Economic Linkages and Implications for Exchange Rate Regimes in East Asia.* London and New York: Routledge Curzon, pp. 15-102.

Kenen, Peter B. 2001. *The International Financial Architecture: What's New? What's Missing?* Washington, DC: Institute for International Economics.

Krumm, Kathie and Homi Kharas. 2003. 'Overview.' Kathie Krumm and Homi Kharas, eds., *East Asia Integrates: A Trade Policy Agenda for Shared Growth.* Washington, DC: World Bank, pp. xv-xliv.

Kuroda, Haruhiko and Masahiro Kawai. 2002. 'Strengthening Regional Financial Cooperation in East Asia.' *Pacific Economic Papers* 51 (October).

Lloyd, Peter. 2002. 'New Bilateralism in the Asia Pacific.' *World Economy* 25(9): 1279-1296.

McCauley, Robert N., San-Sau Fund and Blaise Gadanecz. 2000. 'Integrating the Finances of East Asia.' *BIS Quarterly Review* (December): 83-95.

McKinnon, Ronald I. 2000. 'The East Asian Dollar Standard: Life after Death?' *Economic Notes* 29 (February): 31-82.

McKinnon, Ronald I. 2001. 'After the Crisis, the East Asian Dollar Standard Resurrected.' A paper presented to the international conference on 'Monetary Outlook on East Asia in an Integrating World Economy' (September 5-6), Chulalongkorn University, Bangkok.

Montiel, Peter J. 2004. 'An Overview of Monetary and Financial Integration in East Asia.' Asian Development Bank, ed., *Monetary and Financial Integration in East Asia: The Way Ahead*, Vol. 1. Houndmills and New York: Palgrave MacMillan, pp. 1-52.

Ogawa, Eiji and Takatoshi Ito. 2002. 'On the Desirability of a Regional Basket Currency Arrangement.' *Journal of the Japanese and International Economies* 16: 317-334.

Organisation for Economic Co-operation and Development (OECD). 2003a. *Harmonizing Donor Practices for Effective Aid Delivery, DAC Guidelines and Reference Series.* Development Assistance Committee, Paris.

Organisation for Economic Co-operation and Development (OECD). 2003b. *Regionalism and Multilateral Trading System.* Secretary General, Paris.

Pangestu, Mari and Sudarshan Gooptu. 2003. 'New Regionalism: Options for East Asia.' Kathie Krumm and Homi Kharas, eds., *East Asia Integrates: A Trade Policy Agenda for Shared Growth.* Washington, DC: World Bank, pp. 39-57.

Rajan, Ramkishen and Reza Siregar. 2004. 'Centralized Reserve Pooling for the ASEAN+3 Countries.' Asian Development Bank, ed., *Monetary and Financial Integration in East Asia: The Way Ahead,* Vol. 2. Houndmills and New York: Palgrave MacMillan, pp. 285-329.

Rapkin, David P. 2001. 'The United States, Japan, and the Power to Block: the APEC and AMF Cases.' *Pacific Review* 14(3): 373-410.

Ravenhill, John. 2001. *Asia Pacific Economic Cooperation: The Construction of Pacific Rim Regionalism.* Cambridge: Cambridge University Press.

Scollay, Robert and John Gilbert. 2001. *New Subregional Trading Arrangements in the Asia-Pacific.* Washington, DC: Institute for International Economics.

Scollay, Robert and John Gilbert. 2003. 'Impact of East Asian Regional or Subregional FTAs.' Report for the Australian Department of Foreign Affairs and Trade (May), Canberra.

Stubbs, Richard. 2002. 'ASEAN Plus Three: Emerging East Asian Regionalism?' *Asian Survey* 42(3): 440-455.

Takagi, Shinji and Kenichi Hirose. 2004. 'A Multivariate Approach to Grouping Financially Integrated Economies.' Gordon de Brouwer and Masahiro Kawai, eds., *Economic Linkages and Implications for Exchange Rate Regimes in East Asia.* London and New York: Routledge Curzon, pp. 131-152.

Terada, Takashi. 2003. 'Constructing an 'East Asian Concept' and Growing Regional Identity: From EAEC to ASEAN+3.' *Pacific Review* 16(2): 251–277.

Urata, Shujiro. 2001. 'Emergence of an FDI-Trade Nexus and Economic Growth in East Asia.' Joseph Stiglitz and Shahid Yusuf, eds., *Rethinking the East Asian Miracle.* New York: Oxford University Press, pp.407-459.

Williamson, John. 1999. 'The Case for a Common Basket Peg for East Asian Currencies.' Stefan Collignon, Jean Pisani-Ferry and Yung Chul Park, eds., *Exchange Rate Policies in Emerging Asian Countries.* London and New York: Routledge, pp. 327-343.

Williamson, John. 2000. 'Exchange Rate Regimes for Emerging Markets: Reviving the Intermediate Option.' *Policy Analyses in International Economics*, 60, Institute for International Economics, Washington, DC.

Williamson, John. 2001. 'The Case for a Basket, Band and Crawl (BBC) Regime for East Asia.' David Gruen and John Simon, eds., *Future Directions for Monetary Policies in East Asia.* Sydney: Reserve Bank of Australia, pp. 96-111.

Wong, John and Sarah Chan. 2003. 'China-ASEAN Free Trade Agreement: Shaping Future Economic Relations.' *Asian Survey* 43(3): 507-526.

World Bank. 1998. *East Asia: The Road to Recovery*. Washington, DC.

Wyplosz, Charles. 2004. 'Regional Exchange Rate Arrangements: Lessons from Europe for East Asia.' Asian Development Bank, ed., *Monetary and Financial Integration in East Asia: The Way Ahead*, Vol. 2. Houndmills and New York: Palgrave MacMillan, pp. 241-284.

Yusuf, Shahid, *et al.*, eds. 2003. *Innovative East Asia: The Future of Growth*. Washington, DC: World Bank.

CHAPTER 2

SEQUENCING REGIONAL INTEGRATION IN ASIA*

Richard Pomfret

Europe, the Americas, Sub-Saharan Africa, the Arab world and Australasia have all seen efforts towards regional integration in the last half century, but in East Asia the only regional integration has been in South-East Asia and that has made only limited progress.[1] This history has led to claims that Asia missed out on the benefits from regional integration, and since 1997 there have been proposals for Asian regional integration. The distinctive feature of the proposals is in their sequencing, which starts with monetary integration, in contrast to conventional views of regional integration, which start with trade and place monetary integration near the end of the process.

Despite the lack of policy-driven integration in East Asia, regional interdependence has grown substantially. Fukasaku (1992) describes the increase in intra-Asian trade in the second half of the twentieth century, as the region's economies grew faster than world trade and hence provided the fastest growing markets for one another's exports. More recently, Kawai (2005) has emphasised the combination of external trade

---

* Earlier versions of this chapter were presented at the Singapore Economic Review 50th Anniversary Conference on 4–6 August 2005 in Singapore, the Claremont Regional Integration Workshop in Claremont CA on 25 February 2005 (a revised version was published as Pomfret, 2005a), and at the East Asian Economic Association conference in Hong Kong on 13–14 November 2004. I am grateful to James Dean, Medhi Krongkaew, and other participants at these meetings for helpful suggestions. For comments on earlier drafts, I am also grateful to Paul Bowles, Ian McDonald and Ramkishen Rajan.

[1] In this chapter the terms regionalism and regional trade integration are used to describe a policy–driven process of economic integration, in contrast to market–driven regionalization.

liberalization, domestic structural reform, and market-driven integration (led by Japanese multinational corporations after the 1985 currency realignments) in promoting intra-regional trade, direct foreign investment and financial flows within East Asia, and hence creating a 'naturally' integrated economic zone. Rajan (2005) identifies a similar process emerging between India and China since the turn of the century.

Against this backdrop, a variety of approaches to establishing more formal institutions for regional integration have been proposed. The most dramatic were the calls, following the 1997 Crisis, for an Asian Monetary Fund or even for Asian currency union (Pomfret 2003). Although none of these proposals has yet made substantial progress, monetary cooperation has increased and proposals for quasi-monetary union, ie. less than a full-blown currency union, remain plausible (Kwack 2005).[2] Although negotiations on free trade agreements covering various combinations of Asian countries are taking place simultaneously, the distinguishing feature of East Asian regionalism continues to be a focus on monetary agreements. This is in contrast to the priority given to trade in mainstream economic thinking on the sequencing of regional integration.

The first section of the chapter examines whether East Asia missed out from not participating in the waves of regional trading arrangements during the second half of the twentieth century. Section 2 reviews the steps towards regional integration in East Asia since 1997. The third section assesses the validity of a sequence which puts monetary integration before trade integration. The fourth section analyses the obstacles to regional integration, both in the conventional trade-first sequence and in the Asian money-first sequence, addressing the issue of why so many proposed regional trading arrangements or currency unions amount to nothing. Section 5 applies the analysis to East Asia, and the final section draws conclusions about the prospects for regional integration in Asia.

[2] This view is, however, not universal among leading Asian economists. Nasution (2005, 441) concludes that a regional currency is 'neither desirable nor feasible'.

Regional Integration 1947–1997 — Did Asia Miss Out?

A paradox of the global trading system regulated by the General Agreement on Tariffs and Trade (GATT) and its successor the World Trade Organization (WTO) is that, despite the non-discrimination principle enshrined in the first article of the GATT, discriminatory trading arrangements have flourished. Such arrangements are permitted under the GATT/WTO rules, notably under Article XXIV on customs unions and the Enabling Clause for special treatment for developing countries, but the conditions for these exceptions have seldom been fully met in practice. Many of these arrangements have aimed at promoting regional integration, in apparent conflict with the commitment to multilateralism made by countries acceding to the GATT/WTO.

Since the GATT was signed in 1947, three waves of regionalism have swept the world trading system. During the 1950s and 1960s the 'rush to discrimination' was led by Western Europe, which founded the only substantial new customs union of the second half of the twentieth century and also established a complex network of preferential arrangements with other trade partners.[3] The European customs union was taken as a model by groups of developing countries in Africa, the Caribbean, Central America, and South America, but even the most promising of these arrangements, the East African Community and the Central American Common Market, collapsed during the 1970s.

The first wave of regionalism was resisted by the USA, which remained committed to the multilateral system, and was receding in the 1970s as the European Union became established as a single actor in the global trading system. Successful conclusion of multilateral trade negotiations in the 1961–4 Kennedy Round, in which the members of the European customs union negotiated with a single voice for the first time, and in the 1973–9 Tokyo Round, which first seriously addressed the issue of non-tariff barriers to trade, sent important signals of the leading trading nations' commitment to multilateralism.

[3] For more details on the trading arrangements mentioned in this paper, see Pomfret (2001) and Pomfret (2006).

A second wave of regionalism was initiated by the United States' departures from the GATT nondiscrimination principle in the first half of the 1980s and peaked with the North American Free Trade Agreement (NAFTA) negotiations in the early 1990s, which coincided with the European Union's 1992 project for completing the internal EU market. Although NAFTA was signed and implemented, the EU completed its 1992 program and Australia and New Zealand deepened their free trade area into the Closer Economic Relations (CER), the major trading nations reaffirmed their commitment to the non-discrimination principle with the successful conclusion of the 1986–94 Uruguay Round of multilateral trade negotiations and the establishment in 1995 of the World Trade Organization as the successor to the GATT.

As in the first wave, there was a demonstration effect as groups of developing countries worried about the need to establish and strengthen their own regional groupings.[4] The geographical scope was wider than in the first wave as Latin American regional arrangements such as Mercosur and African customs union in various overlapping incarnations were joined by Asian regional organizations. Among the regional organizations introducing tariff preferences in the 1980s or early 1990s were the Economic Cooperation Organization (ECO), the South Asian Association for Regional Cooperation (SAARC) and the Association of Southeast Asian Nations (ASEAN).

In the opening years of the twenty-first century, a third wave of discriminatory trading arrangements has been gathering force. This is led by Asian countries, which had previously been the strongest bulwarks of non-discrimination — Japan and South Korea within the WTO and China and Taiwan outside the WTO — who were joined, especially under the G.W. Bush administration, by the USA. The collapse of the 1999 WTO meetings in Seattle and the diminishing significance of APEC (including the half-hearted attempt by the USA to kick-start further trade liberalization at the 1999 APEC summit through its P5 initiative with Australia, Chile, New Zealand and Singapore) led to new approaches to

---

[4] Although it was outside the ambit of the WTO, the biggest change in this period was the collapse of a very large regional arrangement, the Soviet–led Council for Mutual Economic Assistance.

trade liberalization in the Asia–Pacific region. Bilateral negotiations were begun in 1999/2000 by Japan with Singapore, South Korea, Canada and Mexico, by South Korea with Chile and New Zealand as well as with Japan, and by Singapore with New Zealand (concluded in 2000), Australia, Canada and other countries.[5]

Although the third wave is seen as a recrudescence of regionalism, many of the bilaterals are not regional. Thailand under Thaksin, for example, began its policy of negotiating bilateral trade agreements with Bahrain and Australia, before moving on to the USA and Japan; this pattern is weakening Thailand's regional trading arrangements by eroding preferential treatment negotiated within ASEAN. South Korea's bilaterals started with Chile and New Zealand, willing collocutors, but hardly regional neighbours and never likely to generate large bilateral trade flows.[6]

As with the second wave, which was characterized by proponents as a 'new regionalism', the third wave has novel features. With respect to tariffs and some non-tariff barriers to trade, the post–Uruguay–Round bar is lower, so effective discrimination requires focus on other aspects. The bilateral agreement negotiated between Singapore and Japan in 2000 focused on areas such as financial services, capital flows and coordination of regulatory systems, which are analytically more difficult areas, often with inherently less transparency than the traditional trade barriers of tariffs or quotas. Although negotiations towards bilateral trade agreements are mushrooming in the Asia–Pacific region, the agreements' coverage and actual implementation are often limited.[7]

---

[5] On the genesis of the new bilateral agreements see Rajan, Sen and Siregar (2001). Bonapace (2004) provides an assessment of agreements in the Asia–Pacific region.

[6] The embracement of bilateral trade agreements by the USA since 2000 has also been global rather than regional, and often driven by a desire to identify and reward political allies rather than by economic considerations.

[7] In general, it is difficult to monitor the progress of these bilateral negotiations. Many countries have long had bilateral arrangements on double taxation, coordinated strategies to fight money laundering and other financial matters without making the claims to be furthering liberalization that the recent bilateral negotiations have attracted. Some negotiations appear to be driven by a desire for progress on a single contentious issue, eg. China has demanded as a precondition for entering into a FTA with Australia that it be granted market economy status by Australia. Singapore and Japan could happily leave

Whether regional/bilateral agreements are becoming a major feature of the global trading system (as opposed to a major preoccupation of trade negotiators) is not as obvious as many observers seem to believe. It is often asserted that, because the number of regional trading arrangements (RTAs) reached an all-time high in the early 2000s, regionalism is more prevalent than ever. Such counting is nonsense because some arrangements are obviously far more important than others and some are totally inconsequential. One reason for the rapid increase in the number of RTAs during the 1990s was the proliferation of bilateral and plurilateral free trade agreements among countries of the former Council for Mutual Economic Assistance; these were primarily a response to regional disintegration, rather than a trend towards regionalism. Another illustration of the meaninglessness of such measures occurred in 2004 when the number of arrangements registered with the WTO declined by about a fifth, mainly due to the accession of eight eastern European countries to the EU;[8] their web of bilateral trading arrangements and preferential agreements with the EU became redundant, although with their incorporation into the EU customs union the degree of regionalism was increased. In contrast, it is arguable that, despite the increased attention being paid to regional arrangements, the hold of multilateralism is stronger than ever as practically all trading nations have now acceded to the WTO, with lower trade barriers and stronger trade dispute settlement procedures.

Perceptions do, however, matter. Supporters of closer economic integration in Asia are concerned that Asia has been left behind in a global movement to regionalism represented by an expanded European Union and a putative Free Trade Area of the Americas.[9] Whether Asian coun-

---

agriculture outside their bilateral, but omitting agriculture is more contentious when they negotiate with a country like Thailand. Similarly, the US refusal to include sugar in its 'free trade' agreement with Australia greatly reduced the trade–creating potential of the agreement.

[8] As a result of the EU enlargement in 2004 the number of RTAs fell from 285 to 229, see the World Bank *Global Economic Prospects 2005*, p.53, n.1.

[9] 'Clearly, the Asian FTA effort is a belated example of a trend that has been widespread throughout the world for some time. Regionalism has become a critical part of the new international trade order. The world has seen a surge in regional arrangements since the

tries suffered from their minimal participation in the first two waves of regionalism is an issue which can be analysed by examining the consequences of those RTAs which did occur.

The customs unions agreed among developing countries in the 1950s and 1960s all failed because they were based on a regional form of import substitution. This inevitably led to conflict over trade diversion, as each member wanted a regional market for its own inefficient industries, but was unwilling to buy the expensive or poor quality import-substitutes being developed by their partners. The only East Asian attempt at such a strategy, ASEAN's promotion of Asean Industrial Projects, broke down for the same reason in the early 1980s. The European customs union had similar strains, especially with respect to farm products, but the political will for greater economic union overcame these trade-diversion costs even in large net economic losers from membership such as the United Kingdom or the Scandinavian countries.[10]

In the second wave of regionalism, supporters of NAFTA, the CER or the deeper EU argued that these were new forms of regionalism going into areas, such as increasing-returns industries, service activities, or policy harmonization, where the analysis of trade creation and trade diversion due to Viner (1950) was inapplicable. For the other RTAs of the 1980s and early 1990s, however, the practical outcomes were minimal for much the same reasons as in the first wave; each partner was unwilling to grant other partners non-trivial preferential access to its own protected markets. The Asian RTAs were especially ineffective. The two largest economies in SAARC, India and Pakistan, withheld MFN treatment from one another. ECO was in abeyance while Iran was at war with Iraq. Most studies find minimal effects on trade for SAARC and ECO or for ASEAN (Greenaway and Milner 2002: 577).

---

early 1990s. The GATT–WTO has been notified of over 250 regional trading agreements up to December 2002' (Naya, 2004, 4).

[10] The UK, Denmark and Sweden remain, however, notably more sceptical of economic union than most other EU members, a position reflected in their remaining outside the euro zone. Pomfret (1986) reviews the trade diversion due to policies towards agriculture, cars, steel, and textiles and clothing in the European customs union.

Despite the novel features of the third wave of regionalism, the thrust of the analysis of the first two waves remains valid. Even in the new areas, multilateral non-discriminatory trade liberalization is usually the best approach not only from a cosmopolitan global perspective, but also for the net economic welfare of the participants in regional arrangements. The lack of transparency and selective coverage of many bilateral agreements make it more likely, given the political economy of trade policy, that trade-creating opportunities will be passed over because they hurt domestic producers while trade diversion will be permitted. Such selectivity might facilitate reaching agreement, but, as happened with most of the first wave RTAs, it will undermine the sustainability of the new bilaterals.

In sum, despite the appearance of rampant regionalism, the vast majority of RTAs signed during the second half of the twentieth century ended in the trashcan. The only significant exceptions were the EU, NAFTA and perhaps the CER and Mercosur. The first two of these are important because they involve most of the largest trading nations, but they are also special cases, as will be argued below. For all other RTAs the economic costs of trade diversion fuelled breakdown. For the Asian countries which did not participate in RTAs, this assessment implies that they did not miss out. Indeed, given the stellar trade-led economic performance of the East Asian economies which embraced multilateralism, it is difficult to imagine how their economies could have performed much better under alternative trade regimes, and easy to imagine how they could have fared worse.

Regional Integration in East Asia 1997–2005

The emergence of Asian regionalism can be dated from 1997, and was partly in reaction to perceived shortcomings of the role of the multilateral institutions, especially the International Monetary Fund, during and after the 1997 Asian Crisis. In contrast to the previous modest steps towards regional trading arrangements by the East Asian countries, regional cooperation in monetary issues received enthusiastic support from some governments. The lead in proposing new institutional responses was taken by Japan, which floated the idea of an Asian Monetary Fund (AMF) at the ASEM Finance Ministers' meeting in Bangkok in September 1997.[11] Substantive progress in monetary coordination (eg. the 2000 Chiang Mai Initiative) was accompanied by calls from some quarters for more drastic monetary integration. The head of the Hong Kong Monetary Authority, Joseph Yam, raised the possibility of an Asian currency unit and the Philippine President Joseph Estrada put the issue on the Agenda of the 1999 ASEAN summit, and several academics, including Robert Mundell, advocated creation of an Asian euro.[12]

The AMF proposal received some support from policymakers outside Japan, but made little progress. Some of the suggested functions for the AMF could be handled within existing institutions; the regional surveillance role, for example, was taken on by the Asian Development Bank (ADB).[13] The fundamental reason for the AMF's lack of progress, how-

---

[11] The Asia–Europe Meeting (ASEM) format was proposed by the EU, which wanted a dialogue with the ASEAN countries plus China, Japan and South Korea., and the first ASEM summit was held in 1996. The Asian participant list revived the East Asian Economic Caucus grouping, proposed by Malaysia in 1990 and subsequently overshadowed by APEC because other countries, notably the USA and Australia, feared that the EAEC would be the nucleus for an East Asian regional trading arrangement. Instead, in the late 1990s, the group's members, now called the ASEAN+3, formed the nucleus of Asian monetary coordination.

[12] For references see Henning (2002) and Eichengreen (2004). More limited currency union has also been considered, especially within Southeast Asia (Madhur, 2002). The adoption of a common currency by twelve EU members, whose outcome became assured in late 1990s and was sealed by the issue of euro banknotes in January 2002, was a positive stimulus. Seeing the euro as evidence of a pattern towards currency consolidation is, however, a selective reading of the European experience as Eastern Europe was undergoing a dramatic monetary disunion as the Czechoslovak, Yugoslav and Soviet currency areas all disintegrated. Europe had more currencies in 2002 than it had a dozen years earlier (Pomfret, 2003).

[13] The IMF's surveillance mechanism is bilateral, so that when the ASEAN countries proposed a surveillance process in 1998 the regional nature of their proposal was innovative. The ASEAN Surveillance Process became operational in March 1999 with a coordinating unit at the ASEAN Secretariat in Jakarta and national units in the ten member countries (Manupipatpong, 2002, 112–5). At a meeting in Sydney in March 1999 the Australian government proposed that a regional surveillance information facility be based at the ADB in Manila, and provided financial assistance through AusAID. Staff of the ADB's Regional Economic Monitoring Unit prepare the *Asia Recovery Report* twice a year and maintain a website at http://www.adb.org/REMU/aric.asp.

ever, was the opposition from other IMF members, notably the USA, to duplication of roles.[14]

A weaker version of the AMF proposal emerged at a meeting of Asia–Pacific finance ministers and central bankers in Manila in November 1997. The fourteen economies represented in Manila were the first six ASEAN members, China, Hong Kong, Japan, South Korea, Australia, New Zealand, Canada and the USA. The Manila Framework called for a regional surveillance mechanism, enhanced economic and technical cooperation in strengthening domestic financial systems and their regulation, and measures to strengthen the IMF's response to financial crises. Although the topics are reminiscent of Japan's AMF proposals, the tone is in terms of supplementing the central role of the IMF.

Support within the region has been mixed. China's role was especially crucial, as it switched from backing the US position in 1997–8 to participating in regional initiatives after 1999.[15] China supported the IMF's approach to the 1997 crisis and its 'mainstay' role was acknowledged at the December 1998 APEC summit in Kuala Lumpur. China, however, felt that it received little practical reward, and relations with the USA soured in the first half of 1999 over the US intervention in Kosovo and bombing of the Chinese embassy in Belgrade.

The most important forum for regional financing arrangements emerged out of meetings begun in March 1999 among the ASEAN+3 group of the ten ASEAN countries plus China, Japan and South Korea. At a meeting of the thirteen countries' finance ministers in Chiang Mai in May 2000 a regional financing arrangement was established with one

[14] The following paragraphs draw on Henning (2002), Manupipatpong (2002) and Murase (2002) for information about the various developments and on Bird and Rajan (2002) for policy options raised in the process. In 2000 the Bank for International Settlements (BIS) established an Asian office in Hong Kong, which could be seen as providing an established international institution to address proposals for an Asian body in areas beyond the IMF's normal competencies; the BIS manages the Asian Bond Fund.

[15] Bowles (2002) contrasts the coolness of Jiang Zemin's visit to Japan in December 1998 with the conciliatory nature of Zhu Rongji's visit in October 2000. Although there is strong evidence of China's willingness to play a leadership role in Asian regionalism since the 1997 crisis, some commentators (eg. Medeiros and Fravel, 2003) interpret China's more active diplomatic engagement since the mid–1990s in a global rather than a regional context.

billion US dollars in commitments. The Chiang Mai Initiative (CMI), which became effective in November 2000, allows countries to swap their local currencies for major international currencies for up to six months and for up to twice their committed amount. The CMI is framed in terms of supplementing the IMF's role insofar as countries seeking liquidity support must also look for IMF assistance, although bilateral swaps under the CMI are not conditional on IMF negotiations being completed. By March 2002 six bilateral swaps, worth $14 billion, had been concluded under the CMI (Manupipatpong 2002: 118), and by the end of 2003 this had increased to sixteen bilateral swaps amounting to $35.5 billion (Wang 2004: 944).

The CMI has the potential to evolve into the role foreseen for the AMF as lender of last resort in crises. CMI commitments already supersede those of its predecessor, the ASEAN swap arrangement, which had been in place since 1977 but at its maximum the facility only amounted to $200 million. With combined reserves of around $800 billion, the ASEAN+3 countries have resources which dwarf the assistance given in 1997–8. The ambiguous relationship to IMF financing could be interpreted as a step towards creating a competing institution, although from the participating countries' public pronouncements it is unclear how far some of them are willing to see the CMI evolve towards an AMF. The relationship of the CMI to the Manila Framework also remains unclear. Although garnering fewer headlines, the Manila Framework remains in place and raises questions of coordinating activities under the CMI and financial activities involving Australia, Canada, New Zealand, the USA and the ASEAN+3.

Monetary policy and exchange rate coordination is less advanced. A case is often made for exchange rate fixity to forestall competitive devaluations by countries competing with one another across a range of traded goods and also to encourage direct foreign investment. In the years before 1997 such fixity was more or less maintained among the ASEAN countries, China, Hong Kong, South Korea and Taiwan by their *de facto* pegs to the US dollar, but this led to, disastrous in some cases, swings against the yen.[16] Despite the experience of 1997–8, the attraction of a dollar peg seems to remain strong in these countries. McKinnon (2004: 326) points out that by early 2004 'the day–to–day volatility of each country's dollar exchange rate is not significantly different from its precrisis level'. Moreover, in all East Asian countries' trade except Japan, the US dollar is the dominant invoice currency (McKinnon 2005). The simplest solution to the competitive devaluation threat would be region-wide pegs to the dollar, or even dollarization, and McKinnon and Schnabl (2002) conclude that East Asia is a 'natural dollar zone'. For many Asians, however, it is unacceptable to have monetary policy determined in the USA, and they see a common currency as the best solution.

Another potential benefit of a larger currency area is reduction of the required level of forex reserves, because offsetting shocks would reduce the need for a lender of last resort (Stockman 2001). A single currency is also advocated as allowing the East Asian countries to speak with a single voice in international financial fora.[17] Despite these benefits and the long-attested finding that East Asia satisfies some of the criteria identified in the optimal currency area literature at least as well as Western Europe (Goto and Hamada 1994), many obstacles to Asian monetary union remain.

Can Monetary Union Lead Regional Integration?

Regional integration theory for at least the last sixty years has focused on trade integration. In the 1980s the concept of deep integration went beyond trade with its focus on policy harmonization, which came to include monetary integration, but it presupposed trade integration as the first step in the regional integration sequence. The five levels of integration developed in the early 1960s by Bela Balassa (1961) — preferential trading arrangements, free trade area, customs union, common market, economic

[16] The third currency phenomenon, as it applies to Southeast Asian countries, is analysed by Bird and Rajan (2002b).

[17] This point, which addresses Japanese concern about its low voting weight in the IMF, has also been raised by Korean economists (Oh and Harvie, 2001, 261).

union — are often treated as a sequencing pattern towards closer integration as well as a taxonomy of deeper and deeper integration.[18] When discussion of monetary integration began in East Asia after 1997, it was in the absence of trade integration, and some proponents saw monetary integration as a step towards promoting trade integration by differentially facilitating intra-regional trade flows.[19] This priority to monetary integration turns the Balassa sequence on its head (Pomfret 2005a).

The two theoretical literatures dealing with trade and monetary integration (customs union theory and optimal currency area theory) developed along distinct tracks. In optimal currency area (OCA) theory, the choice of currency domain involves a cost-benefit analysis trading off microeconomic efficiency against macroeconomic flexibility (Krugman 1993: 4). A common currency by lowering transactions costs increases microeconomic efficiency, but at some point the marginal gains in efficiency from a larger currency area may be offset by the benefits from having an independent monetary policy. For Mundell (1961) this point is where factor mobility ceases to provide an alternative adjustment mechanism. McKinnon (1963) emphasised the degree of openness because in a less open economy money illusion permits the exchange rate to be an effective policy instrument. Kenen (1969) and others lengthened the list of criteria which might be relevant,[20] but the emphasis remained on es-

---

[18] A free trade area (FTA) is where the preferential tariffs are zero on trade among signatories, a customs union is an FTA + common external tariffs, a common market is a customs union + free internal movement of capital and labour, and an economic union is a common market + common economic policies.

[19] Wang (2004, 952–4) starts his discussion of the sequencing issue by observing that: 'The euro area pursued trade integration first, but from a theoretical point of view there is no clear reason for this. . . .Furthermore, there are many good reasons for forming a monetary union before a FTA'. The European trade–first emphasis reflected the historical conditions during the Bretton Woods era of fixed exchange rates, when monetary factors were not an obstacle to trade but tariffs were high; the 1957 Rome Treaty which established the EU customs union did not mention monetary integration. In contrast, the Mercosur free trade area suffered major problems in the 1990s and 2000s from exchange rate volatility between Argentina and Brazil

[20] Alesina and Barro (2002) argue that the trade–off might be mediated by history and by geography, but otherwise their criteria are similar to those in the survey by Tower and Willett (1976) or in the textbook treatment of de Grauwe (2000). Pomfret (2005c) reviews the literature.

tablishing the geographical boundaries at which macro policy becomes effective.

The main benefit from a common currency (or fixed exchange rates) is lower transactions costs. This has long been accepted as the overwhelming argument for mini states (eg. Luxembourg or Brunei) not to have independent currencies. The argument becomes less potent as the currency area becomes large enough to have well-functioning forex (including forward) markets, and the threshold at which this occurs seems to be quite low. A second benefit from a common currency is that in larger currency areas disturbances are likely to be offsetting, so that exchange rate changes are smaller, with less feedback on domestic prices.[21]

The main disadvantage of adopting a common currency is the loss of monetary independence. Eichengreen (1990) compared the adjustment mechanism in US states to that in independent countries. If oil prices fall, output will decline and unemployment will increase in Texas, and the government might like to either increase the money supply, in order to reduce interest rates and stimulate investment, or devalue, in order to encourage non-oil exports and import-competing activities, but the state can do neither. The lack of policy independence is, however, not a big cost for Texas. Although the Texan economy will shrink, the adjustment problem for individuals will be mitigated because the unemployed capital and labour can move to other states. Moreover, in a very open economy like Texas, devaluation would not have much impact because prices and wages immediately increase to wipe out any competitive advantage. Hence Texas as a US state satisfies the Mundell and McKinnon criteria for being in an OCA.

The outcome of the western European policy debate was the establishment of the euro as a common currency, but the process did not parallel predictions of the OCA literature.[22] Although over time the EU did

---

[21] The greater price stability is usually ascribed to random shocks being offsetting. Other mechanisms include reduction in weights of outliers in the CPI and reduction in the ratio of trade (or rather transactions denominated in, potentially volatile, foreign currencies) to GDP.

[22] Attempts to quantify and synthesise the OCA criteria in the 1970s, such as Kreinin and Heller (1974), predicted that Sweden and Switzerland were among the top candidates for

experience greater factor mobility and more open national economies, the pace of monetary integration did not follow these trends, and in the endgame capital controls were abolished as a step towards monetary union rather than monetary union being driven by greater factor mobility (Pomfret 2003). Meanwhile, during the 1990s eastern Europe witnessed substantial monetary disunion as several currency areas disintegrated, despite high levels of economic integration (including factor mobility and the absence of money illusion) among their members.

How to explain these outcomes? Monetary union not only reduces private transactions costs, but also public sector transactions costs. As the EU moves closer to a federal state, it is too difficult to make common polices if internal exchange rates fluctuate. This was first apparent in trying to manage the common agricultural policy after the collapse of the first effort at monetary union in 1976, and this led speedily to a renewed effort to fix internal exchange rates through the European Monetary System which started operation in 1979 (Pomfret 1991; Basevi and Grassi 1993). On the other hand, monetary union is impossible among countries wishing to pursue differing monetary policies. That is why the EU's first effort collapsed in the early 1970s; the large EU members wanted to address problems raised by oil crisis and recession through differing monetary policies and the fixed exchange rate system (the Snake) collapsed. After the political dissolution of Czechoslovakia, Yugoslavia and the Soviet Union, disagreements arose over the conduct of monetary policy which made a common currency unsustainable in each case (Pomfret 2003). In the European experience of the 1990s, the crucial issues concerned who determines the conduct of monetary and fiscal policy, rather than the effectiveness of macro policy as emphasized in OCA theory.

On the benefit side, although it is plausible that a common currency reduces transactions costs, there are no convincing empirical estimates of the magnitude of the savings. The Commission of the European Communities (1990) in measuring the 'costs of non-Europe' estimated large benefits from completing the EU's internal market and from monetary

---

adoption of a European common currency and Italy was one of the countries which least satisfied the OCA criteria (Pomfret, 2004).

union, but the exercise was clearly biased in the direction of finding such benefits in order to justify the policies. Krugman (1993) drew attention to the absence of serious consideration of the nature or magnitude of transactions costs in debates over the international financial system. Frankel and Rose (1998) analysed the two-way causality between economic integration and monetary union, arguing that a common currency promotes closer trade links and more synchronized cycles.[23] One aspect of that paper was addressed in greater depth by Rose (2000), who found that the impact of monetary union on trade was much larger than the impact of fixed exchange rates.

Rose (2000), using a gravity model with a currency union dummy and a large dataset (33,903 bilateral trade observations for 186 countries in 1970, 1975, 1980, 1985 and 1990), found that currency union has a large effect on bilateral trade. Many economists expected the effect to be small because currency conversion costs are low and estimates of the effect of exchange rate volatility on trade are small (Alesina, Barro and Tenreyro 2002: 18), but Rose estimated that, *ceteris paribus*, a common currency more than triples bilateral trade. Because Rose follows an admirable open-access policy with his data, the results could be replicated or challenged very quickly by other researchers.

Rose's sample is smaller than it might appear; of his 33,903 observations, only 320 are classified as 'within currency union' trade and most of these involve a tiny economy and a much larger neighbour. Several authors (Persson 2001; Kenen 2001; Nitsch 2004a) have shown that the countries in currency unions are not from a random draw; currency union members are smaller and more open than their natural comparators, and history (usually in the form of colonial background) matters. When the currency union members are matched with similar countries which are

[23] This is not a theoretical result, but a hypothesis to be tested empirically. More bilateral trade could promote inter–industry specialization and less synchronized cycles, but, using various measures of bilateral trade intensity and cycle synchronization for twenty–one developed economies, Frankel and Rose find a robust positive relationship between the two variables. They interpret this finding as evidence that a common currency promotes bilateral trade and also increases cycle synchronization. The context of Frankel and Rose's paper was to show why actual currency areas always seem to fit OCA criteria better than potential currency areas; in this view, the OCA criteria are endogenous.

not in a currency union, the differential impact on trade is much smaller than when the currency union members are part of a global dataset. Rose and Engel (2002) also argue that members of currency unions are different, but their case is that currency unions are more integrated with one another than similar pairs of countries with independent currencies. When Rose and van Wincoop (2001) introduce country-specific trade resistance measures into their gravity model; the currency union effect on trade is smaller than in Rose (2000), but still substantial. López–Córdova and Meissner (2003), in a study of trade in 1870–1910, find similar quantitative effects to those which Rose found for 1970–90, and they conclude that 'It is reasonable to assert that bilateral trade would be about 3.30 times larger when both countries belonged to a monetary union.'[24]

Alesina, Barro and Tenreyro (2002 Table 8) and Rose (2002) summarize the empirical literature. In the nineteen studies covered by the meta-analysis in Rose (2002), the average effect of currency union is to more than double trade among the members, and this is robust to variations in sample composition and time period, whether fixed or random effects models are used, and to the exclusion of the six studies involving Rose himself. In their less formal analysis of fourteen studies, Alesina et al. reach essentially the same conclusion; the empirical results are heterogeneous, but the trade coefficient is usually statistically significant, and the median estimate of the trade effect is 100 percent. In sum, the cross-section and panel gravity models find that a common currency stimulates trade. Although the magnitude of the common currency effect is still debated, the finding that it is large and statistically significant seems to be robust. The cross-section studies may, however, fail to address the key policy issue: what happens to trade when countries adopt a common currency or when a currency union dissolves?

Analysing time series data for correlations between changing currency union status and bilateral trade flows, Glick and Rose (2002) esti-

[24] Flandreau and Maurel (2001) and Estevadeordal, Frantz and Taylor (2003) also utilize nineteenth century data.

mate that dissolution of a currency union halves bilateral trade.[25] Currency union break-up is, however, usually associated with other events which disrupt trade. Over two-thirds of the sixty cases of post–1947 currency union dissolutions in the Glick–Rose dataset broke up within a decade of the end of a colonial relationship (Nitsch 2003).[26] Even abstracting from non-monetary causes of trade disruption, the specific nature of a currency union dissolution and its accompanying monetary arrangements may be more important than a simple generalizable mechanism of currency union dissolution reducing trade. Schoor (2003) identifies a 15–20 percent decline in CIS trade as being due to the collapse of the ruble zone in 1992–3, but he ascribes this decline mainly to the need for bilateral balancing; if the ruble zone had been replaced by convertible national currencies, as in the Baltic countries, then there would have been no trade loss. In tranquil currency union changes, notably Ireland's secession from its currency union with the UK in 1979 and subsequent participation in the process leading to the euro, the impact on bilateral trade is unclear. Thom and Walsh (2002) find that breaking the currency union did not have an adverse impact on Ireland–UK trade, while Fitzsimmons, Hogan and Neary (1999) find that trade between Ulster and Ireland is greater than predicted by a standard gravity model despite the absence of a common currency after 1979.

The impact on bilateral trade of currency area dissolution and of currency area formation may not be symmetric. For the 'East Asian sequence' the key issue is whether currency area formation boosts trade. The difficulty in providing an empirical answer to this question is that the sole example for over a century of large countries abandoning monetary independence in favour of a common currency is the euro. Episodes of currency union formation other than the euro have been studied, but they involve unbalanced currency unions or small economies and are of

---

[25] In an earlier time series analysis, Pakko and Wall (2001) found a negative but statistically insignificant trade effect, but their dataset was based on 1970–90, when there were few cases of currency union exit and entry. The dataset used by Glick and Rose goes back to 1948 and contains more cases of exit or entry.

[26] The end of the ruble zone, which is not in the dataset, would increase the percentage still further.

limited relevance to any substantial East Asian currency union. Nitsch (2004b) reports his research on the Belgium–Luxembourg currency union, where he found no measurable change in bilateral trade after adoption of the common currency when other factors are taken into account. Nitsch (2004b) analyses the trade effects of currency union on the three countries which entered the CFA franc zone in the 1980s and 1990s; Mali suffered a big decline in trade with other CFA countries, Equatorial Guinea experienced a big increase in such trade, and Guinea–Bissau's trade was largely unchanged, although this may be partly due to the latter's more recent accession (1997, as opposed to 1984 for the other two countries). The net effect of adopting the CFA currency depends entirely on how the three cases are weighted.

The euro's trade impact can be estimated by fitting pre– and post–euro values to a model whose coefficients have been estimated independently. Rose and van Wincoop (2001), using coefficients from their gravity model with country-specific trade resistance measures, estimate that adoption of the euro will boost trade among the Euroland countries by 59 percent, but like any gravity model this may be confounding other determinants of bilateral trade flows in the currency union coefficient.[27] Alternatively, the euro's impact can be estimated by comparing actual trade flows after currency union with counterfactual flows which would have occurred if national currencies still existed. Micco et al. (2003) find a moderate increase in intra-Euroland trade during the first four years of the common currency. Faruqee (2004) reaches a similar conclusion, with the euro raising intra-Euroland trade by around ten percent on most specifications, and most of the impact concentrated in 2001 and 2002. These results reinforce the impression that introduction of the euro had a positive effect on bilateral trade, although the impact is more modest than that predicted on the basis of gravity model analysis.

Maurel (2004) analyses the impact of European monetary integration on bilateral intra-European trade by applying a gravity-type model to a

---

[27] Rose and van Wincoop observe that in a simpler gravity model the predicted increase in trade due to the euro is 250–400 percent. Their trade resistance measures pick up some of the non–currency–union determinants of trade, but may not be picking it all up (or may be picking up too much).

panel of 26 European countries' trade from 1990 to 2000. The dataset allows her to discriminate among EU members and non-members and among a variety of exchange rate regimes. Maurel's conclusion is that current account imbalances and their financing are a constraint on the volume of trade. Currency union is associated with reduction of capital market imperfections and reducing or removing the financing constraint, but the constraint could also be relaxed by fiscal coordination within other monetary settings. As case studies illustrating the argument, she points to the Baltic countries which actively used fiscal policy to address current account imbalances. This argument is similar to the analysis by Flandreau and Maurel (2001) of trade integration in nineteenth century Europe. It is also similar to the argument by Schoors (2003) that the dissolution of the ruble zone was associated with disruption of trade among countries whose balance of payments financing was impeded by the limited convertibility of their national currencies, but currency union dissolution did not disrupt trade of countries with convertible currencies (the Baltic case again). The implication is that currency union can promote trade integration by reducing the current account constraint, but there are alternative routes to the same destination.

If East Asia adopted a common currency, would it have the effect of strengthening regional economic ties? The literature inspired by Rose suggests that this is possible given the large impact of a common currency on bilateral trade flows, but doubts linger as to whether the gravity model analysis identifies the effects of forming a currency union or picks up other effects in the currency union dummy. If the key constraint on trade is the current account balance, then monetary union could promote regional trade, but other measures to reduce capital market imperfections which hamper current account disequilibrium, such as creation of Asian bond markets, could play the same role.[28] The case study literature on the trade effects of currency union formation provides little empirical evi-

[28] This may be an argument for greater integration by Asian countries into global financial markets, centred in the USA and Europe, rather than for regional financial market development. Proponents of the Asian Bond Initiative argue that there is regional bias as well as home bias in financial markets (Wang, 2004, 947), but there is little empirical evidence on this.

dence either way and is too sparse to be conclusive, mainly because there have been so few cases of currency union among large countries in the last century and the prime example, the euro, was too long in preparation[29] and too recent in implementation to provide simple conclusions. Some authors have suggested that globalization and factors such as the growth of e-commerce have reduced the usefulness of minor currencies to their holders (von Furstenbeg 2002; Costa Storti and de Grauwe 2002),[30] but there has been no attempt to determine whether the transactions costs of small currency areas have been rising. In sum, there is a presumption from both theory and empirical work that monetary union promotes bilateral trade, but the foundations for this conclusion remain fairly weak and the magnitude of the effect is unclear.

What are the Obstacles to Regional Integration?

The choice between regionalism and multilateralism is full of paradoxes. Although most of the world's nations have now signed on to the non-discriminatory liberal trade and monetary regimes of the WTO and IMF, their governments frequently sign regional agreements. Despite the political economy forces encouraging politicians to embark on preferential trade policies or other regional integration schemes, strong economic forces work in favour of adherence to the non-discrimination principle. Of the many plans for regional trading arrangements the majority have failed to come to fruition, and among those that did most failed to survive long or exercise a significant economic influence.

The ambiguity in RTA outcomes reflects the classic insight by Viner (1950) that any discriminatory trade policy, such as a customs union or free trade area, is by its nature second-best. One distortion is removed,

---

[29] The adoption of the euro was preceded by a lengthy transition period during the existence of the European Monetary System which began in 1979 and especially after the Maastricht agreement of the early 1990s. The introduction of the single currency officially occurred on 1st January 1999, but for many people only became tangible with the appearance of euro notes and coins on 1st January 2002.

[30] Arnone and Bandiera (2004) argue that electronic money will increase the size of OCAs by undermining the efficacy of monetary policy, but conclude that the current level of e–money use does not pose such a threat.

the differential treatment between a member's domestic products and products from other member countries of the union, but a new distortion is introduced between imports from member and non-member countries which were previously treated equally. The trade creation and trade diversion effects work in opposite directions to leave the direction of change in welfare of the country joining a customs union and of the world theoretically ambiguous. Thus, although a discriminatory tariff reduction, as in a customs union or free trade area, may be welfare-improving, the presumption is that removal of trade barriers on a non-discriminatory basis would be first-best. Vested interests may lobby for tailor-made RTAs that avoid increased competition for domestic producers, but this excision of trade creation only increases the likelihood that the RTA will have a net negative effect and will ultimately fail.[31]

Politicians are often attracted to discriminatory trading agreements for political reasons. Signing a preferential trade agreement is a politically cheap way of signalling friendship. Perhaps the most egregious case in the last half century has been the EU's use of trade preferences as a substitute for its lack of a common foreign policy.[32] This approach led to a complex pyramid of preferences, which left most partners feeling hard done by relative to some other country, and any preferences which threatened EU producers tended to be removed. This last feature also characterized the Generalized System of Preferences for developing countries, which was introduced in 1971 under the slogan of encouraging trade rather than providing aid to poor countries, but whose economic impact was small. Reciprocal agreements like free trade areas or customs unions appear less easy to renege on than unilateral preferences, but they do not have a good record of surviving. Customs unions require agreement on the common external tariff and on the sharing of customs revenues, which reach to the heart of public policy. Free trade areas are easier

[31] Trade diversion, where the source of imports is transferred from a third country to a regional partner, contributes to regional integration without harming established domestic producers, but consumers (including buyers of intermediate products like steel) suffer from discriminatory policies favouring producers who are not the world's most efficient suppliers.

[32] Presidents of Soviet successor states have had an incredible propensity to sign RTAs which are often inconsistent and are never implemented (Pomfret, 2005b).

to agree on, but it is difficult to prevent trade deflection, so that the appearance of policy autonomy towards imports from non-member countries is a mirage.[33]

Some customs unions have survived, but apart from enclaves and other ministates (such as San Marino or Monaco in Europe), they are uncommon. The single example in recent decades is the EU, where the customs union and other common policies, which are partially funded from the customs revenues, are steps towards some kind of political association. In this respect the EU resembles the nation-building exercises of the nineteenth century in Italy, Canada, Germany and Australia, rather than the theoretical model of a customs union among independent nations.

Long-lasting free trade areas are even rarer. Perhaps the most successful were the European Free Trade Area (EFTA) and the Central European Free Trade Area (CEFTA), for both of which the main role was as a way-station en route to most members joining the EU. The best known free trade area is that between the USA and Canada, which evolved into NAFTA when Mexico joined. The US–Canada agreement was special insofar as these were two of the most integrated economies in the world, with low external tariffs and duties of less than five percent on most bilateral trade; removing intra-FTA tariffs facilitated trade with little impact on tariff revenue or on economic activity, and low external tariffs made trade deflection unlikely. NAFTA was a more complex agreement, reflected in its 900 pages. It is in many respects an example of managed bilateral trade with complex rules to protect special interests and, although barriers are fairly low in all three member countries, trade within NAFTA is not free — that would have required a one page agreement. The same caveat applies to the many 'free trade areas' agreed upon elsewhere. In South Asia and Southeast Asia 'free trade areas' have been announced (SAFTA and AFTA) which have restrictions on trade among members. There are very few true free trade areas (ie. with zero

[33] Simple transhipment through the least protected market can be regulated by rules of origin. However, if prices are lower in that market and domestic production exists, then domestic goods will be deflected to higher tariff markets within the FTA.

tariffs on trade among members and autonomous trade policies towards non-members) in the world.[34]

The bilateral trade agreements in the third wave of regionalism are similar to the pseudo free trade areas in that they are selective in coverage. Such selectivity tends to favour excluding products where trade creation is likely, because producer lobbies will resist threats to their competitive position. The ensuing trade diversion bias means that the agreement will have net negative effects for the signatories, and for the world. Viner's analysis explains why economic forces work against such arrangements in practice. The situation is more difficult to analyse when services or non-trade measures are included in the agreement, but a non-discriminatory policy is often first-best and the design of bilateral agreements is likely to be captured by vested interests.

For all of these reasons RTAs are rarely economically beneficial, and tend only to survive when there are over-riding pressures for fuller economic integration (as in the EU) or when liberal external trade policies make the costs minor (as with NAFTA or the CER). This conclusion reinforces the presumption that East Asian countries did not suffer from not participating in RTAs.

What are the obstacles to monetary integration? One lesson from the recent history of monetary union and disunion in Europe is that the OCA literature provides little practical guide to the prospects for monetary union because it assumes a background of optimum monetary policy. The eastern European and former Soviet Union experience indicated that a currency union without appropriate monetary policy instruments is a far worse evil than the higher transactions costs from independent currencies, even when the independent currency covers a small national economy. Western European monetary union also stalled on the monetary

[34] The CER has internal free trade, but the external tariffs of Australia and New Zealand are now so low that there is little opportunity for trade deflection. EFTA, now consisting of Iceland, Liechtenstein, Norway and Switzerland, only makes sense as a free trade area in the context of EFTA members' participation in the European Economic Area with the 25 EU members. The stability of this arrangement, whereby EFTA members get the benefits of free access to the European market without the political elements of EU membership, depends upon the will of the EU – and on the EFTA countries' relative economic insignificance.

policy hurdle in the 1970s and only overcame the hurdle when, in the 1990s most, but not all, of the EU members accepted the loss of sovereignty inherent in a common central bank.

Monetary union also tends to imbed some degree of fiscal policy cooperation. Kenen (1969) argued that in federal states such as the USA or Canada regional idiosyncratic shocks generate automatic and prompt redistribution via fiscal rules, and other federal systems all embody some degree of fiscal insurance.[35] In the EU the problems of operating common fiscal policies when members' contributions and benefits fluctuated with volatile bilateral exchange rate changes were a critical reason for maintaining the momentum for monetary union in 1977–8 and later. This is the problem of transactions costs in public finance identified by Helleiner as a major reason for creating national monies in the nineteenth century.[36]

The close nexus between currency union and both monetary policy and fiscal policy highlights the difficulty in agreeing on currency union among independent countries. Indeed, the global experience for over a century indicates a rule of one country-one currency (Pomfret 2005c). Even in large and diverse countries fiscal pressures lead to a single national currency. For very small states private sector transactions costs may have dictated adoption of another country's currency, and for poor

---

[35] Eichengreen (2004), however, rejects this as a 'pseudo precondition' for monetary union, by which he seems to mean that it is helpful but not strictly necessary.

[36] Helleiner (2003) is one of the most perceptive critics of the inadequacy of OCA theory in capturing actual monetary arrangements. Explaining currency domains in pure political terms, as part of the Westphalian nation state system or for national identity, will not do either; territorial currencies were only established in the 1815–1914 period, long after the first emergence of the nation state. Technical change in minting coins and printing notes in large standardized and hard–to–counterfeit batches was a precondition, but national motives varied. Helleiner focuses on four motives: the macropolicy motive of OCA theory, creating national identity, and the desire to reduce transactions costs in the private sector and in public finance. The transactions costs motives became more important as the monetized economy spread to the working classes and as the state took on more functions and cast its revenue net more widely. These are motives with an economic dimension, which, together with the crucial technical change in using steam presses to mint coins, are firmly rooted in the historical situation following the industrial revolution. Helleiner's explanation of the timing of the formation of monetary domains contrasts with the predictive incapacity of OCA theory.

countries a neo-imperial power may have been able to offer inducements to operate under its monetary umbrella, but otherwise each country had its own currency.

Application to East Asia

The East Asian countries stood apart from the waves of regional trading arrangements in the second half of the twentieth century. ASEAN was the only RTA in the region, and it has had little impact on trade. Northeast Asia was characterized by the non-participation in RTAs by Japan or China or South Korea (or Taiwan or Hong Kong). At the end of the century proposals for regional integration became stronger, and they focused on monetary integration, reversing the conventional view of monetary integration being a final step in economic integration after integration of goods and factor markets.

Advocates of a common Asian currency point to the advantages of exchange rate stability, a more effective lender of last resort and a single voice in global monetary fora, but they have not addressed the institutional question of how the common exchange rate is determined (and hence how monetary policy is conducted for the entire currency area), who would determine when the lender of last resort acts, and who would speak with the single voice.

The short-run practical obstacles to monetary union are illustrated by Eichengreen (2004), who lists four real preconditions for monetary union, in contrast to pseudo conditions such as numerical deficit ceilings or convergence criteria:

- the capacity to delegate monetary policy to an international institution, which should be accountable, representative, efficient and effective;
- a culture of monetary policy transparency;
- open capital accounts;
- a common transmission mechanism from monetary policy to the economy.

The 1997 crisis exposed the variation and weakness of East Asian financial systems, which means that the transmission mechanism will differ from country to country and even if the participating countries agree on monetary policy goals (eg. an inflation target) the effect of monetary policy instruments will vary across countries.[37] There is very little transparency in the region's central banks, many of whom claim to peg to a basket but do not reveal the contents of the basket, which seems to change over time. Political cultures would need to change in many of the Asian countries, including some of the large ones, if the second condition is to obtain.

Several of the East Asian countries restrict capital mobility in some way, but the most important is China, whose current stance is that capital flows are being freed as a preliminary to introducing more exchange rate flexibility. The basic problem is the unhealthy state of China's banking sector, and the official fear that greater exchange rate flexibility would be followed by capital flight and currency collapse. As Prasad et al. (2005) argue, currency collapse is more likely if the authorities put capital account liberalization first, because capital outflow will put unbearable pressure on the exchange rate, much as happened to the Asian countries with fixed exchange rates in 1997. That scenario could well induce a return to capital controls. Meanwhile, the true equilibrium value of the yuan is becoming more and more opaque, and China has artificially low interest rates which encourage excessive bank lending and inefficient investment. Given China's pivotal role in the ASEAN+3, any further move towards monetary union will have to await China sorting out its own macroeconomic policy dilemmas.

Most distant of all is the prospect of agreeing on an international monetary policy institution. If the European Union is becoming a territorial unit as Germany or Italy or Canada did in the nineteenth century and this was a significant motive behind the introduction of the euro, then it is *sui generis* in the current world economy and the euro cannot be seen as a harbinger of further monetary unions. This analysis has implications

[37] Pobre (2004), using quarterly data for 1981–2000 from Korea, the Philippines and Thailand, finds significant differences between the three countries in the magnitude and speed of reaction to monetary shocks.

for the prospects for monetary union in East Asia insofar as discussing the matter as a technical one of economic benefits versus economic costs misses the point of whether any of the independent countries, apart from the very small states are willing to cede national autonomy over monetary and part of fiscal policy to a supranational institution.[38]

This last point is often invoked to say that for monetary union 'economics matters but politics matters more' (Benjamin Cohen in Salvatore, Dean and Willett 2003), but such dichotomous generalizations are just as oversimplified as the OCA literature. Successful regional integration faces the economic obstacles described above and requires political decisions on (a) sharing control over monetary and fiscal policy and (b) the domain over which this sharing will occur.

The question of sharing sovereignty is often phrased in terms of how would the huge variations in economic and demographic size be dealt with and, assuming that China and Japan would be likely to have the largest weight, what are the prospects for genuine trust and cooperation in the near future. The role of former enemies France and Germany in European integration was crucial, in part because both accepted the higher goal of cementing peace by economic integration. The continuing antipathy between China and Japan on many levels (highlighted by the riots at the 2004 Asian soccer championship finals when Japan defeated China in Beijing and the April 2005 protests in China about Japanese history books) suggests how different the Asian situation today is to that of Europe half a century ago. Relations between South Korea and Japan are also far from warm. Widespread opposition in both China and Korea to Japan obtaining a permanent seat on the UN Security Council is an example of regional non-cooperation.

Although the recent push towards Asian regionalism has been in the ASEAN+3 framework, the question of what constitutes the Asian region

---

[38] Currently Brunei has ceded monetary policy authority to Singapore and Timor Leste uses the US dollar. Future developments could include a baht zone, incorporating Laos, or a Greater China currency zone with monetary policy determined in Beijing, but it is difficult to imagine many other Asian examples. The new members of the EU in 2004 were willing to accept eventual adoption of the euro as a condition for EU membership, because they had similar monetary policy goals to existing EU members and because they recognized that they were joining a union with common policies.

remains open. Should South Asia be included? If India continues to grow rapidly, it could provide a counterweight to China and Japan, which may make decision-making easier. If India is included, should the other South Asian countries be part of the currency area? Perhaps here, the euro zone does provide a lesson, in that membership could be voluntary and as long as the core countries agree (France/Germany or China/Japan), then the monetary union has critical mass.

The aim is not to predict future alignments, but simply to point out that the geographical boundaries of Asian regionalism remain fluid. To the southeast it is unclear where 'Asia' ends. In the early 1990s under Keating Australia moved substantially closer to its East Asian neighbours, but since 1996 under Howard it appeared to move away, although there have been recent signs of this being reversed.[39] In terms of GDP if not population, Australia could also be a significant counterweight to the China/Japan core, much as in Euroland Italy and Spain are large enough to provide a balance against Franco–German hegemony.

Conclusion

The regional integration agenda in East Asia was kick-started by the post–1997 currency union debate. Although bilateral trade negotiations have been flourishing in the first half of the present decade, in terms of integrating the broader regional economy they have been limited in terms of both geographical and sectoral coverage and have been bewildering in their bilateral rather than truly regional format.[40] Monetary agreements,

[39] Closer relations were fostered by economic complementarity as Australia provided coal, iron and other primary products to the fast–growing economies of Northeast Asia. Relations with Malaysia were tetchy, reflected in the controversy in the late 1980s and early 1990s over whether the EAEC or APEC should be the vehicle for regional cooperation. The bad relations were reinforced by Australian participation in the invasion of Iraq, although they appear to be better under Abdullah Badawi than under Mahathir Mohamad. Australia–Indonesia relations soured when Australia led the UN peacekeeping force to East Timor in 1999, but they also may be improving under Susilo Bambang Yudhoyono.

[40] Scollay and Gilbert (2001) emphasised the tangled web nature of the new wave of bilaterals in Asia, and the pattern has if anything become more confused and less regionally integrated since they wrote. Desker (2004) has a more positive view of the potential

the Chiang Mai Initiative in particular, have been more concrete and potentially far-reaching. The urgency of pursuing regional initiatives towards monetary integration has been underlined since the turn of the century by a feeling that reform of the international financial architecture and the IMF, which was in the air after the 1997 Asian Crisis has now gone off the G8 radar screen (Wang 2004: 940). This juxtaposition raises the question of whether Asian economic integration could be led by monetary integration, with trade integration being pulled along later.

This paper argues that there is evidence to support the claim that monetary union can facilitate bilateral trade and hence be a first step towards regional integration. However, monetary integration is difficult, because actual currency union involves far more than simply satisfying conditions set out in OCA theory. Even from a short-run technical perspective, key East Asian countries need to reform their financial sectors and change macroeconomic policy cultures before monetary union would work. More fundamentally, the close nexus between currency union and both monetary policy and fiscal policy highlights the distance that East Asia has to go before an Asian currency union is seriously on the political agenda. Monetary policy has to be ceded to a single central bank (or equivalently to a rigid rule). Moreover some degree of fiscal insurance may be necessary to convince all countries of the benefits. Yet, in East Asia the political will to give up national autonomy over macro policies is far away. The situation where an Asian supranational authority would operate a budget on a par with that of the European Commission seems even more distant.

---

of trade agreements to create a 'lattice network' across East Asia, and also to improve the security situation.

References

Alesina, Alberto and Robert J. Barro (2002): Currency Unions, *Quarterly Journal of Economics* 117(2), 409–436.

Alesina, Alberto, Robert J. Barro and Silvana Tenreyro (2002): Optimal Currency Areas, *Harvard Institute of Economic Research Discussion Paper No. 1958*, June — published version in Mark Gertler and Kenneth Rogoff, eds. (2003): *NBER Macroeconomics Annual 2002* (MIT Press, Cambridge MA).

Arnone, Marco, and Luca Bandiera (2004): Monetary Policy, Monetary Areas, and Financial Development with Electronic Money, *IMF Working Paper WP/04/122*, July.

Balassa, Bela (1961): *The Theory of Economic Integration* (Richard D. Irwin, Homewood IL).

Basevi, Giorgio, and Silvia Grassi (1993): The Crisis of the European Monetary System and its Consequences for Agricultural Trade, *Review of Economic Conditions in Italy* 46 (June), 81–104.

Bird, Graham, and Ramkishen Rajan (2002a): The Evolving Asian Financial Architecture, *Essays in International Economics*, No. 226 (International Economics Section, Princeton University NJ), February.

Bird, Graham, and Ramkishen Rajan (2002b): Optimal Currency Baskets and the Third Currency Phenomenon: Exchange Rate Policy in Southeast Asia, *Journal of International Development*, 14, 1053–1073.

Bonapace, Tiziana (2004): Free Trade Areas in the ESCAP Region: Progress, Challenges and Prospects, paper presented at the Asian Development Bank High–Level Conference on Asia's Economic Cooperation and Integration, Manila, 1–2 July.

Bowles, Paul (2002): Asia's Post–Crisis Regionalism: Bringing the State back in, keeping the (United) States out, *Review of International Political Economy* 9(2), 230–256.

Commission of the European Communities (1990): One Market, One Money, *European Economy* 44 (October).

Costa Storti, Claudia, and Paul de Grauwe (2002): Electronic Money and the Optimal Size of Monetary Unions, paper presented at the Fordham/CEPR conference on the Euro and Dollarization, New York, 5–6 April.

De Grauwe, Paul (2000): *The Economics of Monetary Union*, Fourth Revised Edition (Oxford University Press, Oxford UK).

Dean, James (2004): Adopting the Euro: Tradeoffs and challenges facing the new EU–ten, *Journal of Policy Modeling* 26(7), 759–768.

Desker, Barry (2004): In Defence of FTAs: From purity to pragmatism in East Asia, *The Pacific Review* 17(1), 3–26.

Eichengreen, Barry (1990): One Money for Europe? Lessons from the U.S. Currency and Customs Union, *Economic Policy* 10 (April), 117–187.

Eichengreen, Barry (2004): Real and Pseudo Preconditions for an Asian Monetary Union, paper presented at the Asian Development Bank High–Level Conference on Asia's Economic Cooperation and Integration, Manila, 1–2 July.

Estevadeordal, Antoni, Brian Frantz and Alan Taylor (2003): The Rise and Fall of World Trade, 1870–1939, *Quarterly Journal of Economics* 118(2), 359–407.

Faruqee, Hamid (2004): Measuring the Trade Effects of EMU, *IMF Working Paper WP/04/154*, August.

Fitzsimmons, Emla, Vincent Hogan and J. Peter Neary (1999): Explaining the Volume of North–South Trade in Ireland: A Gravity Model Approach, *Economic and Social Review* 30(4), 381–401.

Flandreau, Marc, and Mathilde Maurel (2001): Monetary Union, Trade Integration and Business Cycles in 19th Century Europe: Just do it, *CEPR Discussion Paper No. 3087.*

Frankel, Jeffrey, and Andrew Rose (1998): The Endogeneity of the Optimum Currency Area Criteria, *Economic Journal* 108 (July), 1009–1025.

Fukasaku, Kiichiro (1992): Economic Regionalisation and Intra–Industry Trade: Pacific–Asian Perspectives, *OECD Development Centre Technical Paper No.53*, February.

Glick, Reuven and Andrew Rose (2002): Does a Currency Union affect Trade? The Time–Series Evidence, *European Economic Review* 46(6), 1125–1151.

Goto, Junicho, and Koichi Hamada (1994): Economic Preconditions for Asian Regional Integration, in Takatoshi Ito and Anne Krueger, eds., *Macroeconomic Linkage: Savings, Exchange Rates, and Capital Flows* (University of Chicago Press, Chicago IL), 359–385.

Greenaway, David, and Chris Milner (2002): Regionalism and Gravity, *Scottish Journal of Political Economy* 49(5), 574–585.

Helleiner, Eric (2003): *The Making of National Money* (Cornell University Press, Ithaca NY and London).

Henning, C. Randall (2002): East Asian Financial Cooperation, *IIE Policy Analyses in International Economics* 68 (Institute for International Economics, Washington DC), October.

Kawai, Masahiro (2005): East Asian Economic Regionalism: Progress and challenges, *Journal of Asian Economics*, 16(1), 29–55.

Kenen, Peter (1969): The Theory of Optimum Currency Areas: An Eclectic View, in Robert Mundell and Alexander Swoboda, eds., *Monetary Problems of the International Economy* (University of Chicago Press, Chicago), 41–60.

Kenen, Peter (2002): Currency Unions and Policy Domains, in David M. Andrews, C. Randall Henning and Louis W. Pauly, eds., *Governing the World's Money* (Cornell University Press, Ithaca NY), 79–104.

Kreinin, Mordechai, and H. Robert Heller (1974): Adjustment Costs, Optimal Currency Areas, and International Reserves, in Willy Sellekaerts, ed., *International Trade and Finance: Essays in Honour of Jan Tinbergen* (Macmillan, London), 127–140.

Krugman, Paul (1993): What do we Need to Know about the International Monetary System? *Essays in International Economics* No. 190 (International Economics Section, Princeton University NJ), July.

Kwack, Sung Y. (2005): Exchange Rate and Monetary Regime Options for Regional Cooperation in East Asia, *Journal of Asian Economics*, 16(1), 57–75.

López–Córdova, J. Ernesto, and Christopher Meissner (2003): Exchange–Rate Regimes and International Trade: Evidence from the Classical Gold Standard Era, *American Economic Review* 93, 344–353.

Madhur, Srinivasa (2001): Costs and Benefits of a Common Currency for ASEAN, *ERD Working Paper No.12*, Asian Development Bank, Manila, May.

Manupipatpong, Worapot (2002): The ASEAN Surveillance Process and the East Asian Monetary Fund, *ASEAN Economic Bulletin* 19(1), 111–122.

Maurel, Mathilde (2004): Current Account Constraint as a Barrier to International Trade: The evidence from the European enlargement process, *Economic Systems* 28, 301–317.

McKinnon, Ronald (1963): Optimum Currency Areas, *American Economic Review* 53, 717–725.

McKinnon, Ronald (2004): The East Asian Dollar Standard, *China Economic Review* 15, 325–330.

McKinnon, Ronald (2005): Trapped by the International Dollar Standard, *Journal of Policy Modeling* 27(4), 477–486.

McKinnon, Ronald, and Gunther Schnabl (2002): Synchronized Business Cycles in East Asia: Fluctuations in the Yen/Dollar Exchange Rate and China's Stabilizing Role, unpublished ms available at http://www.stanford.edu/~mckinnon/ or at http://uni–tuebingen.de/uni/wwa/homegs.htm — published in *The World Economy*, August 2003, 1067–88, and forthcoming as a chapter in Ronald McKinnon, *Exchange Rates under the East Asian Dollar Standard: Living with conflicted virtue* (MIT Press, Cambridge MA).

Medeiros, Evan, and M. Taylor Fravel (2003): China's New Diplomacy, *Foreign Affairs* 82(6), 22–35.

Micco, Alejandro, Ernesto Stein and Guillermo Ordonez (2003): The Currency Union Effect on Trade: Early evidence from EMU, *Economic Policy* 37 (October), 315–356.

Mundell, Robert (1961): Theory of Optimum Currency Areas, *American Economic Review* 51, 657–665.

Murase, Tetsujui (2002): *A Zone of Asian Monetary Stability* (Asia Pacific Press, Canberra).

Nasution, Anwar (2005): Monetary Cooperation in East Asia, *Journal of Asian Economics* 16, 422–442.

Naya, Seiji (2004): Japan in Emerging East Asian Regionalism, *East Asian Economic Perspectives* 15(2), 1–16.

Nitsch, Volker (2002): Honey, I shrunk the Currency Union Effect on Trade, *The World Economy* 25(4), 457–474.

Nitsch, Volker (2003): Have a break, Have a . . .National Currency: When do Monetary Unions fall apart? paper presented at the Workshop on Monetary Unions after EMU at the CESifo Venice Summer Institute, 21–22 July 2003 and circulated as CESifo working paper 1113 [available online at http://www.cesifo.de].

Nitsch, Volker (2004a): Comparing Apples and Oranges: The Effect of Multilateral Currency Unions on Trade, in Volbert Alexander, Jacques Mélitz, and George M. von Furstenberg, eds., *Monetary Unions and Hard Pegs: Effects on Trade, Financial Development, and Stability* (Oxford University Press, Oxford), 89–100.

Nitsch, Volker (2004b): Currency Union Entries and Trade, paper prepared for the conference 'Globalization of Capital Markets: An Anglo–German Perspective' held at the Free University Berlin, 5–6 March 2004.

Ogawa, Eiji (2001): A Regional Monetary Fund and the IMF, *The Journal of the Korean Economy* 2(2), 229–248.

Oh, Junggun, and Charles Harvie (2001): Exchange Rate Coordination in East Asia, *The Journal of the Korean Economy* 2(2), 249–296.

Pakko, Michael, and Howard Wall (2001): Reconsidering the Trade Creating Effect of Currency Unions, *Federal Reserve Bank of St. Louis Review.*

Persson, Torsten (2001): Currency Unions and Trade: How Large is the Treatment Effect? *Economic Policy* 16(33), 433–448.

Pobre, Mervin (2004): The Monetary Transmission in East Asia, *Asia–Pacific Journal of Economics and Business* 8(2), 16–41.

Pomfret, Richard (1986): The Trade–diverting Bias of Preferential Trading Arrangements, *Journal of Common Market Studies* 25 (December), 109–117.

Pomfret, Richard (1991): The Secret of the EMS's Longevity, *Journal of Common Market Studies* 29 (December), 623–633.

Pomfret, Richard (2001): *The Economics of Regional Trading Arrangements* (Clarendon Press, Oxford, 1997; paperback edition with new Preface, Oxford University Press, Oxford, 2001).

Pomfret, Richard (2003): Currency Unions in East Asia: Lessons from Europe, *Asia–Pacific Journal of Economics and Business* 7(1), 4–17.

Pomfret, Richard (2004): Why does Optimal Currency Area Theory fail to predict Changes in Currency Areas? in Michael Plummer, ed., *Empirical Methods in International Economics: Essays in Honor of Mordechai (Max) Kreinin* (Edward Elgar, Cheltenham UK), 53–71.

Pomfret, Richard (2005a): Sequencing Trade and Monetary Integration: Issues and application to Asia, *Journal of Asian Economics* 16(1), 105–204.

Pomfret, Richard (2005b): Trade Policies in Central Asia after EU Enlargement and before Russian WTO Accession: Regionalism and integration into the world economy, *Economic Systems* (March), 32–58.

Pomfret, Richard (2005c): Currency Areas in Theory and Practice, *Economic Record* 81(253), 166–176.

Pomfret, Richard (2006): Regional Trade Agreements, in Michele Fratianni and Alan Rugman, eds., *Regional Economic Integration* (Elsevier, Amsterdam), 39–54.

Prasad, Eswar, Thomas Rumbaugh and Qing Wang (2005): Putting the Cart before the Horse? Capital Account Liberalization and Exchange Rate Flexibility in China, *IMF Policy Discussion Paper 05/1*, January.

Rajan, Ramkishen (2005): Will Asia come together? *Business Times* (Singapore) 1 February 2005.

Rajan, Ramkishen, Rahul Sen and Reza Yamore Siregar (2001): *Singapore and Free Trade Agreements: Economic Relations with Japan and the United States* (ISEAS Publications, Singapore).

Rose, Andrew (2000): One Money, One Market: The Effect of Common Currencies on Trade, *Economic Policy* 30 (April), 7–33.

Rose, Andrew (2002): The Effect of Common Currencies on International Trade: A meta–analysis, April 8 version from haas.berkeley.edu/~arose – subsequently published in Volbert Alexander, Jacques Mélitz, and George M. von Furstenberg, eds. (2004): *Monetary Unions and Hard Pegs: Effects on Trade, Financial Development, and Stability* (Oxford University Press).

Rose, Andrew, and Charles Engel (2002): Currency Unions and International Integration, *Journal of Money, Credit and Banking* 34(4), 1067–1089.

Rose, Andrew and Eric van Wincoop (2001): National Money as a Barrier to Trade: The Real Case for Monetary Union, *American Economic Review* 91(2), 386–390.

Salvatore, Dominick, James Dean and Thomas Willett, eds. (2003): *The Dollarization Debate* (Oxford University Press, Oxford and New York).

Schoors, Koen (2003): The Effect of Soviet Monetary Disintegration on the Collapse of Trade between Members of the Commonwealth of Independent Sates, *Economic Systems* 27(1), 1–26.

Scollay, Robert, and John Gilbert (2001): New Regional Trading Arrangements in the Asia–Pacific, *Policy Analyses in International Economics* 63 (Institute for International Economics, Washington DC).

Stockman, Alan (2001): Optimal Central Bank Areas, Financial Intermediation, and Mexican Dollarization, *Journal of Money, Credit and Banking* 33(2), 648–666.

Thom, Rodney and Brendan Walsh (2002): The Effect of a Currency Union on Trade: Lessons from the Irish Experience, *European Economic Review* 46(6), 1111–1123.

Tower, Edward and Thomas Willett (1976): The Theory of Optimum Currency Areas and Exchange–Rate Flexibility, *Princeton Special Papers in International Economics*, No. 11 (International Finance Section, Princeton University), May.

Viner, Jacob (1950): *The Customs Union Issue* (Carnegie Endowment for International Peace, New York).

von Furstenbeg, George (2002): One Region, One Money: The Potential Contribution of Currency Consolidation to Financial Stability in the Developing World, in Michele Fratianni, Paolo Savona and John Kirton, eds., *Governing Global Finance: New Challenges, G7 and IMF Contributions* (Ashgate, Aldershot UK).

Wang, Yunjong (2004): Financial Cooperation and Integration in East Asia, *Journal of Asian Economics* 15, 939–955.

CHAPTER 3

ASEAN+3: IS AN ECONOMIC COMMUNITY IN THEIR FUTURE?

James Angresano

'Behind the economic importance [of the China–ASEAN Free Trade Area membership] is the deeper political implications caused by trade liberalization between ASEAN and the PRC, or it will be difficult to answer, for example, why Japan, ASEAN's oldest dialogue partner that has a huge economic scale and close economic ties with both Southeast Asia and mainland China, has not been in the game [prior to 2002]. Hence, the above-mentioned questions can not be answered solely from an economic perspective' (Huang 2001).

ASEAN[1] currently is at numerous stages of political and economic integration and cooperation both among its members, and between ASEAN and the three large northeast Asian countries (China, Japan and South Korea), as well as with other Asian, European and North American countries. ASEAN is the core member of the Asia Pacific Economic Cooperation Forum (APEC), an extra-regional forum designed to build a Pacific community. ASEAN has also created the ASEAN regional forum to discuss political and security issues with the USA, China, Russia, France, and Britain. ASEAN has expanded its economic horizons through initiating the Asia–Europe Summit Meeting. Of special interest are the ongoing discussions to widen integration by formalizing closer trade and monetary relations among ASEAN and three of its 'dialog partners:'

[1] ASEAN members include Brunei, Cambodia, Indonesia, Laos, Malaysia, Myanmar, Thailand, the Philippines, Singapore, and Vietnam.

China, Japan, and South Korea (this partnership is hereafter referred to as ASEAN+3). These discussions began in 2002 when ASEAN leaders began studying the feasibility of forming an ASEAN Economic Community by 2020 that would include these three neighboring economic powers.

The European Union (EU) began with a series of agreements among only six countries with the common political and economic objectives of establishing closer trade relations so as to foster common economic interests that would supplant political and military competition (Wyplosz 2001: 151). The EU's post–1951 experience indicates that favorable economic growth and development has occurred concurrent with EU integration, and analysts argue that integration has contributed quite positively to this successful performance.[2] European integration has included such market-oriented reforms as reduced tariff and non-tariff barriers, easier cross-border transport, a stronger competition policy, and a common currency. This success makes the issue of whether some features of the EU development and integration experience offer lessons for ASEAN +3 integration. Authorities considering the feasibility of forming the ASEAN+3 Economic Community can broaden their understanding of integration's implications for ASEAN members by studying the European Union development and integration experience to see if it might offer them useful lessons.

This chapter will argue that EU integration offers ASEAN+3 political and security lessons concerning the maintenance of regional stability. There are also both positive and negative lessons pertaining to political and economic issues and indications that there can be limits to integration beyond which some members, whose economies' performance trend is unfavorable, might object to proposals for deeper and wider integration. However, the existence of some specific lessons does not mean that the EU provides any institutional blueprint for deeper and wider integration that ASEAN+3 could seek to emulate. This is due to the 'contextual specificity' of institutions. In fact, ASEAN+3 policy makers have consistently demonstrated a clear understanding that it is unwise to transplant in a wholesale manner institutions and corresponding rules

---

[2] This will be discussed in Section Two.

from another economy — particularly a Western economy — to their own country and expect favorable outcomes to ensue.

This chapter utilizes an evolutionary–institutional perspective for analyzing some integration and development cases.[3] Section One examines the EU's development and integration experience — particularly the relationship between the deepening and widening of integration and the economy's performance — and recent controversies over proposals to deepen and widen EU integration further. This description of the EU experience will elucidate lessons that may be useful for ASEAN authorities. The same is the case for the following section which presents common aspects of the Japanese and Chinese development experiences. It is noted that neither of these countries was integrated politically or economically with any other country as they developed. This isolation may explain the two countries' cautious response to recent invitations to integrate with ASEAN. In Section Three the evolution of ASEAN, its economic performance, and its evolving political and economic relationships with China, Japan and South Korea are presented. The chapter concludes by suggesting lessons the EU integration experience provides for ASEAN+3.

The EU Development and Integration Experience

Integration of EU members was part of a development strategy with multiple goals, especially the strong desire to improve political relations among members so as to reduce nationalism and the likelihood of war. However, at the time of the European Coal and Steel Community's inception in 1951 there was little economic theory upon which to base institutions and rules pertaining to integration.[4] Member country authorities

---

[3] For a detailed treatment of this perspective see Angresano, 1996.

[4] Early writers looked upon discriminatory trade arrangements from the point of view of the nation granting the preference. Adam Smith had argued in favor of preferential trade agreements on a bilateral basis, arguing that the recipient of preferential treatment could benefit. Robert Torrens argued that benefits could be derived for a nation from discriminatory trade policies if it could establish a 'nationally optimum tariff' along the lines of a price-discriminating monopolist. In 1950 Jacob Viner's pioneering work identified that preferential trade arrangements could have both benefits (trade creation) and costs (trade

and their advisors chose to adopt some unique supranational institutions and rules for integration in response to their particular historical, political, and socio-economic conditions. They did not adhere to any blueprint for development and integration such as the model of a 'free market economy.' Since 1951 the EU has simultaneously been one economy and between 6 and 25 member state economies. Both the EU and its members are continually evolving: although integration has deepened and widened, each participating economy's degree and pace of political, economic, and social integration has varied.

The commitment to integrate was stimulated by centuries of war and the underdeveloped state of European economies after World War Two.[5] The French were at the center of the integration process. They sought a Franco-German *rapprochement* that would not impose harsh economic suppression on Germany (which had been the case with the Treaty of Versailles penalties), thereby avoiding adverse economic effects on Germany's natural trading partners along its western and southern borders. The Benelux countries and Italy endorsed the French position. The political, economic and social challenges that ensued from the subsequent decision to form the European Coal and Steel Community (ECSC) required authorities from these six countries to design appropriate institutions and corresponding rules. United States defense spending, by guaranteeing the military protection necessitated by the Cold War, obviated the necessity for the ECSC to allocate substantial resources toward common institutions for its own military defense. The USA aid facilitated the establishment of supranational institutions that would achieve the community's political, security and economic objectives.

---

diversion), and consequently global welfare needed to be considered in evaluating the net economic impact of economic integration among nations. For further discussion see Pomfret, 2001: 176-182.

[5] One scholar notes that 'Walter Hallstein, the first president of the Community, frequently said that the common market was in politics, not in business. That is, the common market was primarily formed not to gain the considerable economic advantages envisioned, but to meet the political challenges of post war Europe. A political solution to Franco-German animosity had to be found; a European effort to face up to the Soviet military-strategic challenge was a necessity; and a way to fend off American economic domination was considered essential. Although not the only factor, the European Community was important in achieving all these goals' (Krause 1999: 5-6).

Subsidiary to the political and security objectives was the desire among smaller ECSC members to realize anticipated dynamic benefits of integration, particularly economies of scale. Prior to the French and Dutch rejection of the proposed EU Constitution in 2005, larger members had been giving higher priority to establishing institutions and rules designed to promote deeper and wider integration for purposes of maintaining stability and security. Meanwhile smaller EU members, in hopes that deeper integration would benefit them, have emphasized establishment of institutions that would promote greater economic integration and unilateralization of trade negotiations. Without any comparable integration case, and armed with only modest economic theory pertaining to integration, ECSC authorities developed a new philosophical basis for their integrated economy. They drew heavily on the contextual, pragmatic philosophy of Robert Schuman, who proposed a supranational principal institution, the High Authority, to address primary political, security, and economic problems. The Schuman proposal, by giving the ECSC control over iron ore and coal, made it materially impossible for a war to occur between France and Germany.

Over the past five decades the philosophy towards integration has reflected shifting attitudes among member nation authorities towards the efficacy of centralized supranational and state institutions — versus markets — for resolving pressing political, economic and social problems. While some members held a bias in favor of economic management, state intervention, and increased government expenditures, others advocated less centralized control and greater reliance upon market forces. Since the early 1990s the dominant philosophy shifted in favor of market forces, as is evident in the removal of many internal trade barriers to permit a freer flow of resources within the integrated economy, and in the adoption of a single currency — albeit at the price of greater federalization of the EU.

On the other hand, leading EU authorities have also maintained some protective barriers, particularly towards agricultural interests, that have created a deadlock in the most recent round of WTO trade negotiations. At the center of the dispute are EU farmers, particularly those from France, who receive about Euro 50 billion in annual subsidies. They remain 'vehemently opposed' to reductions in the current system of subsidies (Wright 2005). As a result, the EU's position at the WTO appears quite contradictory to some observers, being simultaneously a regional trading arrangement striving to deepen integration for economic benefits and a trading bloc that resists reducing protective barriers that deny its citizens lower priced goods and export opportunities to non EU nations.[6] One observer argues that the EU's refusal to reduce agricultural protection beyond what it proposed at WTO trade negotiations in 2003 is 'a signal of the declining relevance of an aging continent whose arrogance is a transparent mask for fear' (Bowring 2005).

EU authorities have defended the usefulness of centrally controlled common policies not only for agriculture, but for transport, social, and regional purposes in achieving greater political, economic, and social integration. Jacques Delors describes the philosophy underlying the establishment of common policies, contending that integration of European countries was to be 'an instrument not merely to promote economic ends, but [also] like Jean Monnet argued . . . [to provide] a stepping stone to the creation of a democratic socialist European super state that [would] be able to maintain the cultural identity of European civilization against the capitalist threat of the USA and Japan and the Communist threat of the USSR' (Price 1989: 40). In this regard EU authorities have been supported by social concerns stemming from a social structure that, in contrast to ASEAN+3, has considerable trade and professional union membership, which strongly favors significant redistribution policies and job security.

Institutional adaptation to the deepening and widening of integration, a reflection of EU leaders' willingness to compromise so as to reconcile differences among members, has coincided with the need for an executive branch (Commission), principal decision-making body (Council), arbiter for disputes (Court), democratically elected consultative body (Parliament), and, most recently, monetary control and policy (European Central Bank). These idiosyncratic institutions have been designed to address such challenges of governance as maintaining static consistency

[6] The EU does not stand alone in its unwillingness to maintain agricultural barriers. Japan, South Korea, and the United States retain high barriers as well.

(satisfied by the Court) as well as dynamic stability. The latter has been problematic due to the massive institutional adaptations necessitated by the distributional implications of enlargement.

Among the rules governing ownership and control of EU resources have been the numerous discriminatory external trade agreements between the EU and non-members. Given its growing bargaining power from an enlarged economy, in virtually every case of 'preferential trade agreements' the EU has been effective in setting tariffs and antidumping duties on what EU analysts considered to be 'unfairly cheap' imports of what the EU classifies as 'sensitive products' — especially cereals, dairy products, sugar, and footwear products. In the case of agreements with poor countries, it appears that EU preferential trade agreements have contained far more form than substance, with relatively modest benefits offered to selected non-EU members (e.g., North African countries), while trade diversion has been experienced by these non-EU countries in some cases.[7] This is primarily due to the EU's imposing tariffs and anti-dumping measures well above the world average on textiles and clothing products, as well as on 'sensitive' agricultural products.[8]

As one economy the EU has featured regulated markets that are protected, which in some cases have been in violation of GATT or WTO principles. The EU has extended most favored nation status to only six countries, from which it receives about one third of its imports, with a wide range of tariff rates and other conditions imposed on the rest of the world according to the political and social relationship between each country and the EU (Sapir 1998). A case in point is the 1993 'banana regime', which created a single EU market in bananas. Some non-EU member banana producers suffered from a discriminatory preferential

---

[7]See ECPDM (1999), and Stevens and Kennan (2000). EU trade barriers imposed against poorer countries typically have been highest for products that poorer countries have a comparative advantage producing. In the case of Egypt, changes in market share of Egyptian exports over time indicates that there has been slower export growth, and even a decline, for products that Egypt is relatively more efficient at producing due to EU non-tariff barriers. See Ghoneim (2000).

[8] One criticism of EU trade policy is that it is a 'hub and spoke approach' whereby its preferential agreements with poorer countries 'ensures an open door for European exporters in expanding foreign markets' but may be 'welfare deteriorating' for the poorer countries who sign such agreements (Busse 2001).

trade agreement that allocated production quotas to overseas territories (an EU historical legacy) eligible to receive EU Common Agricultural Policy price supports (Pomfret 2001: 132). The EU can counter criticism of its trade restrictions by pointing to its listed tariffs as being perhaps the lowest of any major economy in the world. However, coinciding with the reduction of EU tariffs have been rising non-tariff barriers — particularly the greater use of anti-dumping measures.

The degree to which integration has contributed favorably or unfavorably to both freer worldwide trade and the performance of the EU economy has been the subject of numerous studies. Each study has attempted to isolate one of the following effects that EU integration has had on both EU member countries and the rest of the world:[9] trade creation and trade diversion; dynamic effects such as economies of scale and productivity; foreign direct investment; changes in intra-EU regional disparities; reduced transactions costs; macroeconomic stability; enlargement; bargaining power of the EU in GATT and WTO negotiations; and costs born by non-EU countries. In addition, attempts have been made to identify non-economic benefits and costs EU members have realized from integration.

Most evidence indicates that integration has contributed to a net positive trade creation for the EU, although there are conflicting estimates of the extent to which trade creation has or has not outweighed trade diversion, measured in terms of either relative magnitudes or the net magnitude of the change in costs on newly traded or diverted goods (Kreinin 1972; Balassa 1975; Robson 1984; Pomfret 1997; Panagariya 2000). It appears that the positive static welfare effects have been modest (i.e., a small net trade creation effect).[10] There also is convincing evidence that EU integration has positively affected medium-term economic growth through improving an investment climate that attracts capital formation, which, in turn, promotes greater worker productivity and higher rates of

---

[9] Two methodological approaches typically have been taken. One relies upon counterfactual analysis within a partial or general equilibrium model framework, while the other concerns ex post studies using gravity equations (see Panagariya 2000: 325).

[10] Baldwin and Venables (1995) argue that the reason for the 'modest' positive welfare effects post 1992 is that there were already no tariffs on internal trade, and thus trade creation did not occur after completion of the internal market.

economic growth (Baldwin and Wyplosz 2003). The experience of Ireland, Portugal and Spain post accession to the EU supports this conclusion, as does a comparison of the growth rates of EU members France, Germany and Italy versus non-member UK between 1950 and 1973. Such was not the case for Greece, however, although this has been attributed to that country's poor macroeconomic policies (Baldwin and Wyplosz 2003).

While dynamic effects such as increased economies of scale, higher worker productivity and lower production costs were realized after the formation of the European Economic Community in 1957, no convincing study has identified the causal effect of European integration. This is due to the problem of distinguishing correlation from causality as researchers seek to 'disentangle the effect of the regional integration from other changes in the economy' (Baldwin and Venables 1995). Due to this problem most methodologies analyzing the effects of EU integration do not attempt to include dynamic effects.[11] Nevertheless, two noteworthy studies (Cecchini 1988; Gasiorek, Smith and Venables 1988) forecast substantial dynamic effects from the integration of national markets into a single European market in 1992, with the 'main source of potential gain appear[ing] to be scale induced reductions in average cost' (Gasiorek, Smith and Venables 1992).[12] Further, empirical and theoretical studies for Canada (Wonnacott, Wonnacott 1967; Cox, Harris 1985) attributing the realization of economies of scale to integration have been convincing. This is not surprising, given that the Canadian–USA example is a classic small nation-large nation case in which the small nation would be expected to benefit substantially from integration due to its becoming able to achieve greater economies of scale.

The effect of EU integration on productivity benefits and increases in foreign direct investment has also been difficult to identify, although correlations between deeper integration and modest positive indicators for both factors throughout the EU have been observed. Some analysts argue

---

[11] Analytical techniques used in an attempt to isolate the effects of integration include computable equilibrium models and econometric evaluations, each of which has strengths and weaknesses.

[12] These gains were attributed to the competitive-inducing effects of integration which reduced the degree of imperfect competition throughout the EU.

that the stimulus for foreign direct investment throughout the EU during the 1980s was the fear among investors from non-EU countries that 'Fortress Europe' would impose greater barriers to such investment after the completion of the internal market. Some reduction in regional disparities within the EU, however, can be attributed to the establishment of the Social, Structural and Regional Funds designed to achieve that purpose. There is also evidence of some convergence of per capita national incomes among the ECSC members (Ben–David 1993).

Greater macroeconomic stability is attributable in part to greater intra-EU trade which has reduced external economic dependence and adverse effects from external shocks (Letiche 2000: 276).[13] In addition, there is expanding recognition that 'the relationship between monetary integration and economic integration (and political integration) is two-way and mutually reinforcing' (Pomfret 2003). Although the literature is still in an early stage, it has been anticipated that the single currency may yield many benefits. One is the potential to promote internal trade by modest amounts due to expected reduced transactions costs (some estimate as much as 0.4 percent of the EU GDP) and greater exchange-rate stability (Rose 2000). It is also expected that an additional benefit from the single currency will be to induce a greater degree of fiscal policy cooperation. A third benefit is that a common currency may be the 'best solution' for the threat of competitive devaluation (Pomfret 2003). Finally, evidence indicates that integration to the economic and monetary union level has contributed to reducing the cost of capital for firms in the euro area (Bris et al. 2004).

There have been consistent findings concerning the impact of enlargement. Following each of the three pre 2004 enlargements there was a modest negative welfare effect on existing members from the Common Agricultural Policy, the magnitude of the effect depending upon the size of members' agricultural sector. Another finding is that trade diversion effects encountered by the three new Mediterranean

[13] In support of this conclusion Letiche (2000: 276) points out that in 1950 the average ratio of exports to GDP of the ECSC and EC members was about 35 percent but that by 2000 this percentage had declined to 15 percent (both percentages include intra-union trade).

members in the 1980s also were due to the Common Agricultural Policy (Pomfret 2001: 264, 277). Awareness of these costs associated with integration, as well as anticipated non economic costs of integrating with other countries, could induce newer entrants to the EU to seek larger economic incentives than had prior accession countries (Baldwin 1995). On the other hand, the 2004 enlargement has stimulated fears in France, Germany and the Netherlands that further increases in their respective unemployment rates will ensue due to anticipated loss of jobs to workers from the new Central and East European members. For support, critics point to substantial wage differentials between these three countries' labor markets and those in the 10 new members (e.g., labor costs are estimated to be six times greater in Germany than in neighboring Poland in certain industries).

Integration appears to have enhanced the EU's ability to gain an advantage in bilateral agreements with smaller economies, as well as in worldwide negotiations. In GATT and WTO rounds of negotiations the EU's ability to use its bargaining power to further its own interests at the expense of the rest of the world has been most apparent in its ability to maintain the restrictive Common Agricultural Policy. Studies also indicate that the deepening and widening of EU integration have contributed to a more vigorous use of anti-dumping claims against non-EU members (Eeckout 1997; Hindley and Messerlin 1993). EU external policies, including preferential trade arrangements between the EU and its 'overseas territories', the trade restrictions and subsidies associated with the Common Agricultural Policy, and other features of the EU's RTA, have led some analysts to argue that the benefits of EU integration have come at the expense of the rest of the world (Sampson and Snape 1980). Some Asian countries believe they have suffered the effects of trade diversion (Plummer and Jones 2004: 831; Lee 2003; Geithner and Nankani 2002). EU non-tariff barriers have contributed to trade diversion and mitigated gains for countries such as Egypt from its bilateral agreement with the EU. One study concerning Egypt's bilateral agreement with the EU demonstrates a declining market share of Egyptian exports following the implemenation of the agreement, particularly products for which Egypt enjoys a comparative advantage *vis-à-vis* the EU (Ghoneim 2000).

Concerning non-economic effects integration, EU analysts seem to agree that the EU's integration experience has provided an example to the rest of the world that political and economic integration can promote a better sense of community while contributing to the realization of substantial political, security, and social benefits. After millennia of wars, EU members have been at peace with one another for over 50 years. Providing fewer resources for security has enabled EU members to provide their citizens with extensive social insurance and welfare schemes that have contributed significantly to the alleviation of poverty and to a high Human Development Index in most member nations. Although there are some non-economic costs born by new EU members during accession (Baldwin 1995), these appear to have been outweighed in Europe by positive non-economic effects of integration. For example, feelings of nationalism and regional hostility, while difficult to quantify, appear to have diminished substantially throughout the EU over the past half century.

On the other hand, offsetting the material and non economic benefits attributed to EU integration is the political reality that deeper and wider integration conflicts with the nation state's desire for self determination while democratic politics is driven by interest groups who seek to directly affect policy decisions. This condition has created a 'political trilemma' for the world economy in general and the EU in particular. Dani Rodrik argues that this trilemma exists because deeper economic integration, the nation state, and democratic politics are 'mutually incompatible' (Rodrik 2002). This is relevant for some EU members who believe that deeper integration of economies to the point where the existence of unregulated markets without sufficient compensation for those adversely affected by external economic forces, combined with adherence to rules such as those imposed by the EMU Maastrict requirements has placed their policy makers in a 'golden straightjacket' (Rodrik 2002). The French and Dutch rejections of the EU Constitution appear to be a reaction to this emerging belief.

The inability of France, Germany, and Italy to adhere to the 3 percent of GDP Maastricht budget deficit convergence rule, combined with persistent unemployment and low growth in these countries, has become a source of friction within the EU. Some Italian critics have called for the nation to leave the EMU and reintroduce the lira to enable Italian policy makers to have discretionary monetary policy available as a macroeconomic policy tool. The French have been particularly aggressive in blaming economic liberalization created by deeper and wider global and EU integration for their economic problems as well as for their perceived loss of some social and cultural identity. In response to recent attempts by foreign firms to acquire French firms (e.g., PepsiCo's pursuit of Danone) the government announced that it was planning to identify '10 strategic sectors' that it would protect from foreign takeover, even if such a move was in violation of EU freedom of capital movement rules (Bowley 2005). These reactions reflect the growing realization throughout the larger original 15 EU members that '[t]he liberal regime within Europe, combined with the protectionist regime toward the rest of the world, worked pretty well when we could dictate the terms of trade . . . One of the things that we have had to realize in the age of globalization is that that is no longer the case' (Bowley 2005). As is the case for France, Italy and the Netherlands, two Asian economic powers, Japan and China, are adjusting their attitudes towards integration in the face of globalization pressures — albeit in a different direction.

The Development Experience of Japan and China

Although Japan's development experience (early 1950s — early 1990s), as well as that of China after 1949 have distinctive aspects,[14] common features will be discussed below — particularly as they pertain to attitudes towards European-style integration. These features include bold decisions implemented quickly, particularly innovative and pragmatic development policies guided by the state and a lengthy (at least 25–year) period of rapid GDP, export, and FDI growth that did not coincide with political and economic integration. Neither Japan nor China had favorable political or economic experiences with Western nations prior to the early 1950s. Their respective colonial and neocolonial relationships with Europe and the USA reinforced their inward-looking insti-

[14] For a detailed treatment of the Japanese and Chinese development experiences from the evolutionary-institutional perspective see Angresano 1996 and 2003.

tution building and development strategies. Both countries have borrowed and purchased Western technology freely, but have grafted this technology carefully onto their cultures without adopting European values.[15] Japan was able to do this despite the influence of the Occupation Authority on institutional change and the country's 1946–1952 development strategy. Post–1949 China carefully studied the development experiences of both Western and Eastern Europe and Latin America — particularly where World Bank and IMF policies had been introduced, before choosing their innovative development strategy that countered the standard recipe advocated by these international financial agencies (Angresano 2005).

Both countries have demonstrated a considerable unwillingness to give up sovereignty for integration purposes. A strong preference in both countries for close economic relations with an insider network and the ability to form what are in effect viable cartels have further discouraged political or economic integration except for unilateral trade relations and the encouragement (particularly in China) of foreign direct investment. In both cases, this preference is grounded in ethnocentric social attitudes common to both countries, which include a desire to maintain cultural homogeneity, and in each country's historical experiences with Western colonial powers. Japan suffered the humiliating effects of USA gunboat diplomacy in the mid 19th century. Similarly, China's experience with the 1840–41 Opium War and with colonial powers who carved the country into colonies and forcibly imposed 'unequal treaties' influenced its decision to close its economy throughout the 1949–1978 period (Chow 2002). One-party control in China and the continual political control held by the Liberal Democratic Party in Japan (1952–1994) provided the political stability and power to establish and maintain international economic policies that promoted economic, social and political interests, albeit with the sacrifice of some economic efficiency. For Japan and China (as well as for ASEAN members) the achievement of favorable

[15] Japanese and Chinese policy makers are very familiar with European economies and integration, particularly because many students of economics and agency workers (Ministry of International Trade and Industry, Committee for Restructuring the Economic System) attended universities in Europe, especially Oxford and Cambridge.

economic performance without substantive political reform during their respective growth and development periods since the mid 1950s has demonstrated that — quite contrary to the *aquis communitaire* of the EU — political reform may not be necessary for economic growth and development.

Most Japanese and Chinese principal institutions and working rules that were implemented during their bursts of development had few counterparts outside their countries. Particularly distinctive were Japan's Ministry of International Trade and Industry, *keiretsu*, Postal Savings Bank, and *sogo shosha* and China's township and village enterprises and special economic zones (whose rules differed radically from those applied to the rest of the economy). In both countries the unique institutional development corresponded to the needs of their respective initial economic and political realities, especially by being compatible with ruling authority interests. China in particular 'highlights the context-specificity of what worked and what did not' (Qian 2003: 331). The importance and effectiveness of the unique institutions in advancing economic development reinforced Japan's and China's aversion to integration, supranational institutions, and the modification of domestic institutions and rules.[16]

Perhaps the most significant common feature of these economies has been state guidance of the economy with strong central decision-making. Any foreign ownership of assets was based upon rules established on Japanese or Chinese terms. Strong state guidance permitted the gradual introduction of market-oriented economic activities and facilitated means of inducing high savings and investment rates, controlling the allocation of credit, and minimizing capital flight. Pragmatism (essentially, the adoption of whatever worked and preference for common sense and experience over ideologies or abstract theoretical economic models) was a

---

[16] As in Japan and China, there were contextually specific institutions in EU nations that contributed favorably to each member's post 1945 rapid growth period. These included corporatist wage bargaining (particularly in Sweden), the Planning Commission which facilitated indicative planning (France), and corporatism as in Germany where the Council of Economic Experts recommended a gradualist growth strategy involving a social contract between the major macroeconomic actors: the government, central bank, unions, and employers.

consistent characteristic of both countries' development strategies. In each case the state played a development role in devising a pragmatic strategy based upon strong state-private sector cooperation, allocation of investment funds, and protection from foreign competition through rules pertaining to trade and foreign direct investment. In Japan's case state authorities were receptive to advice from private sector leaders.

The dramatic and unprecedented economic performance of each economy is well documented, particularly the average annual real GDP growth rate of 10 percent in Japan during 1955–1970 (OECD 1989) and over 9 percent in China since 1978 (Chow 2002), as well as substantial reductions in the incidence of poverty. Although there were radical differences between property rights in the two countries, both development strategies promoted the institutions, rules, and incentives that stimulated rates of innovation and investment to generate unprecedented rates of sustained GDP growth.[17] Initial success stimulated a circular and cumulative causation process that first accelerated, and then helped sustain economic growth and development.

It has been argued that China has 'integrated' into the global economy through foreign direct investment, gradually opening its economy prior to its WTO entry, and has made market access and tariff commitments to the WTO that 'exceed those made by any member that has joined the WTO since 1995' (Prybla 2003). Similarly, analysts point out that Japan has become a more 'open' economy than any other OECD economy.[18] Nevertheless, for both countries the favorable development experiences can in no way be attributed to European-style integration. A case in point is that the high percentage of China's poverty reduction had occurred by the mid 1980s, and this reduction has been attributed to agricultural growth. There has been only a modest reduction in poverty since the dramatic early 1990s increases in foreign trade and investment (Bardhan 2005). For political and economic reasons, however, both

[17] Analysis of cross-country variation in growth point to the importance of 'institutions, geography, economic and political structures, policies and governance' as the key contributing factors to such differences (Wacziarg 2002; Rodrik et al. 2002; Qian 2003).

[18] This assertion was made by Erik Ramstetter, Chief, Research Division, International Centre for the Study of East Asian Development.

countries have taken steps in recent years towards integration with their Southeast Asian neighbors and with the WTO (see following section).

Among the common factors credited with contributing to the impressive performance of the Japanese and Chinese economies were the high priority given to education; low population growth rates; the avoidance of the European problem of rising government expenditures as a percentage of GDP (which has considerably reduced investment and job creation within the EU); the ability to take advantage of the product life cycle for goods in which each country had a comparative or competitive advantage; an ethnic-cultural-linguistic feature that promoted homogeneity and respect for authority; high rates of investment in infrastructure; and (in China post 1993) foreign direct investment.[19] The Japanese and Chinese experiences, because they succeeded while differing materially from Western strategies, demonstrate an important lesson in economic growth analysis. The lesson is that 'there is no miracle cure, and that achieving high rates of growth requires the confluence of many specific policies and hard to satisfy conditions' (Wacziarg 2002: 916–917). The reverse is also true: when non-Asian countries have tried to implement the Japanese and Chinese development strategy, they typically have been unsuccessful. The experiences also demonstrate that achievement of political security and economic development have been experienced by countries that until recent years avoided political and economic integration.

The Evolution of ASEAN and ASEAN+3

Political factors partly explain the modest degree of integration achieved among the ASEAN+3 countries by 2005. Nearly all of these countries have 'not been characterized by close associations among its very diverse peoples and political systems, but by political fragmentation and external interference and domination' (Frost 1990: 2). In contrast to the EU there

[19] If the behavior of foreign direct investors is any indication of improved institutions, China's development strategy and policies merit considerable attention, especially given the meteoric rise in FDI there as China has become the world's largest FDI recipient, and it ranks second in a recent FDI confidence survey.

has not been close cohesion fostered by any 'Asian' solidarity.[20] Politically, there has been little experience with parliamentary democracy in a Western sense. Rather, one party has tended to dominate each system within a hierarchical authoritarian political structure with particular emphasis placed upon maintenance of political stability and continuity. Unlike Europe where the impetus for integration was 'generated by the wish to overcome lasting contention amongst the founding members', the underlying motivation for the creation of ASEAN was driven by 'external factors . . . of a political [and security] nature' (Gramegna 1997). During the early 1960s anti-communist fears concerning potential Vietnam aggression were particularly strong. In 1967 when their respective political stability was believed to be at risk Indonesia, Malaysia, the Philippines, Singapore, and Thailand formed The Association of Southeast Asian Nations (ASEAN) in response to a perceived military threat from Vietnam. This fear was heightened in the mid 1970s due to the power void created by the USA departure from Vietnam. Also threatened by insurgency movements, the five founding members greatly desired to promote regional peace, stability, and security and avoid balkanization. In this respect ASEAN was similar to the early years of European integration when the ECSC was 'held together by political fear' (Krause 1999: 5) rather than by a desire to benefit from economic integration. Some of this fear has since been alleviated. At the First ASEAN Summit in 1976 members signed the Treaty of Amity and Cooperation (TAC), a non-aggression pact aimed at promoting regional stability; in 1993 the ASEAN Regional Forum was established to foster dialogue and consultation on political and security issues while building confidence in preventive diplomacy for the region;[21] and enlargement has widened integration to include ten members, among them Vietnam which became an ASEAN member in 1995.

From its inception ASEAN was not established to pursue supranational objectives, and its leaders insisted that economic and political mat-

[20] Some of my Chinese and Japanese students have commented that 'Asian' is an American political term and that people in Southeast Asian countries identify almost exclusively with national interests and culture.

[21] In addition to ASEAN members participants include Australia, Canada, China, the European Union, and the USA, among other countries.

ters be kept separate. Consequently, economic interests of ASEAN members remained national. While there was no attempt to pursue economic integration in the European sense, members were not averse to modest forms of economic cooperation. There was, however, an understanding that ASEAN cooperative ventures should focus on national development as the primary means for regional economic development. Thus, in its first decades the organization exhibited few characteristics of economic integration. Some believe that the token economic cooperation that did exist was only a cover for ASEAN's anti-communist political intentions, although the oil shock of 1973 briefly stimulated some interest in more substantive economic cooperation. There was, however, 'no economic content until the 1977 summit, and the trade preferences and coordinated industrial policies introduced then and during the early 1980s proved ineffective' (Pomfret 2001: 102).

The general lack of interest in substantive political and economic integration is indicated by ASEAN's organizational structure. Unlike the EU, ASEAN's (modest) political and economic cooperation have occurred 'without relying on an institutional framework' designed to foster integration (*The Japan Times* 2003). From its inception ASEAN, as an administrative body, has been quite decentralized so as not to interfere with member nations' desire for political independence.[22] ASEAN's institutions have been 'consciously kept diffuse, decentralized, and under national control' (Palmer and Reckford 1987: 109).[23] ASEAN nations' leaders have expressed no interest in any 'institutional frameworks that might give potential Asian superpowers . . . a major voice in their national affairs' (Letiche 2000: 285). The lack of interest in building supranational institutions is also due to the fear that such institutions, in creating a higher level of governance, provide prime vehicles for corruption and the abuse of power. There are no politically integrated groups, and

[22] It has been noted that during the Singapore Foreign Minister's recollection of the first meeting in 1967 he stated that 'at that time we ourselves having launched ASEAN, were not quite sure where it was going or whether it was going anywhere at all' (Frost 1990: 5).

[23] Until the Third Summit of 1987 there was no Secretary General of ASEAN. Rather, an undistinguished diplomat held the position of Secreatry General of the ASEAN Secretariat, and thus was essentially a 'mailbox' rather than a person of authority.

therefore no counterpart to the EU Court of Justice or Parliament. The ASEAN Secretariat staff numbers just over 100, as opposed to the roughly 24,000 staff members employed by the European Commission. Overall, ASEAN's principal institutions and their impact upon members' economies make it clear that 'ASEAN is certainly not the Treaty of Rome' (Palmer and Reckford 1987: 37), and that ASEAN was not instituted for economic reasons.

ASEAN's structure has been described as being that of a 'pure intergovernmental organization' without a large bureaucratic decision making body. In a manner consistent with member nations' preference for gradual, pragmatic changes and the value placed on maintaining their own sovereignty, ASEAN's decisions are made by members' foreign ministers on the basis of consensus or unanimity. Each ASEAN member 'has learned to respect each other's political system and domestic affairs and appreciate the fact that no single state has the right to impose its will on fellow members' (Gramenga 1997). One observer describes ASEAN decision making as similar to the 'the Malay cultural practice of consultation and consensus building as an operational process . . . and includes the hardened policy of non-interference in the internal affairs of fellow members' state affairs' (Jones 2004: 141). The result has been modest and gradual progress, 'in keeping with the style of the participants' (Palmer and Reckford 1987: 47). However, such a consensus building process bent on non interference has meant that decisions are made through agreement with the lowest common denominator.

The emphasis placed on its own national policies by each member towards trade, agricultural production, state-owned enterprises, foreign investment, and joint ventures limited the extent of economic cooperation during ASEAN's first two decades when intra ASEAN trade remained low (about 15 percent). Economic integration efforts were modest and fairly ineffective. During the late 1970s members' import substitution policies mitigated intra-ASEAN trade, which, as a percentage of members' total trade, actually declined by 1989 to under 10 percent if reexporting from Singapore is not included (Pomfret 2001: 300). Another factor limiting expansion of intra-ASEAN trade until very recently is that the ASEAN+3 nations 'still view themselves as distinct and competitive' (Letiche 2000: 285). Even though member countries' economies have been complementary, until the past few years it was an inter-industry type of complementarities producing inter-industry goods such as oil, rubber and other natural resources. Further, ASEAN member economies are relatively small and their foreign trade orientation (about two thirds of this trade) has been towards richer trading partners outside of the region, such as Japan, the USA and the EU.[24] Thus, unlike that of EU members, the composition of output and trade orientation of ASEAN economies limited the potential gains from economic integration. Attempts by ASEAN members' policy makers to establish cooperative industrial strategies to create vertically integrated ASEAN industries were unsuccessful. For example, when Malaysia sought to establish its own automobile industry, it effectively ended the attempt to promote complementary production in the auto industry throughout ASEAN.

While the performance of the individual economies of ASEAN's original members improved dramatically in terms of standard economic indicators from ASEAN's formation until the late 1990s, little credit has been given to integration for contributing appreciably to that success. One analyst argues that '[t]he economic importance of the association [ASEAN], however, could be said to derive more from the rapid growth and development performance of some of its member economies than the collective strength and cohesion of the association itself' (Chaterjee 1990: 58). It appears that policy shifts towards export promotion, development of labor-intensive industries (particularly electronics), and foreign direct investment from the USA and Japan deserve much credit. The major success attributable to integration has been the achievement of greater political and regional stability. The combination of ASEAN's formation, the TAC, and the USA departure from the region in the mid1970s have coincided with an absence of aggression throughout the region over the past four decades. This stability has had positive economic benefits. In the case of Japanese investors, the maintenance of a 'relatively stable political climate' (Daquila 2002: 10) has been the most important factor stimulating their FDI throughout ASEAN countries.

---

[24] It has been estimated that EU exports to NEAC plus ASEAN trade with the EU will be about 10 percent of the EU's total shortly after the 2004 accession, while NEAC and ASEAN exports to the enlarged EU are predicted to about 20 percent (Lee 2003).

Even though during the early 1980s ASEAN integration resembled that of the EU more than that of any other integrated group of economies, by the mid 1990s ASEAN remained less integrated than NAFTA as members retained inward-looking protective measures *vis-à-vis* one another. The success of export promotion policies stimulating individual members' economic growth and development contributed to a 1992 proposal for integrating deeper by forming the ASEAN Free Trade Area (AFTA). AFTA was intended to reduce tariffs on all trade among members to less than 5 percent within fifteen years, albeit with the innumerable exclusions upon which each member nation insisted. Few substantive reforms occurred, however, until 1997 when the Asian financial crisis coincided with a worldwide recession to affect ASEAN member exports adversely. These negative events stimulated a change in ASEAN members' attitudes in favor of deepening integration through closer financial cooperation and trade relations. The attitudinal change was due in part to collective dissatisfaction with both the timing of the IMF's response to the crisis and what Asian countries believed to be inappropriate loan conditions imposed by the IMF. This dissatisfaction spurred Asian economic authorities to conclude that without closer financial cooperation 'their financial markets and institutions were insufficiently prepared to manage globalized capital flows' (Wang and Anderson 2003: 89) and thus individual members were unable to prevent the loss of confidence that stimulated capital flight. Japan and the EU[25] provided funds for technical advice and to study the implications of some integrated financial arrangements.

In May 2000, ASEAN members' finance ministers signed the Chiang Mai Initiative, along with the finance ministers from China, Japan and South Korea. This agreement indicated a willingness on the part of these three Asian economic powers to cooperate with ASEAN for the establishment of a regional framework for monetary and financial cooperation. The Chiang Mai Initiative was designed to strengthen the countries'

[25] To assist Asian countries in recovering from the 1997 financial crisis, and to mitigate the chances for a similar recurrence, the EU established The Asian-Europe Meeting (ASEM) Trust fund at the World Bank. This fund provided the means to obtain expert financial advice and technical assistance for strapped Asian countries desiring to restructure their financial sector (*Single Market News* 1998).

financial systems by mitigating problems ensuing from unfavorable balance of payments and short-term liquidity conditions. It expanded an existing currency-swap network by increasing the size of the swap arrangements and creating a larger network of bilateral swap agreements among the ASEAN+3 countries (Wang and Andersen 2003: 90). Under the agreement countries were permitted 'to swap their local currencies for major international currencies for up to six months and for up to twice their committed amount' (Pomfret 2003). Since then not only has this initiative contributed to greater exchange rate and financial stability in the region, but it has sent signals to financial markets that confidence and liquidity problems inherent before and during the 1997 crisis have been significantly reduced by the ASEAN+3 monetary cooperation.[26]

This successful outcome, for which credit has been given to the 'will and vision of its leaders' (Gramenga 1997), encouraged ASEAN+3 finance ministers during the spring of 2005 to pursue closer financial cooperation. It was agreed to enhance the economic surveillance process, adopt a closer, collective decision making process towards bilateral swap arrangements, to increase the size of available swaps by up to 100 percent from $1 billion to $2 billion, and to double the size of the swaps (from 10 percent to 20 percent) that could be withdrawn without them coming under an IMF program. ASEAN members, however, are not prepared to pursue formation of a monetary union with a single currency, although 'economically it is rather close to fulfill[ing] the criteria of convergence.' As a result, ASEAN members are now in position to peg their currency among themselves, while 'float[ing] their respective currencies with the rest of the world' (Mittal 2004).

After 1997 ASEAN authorities also began more serious pursuit of closer economic relations among themselves. The impetus to work towards overcoming fears that such relations would lead to conflicts among members' special interests groups[27] came from other factors besides the financial crisis. ASEAN members also were reacting to per-

---

[26] Confidence has been strengthened due to the regional monetary cooperation by the significant amount of combined foreign exchange reserves (about $800 billion) held by ASEAN+3 (Pomfret 2003).

[27] Such as those which have arisen in NAFTA between lumber and wheat producers in the United States and Canada.

ceived bullying tactics used for decades by the World Bank, IMF and USA to influence ASEAN members' economic agenda, believing that collective action was more likely to enable members to attain their goals (Tourk 2004: 884). Improved political stability and the institutionalization of the ASEAN summit meetings (to occur every three years) contributed to speeding up the implementation of harmonized standards concerning some traded goods (e.g., electrical and electronic products), environmental cooperation, and trade and investment liberalization measures envisioned in the AFTA agreement (Daquila 2002).

There has been considerable integration success in the achievement of closer environmental protection cooperation for monitoring cross border pollution, better coordination of efforts to reduce haze pollution, and improved management of water resource and fisheries. Since the late 1990s the growth of FDI throughout ASEAN has exceeded the world average as ASEAN members were the recipients of more than $25 billion FDI in 2004. Intra ASEAN trade has increased, albeit modestly, to account for almost 23 percent of members' total foreign trade.[28] To increase this percentage ASEAN authorities will need to reduce obstacles inhibiting higher incidences of intra ASEAN trade that include large differences in members' tariff structures, the Western orientation of ASEAN members' trade, and only modest support for preferential trading schemes introduced throughout the region.

ASEAN leaders have openly declared their intention to overcome these obstacles by satisfying these agreements through 'fast track acceleration of regional integration' (Joint Media Statement of the Thirty-Seventh ASEAN Economic Ministers Meeting 2005). The agreements include (1) completing the measures proposed in the AFTA agreement, especially those pertaining to greater intra-regional trade liberalization through preferential trading arrangements and a common effective preferential tariff; (2) implementing measures to liberalize trade in services and increase intra ASEAN investment through the provisions contained in the ASEAN Investment Area scheme; and (3) promoting the

---

[28] A high proportion of intra ASEAN trade continues to be between Singapore and Malaysia and between Singapore and Indonesia. Singapore offers its port and other services needed by Malaysia for its exports in exchange for basis resources from Malaysia Singapore needs, particularly water.

ASEAN Industrial Cooperation scheme which permits joint ventures between ASEAN nationals and foreign investors whose products or services will be given tariff preferences. For some agreements the timetable has been accelerated, as in the case of tariff reductions where the more economically advanced ASEAN members have agreed to remove import tariffs for products in 11 priority sectors by 2007 which would be 3 years ahead of schedule.

According to the AFTA agreement the deadline for tariff reduction was first set for 2008. However, after enlargement which included Vietnam, Laos, Cambodia, and Myanmar, the deadline was moved forward to 2003, and later to 2000.[29] In the year 2002 the Initiative on ASEAN Integration was launched. It included unilateral and voluntary tariff reduction, particularly by the older ASEAN members. An ASEAN fund in excess of $55 million was established to assist new members in areas such as infrastructure, human resource development, information and communications technology, and regional economic integration. Despite these provisions to deepen integration, since 2002 AFTA has been more of a preferential trade area with lower tariffs among its members relative to the rest of the world than a free trade area that eliminates tariffs and non-tariff barriers on goods produced by members for intra-AFTA trade.

Nevertheless, consideration of forming an East Asian Community that would be comprised of all Southeast Asian countries, China, Japan and South Korea began in 2002. Each of these three economic powers soon made it clear thereafter that they were not interested in integrating to such a degree, particularly in an economic union that would include both of its two main northeast Asia rivals. Undeterred, a year later ASEAN members signed an agreement designed to achieve an ASEAN Economic Community by 2020 that would be similar to the EU. This economic community would be based upon economic cooperation, political and security cooperation, and socio-cultural cooperation.

In the meantime ASEAN has continued to pursue establishment of closer political, financial and economic ties through proposals that would establish three separate free trade areas between ASEAN and China (ACFTA), Japan, and South Korea. Among factors motivating ASEAN+3

[29] This decision was negated by the 1997 finanical crisis.

authorities to consider integrating have been the threats of rising protectionist provisions and disputes within the WTO that have stalled world trade negotiations, the 2004 EU enlargement and fears of more trade diversion effects,[30] the continued North Korean threat to regional stability, the desire by each of the 3 Northeast Asian countries not to be left out if ASEAN were to reach a integration agreement with either or both of its Northeast Asian rivals, and perhaps the conclusion reached by some analysts that in order for ASEAN to realize the benefits offered by a free trade area, a 'major economic power' able to be the dominant consumer of the products exported by other members is required as a member (*The Japan Times* 2005).

ASEAN and Chinese authorities signed the ASEAN-China Free Trade Area (ACFTA) agreement in 2004. ACFTA's potential political importance lies in its being a sign that the 'historical feud and political clashes between ASEAN member states and the PRC are no longer one of the most important factors influencing ASEAN-PRC relations' (Huang 2001). China sees ACFTA as a means to marginalize Taiwan, thereby serving as a peaceful means of eventual reunification. Further, Chinese authorities may believe ACFTA provides a means for China to replace Japan and South Korea as the dominant political and economic power in Southeast Asia. ACFTA is intended to serve as a means to not only improve links with trade and foreign direct investment through liberalizing rules for bilateral trade, investment and services among ACFTA members, but to yield substantial economic benefits to both China, which is now ASEAN's fifth largest trading partner, and ASEAN which is China's sixth largest trading partner. From an economic perspective Chinese cooperation with ASEAN creates a trading arrangement with a population that exceeds $1.85 billion, GDP of more than $2 trillion, and a pre-FTA trade volume of about $1.2 trillion. The Chinese anticipate ACFTA would 'promote intra-ethnic trade between mainland Chinese and overseas Chinese living in ASEAN countries through existing busi-

[30] One study indicates that the trade diversion effects on ASEAN and NEAC from the 2004 EU enlargement will be very modest, although the textiles and apparel and the services sectors will suffer the most (Lee 2003).

ness networks. Such networks [give] ACFTA a unique Chinese characteristic as a regional cooperative framework' (Youn 2003).

Both ASEAN and China expect economic benefits through trade creation, higher GDP growth and greater productive efficiency resulting from intensified domestic competition, and a wider range of internal industrial complementarities. Prior to 2002 there were estimates that due to the complementarity of the ASEAN and Chinese economies, reduced trade and investment barriers would boost ASEAN GDP by 1 percent if bilateral trade with China achieves its potential to grow to 50 percent (Hang 2001), while also stimulating intra ACFTA trade and FDI. This positive forecast was realistic. In 2002 ASEAN-China trade 'jumped by 31.8 percent to a record high 54.8 billion US dollars' (China.org 2003), and has continued to increase — growing by 25 percent from mid 2004 to mid 2005. Meanwhile China's FDI into ASEAN increased from $189 million in 2003 to over $225 million in 2004 (Joint Media Statement of the Thirty-Seventh ASEAN Economic Ministers Meeting 2005).

The ACFTA programs implemented to enhance mutual benefits indicate a strong commitment to deeper integration between ASEAN and China. The Early Harvest Program that was introduced in 2004 lowered tariffs below average AFTA levels for some traded products such as live animals, meat, fish, dairy produce, vegetables, fruits and nuts. A local/cumulative content requirement agreement has been reached whereby a 40 percent minimum is required. Perhaps in response to this requirement the ACFTA agreement now also includes a dispute settlement mechanism that is to be implemented by the end of 2005.

The progress towards ASEAN integration with Japan has been considerably slower than with China even though Japanese attitudes towards integration have shifted in recent years — partly driven by geopolitical interests that includes its desire to protect the independence of Taiwan. Japan did officially propose formation of a free trade agreement with ASEAN in early 2002. This proposal remains under study with slow progress towards achieving a substantive agreement. Japan and ASEAN have signed a Common Economic Partnership agreement to increase trade through liberalizing trade terms, and ASEAN authorities encouraged Japan to consider accession to the TAC. Meanwhile the two sides are pooling experts to study the feasibility of an ASEAN–Japan free trade area. Substantive progress remains elusive in this regard as well. One reason is that Japan appears to favor bilateral trade agreements over a regional trading arrangement. The country signed an 'Economic Agreement for a New Age Partnership' with Singapore in 2002, Japan's first bilateral free trade agreement. In 2004 Japan concluded a bilateral FTA with Mexico, and 'is now actively pursuing FTA negotiations with Thailand, Malaysia, the Philippines and South Korea' (Tourk 2004: 876).

Except for closer financial ties ensuing from the Chiang Mai Initiative, there has been very modest substantive trade and security agreements between ASEAN and South Korea. This has been due to South Korea's preference for the multilateral trade negotiation framework over regional economic blocs, as South Korea has maintained its commitments to trade liberalization at the global level. However, the country is becoming more open minded to integration in the face of changing patterns of FDI, deeper and wider ASEAN integration, and the potential to use ASEAN membership as a foreign policy tool to boost regional political power as growing distrust of the USA spreads throughout the region in the wake of the war with Iraq.[31] South Korea's and Japan's growing interest in considering integration, as well as the formation of ACFTA, lends credence to the vision of an East Asian Community. Those East Asian authorities interested in pursuing this possibility can use the respective experiences of EU development and integration, and Japanese and Chinese development, to draw some useful lessons.

Lessons and Conclusions

The EU experience offers ASEAN+3 a number of integration lessons. Some are positive lessons indicating actual and potential benefits from wider and deeper integration that could make integration more appealing to ASEAN+3. Given that the original intent of European integration

[31] To gain experience with the effects of integration South Korea formed a free trade area with Chile in 2002. In the face of considerable agricultural and labor union resistance within South Korea the degree of trade liberalization between the two countries has thus far been modest.

was a political project to avoid war, the first lesson is that deeper and wider integration contributed to the reduction of hostility, heightened political security, and thereby enhanced overall regional stability. This lesson is relevant to ASEAN, since like the EU, ASEAN members initiated integration for political and security reasons. One analyst argues that for ASEAN to realize this integration benefit to a greater degree 'as regional identity evolves, nationalist sentiments must be reduced' (Cheow 2005). However, for the ASEAN+3 countries molding any 'Asian identity' will be difficult. This is partly due to 'historical, territorial and political disputes, [which have been contributing to] a wave of nationalism [that] is sweeping Japan, the Koreas and China' (Cheow 2005). On the other hand if such disputes can be reconciled there is another lesson ASEAN+3 can learn from the EU (and NAFTA as well). This is that integration can serve as a foreign policy instrument. Some observers believe that ASEAN's agreement to establish ACFTA follows from this lesson, as they recognize China's key position in defusing the North Korean threat.

There are positive economic lessons from the EU experience. Among them is the reasonable expectation that positive net static trade creation effects will ensue post integration, albeit at the expense of non-members. ASEAN+3 members could avoid more trade diversion by increasing intra ASEAN+3 trade, and this can be accomplished through deeper trade and wider integration. ASEAN+3 countries believe they have paid the price of trade diversion that has resulted from EU integration and the formation of NAFTA (especially from rules of origin), and therefore these countries may see integration at a loose free trade area level as a means for self-defense against the growing trend toward RTAs with strong countervailing power in worldwide trade negotiations.

Before ASEAN+3 members could expect to enjoy trade creation benefits to the same degree as the EU, however, intra ASEAN+3 trade would need to rise well above its current level of roughly 25 percent to approximate the more than 65 percent of intra 'community' trade engaged in by the EU. Some recent decisions by individual ASEAN members do not appear encouraging in this regard as fragmentation has been occurring. For example, some ASEAN countries are taking the bilateral free trade area approach by forming bilateral free trade agreements (e.g. Singapore entering into a free trade area with New Zealand). This has prompted leaders from Malaysia and Indonesia to protest that 'Singapore's bilateral trade talks would undermine ASEAN unity' (Daquila 2002). Another positive economic lesson is that there is a correlation between the deepening and widening of integration and dynamic economic benefits. In particular, based upon the EU's influence at WTO negotiations ASEAN+3's bargaining power in trade negotiations should be expected to increase considerably.

One analyst argues that EU monetary cooperation offers lessons to ASEAN+3 that 'have more applicability . . . than is customarily recognized' (Letiche 2000: 277). There are the widely recognized benefits of reduction in transactions costs and inducement to higher levels of FDI after currency instability among the 12 EMU was eliminated. Further, it has been argued that monetary cooperation that includes a common currency also would increase the bargaining power of ASEAN+3 in international financial and trade negotiation meetings, as well as being the 'best solution' to the threat of competitive devaluation (Pomfret 2003).

There are some qualifications that merit consideration before assuming that the positive lessons from the EMU should stimulate ASEAN+3 members to consider pursuing such a deep degree of integration. The first is that the main EU objective in forming a monetary union has been exchange rate stability among its members in order to achieve deeper trade integration. ASEAN+3 is more interested in exchange rate stability vis a vis the rest of the world, and to achieve it with a 'minimum of rules' (Wyplosz 2001), than with exchange rate stability within the region. Second, the sequence followed by the EU has been (1) the establishment of common trade agreements, with (2) supernational institutions offering proposals and taking responsibility for dispute settlement, followed by (3) earlier means to achieve exchange rate stabilization (the European Monetary System), then (4) rules permitting a freer flow of capital across borders was implemented, and finally (5) the formation of EMU (Chino 2002). Thus, it was closer trade relations that necessitated closer monetary cooperation. ASEAN's sequence since 1997 has been a desire to avoid another financial crisis by stabilizing their exchange rates through the type of monetary cooperation contained in the Chiang Mai

Initiative, with only modest regional trade agreements. Perhaps a lesson ASEAN+3 authorities can draw is that, given that its objectives, needs and acceptable means (in terms of the degree of political integration it will endure) differ substantively from those of the EU, they should 'pursue a sequence oriented to its own needs and circumstances' (Chino 2002). In pursuing this sequence they can also consider the final EMU lesson, namely that it took the EU over four decades to establish a successful monetary union and the corresponding institutions required. One analyst notes that 'given the political and economic fragility of ASEAN countries it might take them much longer' (Mittal 2004).

There are also some negative lessons from the EU integration experience that could make deeper and wider integration less appealing to ASEAN+3 authorities. The first is that the EU experience indicates that considerable political and policy maker integration (with a strong willingness to compromise and adapt to differences among member nations) is required to form a successful EMU, as well as to achieve other benefits offered by integration (Plummer and Jones 2004: 841). Further, there is a corresponding loss of individual member sovereignty and identity from integrating at the monetary union level. However, the political differences among the ASEAN+3 nations, and the requirement that they abandon their sovereignty considerably by giving up macroeconomic policy independence in exchange for agreeing to the monetary rules imposed by a central bank while adopting a single currency, reduce the net benefits (and likelihood) of their moving to such a level in the near future. Unfortunately for the region 'there are no historical grounds to believe that East Asian economies will experience any such political unification,' nor that its citizens would be able and willing to 'forge common bonds that transcend nationality' with other member nations (Mittal 2004).

The second negative lesson from the ASEAN+3 viewpoint is that 'institution building is crucial' (Chino 2002). Deeper and wider integration requires a highly developed supranational institutional structure. ASEAN alone does not have such a structure, nor is there any indication that there is the political will to develop one. Rather, ASEAN+3 authorities may use the recent rejection of the EU Constitution to resist integrated institutions, as Rodrik's 'trilemma' would predict. That is, these authorities may conclude that there are limits to integration beyond which some members, whose economies' performance trends and fiscal balances are unfavorable, will strongly object to proposals for deeper and wider integration. ASEAN+3 authorities might prefer to avoid Rodrik's 'golden straightjacket' that rules such as the EMU convergence criteria would impose if applied too strictly to members of a monetary union.

There is a also a negative lesson from the EU's aloof, elitist, and 'technocratic' decision making process concentrated at the ministerial level without widespread public support — namely that 'the EU developed a 'democratic deficit', resulting in the well-known disaffection among many electorates in Western Europe [e.g., the French and Dutch] that have stymied more comprehensive political integration and monetary unification' (Sunchindah 2005). However, this problem may not be serious for most ASEAN+3 countries since strong democratic input is rarely a feature of their political or economic policy decision making.

The final negative lesson, however, poses a serious inhibiting factor to ASEAN's current members willingness to integrate with the three East Asian countries. It is that wider integration will result in reduced political power for the original ASEAN members over integration rules. Once again the French and Dutch rejection of the EU Constitution is relevant. These two countries were among the six original founding members, 'who remember when the EU was a small, tightly knit entity' and fear a growing inability to exert their influence in a much larger European Union (Cheow 2005).

How ASEAN+3 authorities weigh these lessons and decide if there will be net benefits (or costs) from deeper and wider integration will influence the path integration follows in the region. Benefits from reduced regional tension and the likelihood of war, trade creation, some dynamic economic effects, and the lower transactions costs and greater exchange rate stability from monetary cooperation may not outweigh their perceived costs of deeper and wider integration. These costs include those associated with deeper political integration, creating supranational institutions while giving up some sovereignty in the process,[32] and facing reduced macroeconomic policy instruments if much closer monetary cooperation was established. There are two other factors that might limit the appeal of deeper and wider integration throughout the region. One is that the positive development indicators experienced by individual ASEAN+3 economies have not been attributed to integration — particularly in Japan and China. Rather, analysts have pointed to export promotion, foreign direct investment, and building culturally specific institutions as being the main factors enabling the economies of Japan and China to develop while protecting their respective sensitive interests, and without having to integrate for bargaining purposes. Second, ASEAN+3 authorities are (unlike the EU) not interested in using integration as a means to achieve economies of scale or to aid their agricultural sectors because these are not problems for them, in the same way that they were for the original EU members.

It would therefore be reasonable to expect that the net effect of the integration provided by the EU experience could encourage ASEAN+3 authorities to pursue modest deepening and widening of integration limited to a loose free trade agreement, environmental cooperation, and closer monetary cooperation that focuses on stabilizing members exchange rates vis a vis the ROW. A pertinent EU lesson is relevant, namely that deepening and widening of economic integration 'is always easier during good economic times,' so that ASEAN+3 authorities must 'choose the 'correct' moment to launch its regional project and proceed decisively during good economic times' (Cheow 2005). It is also reasonable to expect ASEAN+3 authorities to conclude that the considerable loss of sovereignty is not worth the economic benefits that significantly deeper and wider integration could be expected to yield. However, considering some potential economic benefits and the threat of regional political instability, ASEAN authorities appear likely to pursue more integrated security cooperation (within the context of TAC) that will encom-

---

[32] This forecast is further supported by the strong desire among these countries to preserve their sovereignty. The aversion to increased political integration is evident in the steadfast insistence upon the separation of political and economic issues in ASEAN negotiations.

pass China, Japan, and South Korea. To gain political support from their constituents for such integration they can point to appropriate lessons drawn from the EU integration experience.

Progress towards achieving the goals of ACFTA and movement toward an ASEAN+3 Community can be expected to evolve slowly, and simultaneously, although at different paces, as chosen institutional responses to regional economic and political problems. In any case, each country's economic, political and cultural interests, rather than any ASEAN+3 solidarity comparable to that in Europe, will drive the future path of integration in the region. The final outcome of integration among ASEAN+3 ultimately will be determined by the political will and economic objectives of concerned political authorities.

References

Angresano, J. (1996). *Comparative Economics*, 2nd ed. Prentice Hall, Upper Saddle River, NJ.

Angresano, J. (2005). China's Development Strategy: A Game of Chess that Countered Orthodox Development Advice. *Journal of Socio-Economics* 34: 471-498.

Angresano, J., Zhang, B., and Zhang, M. (2002). China's Rapid Transformation: The Role of FDI. *Global Business and Economics Review* 4: 223-242.

Balassa. B., ed. (1975). *European Integration*. North-Holland, Amsterdam.

Baldwin, R. (1995). A Domino Theory of Regionalism, in Baldwin, R., Haaparnata, P., and Kiander, J. (eds.), *Expanding Membership of the European Union*. Cambridge University Press, Cambridge: 25-53.

Baldwin, R. and Venables, A.J. (1995). Regional Integration, in Grossman, G.M. and Rogoff, K. (eds.), *Handbook of International Economics*, Vol. 3. North-Holland, Amsterdam: 1598-1641.

Baldwin, R. and Wyplosz, C. (2003). *The Economics of European Integration*. McGraw Hill, New York.

Ben-David, D. (1993). Equalizing exchange: Trade and liberalization and income convergence. *Quarterly Journal of Economics* 108: 653-679.

Bhagwati, J. (1995). U.S. Trade Policy: The Infatuation with Free Trade Areas, in Bhagwati, J. and Krueger, A.O. (eds.), *The Dangerous Drift to Preferential Trade Agreements*. American Enterprise Institute for Public Policy Research, Washington, DC: 1-18.

Busse, Matthias. (2000). The Hub and Spoke Approach of EU Trade Policy. *Intereconomics* 35: 153-154.

Cecchini, P., Catinat, M., and Jacquemin, A. (1988). *The European Challenge 1992: The Benefits of a Single Market*. Wildwood, Aldershot, England.

Chow, G. C. (2002). *China's Economic Transformation*. Blackwell, Oxford.

Cox, D. and Harris, R. (1985). Trade Liberalization and Industrial Organization: Some estimates for Canada. *Journal of Political Economy* 93: 115-145.

ECDPM. (1999). The EC's Impact Studies on Regional Economic Partnership Agreements. (Lomé Negotiating Brief No. 5). ECDPM, Maastricht.

Frost, F. (1990). Introduction: ASEAN since 1967 — Origins, Evolution and Recent Developments, in Broinowski, A. (ed.), *ASEAN into the 1990s*. St. Martin's Press, New York: 1-31.

Gasiorek, M., Smith, A., and Venables, A.J. (1992). 1992: Trade and Welfare; A General Equilibrium Model. *Centre for Economic Policy Research Discussion Paper 672*.

Geithner, T. and Nankani, G. (2002). Market Access for Developing Country Exports - Selected Issues. Report prepared by the Staffs of the IMF and the World Bank. IMF, Washington, DC.

Ghoneim, A. (2000). *Determinants of the Egyptian Exports Market Access to the European Union*. Center of Economic and Financial Research Studies, Cairo.

Hindley, B. and Messerlin, P. (1993). Guarantees of Market Access and Regionalism, in Anderson, K. and Blackhurst, R. (eds.), *Regional Integration and the Global Trading System*. Harvester Wheatsheaf, London.

Jones, E. (2003). Idiosyncrasy and integration: suggestions from comparative political economy. *Journal of European Public Policy* 10: 140-158.

Jones, Michael E. (2004). Forging an ASEAN Identity: The Challenge to Construct a Shared Destiny. *Contemporary Southeast Asia* 26: 140-154.

Krause, L.B. (1999). *U.S. Economic Policy toward the Association of Southeast Asian Nations*. Brookings Institution, Washington, DC.

Kreinin, M. (1972). Effects of the EEC on Imports of Manufactures. *Economic Journal* 82: 897-920.

Lee, H. (2003). EU Enlargement and Its Impact on East Asia. Unpublished paper presented at the EU-Asia Links and Lessons Workshop Program, Johns Hopkins University Bologna Center and ICSEAD, 12 May.

Letiche, J.C. (2000). Lessons from the euro zone for the East Asian economies. *Journal of Asian Economics* 11: 275-300.

Mittal, Rashi. (2004). ASEAN Monetary Union-A Possibility? unpublished manuscript, May, Stanford University.

OECD. (1989). *Historical Statistics: 1960-1987*. OECD, Paris.

Palmer, R.D. and Reckford, T.J. (1987). *Building ASEAN: 20 Years of Southeast Asian Cooperation*. Praeger, New York.

Panagariya, A. (2000). Preferential Trade Liberalization: The Traditional Theory and New Developments. *Journal of Economic Literature* 38: 287-331.

Plummer, Michael and Jones, Erik. (2004). EU and Asia: Links and Lessons. *Journal of Asian Economics* 14: 827-842.

Pomfret, R. (1997). The Economic Co-operation Organization: Current status and future prospects. *Europe-Asia Studies* 49: 657-667.

Pomfret, R. (2001). *The Economics of Regional Trading Arrangements*. Oxford University Press, New York.

Pomfret, R. (2003). Formation and Dissolution of Monetary Unions: Evidence from Europe, and Lessons for Elsewhere. Paper presented at the Australian Economists' Conference, Canberra, 29-30 September.

Price, V.C. (1989). *Whose Europe?* The Institute of Economic Affairs, London.

Prybla, J. (2003). Review of Nicholas R. Lardy, Integrating China Into the World Economy. *Journal of Comparative Economics* 31: 159-162.

Qian, Yingui. (2003). How Reform Worked in China, in Rodrik, Dani (ed.), *In Search of Prosperity*. Princeton University Press, Princeton: 297-333.

Robson, P. (1984). *The Economics of International Integration*, 2nd ed. George Allen and Unwin, London.

Rodrik, D., Subramanian, A., and Trebbi, F. (2002). Institutions Rule: The Primacy of Institutions Over Geography and Integration in Economic Development. *NBER Working Paper No. W9305.*

Rose, A. (2000). One Money, One Market: The Effect of Common Currencies on Trade. *Economic Policy* 30: 9-45.

Sapir, A. (1998). The Political Economy of EC Regionalism. *European Economic Review* 42: 717-732.

Smith, A. and Venables, A.J. (1988). Completing the Internal Market in the European Community: Some Industry Simulations. *Centre for Economic Policy Research Discussion Paper 233.*

Stevens, C. and Kennan, J. (2000). Analysis of EU Trade Arrangements with Developing and Transition Economies. Report prepared for the Institute of Development Studies. Institute of Development Studies, Brighton.

Tourk, K. (2004). Political Economy of East Asian Integration. *Journal of Asian Economics* 15: 843-888.

Wacziarg, R. (2002). Review of Easterly's *The Elusive Quest for Growth. Journal of Economic Literature* 40: 907-918.

Wang, S. and Andersen, L. (2003). Regional Financial Cooperation in East Asia: The Chiang Mai Initiative and Beyond. *Bulletin on Asia-Pacific Perspectives 2002/2003*: 89-99.

Wonnacott, P. and Wonnacott, R. (1967). *Free Trade between the United States and Canada: The potential economic effects.* Harvard University Press, Cambridge, MA.

Wyplosz, C. (2001). A Monetary Union in Asia? Some European Lessons, in Gruen, David and Simon, John (eds.), *Future Directions for Monetary Policies in East Asia.* Reserve Bank of Australia: 124-155.

Internet Sources

Bardhan, P. (2005). China and India: Giants unchained? Not so fast. 2 November, www.iht.org

Beng, L.C. (1997). European and ASEAN Integration Processes: Similar Models? 8 May, www.unu.edu

Bowley, G. (2005). Globalization drives a wedge into EU. www.iht.org

Bowring, P. (2005). Europe's self-sabotage on trade. 1 November, www.iht.org

Bris, A., Koskinen, Y., and Nilsson, M. (2004). The Real Effects of the Euro: Evidence from Corporate Investments. www.cepr.org

Cheow, E.T.C. (2005). EU Lessons for East Asian Regionalism, *The Japan Times.* 25 June, www.japantimes.com

China (2003). China - ASEAN to Implement Tariff Reduction Program in 2005. www. China.org.cn/english/BAT/56731.htm

Chino, T. (2002). Monetary and Financial Cooperation in East Asia: Lessons from Europe. 5 July, www.adb.org

Daquila, T.C. (2002). ASEAN's Economic Performance: Reviewing the Past Looking to the Future, *Harvard Asia Quarterly Online*. http://www.haqonline.org

Eeckhout, P. (1997). European Anti-dumping Law and China, *European Integration online Papers (EIoP)*. http://econpapers.repec

Gramegna, P. (1997). European and ASEAN Integration Processes: Similar Models? 8 May, www.unu.edu

Huang, K.B. (2001). The China-ASEAN Free Trade Area: Background, Framework and Political Implications. www.dsis.org.tw/peaceforum/papers/20002/APE02020001e.htm

Joint Media Statement of the Thirty-Seventh ASEAN Economic Ministers Meeting. (2005). 28 September, www.aseanscc.org

Single Market News. (1998). EU support to help track Asian financial crisis: European network of financial experts to be established. http://europa.eu.int

Sunchinah, A. (2005). Mid-life Reflections on ASEAN and the EU, *Jakarta Post*. 9 March, www.aseansec.org

The Japan Times. (2003). East Asia on Economic Integration Road. 13 November, www.japantimes.com

Wright, T. (2005). France digs in heels on farm subsidies. 20 October, www.iht.org

Youn, J.K. (2003). The Political Economy of the China-ASEAN Free Trade Area: Regionalism with Chinese Characteristic. Hcs.harvard.edu/-heas/conference/youn.htm

CHAPTER 4

STOCK MARKET PERFORMANCE IN ASEAN: IS INSTITUTIONAL INTEGRATION WARRANTED?

Reid W. Click and Michael G. Plummer[1]

All countries of the Association of Southeast Asian Nations (ASEAN) grouping, from the most to the least developed, have been working diligently to enhance the strength, efficiency, and depth of their financial systems. Development of the financial sector has been a salient policy goal of most member-states at least since the mid-1980s, but the urgency and determination with which ASEAN governments have focused on capital-market reform has increased dramatically with the advent of the Asian Currency Crisis in July 1997. ASEAN leaders now place financial reform among their most important and pressing economic policy goals. The proposal to create an ASEAN Economic Community (AEC) in 2002 had financial development and integration at its heart.

Since the financial systems of all ASEAN countries are mainly based on banking, reform in this area has been the most crucial, especially because it was the banking sector that bore the brunt of the financial crisis. ASEAN countries have been trying to diversify their heavy reliance on the banking sector in favor of other financial intermediation vehicles, including equity and fixed-income markets. It is only natural for banks to play an even more central role in developing countries than

---

[1] This paper was initiated while the authors were Visiting Researchers at The International Center for the Study of East Asian Development (ICSEAD) in Kitakyushu, Japan. It draws substantially from Click, Reid W. and Michael G. Plummer, 2005, 'Stock Market Integration in ASEAN,' *Journal of Asian Economics* 16(1), 5-28. We are grateful for financial support from ICSEAD during this period and for valuable comments from Eric Ramstetter, Kiyotaka Sato, Oleksandr Movshuk, Atsuko Matsuoka, and other seminar participants at ICSEAD. We are also grateful for comments from participants at the 2003 Southern Economics Association meetings.

they do in developed countries. The information asymmetry that exists between borrowers and lenders, with borrowers having much more information than lenders, is more pronounced in the case of developing countries, and this constitutes one reason why banks need to play a prominent role especially at the early stages of development.[2] Moreover, given the economies of scale related to fixed income and equity markets and complications related to enabling financial infrastructure, diversification of capital markets can be difficult. However, a one-pillar, bank-dominated financial system holds many risks, including possible efficiency losses and increased systemic risk. Importantly, it limits the way in which a financial system can price risk efficiently, and reduces the options open to investors and borrowers. Hence, the development of alternative markets could be extremely important for the long-run growth and development of the financial sector, as well as the entire economy.

This paper examines stock market integration in Indonesia, Malaysia, the Philippines, Singapore, and Thailand in the aftermath of the Asian financial crisis. These five countries are the original members of ASEAN, which now also includes Brunei Darussalam, Cambodia, Laos, Myanmar, and Vietnam. Over the past few years, ASEAN member countries have made tremendous progress in forming a free trade area and investment zone — witness the ASEAN Free Trade Area (AFTA) and the ASEAN Investment Area (AIA). As part of the process of creating the AEC, the region is now examining the possibility of capital market integration for national bond markets and stock markets alike. ASEAN countries, in fact, are beginning to discuss the feasibility of a currency union as well, which suggests that the countries are interested in multilateral approaches to many regional economic and financial issues. The five original ASEAN countries (the ASEAN-5) are the most likely candidates to undertake integrative measures first, and therefore provide the focus for this paper.

Integration in the ASEAN capital markets may include initiatives to coordinate the five national capital markets that already exist, or at an extreme may involve the creation of supranational regional bond and

---

[2] As markets develop, information becomes more open and standardized, and financial systems become more transparent, this asymmetry becomes less important and development of other forms of finance more appropriate.

stock exchanges.[3] The issue is integration as opposed to capital market development more generally, although one motivation for integration is typically to foster development of the market. ASEAN policymakers are weighing the benefits of financial market integration in the same way as European Union policymakers prior to monetary unification. With respect to unification in Europe, Kleimeier and Sander (2000) point out that there are really two kinds of benefits: first, benefits of regional integration of the type studied in the Cecchini Report (Cecchini 1988); and second, benefits of integrating the region with global financial markets. Although Kleimeier and Sander (2000) examine banking, the point is generalizable to stock and bond markets as well. ASEAN policy makers are naturally wondering what gains might be available to their region.

Interest in stock market integration arises primarily because financial theory suggests that an integrated regional stock market is more efficient than segmented national capital markets. Capital market efficiency in Southeast Asia has become even more important after the Asian financial crisis of 1997-1998, so we focus on the post-crisis period to-date, using high-frequency data. Southeast Asian countries are specifically seeking to reduce the traditional dependence of firms on bank loans rather than bond and stock issuances, and at the same time are seeking new capital from outside the region.

With an integrated regional stock market, investors from all member countries will be able to allocate capital to the locations in the region where it is the most productive. With more cross-border flows of funds, additional trading in individual securities will improve the liquidity of the stock markets, which will in turn lower the cost of capital for firms seeking capital and lower the transaction costs investors incur. These suggest a more efficient allocation of capital within the region.

From the perspective of a portfolio investor outside the region, stock market integration suggests that separate markets move together and have high correlations, so there is less benefit from portfolio

[3] A separate paper (Plummer and Click, 2005) examines the bond markets (and see the references therein). This paper uniquely focuses on stock markets.

diversification across countries. However, an integrated regional stock exchange will be more appealing to investors from outside the region who would find investment in the region easier or more justifiable. As shares become more liquid and transaction costs fall, fund managers become increasingly willing to take positions in the stocks. In addition, outside investors may take notice of the regional stock exchange instead of dismissing a collection of small national exchanges: the whole (one regional stock exchange) might be greater than the sum of the parts (individual country exchanges). For example, Freeman (2000) makes the argument that total equity market capitalization is important to investment managers outside the region: 'Institutional investors with global portfolios may simply dispense altogether with equity markets that have low asset allocation recommendations, as resources — such as research — are limited (p. 2).' He suggests that, except for Malaysia and Singapore, equity markets in Southeast Asia may be edging toward irrelevance, and that one way to overcome the problem is to band together. Thus, an integrated stock market within the ASEAN-5 will help link the region with the world stock markets and bring more capital into the countries from abroad. This will allow ASEAN companies to expand their shareholder base and lower their cost of capital even further.

In addition to interest from policy makers and investment practitioners, stock market integration also carries interest from an academic perspective. Recent advances in time series analysis allow investigation of 'long run' equilibrium among stock markets using the methods of cointegration. As Kasa (1992) points out, stock markets that are cointegrated have a long-run relationship, so long-run correlations of returns are higher than short-run correlations typically examined. If n variables have p cointegrating relationships, they have n-p common trends. When n-p = 1, as in the case of the five developed-country stock indices investigated in Kasa (1992), correlations of returns converge to unity and there is no diversification potential in the long-run. In this situation, the individual stock markets are completely and perfectly integrated. However, Richards (1995) points out that a major reason for the findings in Kasa (1992) is an inappropriately long lag length used in the estimation process. With shorter lags, Richards (1995) finds that the five developed-country stock indices are not cointegrated, leaving a full set of n (= 5) common trends. In this situation, the individual stock markets are completely segmented.

Following Kasa (1992) — and, to a lesser extent, Richards (1995) — the technique of multivariate cointegration has been used extensively to study financial market integration around the world. For example, Corhay, Tourani Rad, and Urbain (1993) examine integration in five European stock markets over the period 1975-1991 and find one cointegrating vector. Chung and Liu (1994) consider a system including the US and five East Asian markets (Japan, Taiwan, Hong Kong, Singapore, and South Korea) over the period 1985-1992 and find two cointegration relationships. This and other studies of stock market integration in Asia are surveyed below. Recently, in what is apparently the only study of Latin America, Chen, Firth, and Rui (2002) apply the technique to study integration among Argentina, Brazil, Chile, Colombia, Mexico, and Venezuela over the period 1995-2000 and find that there is generally just one cointegrating vector.

This paper specifically considers whether the stock markets of Indonesia, Malaysia, the Philippines, Singapore, and Thailand are currently cointegrated. We examine the period after the Asian financial crisis, specifically July 1, 1998 through December 31, 2002, in order to consider the recent experiences of the ASEAN-5 markets rather than a long history.[4] The database thus suffers from being a short four-and-a-half year span of time from which to extract a long-run relationship, but also has the advantage of being a well-defined period during which we can reasonably say that there have been few structural breaks or shifts in the data. Since this is financial market data rather than macroeconomic data, four-and-a-half years should be a long enough time span to uncover the long-run equilibrium; financial markets are typically thought to achieve equilibrium quite quickly in contrast to macroeconomic markets characterized by price/wage stickiness, long-term contracts, adjustment costs, and other rigidities.

---

[4] For a thorough analysis of the pre-crisis period 1986-1996, see Sharma and Wongbangpo (2002).

There are three key features in our modeling strategy. One is that we consider both daily data and weekly (Friday or end-of-week) data over this period in order to examine what happens as analysts move from higher-frequency to lower-frequency data. In particular, we consider whether the lower-frequency data contains less noise and relatively more information to estimate a long-run relationship. A second feature is that we consider data denominated in local currencies, in US dollars, and in Japanese yen. Analysis is often done in local currencies, but investors outside the ASEAN countries have to convert local currency returns into their home currencies, of which the dollar and the yen are the most widely used. In the period before the Asian financial crisis, the ASEAN countries were typically pegging their exchange rates to the US dollar. This meant that the choice of local currency versus the US dollar did not matter much, but the stock market values denominated in yen were of course sensitive to fluctuations in the yen/dollar exchange rate. Currency issues have become more important in the aftermath of the Asian financial crisis, as countries have allowed their currencies to float against the US dollar (with the notable exception of Malaysia, discussed below). A third feature is that we carefully examine the lag structures of the models, and estimate cointegrating relationships in models with differing lag lengths. This allows us to determine whether our results are sensitive to the number of lags chosen.

With five stock market variables, the number of common trends (n-p) can range from one to five, and this range forms something of a continuum from perfect integration to complete segmentation.[5] If the stock markets are not cointegrated, resulting in five common trends, we infer that they are nationally segmented in the economic sense, and are not yet suitable for a supranational regional stock market. However, if these stock markets are cointegrated in the econometric sense, we infer that they are integrated in the economic sense. If the number of common trends is more than one, we conclude that there is a degree of

[5] Rangvid (2001) points this out by proposing that an increasing number of cointegrating relationships indicates that stock markets become more integrated over time because they are being increasingly driven by the same common stochastic trends.

interdependence somewhat short of complete convergence, so policy initiatives to further integrate the stock markets are appropriate. If the number of common trends is exactly one, we conclude that the stock markets are completely, perfectly integrated and are ready for the establishment of a supranational regional stock market.

The empirical results in this paper demonstrate that the ASEAN-5 stock markets in the period after the Asian financial crisis are cointegrated whether analyzed using daily data or weekly data, and whether analyzed in local currencies, the US dollar, or the Japanese yen. In addition, the finding does not depend on the number of lags used in estimation once a relevant range of lags is determined. The stock markets are thus not completely segmented by national borders. However, there is only one cointegrating vector among the five stock markets, leaving four common trends among the five variables. The ASEAN-5 stock markets are thus integrated in the economic sense, but integration is far from complete. Once again, this finding is robust to the frequency of the data, the currency denomination considered, and the lag lengths chosen. Perhaps surprisingly, the coefficients in the cointegrating vectors are remarkably similar across all forms of the model, suggesting that data frequency, currency denomination, and lag length have relatively little impact on the long-run equilibrium estimated. We therefore qualitatively examine and discuss the cointegrating vector in some depth, and conclude that the coefficients are reasonable for the stock markets being considered. On a policy level, we suggest that initiatives to further integrate the stock markets are feasible, and in fact desirable. From the perspective of the international portfolio investor, benefits of international portfolio diversification across the five markets are reduced but not eliminated.

This paper is organized into four sections. After this introduction, Section 2 provides background on stock markets and integration in ASEAN. The first subsection considers public policies pertaining to ASEAN stock markets, with an emphasis on integrative efforts, and the second subsection surveys the academic literature on Southeast Asian stock market integration. Section 3 then considers the empirical analysis of stock market integration in ASEAN after the Asian financial crisis.

The subsections consider data sources, short-run correlations of returns, unit root tests, lag length tests, and, most importantly, cointegration results. The final section is the conclusion.

Background

The stock markets of the ASEAN-5 countries generally have market capitalizations in line with their stages of development. Using 2000 data,[6] Singapore and Malaysia have market capitalizations as a percent of gross domestic product quite similar to the United States; 165.7 percent and 130.4 percent, respectively, versus 153.5 percent for the U.S. The Philippines, where stock market capitalization is 69.9 percent of GDP, is quite similar to the level of Japan, at 65.2 percent. Thailand and Indonesia are the smallest markets, at 24.1 percent and 17.5 percent, respectively, but not out of line with emerging markets around the world. These figures suggest that there is a general level of equity market development that may be conducive to integration. In contrast, the stock markets of Brunei Darussalam, Cambodia, Laos, Myanmar, and Vietnam are either under-developed or non-existent.

Public Policies on ASEAN Stock Markets

Attempts to coordinate ASEAN stock markets are not new. Wellons (1997: 28) points out that the ASEAN-5 countries agreed to form the Federation of ASEAN Stock Exchanges in 1978, but never followed through. The Singapore and Malaysian stock markets were fairly well linked at this time, as many Malaysian registered companies traded on the Stock Exchange of Singapore (SES). However, financial crises in Singapore during 1985-1986 spilled over into Malaysia, and actually caused dis-integration of the stock markets.

---

[6] Data on stock market capitalization come from the Standard & Poor's Emerging Stock Markets Factbook 2001. The market capitalizations of the markets are as follows: Singapore, $152 billion; Malaysia, $117 billion; the Philippines, $52 billion; Thailand, $29 billion; and Indonesia, $27 billion. For comparison, the market capitalizations of the U.S. and Japan are $15,104 billion and $3,157 billion, respectively. Data on GDP come from the World Development Indicators of the World Bank.

In 1989 the government of Malaysia delisted Malaysian companies from the SES. The decision to delist first appeared in the budget speech of the Minister of Finance on October 27, 1989. Sun, Tang, and Tong (2002) report that:

> He cited the need for the KLSE [Kuala Lumpur Stock Exchange] to develop its own identity and to become a leading regional finance center. To achieve that, a total separation from the SES could not be avoided. The second reason, as cited by the Minister, was to minimize the high correlation between the two markets. The Malaysian government has long been wary of developments in Singapore affecting the KLSE.

Similarly, according to Bank Negara Malaysia (1999), the 'move represented the Government's effort to develop the domestic capital market by establishing KLSE as an independent exchange, to confine dealings in Malaysian counters to the local exchange, to attract international investors as well as to reduce the market's vulnerability to unfavorable developments on the SES (p. 316).' In response to the Malaysian government's action, the SES almost immediately announced a similar delisting of Singaporean companies from the Malaysian Stock Exchange and a plan to develop an over-the-counter market to trade Malaysian stocks. The over-the-counter market, known as CLOB International, actually functioned up until September 1998, when the government of Malaysia announced that all dealings in shares listed on the exchange must be done through the KLSE or one recognized by KLSE.[7]

Wellons (1997) also points out that the Singapore Declaration of 1992 'raised the prospect of stronger capital market cooperation as part of an effort to direct ASEAN economic cooperation (p. 28).' More generally, presidents of stock exchanges in the region call for

---

[7] For more on the 1989 delistings and the history of CLOB, see Sun, Tang, and Tong (2002).

cooperation from time to time to facilitate cross-border trading. 'In 1993, for example, the SES president said that the time had come to promote intra-ASEAN markets. He saw the opportunity to cross-list and trade a handful of larger stocks on markets throughout ASEAN. (p. 28)' In 1995, 'the president of the Thai exchange urged closer cooperation among exchanges in the region (p. 28)' to boost poor trading volumes. And, according to Freeman (2000), the governor of the Bank of Thailand 'proposed a joint venture between the Bangkok, Kuala Lumpur and Singapore equity markets (p. 9)' in 2000.

The dream of a regional stock market in ASEAN has not come to fruition, and there are reasons to believe that markets remain institutionally segmented. In particular, Malaysia's imposition of selective currency and capital controls in dealing with Asian financial crisis (which went into effect on September 1, 1998) suggested that the stock market in Malaysia, which had been well integrated with Singapore, would be separated from both world and regional stock markets.[8] The exchange controls eliminated access to the ringgit by non-residents from sources in Malaysia and abroad, effectively closing down the offshore ringgit market.[9] The ringgit was also pegged to the US dollar at the same time, and the peg has been successfully maintained since then. Some capital controls have been relaxed, suggesting that the Malaysian stock market is not completely segmented from world and regional stock markets. Initially, capital controls required foreigners to hold stocks for at least 12 months, but this was replaced with a 10 percent repatriation levy in February 1999. The KLSE was dropped from the Morgan Stanley Capital International index in late 1998, but was re-added at the end of May 2000. Currently, the Philippines has the most extensive capital controls on portfolio investments of the ASEAN-5, generally imposing a ceiling on foreign ownership of 40 percent and in some cases requiring a separate class of shares (Standard & Poor's, 2001).

[8] See Kaplan and Rodrik (2001) and Johnson and Mitton (2003) for discussion of the Malaysian capital controls. Kaplan and Rodrik (2001) confirm Malaysia's segmentation and compare economic indicators in Malaysia to those in Korea and Thailand (two countries which did not adopt capital controls). Johnson and Mitton (2003) show that the capital controls provided a screen behind which favored firms could be supported.

[9] For more on this, see Bank Negara Malaysia (1999).

Academic Literature

The issue of stock market integration in Southeast Asia has also been studied in the academic empirical finance literature, particularly using the techniques of cointegration. The main issue being addressed is whether individual stock markets are highly (positively) correlated, although more recently the issue has been recast to address 'contagion' across markets. There are several other aspects being examined as part of this general issue. One considers what the appropriate econometric technique for examining the correlations should be. A second addresses the time period to examine, and whether there have been changes over time such as convergence of markets or structural breaks or shifts in relationships (such as those related to liberalization of equity markets or to financial crises). A third is whether the empirical analysis should be conducted in the local currencies, US dollars, Japanese yen, or some other unit. A fourth is whether the local markets are influenced by the U.S. market, or the Japanese market, or both.

Taken together, the conclusions in the literature regarding the integration of Southeast Asian stock markets are contradictory. This might be partially attributable to different methodologies, even when using cointegration techniques. Since several studies have examined Asian stock markets in the light provided by Kasa (1992), we restrict our focus to these. Conflicting and inconclusive results are still apparent, due in part to the wide range of sample periods and sampling frequencies considered; the selection of countries considered; and the exact modeling strategy being implemented.

The earliest study of Asian stock market integration utilizing multivariate cointegration is probably Chung and Liu (1994), investigating the U.S., Japan, Taiwan, Hong Kong, Singapore, and South Korea. Using weekly data denominated in local currencies over the period 1/7/85–5/18/92, they find 1, 2, and 4 cointegrating vectors in models with 12, 24, and 36 lags, respectively, noting that 'the number of cointegrating relationships is sensitive to the choice of lag length (p. 248).' After inspection of each model's forecasting performance (rather than inspection of the lag structure), they settle on the model with 24 lags and two cointegrating vectors.

DeFusco, Geppert, and Tsetsekos (1996) examine weekly data for January 1989–May 1995 denominated in U.S. dollars. They conclude that there is no cointegration in a block of Asia-Pacific countries consisting of U.S., Korea, Philippines, Taiwan, Malaysia, and Thailand. They also conclude that there is no cointegration in the other two other regions they examine, thus capital markets are segmented.

Masih and Masih (1999) use daily data over 2/14/92–6/19/97 denominated in real US dollars (although they do not explain the conversion to real values for daily data). They find cointegration in a block of OECD and Asian countries including the United States, Japan, UK, Germany, Singapore, Malaysia, Hong Kong, and Thailand, but conclude that there is at most one cointegrating vector, leaving seven independent common stochastic trends.

Manning (2002) examines both weekly and quarterly data over January 1988–February 1999, denominated in both local currency and in US dollars. The system includes Hong Kong, Indonesia, Japan, South Korea, Malaysia, Philippines, Singapore, and Thailand, and alternately includes/excludes the United States. The general conclusion is that there are two common trends, indicating 'partial convergence' of the indices.

Phylaktis and Ravazzolo (2005) examine monthly data for January 1980–December 1998 (split into two periods: 1980–1989 and 1990–1998) denominated in local currency, US dollars, and real US dollars. The sample consists of the United States, Japan, Hong Kong, South Korea, Malaysia, Singapore, Taiwan, and Thailand, and cointegration is found for both subperiods in all units of measurement. However, relatively few countries participate in the cointegrating vectors. This leads Phylaktis and Ravazzolo to conclude that the stock markets under investigation are not linked. A subsystem consisting of Taiwan, Thailand, Japan, and the United States seems to reveal the strongest financial integration. In this subsystem, the estimated common trends suggest that the United States has influence in the Pacific Rim, but that Japan and — interestingly — Thailand play more significant roles.

Sharma and Wongbangpo (2002) examine monthly data from January 1986 through December 1996 for the ASEAN–5 markets denominated in local currencies. They find a long-run cointegrating relationship among the stock markets of Indonesia, Malaysia, Singapore, and Thailand, but conclude that the Philippine market does not share the relationship. Furthermore, there is only one cointegrating vector among the four markets, leaving three common trends. One particularly interesting finding is that Malaysia and Singapore move together one-for-one in the cointegrating vector, ostensibly because of the distribution of inward foreign direct investment flows, the strength of trade between the two economies, the geographical proximity, and cultural factors (p. 307).

Taking these five studies together, it is certainly not clear what to expect for stock market integration in ASEAN in the aftermath of the Asian financial crisis. A few additional studies use cointegration techniques to determine whether the local markets are influenced by the US market, or the Japanese market, or both, and generally add to the confusion (see Fernandez–Serrano and Sosvilla–Rivero 2001, Jang and Sul 2002,[10] and Darrat and Zhong 2002). In addition, VAR approaches using differenced data without a cointegrating constraint offer even more positions. Two such studies are worth mentioning.

Dekker, Sen, and Young (2001) use daily data in local currencies and US dollars over the period 1987–1998 in ten-variable VARs to examine linkages among US, Japan, and eight other countries' stock markets including Malaysia, Philippines, Singapore, and Thailand. The results indicate that the four ASEAN markets are linked to the US market, which exerts a great deal of influence, but that the Japanese market is segmented. Furthermore, the Malaysian, Singapore, and Hong Kong markets are closely linked, but the Philippine and Thai markets are segmented.

Tan and Tse (2002) use daily data in local currencies over 1988–2000 in a nine-variable VAR to examine the linkages among US, Japan, and

---

[10] Jang and Sul (2002) also offer bivariate cointegration tests among the three ASEAN-5 markets studied. Thailand and Indonesia are cointegrated during the crisis and well after the crisis; Thailand and Singapore are cointegrated immediately after the crisis and maybe well after the crisis; Indonesia and Singapore may be cointegrated before the crisis but not during or afterwards.

seven Asian stock markets including Malaysia, Philippines, Singapore, and Thailand. By truncating the data at the end of 1996 and restarting the data in mid–1998 to create a pre-crisis and post-crisis comparison, they find that markets appear to be more integrated after the crisis than before, and that Asian markets are most heavily influenced by the United States but that the influence of Japan is increasing. The most noteworthy effect among the ASEAN–5 is that Malaysia is apparently an outlier; Malaysia is less affected by the United States and Japan after the crisis, which can be attributed to the influence of its capital and currency controls, but Singapore and Malaysia still affect each other strongly, which can be attributed to geographic proximity, economic linkages, and structural symmetry.

Empirical Examination

This section considers the empirical characteristics of the ASEAN–5 stock indices. The indices themselves, denominated in local currencies, are considered first. However, the indices are also converted into US dollars and into Japanese yen in order to have the indices in common currency units.[11] The distinction between local currency comparisons and common currency comparisons deserves some discussion. There is a preference for looking at the relationships among the local currency indices when the only question is whether the local currency indices themselves are interdependent. Theoretically, however, this is a comparison of dissimilar units (currencies), and if the units themselves behave differently (as would be the case when inflation rates are different across currencies or when real exchange rate changes alter the relative values of currency units) then conclusions may not be valid. Hence, there are compelling reasons to convert the stock price indices into a common measuring unit, but that raises the question as to which currency should be chosen.

The typical analysis of markets using a common currency considers

---

[11] We cannot convert from nominal currency units to real currency units because price level data do not exist at daily or weekly frequency. However, the stock market and exchange rate data are not materially influenced by inflation during the short time period under consideration, so such an adjustment would not be essential anyway.

the behavior of stock indices from the perspective of an outside investor who values the portfolio in terms of US dollars or other home currency. These converted series implicitly represent the sum of the returns on two assets: the stock index and the currency. This raises the possibility that some portion of interdependence across (local-currency-denominated) domestic markets will not be captured if exchange rates offset economic shocks that in reality tie the domestic markets together. From the perspective of the outside investor, however, the dollar value of the stock is what matters, and an unhedged foreign stock is precisely an asset containing both the local currency stock index and the dollar/local currency exchange rate. This combination thus accounts for any stock market changes that are in fact induced by exchange rate changes, which would be important to outside investors.[12] However, the conversion to a common currency also raises the possibility that the converted indices will uncover interdependence simply based on the behavior of the outside currency, such as general depreciation of the dollar against all local currencies. Hence, the choice of outside currency may affect the results, which suggests that we try more than one. We have furthermore not abandoned our interest in the local currency indices, as the indices denominated in local currencies are obtainable when the currency component is hedged with an offsetting position in foreign currency derivatives.

On conceptual grounds, we thus have an interest in examining stock market integration in both local currencies and in a common outside currency, and furthermore in more than one common outside currency. During the period under investigation, the ASEAN currencies were generally floating against the US dollar, with the notable exception of the Malaysian ringgit (which was pegged to the US dollar). The Japanese yen is the dominant Asian currency in the region. In order to ensure that our results are not influenced by the behavior of the US dollar, or by the ringgit peg to the US dollar, we therefore consider the Japanese yen as the logical alternative common currency. Our analysis thus

---

[12] In other words, some of the movements in the stock price index might reflect the foreign exchange exposure of listed firms. For more on this, see Chapter 7 of Click and Coval (2002).

simultaneously considers local currency stock indices, the US dollar value of the local currency indices, and the Japanese yen value of the local currency indices.

The data consist of daily stock index quotes in local currencies over the four-and-a-half-year period from July 1, 1998 through December 31, 2002, for a total of 1175 observations. From this, we also consider weekly stock index data by taking the Friday (or other end of week) observations over the same period, for a total of 235 observations. We begin with mid–1998 because the bulk of the Asian financial crisis had ended by then.[13] The data are from Datastream, and represent composite stock price indices in Indonesia, Malaysia, Philippines, Singapore, and Thailand. We convert the local currency index into US dollars [Japanese yen] by multiplying the local currency index level by the dollars-per-foreign-currency [yen-per-foreign-currency] exchange rate, also obtained from Datastream.

Table 4.1 presents the simple correlation coefficients among the five stock markets. Panel A utilizes the daily data and Panel B utilizes the weekly data, and within each panel is a matrix for correlations of data denominated in local currency units, US dollars, and Japanese yen. Overall, the correlations are not very high — averaging just 0.336. Comparing the daily correlations to the weekly correlations suggests that correlations may be higher for the weekly data; the average correlation for the daily data is 0.294 and the average for the weekly data is 0.379. Among the 30 correlations, only 4 are lower in the weekly data than in the daily data. Although we do not know whether this difference is statistically significant, it seems plausible that correlations among the five stock markets rise when moving from higher-frequency to lower-frequency data.

---

[13] Tan and Tse (2002) use mid-1998 as the beginning of the post-crisis period. The crisis may or may not have been 'over' at that date, however. Jang and Sul (2002) begin the post-crisis period earlier, on February 1, 1998, because the Thai, Indonesian, and Korean currencies reached record lows in January. Additional adjustments were yet to come, such as Malaysian currency and capital controls introduced September 1, 1998.

Table 4.1. Short-run Correlations of Stock Index Returns (1 July 1998 through 31 December 2002)

Panel A: Daily Data

Local Currency

	Indonesia	*Malaysia*	*Philippines*	*Singapore*
Malaysia	0.17			
Philippines	0.25	0.14		
Singapore	0.27	0.29	0.28	
Thailand	0.28	0.28	0.28	0.43

U.S. Dollars

	Indonesia	*Malaysia*	*Philippines*	*Singapore*
Malaysia	0.19			
Philippines	0.27	0.14		
Singapore	0.26	0.25	0.28	
Thailand	0.30	0.26	0.32	0.44

Japanese Yen

	Indonesia	*Malaysia*	*Philippines*	*Singapore*
Malaysia	0.26			
Philippines	0.32	0.27		
Singapore	0.31	0.37	0.38	
Thailand	0.33	0.34	0.38	0.48

Panel B: Weekly Data

Local Currency

	Indonesia	*Malaysia*	*Philippines*	*Singapore*
Malaysia	0.22			
Philippines	0.36	0.26		
Singapore	0.30	0.27	0.37	
Thailand	0.44	0.28	0.50	0.56

U.S. Dollars

	Indonesia	*Malaysia*	*Philippines*	*Singapore*
Malaysia	0.20			
Philippines	0.42	0.25		
Singapore	0.36	0.25	0.40	
Thailand	0.46	0.27	0.54	0.59

Japanese Yen

	Indonesia	*Malaysia*	*Philippines*	*Singapore*
Malaysia	0.21			
Philippines	0.41	0.34		
Singapore	0.35	0.36	0.47	
Thailand	0.45	0.32	0.55	0.60

The concern that correlations will converge to unity in the long run is precisely the motivation for using cointegration analysis to examine the long run relationship.

In preparation for cointegration analysis, the univariate properties of the stock index data need to be examined to verify whether the data series are nonstationary, or contain a unit root. Table 4.2 presents Augmented Dickey–Fuller (ADF) and Phillips–Perron tests allowing for a constant in the regression but no time trend. Once again, Panel A utilizes daily data and Panel B utilizes weekly data. The tests suggest that all of the series contain unit roots; the hypothesis of a unit root cannot be rejected at the 5 percent level for any of the 60 tests (and cannot be rejected at the 10 percent level for 58 of the tests). The number of lags utilized in the reported ADF tests is chosen using the Akaike Information Criterion, but the unit root finding is really invariant to the number of lags chosen. The number of lags in the reported Phillips–Perron tests is set to four, but again the results are invariant to the number of lags chosen. Since all series are nonstationary, cointegration analysis is appropriate.

The number of lags in the vector autoregression (VAR) used to estimate the cointegrating relationship is an important issue because the number of lags has been shown to affect the number of cointegrating vectors detected (e.g., Richards 1995). Table 4.3 thus presents lag length tests from VARs of different orders. It considers the Akaike Information Criterion (AIC), the Schwartz Bayesian Criterion (SBC), and Likelihood Ratio Tests of exclusion restrictions on incremental lags that are distributed χ^2 with 25 degrees of freedom.

With daily data (analyzed in Panel A), most statistics suggest that only one lag is appropriate in the VAR. The AIC indicates that some additional information may be captured around the one week lag: the minimum AIC occurs at 6 days of lags for the estimation in local currency and 5 days of lags for estimation in U.S. dollars and Japanese yen. However, the SBC achieves minima at one lag in all three daily models, and the likelihood ratio tests indicate that no additional lags beyond the first are statistically significant.

Table 4.2. Unit Root Tests (1 July 1998 through 31 December 2002)

Panel A: Daily Data

			ADF test		*Phillips-Perron test*	
		lags	τ_μ	ρ	τ_μ	ρ
Local Currencies						
	Indonesia	1	-1.19	0.998	-1.19	0.998
	Malaysia	15	-2.10	0.995	-1.92	0.995
	Philippines	10	-1.24	0.998	-0.70	0.999
	Singapore	1	-1.56	0.997	-1.57	0.997
	Thailand	19	-2.46	0.992	-2.23	0.994
U.S. dollars						
	Indonesia	1	-1.25	0.998	-1.23	0.998
	Malaysia	5	-2.12	0.995	-2.08	0.995
	Philippines	11	-0.92	0.999	-0.39	0.997
	Singapore	1	-1.43	0.997	-1.44	0.997
	Thailand	2	-1.96	0.995	-1.87	0.996
Japanese yen						
	Indonesia	23	-1.81	0.996	-1.27	0.998
	Malaysia	5	-2.21	0.993	-2.15	0.993
	Philippines	11	-1.12	0.998	-0.68	0.999
	Singapore	1	-1.50	0.996	-1.54	0.996
	Thailand	12	-2.27	0.993	-1.90	0.995

Table 4.2 (*Continued*)

Panel B: Weekly Data

			ADF test		Phillips-Perron test	
		lags	τ_μ	ρ	τ_μ	ρ
Local Currencies						
	Indonesia	7	-1.57	0.983	-1.32	0.988
	Malaysia	2	-2.18	0.976	-2.03	0.979
	Philippines	2	-1.35	0.986	-1.13	0.993
	Singapore	1	-1.60	0.984	-1.63	0.984
	Thailand	4	-2.35	0.960	-2.40	0.964
U.S. dollars						
	Indonesia	2	-1.48	0.984	-1.43	0.987
	Malaysia	7	-2.83*	0.968	-2.14	0.977
	Philippines	2	-0.92	0.993	-0.75	0.997
	Singapore	1	-1.52	0.985	-1.55	0.986
	Thailand	4	-2.09	0.970	-2.05	0.974
Japanese yen						
	Indonesia	3	-1.71	0.981	-1.50	0.986
	Malaysia	7	-2.79*	0.957	-2.17	0.970
	Philippines	2	-1.14	0.990	-1.04	0.994
	Singapore	1	-1.68	0.976	-1.61	0.978
	Thailand	4	-1.99	0.968	-2.05	0.971

* significant at the 10% level; ** significant at the 5% level; *** significant at the 1% level

In addition to the likelihood ratio tests reported in Table 4.2, we also calculated likelihood ratio tests of 5 lags versus 1 lag and 6 lags versus l lag, yet still cannot reject the null hypothesis that coefficients on the blocks of additional lags are null hypothesis that coefficients on the blocks of additional lags are jointly zero.[14] We therefore estimate the cointegrating vector in two different VARs — one with 1 lag and another with 5 lags — in order to see what effect the number of lags might have on the cointegration analysis.

We examine weekly data because we are interested in the effects of moving from higher-frequency to lower-frequency data. However, it is also somewhat more appropriate given that daily data may reveal some information at the one week lag but not before then. Utilizing weekly data may therefore be a more parsimonious way to estimate a VAR and cointegrating relationships. The lag length tests of weekly data reported in Panel B of Table 4.3 are broadly consistent with the daily data, but with some reversals of particular tests. With the weekly data, both the AIC and the SBC indicate that only one lag is appropriate. However, the likelihood ratio tests suggest that two lags may be appropriate for the local currency model and three lags might be appropriate for the dollar and yen models. In fact, likelihood tests of 3 lags versus 1 lag reject the hypothesis that coefficients on the blocks of additional lags are jointly zero for all three models. In local currency $\chi^2(50) = 74.23$, which is significant at the 5 percent level. In US dollars, $\chi^2(50) = 72.52$, which is significant at the 5 percent level. And in Japanese yen, $\chi^2(50) = 78.69$, which is significant at the 1 percent level. As a result, we estimate the cointegrating vector using the weekly data in three different VARs — 1 lag, 2 lags, and 3 lags — to see once again what effect the number of lags might have on the cointegration analysis.

---

[14] The likelihood ratio test of 5 lags versus 1 lag is distributed $\chi^2(100)$ and the likelihood ratio test of 6 lags versus 1 lag is distributed $\chi^2(125)$. The critical values for the 90 percent confidence level are 118 and 140, respectively. For local currency, $\chi^2(100) = 46.90$ and $\chi^2(125) = 64.02$. For U.S. dollars, $\chi^2(100) = 44.00$ and $\chi^2(125) = 48.55$. For Japanese yen, $\chi^2(100) = 38.71$ and $\chi^2(125) = 43.63$.

Table 4.3. Lag Length Tests (1 July 1998 through 31 December 2002)

Panel A: Daily Data

	===== *Information Criteria* =====			=== *Likelihood Ratio Tests* ===	
	lags	AIC	SBC	comparison	$\chi^2(25)$
Local Currency	10	-48292	-46990	11 vs. 10 lags	1.91
	9	-48313	-47146	10 vs. 9 lags	4.05
	8	-48299	-47261	9 vs. 8 lags	1.89
	7	-48314	-47406	8 vs. 7 lags	9.12
	6	-48336#	-47551	7 vs. 6 lags	8.12
	5	-48328	-47669	6 vs. 5 lags	17.32
	4	-48317	-47784	5 vs. 4 lags	10.24
	3	-48332	-47927	4 vs. 3 lags	8.16
	2	-48324	-48044	3 vs. 2 lags	7.94
	1	-48262	-48110#	2 vs. 1 lag	20.95
U.S. Dollar	10	-47043	-45751	11 vs. 10 lags	2.51
	9	-47046	-45880	10 vs. 9 lags	7.96
	8	-47032	-45993	9 vs. 8 lags	5.63
	7	-47063	-46150	8 vs. 7 lags	2.13
	6	-47080	-46295	7 vs. 6 lags	3.52
	5	-47082#	-46423	6 vs. 5 lags	4.74
	4	-47065	-46534	5 vs. 4 lags	9.05
	3	-47080	-46675	4 vs. 3 lags	3.16
	2	-47074	-46795	3 vs. 2 lags	2.25
	1	-46992	-46840#	2 vs. 1 lag	29.95
Japanese Yen	10	-46641	-45348	11 vs. 10 lags	4.55
	9	-46651	-45485	10 vs. 9 lags	5.97
	8	-46643	-45604	9 vs. 8 lags	7.14
	7	-46670	-45757	8 vs. 7 lags	3.80
	6	-46679	-45893	7 vs. 6 lags	8.06
	5	-46682#	-46023	6 vs. 5 lags	5.09
	4	-46659	-46127	5 vs. 4 lags	9.08
	3	-46670	-46265	4 vs. 3 lags	4.71
	2	-46663	-46385	3 vs. 2 lags	2.18
	1	-46631	-46479#	2 vs. 1 lag	23.07

Table 4.3 (*Continued*)

Panel B: Weekly Data

	===== *Information Criteria* =====			=== *Likelihood Ratio Tests* ===	
	lags	AIC	SBC	comparison	$\chi^2(25)$
Local Currency	4	-7779	-7415	5 vs. 4 lags	23.11
	3	-7797	-7521	4 vs. 3 lags	28.46
	2	-7808	-7618	3 vs. 2 lags	36.61*
	1	-7817#	-7714#	2 vs.1 lag	38.48**
U.S. Dollar	4	-7495	-7132	5 vs. 4 lags	25.82
	3	-7516	-7239	4 vs. 3 lags	26.67
	2	-7521	-7331	3 vs. 2 lags	41.31**
	1	-7538#	-7434#	2 vs.1 lag	31.92
Japanese Yen	4	-7424	-7061	5 vs. 4 lags	21.26
	3	-7450	-7173	4 vs. 3 lags	22.53
	2	-7455	-7265	3 vs. 2 lags	41.82**
	1	-7465#	-7362#	2 vs.1 lag	37.72*

# denotes minimum value
*significant at the 10% level; ** significant at the 5% level; *** significant at the 1% level

Having established the unit root characteristics of the data and identified relevant ranges for lag length, we are ready to proceed with the examination of cointegration. In this section, we consider two inter-related pairs of questions. First, are the ASEAN–5 stock markets cointegrated? If so, how many cointegrating relationships are there? To answer these questions, we rely on the λ_{max} and λ_{trace} statistics. The λ_{max} statistic tests the null hypothesis that the number of cointegrating vectors is r (ranging from 0 to 4) against the alternative of $r+1$cointegrating vectors. The λ_{trace} statistic tests the null hypothesis that the number of distinct cointegrating vectors is less than or equal to r against a general alternative.

Conditional on finding cointegrating relationships, the second pair of questions considers the cointegrating vectors. Which countries participate in the cointegrating relationships? What are the coefficients in the cointegrating vectors, and do they have reasonable magnitudes for interpretation? To answer these, we first conduct individual exclusion tests of the null hypothesis that the coefficient on a variable in the cointegrating vector is zero. These tests are distributed χ^2 with one degree of freedom. For any coefficients that are statistically significant, we qualitatively assess the magnitudes for economic significance.

Table 4.4 reports the results of the cointegration analysis. Panel A again considers daily data, and reports the results for VARs with 1 lag and with 5 lags. Panel B again considers weekly data, and reports the results for VARs with 1, 2, and 3 lags. Within each panel and lag length, models are estimated using the three currency denominations: local currencies, the dollar, and the yen. There are thus 15 VARs estimated, and the results are astonishingly consistent across all versions.

Tests for cointegration utilize both the λ_{max} and λ_{trace} statistics, reported on the left of the various tables. Models denominated in local currencies are estimated without a constant in the cointegrating vector because an exclusion test of the hypothesis that the constant is zero could not reject the null for any of the specifications. Models denominated in US dollars and yen are estimated with a constant in the cointegrating vector because exclusion tests of the hypothesis that the constant is zero reject the null for all of the specifications. The inclusion of a constant in the cointegrating vector alters the critical values of the λ_{max} and λ_{trace} statistics; we use Table B of Enders (1995: 420) for both sets of critical values. Taken together, the λ_{max} and λ_{trace} statistics consistently (and somewhat overwhelmingly) indicate that there is only one cointegrating vector regardless of data frequency, currency denomination, and lag length.

Since cointegration determines whether the different stock markets have a long run relationship, coefficients in the cointegrating vector can tell us *how* the stock markets are related in the long run. To the right of the λ_{max} and λ_{trace} statistics, the cointegrating vectors are reported along with exclusion tests of each variable. The reported cointegrating vectors (only one for each model) are normalized around Indonesia; in addition to being the first country alphabetically, it is also the smallest stock market and cointegrating vectors might be usefully interpreted in that context. Taken together, the coefficients appear remarkably similar across all versions of the model. As mentioned above, one difference among the models is that the local currency versions exclude a constant from the cointegrating vector while the US dollar and yen versions include a constant.[15] Another difference between the local currency models and the US dollar and yen models is that the coefficients in the former are generally a bit larger in absolute value than the coefficients in the latter. Since we cannot say whether these differences are statistically significant, we consider the qualitative implications of all models taken together. The exclusion tests of the variables suggest that each variable indeed participates in the long-run cointegrating vector; no country's stock market index should be removed from the analysis. Note that this is in contrast to the results in Sharma and Wongbangpo (2002), which suggest that the Philippine market should be excluded from the analysis.

Since the cointegrating vectors are all normalized around Indonesia, we can easily rewrite the cointegrating vector as if the Indonesian stock index were the dependent variable and all other variables were independent variables. Since the coefficients are similar across all models, we consider a representative cointegrating vector:

$$INDON = -3.1\ MALAY - 1.8\ PHILI + 3.3\ SINGA + 3.3\ THAIL$$

which is, in fact, simply a collection of the average coefficients across the fifteen models. The long-run relationship suggests that a 1 percent increase in the Malaysian stock index lowers the Indonesian index by 3.1 percent, and a 1 percent increase in the Philippine stock index lowers the Indonesian index by 1.8 percent. Similarly, a 1 percent increase in the Singapore or Thai stock index increases the Indonesian index by 3.3 percent.

[15] The table reveals that the constant in the US dollar models is between 7.9 and 8.9, averaging 8.7. The yen models have a constant ranging from 13.0 to 15.2, averaging 14.2. Not much importance can be attributed to these, as they are simply constants in the levels of the stock market indexes, so we do not consider them further.

Table 4.4. Analysis of Cointegration (1 July 1998 through 31 December 2002)

Panel A: Daily Data

VAR with 1 Lag (1 day)

	===== *Cointegration Tests* =====				============= *Cointegrating Vectors (Exclusion Tests)* =============					
Model	H_0	λ_{max}	H_0	λ_{trace}	Indonesia	Malaysia	Philippine	Singapore	Thailand	Constant
Local Currency	r=0	75.19***	r=0	113.03***	1.000 (8.60***)	3.792 (35.16***)	2.012 (9.42***)	-3.452 (25.00***)	-3.768 (52.36***)	
	r=1	18.38	r≤1	37.84						
	r=2	10.03	r≤2	19.46						
	r=3	8.30	r≤3	9.43						
	r=4	1.13	r≤4	1.13						
U.S. Dollar	r=0	74.82***	r=0	107.68***	1.000 (12.37***)	3.199 (41.92***)	1.727 (20.93***)	-3.230 (33.49***)	-3.344 (54.53***)	7.937 (7.94***)
	r=1	12.76	r≤1	32.86						
	r=2	9.97	r≤2							
	r=3	8.05	r≤3	10.12						
	r=4	2.07	r≤4	2.07						
Japanese Yen	r=0	62.50***	r=0	91.97***	1.000 (15.17***)	2.715 (31.78***)	1.421 (14.59***)	-3.086 (29.74***)	-2.827 (46.31***)	12.965 (10.07***)
	r=1	13.08	r≤1	29.48						
	r=2	8.61	r≤2	16.40						
	r=3	5.12	r≤3	7.79						
	r=4	2.67	r≤4	2.67						

Table 4.4 (*Continued*)

VAR with 5 Lags (5 days)

	===== *Cointegration Tests* =====				============= *Cointegrating Vectors (Exclusion Tests)* =============					
Model	H_0	λ_{max}	H_0	λ_{trace}	Indonesia	Malaysia	Philippines	Singapore	Thailand	Constant
Local Currency	r=0	66.62***	r=0	102.30***	1.000 (8.89***)	3.581 (29.57***)	1.994 (9.42***)	-3.431 (23.95***)	-3.752 (48.20***)	
	r=1	17.80	r≤1	35.68						
	r=2	9.09	r≤2	17.88						
	r=3	8.01	r≤3	8.79						
	r=4	0.78	r≤4	0.78						
U.S. Dollar	r=0	59.90***	r=0	94.13***	1.000 (13.03***)	2.671 (28.35***)	1.500 (16.00***)	-2.903 (27.59***)	-3.116 (44.75***)	8.941 (10.67***)
	r=1	13.95	r≤1	34.23						
	r=2	9.92	r≤2	20.28						
	r=3	7.97	r≤3	10.36						
	r=4	2.39	r≤4	2.39						
Japanese Yen	r=0	53.17***	r=0	83.28***	1.000 (13.75***)	2.548 (24.37***)	1.429 (13.18***)	-3.141 (27.48***)	-2.851 (39.56***)	15.189 (12.57***)
	r=1	13.39	r≤1	30.11						
	r=2	7.81	r≤2	16.72						
	r=3	6.10	r≤3	8.91						
	r=4	2.81	r≤4	2.81						

Table 4.4 (*Continued*)

Panel B: Weekly Data

VAR with 1 Lag (1 week)

	===== *Cointegration Tests* =====				============= *Cointegrating Vectors (Exclusion Tests)* =============					
Model	H_0	λ_{max}	H_0	λ_{trace}	Indonesia	Malaysia	Philippines	Singapore	Thailand	Constant
Local Currency	r=0	78.57***	r=0	118.75***	1.000 (8.45***)	3.995 (36.81***)	2.337 (12.15***)	-3.769 (28.57***)	-4.161 (56.98***)	
	r=1	21.20	r≤1	40.17						
	r=2	10.10	r≤2	18.97						
	r=3	8.18	r≤3	8.87						
	r=4	0.70	r≤4	0.70						
U.S. Dollar	r=0	74.08***	r=0	110.09***	1.000 (13.36***)	3.015 (38.88***)	1.753 (22.63***)	-3.192 (35.16***)	-3.396 (55.43***)	8.684 (10.28***)
	r=1	15.13	r≤1	36.00						
	r=2	9.98	r≤2	20.87						
	r=3	8.78	r≤3	10.89						
	r=4	2.11	r≤4	2.11						
Japanese Yen	r=0	63.80***	r=0	95.03***	1.000 (14.10***)	2.905 (32.96***)	1.698 (18.87***)	-3.434 (33.82***)	-3.132 (48.22***)	14.607 (11.78***)
	r=1	14.08	r≤1	31.23						
	r=2	7.93	r≤2	17.15						
	r=3	6.44	r≤3	9.22						
	r=4	2.78	r≤4	2.78						

Table 4.4 (*Continued*)

VAR with 2 Lags (2 weeks)

	Cointegration Tests				Cointegrating Vectors (Exclusion Tests)					
Model	H_0	λ_{max}	H_0	λ_{trace}	Indonesia	Malaysia	Philippines	Singapore	Thailand	Constant
Local Currency	r=0	50.86***	r=0	87.15***	1.000 (8.70***)	3.150 (20.31***)	1.762 (7.13***)	-3.103 (18.56***)	-3.310 (31.91***)	
	r=1	18.73	r≤1	36.29						
	r=2	10.14	r≤2	17.56						
	r=3	7.10	r≤3	7.41						
	r=4	0.32	r≤4	0.32						
U.S. Dollar	r=0	52.79***	r=0	89.71***	1.000 (14.72***)	2.428 (24.25***)	1.315 (13.44***)	-2.671 (25.71***)	-2.839 (36.24***)	8.848 (11.67***)
	r=1	15.84	r≤1	36.92						
	r=2	11.52	r≤2	21.08						
	r=3	7.52	r≤3	9.57						
	r=4	2.05	r≤4	2.05						
Japanese Yen	r=0	47.77***	r=0	79.77**	1.000 (15.58***)	2.289 (20.85***)	1.218 (10.21***)	-2.836 (24.24***)	-2.603 (33.03***)	14.548 (12.73***)
	r=1	14.73	r≤1	32.00						
	r=2	8.72	r≤2	17.27						
	r=3	6.24	r≤3	8.55						
	r=4	2.30	r≤4	2.30						

Table 4.4 (*Continued*)

VAR with 3 Lags (3 weeks)

	===== *Cointegration Tests* =====				============= *Cointegrating Vectors (Exclusion Tests)* =============					
Model	H_0	λ_{max}	H_0	λ_{trace}	Indonesia	Malaysia	Philippines	Singapore	Thailand	Constant
Local Currency	r=0	49.09***	r=0	92.17***	1.000 (5.70**)	4.010 (19.50***)	2.436 (8.96***)	-3.945 (18.52***)	-3.945 (25.51***)	
	r=1	23.43	r≤1	43.08						
	r=2	12.17	r≤2	19.65						
	r=3	7.28	r≤3	7.48						
	r=4	0.20	r≤4	0.20						
U.S. Dollar	r=0	44.94***	r=0	82.62**	1.000 (8.83***)	3.041 (21.14***)	1.769 (14.37***)	-3.332 (22.80***)	-3.229 (24.57***)	8.856 (7.18***)
	r=1	18.72	r≤1	37.68						
	r=2	10.50	r≤2	18.96						
	r=3	6.64	r≤3	8.46						
	r=4	1.81	r≤4	1.81						
Japanese Yen	r=0	42.22***	r=0	76.04**	1.000 (6.72***)	3.774 (22.46***)	2.310 (15.85***)	-4.339 (24.63***)	-3.604 (22.92***)	13.863 (4.82**)
	r=1	17.01	r≤1	33.82						
	r=2	8.30	r≤2	16.81						
	r=3	6.73	r≤3	8.51						
	r=4	1.78	r≤4	1.78						

* significant at the 10% level; ** significant at the 5% level; *** significant at the 1% level

Since Indonesia is the smallest market, the (rather large) coefficients appear reasonable because they suggest that Indonesia is heavily influenced by the largest markets (Malaysia, Singapore, and Thailand) and somewhat less influenced by the smaller Philippine market. Admittedly, the high magnitude of the coefficient on Thailand is somewhat puzzling, but is consistent with results in Phylaktis and Ravazzolo (2005) concerning the influence of Thailand.

It is particularly interesting that Indonesia is inversely related to Malaysia and the Philippines, as economic integration usually implies that markets move together with a positive correlation coefficient. However, there are some circumstances in which markets will be systematically inversely related; a macroeconomic shock which is favorable for Malaysia and the Philippines but unfavorable for Indonesia will produce such a result. One such shock might be an oil price shock. Indonesia is the region's largest oil exporter and the Philippines imports more oil as a percent of GDP than any other country in Southeast Asia, so perhaps it is not surprising that Indonesia and the Philippines are inversely related. The oil story cannot be comprehensive, however, as Malaysia also exports oil but is empirically negatively related to Indonesia, and both Singapore and Thailand import oil but are empirically positively related to Indonesia. To further complicate the interactions, Singapore refines a great deal of both Malaysian and Indonesian oil. However, other shocks most likely provide part of the explanation. For example, with integrated markets a productivity shock in one country that induces capital inflows (outflows) from (to) the other countries would cause stock prices to move in opposite directions. Note that the markets of Malaysia and the Philippines are also negatively related to each other, which might again be explained by oil shocks. On the whole, then, inverse relationships may not be too disturbing.

To convey the sense of proportions, as well as consider another perspective, we can re-normalize the cointegrating vectors around a different country. We briefly consider normalization around Singapore, the largest market. The representative cointegrating vector can be rewritten:

$$SINGA = 0.3\ INDON + 0.9\ MALAY + 0.5\ PHILI - 1.0\ THAIL$$

and reinterpreted. By virtue of the fact that Singapore and Thailand have the same coefficient in the cointegrating vector, Thailand (the second smallest market) can be easily substituted for Singapore. Thus, the Singapore and Thai stock indices are positively affected by the Indonesian, Malaysian, and Philippine indexes with fairly reasonable magnitudes. For example, a 1 percent increase in the Malaysian market is associated with 0.9 percent increase in the Singapore and Thai markets. Thus, Malaysia and Singapore move approximately one-to-one with each other, and Malaysia and Thailand move approximately one-to-one with each other. The Singapore and Thai markets are less affected by changes in the Philippine and Indonesian markets. Finally, a 1 percent increase in the Thai stock market is associated with a 1 percent decrease in the Singapore stock market, and vice versa. The fact that Thailand and Singapore move one-to-one inversely with each other again seems puzzling, but probably reflects structural asymmetries and shocks which are favorable for Thailand and unfavorable for Singapore (and vice versa). For example, Thailand has a large agricultural sector and Singapore does not, so agricultural price shocks will have opposite effects in Thailand and Singapore.[16]

Taken together, the results of cointegration analysis convincingly reveal that the ASEAN–5 stock markets are cointegrated, and have only one cointegrating relationship. In addition, all five countries participate in the cointegrating relationship. Finally, the magnitudes of the coefficients in the cointegrating vector are all reasonable, although some puzzles remain. One puzzle is with regard to the magnitude associated with Thailand, an otherwise small market. This effect has been detected by previous researchers (primarily Phylaktis and Ravazzolo 2005), but there is still no clear explanation. Another puzzle involves inverse relationships among some market pairs, since the main idea was that markets would move together with a positive association. Although a story about oil shocks works well between Indonesia and the Philippines (and possibly between Malaysia and the Philippines), there must be other

[16] For more on structural asymmetries, see Plummer (2003).

shocks with asymmetric effects in the markets between Indonesia and Malaysia and between Singapore and Thailand.

It is worth pointing out once again that these results are completely robust to the frequency of the data (daily versus weekly), the currency denomination examined (local currencies, US dollars, or yen), and the number of lags chosen for the VAR (within an appropriate range indicated in pre-testing). Such consistent results are rare in time series studies of this type, but may not be too surprising in this particular case. It is intuitively appealing that cointegration is able to pick out a long run relationship equally well from daily and weekly data. Similarly, it is intuitively appealing that the currency denomination does not matter. Although somewhat surprising on theoretical and institutional grounds, the finding most likely reflects a strong relationship in the underlying stock markets which is not substantially altered when the effects of exchange rates are included. Finally, it is also appealing that the cointegrating relationship is reasonably invariant to small changes in the number of lags utilized in the VAR. This suggests that we can have some confidence in the cointegrating relationship, in contrast to what the debate between Kasa (1992) and Richards (1995) might suggest.

Conclusion

The empirical results in this paper demonstrate that the stock markets of Indonesia, Malaysia, Philippines, Singapore, and Thailand in the period after the Asian financial crisis (July 1, 1998 through December 31, 2002) are cointegrated whether analyzed using daily data or weekly data, and whether analyzed in local currencies, the US dollar, or the Japanese yen. In addition, the finding does not depend on the number of lags used in estimation over a reasonable range. The stock markets are thus not completely segmented by national borders. However, there is only one cointegrating vector among the five stock markets, leaving four common trends among the five variables. We therefore conclude that ASEAN–5 stock markets are integrated in the economic sense, but that integration is not complete. Exclusion tests of the variables suggest that each country index participates in the long-run cointegrating vector, so no market should be removed from the analysis. In addition, the coefficients in the cointegrating vector are remarkably similar across all versions of the models, and are reasonable in magnitude and interpretation.

One implication of cointegration is that there is less long-run diversification benefit from investing in all five countries than the short-run correlation coefficients indicate. On a policy level, cointegration suggests that initiatives to further integrate the stock markets are quite feasible, and in fact desirable from the standpoint of efficiency. In particular, since there is less long-run diversification benefit from investing across all five countries, a regional stock exchange will nudge investors to spread their money into smaller markets where they otherwise may not. In fact, investors from outside the region may value the benefits of a regional stock exchange (such as higher liquidity and lower transaction costs) and allocate more capital to the region than they otherwise would. This will allow ASEAN companies to expand their shareholder base and lower their cost of capital.

From the stock market perspective, regional integration suggests that even currency unification would be feasible. Although this issue needs to consider other financial and macroeconomic issues as well,[17] the point here is that efficient flows of capital across borders within the region have the capacity to mitigate the effects of any asymmetric macroeconomic shocks. The inverse relationships in cointegrating vectors among some stock market pairs suggest that such cross-border flows are already occurring. Stock market integration is thus an important component of overall economic integration and might be a useful precondition for monetary unification.

[17] For more on the issue of ASEAN currency unification, see Eichengreen and Bayoumi (1999), Bayoumi, Eichengreen, and Mauro (2000), Bayoumi and Mauro (2001), Ling (2001), Zhang, Sato, and McAleer (2001), Madhur (2002), and Plummer and Click (2005). These studies typically examine the nature of national aggregate supply shocks to determine whether they are positively correlated across countries (and thus more characteristic of an optimal currency area).

References

Bank Negara Malaysia, 1999. *The Central Bank and the Financial System in Malaysia.* Kuala Lumpur, Bank Negara Malaysia.

Bayoumi, Tamim, Barry Eichengreen, and Paolo Mauro, 2000. On Regional Monetary Arrangements for ASEAN. *Journal of the Japanese and International Economies* 14, 121–148.

Bayoumi, Tamim, and Paolo Mauro, 2001. The Suitability of ASEAN for a Regional Currency Arrangement. *The World Economy* 24, 933–954.

Cecchini, Paolo, 1988. *The Costs of Non-Europe.* Bruxelles, Commission of the European Communities.

Chen, Gong-meng, Michael Firth, and Oliver Meng Rui, 2002. Stock Market Linkages: Evidence from Latin America. *Journal of Banking & Finance* 26, 1113–1141.

Chung, Pin J., and Donald J. Liu, 1994. Common Stochastic Trends in Pacific Rim Stock Markets. *Quarterly Review of Economics and Finance* 34, 241–259.

Click, Reid W., and Joshua D. Coval, 2002. *The Theory and Practice of International Financial Management.* Prentice–Hall.

Corhay, A., A. Tourani Rad, and J.-P. Urbain, 1993. Common Stochastic Trends in European Stock Markets. *Economics Letters* 42, 385–390.

Darrat, Ali F., and Maosen Zhong, 2002. Permanent and Transitory Driving Forces in the Asian-Pacific Stock Markets. *The Financial Review* 37, 35–52.

DeFusco, Richard A., John M. Geppert, and George P. Tsetsekos, 1996. Long-Run Diversification Potential in Emerging Stock Markets. *The Financial Review* 31, 343–363.

Dekker, Arie, Kunal Sen, and Martin Young, 2001. Equity Market Linkages in the Asia Pacific Region: A Comparison of the Orthogonalized and Generalised VAR Approaches. *Global Finance Journal* 12, 1–33.

Eichengreen, Barry, and Tamim Bayoumi, 1999. Is Asia an Optimum Currency Area? Can It Become One? Regional, Global and Historical Perspectives on Asian Monetary Relations. In *Exchange Rate Policies in Emerging Asian Countries*, edited by Stefan Collignon, Jean Pisani–Ferry, and Yung Chul Park. London and New York, Routledge, 347–366.

Enders, Walter, 1995. *Applied Econometric Time Series.* John Wiley & Sons, Inc.

Fernández–Serrano, José L., and Simón Sosvilla–Rivero, 2001. Modelling Evolving Long-Run Relationships: The Linkages Between Stock Markets in Asia. *Japan and the World Economy* 13, 145–160.

Freeman, Nick J., 2000. A Regional Platform for Trading Southeast Asian Equities: Viable Option or Lofty 'Red Herring'? Institute of Southeast Asian Studies Working Paper No. 4. Available at http://www.iseas.edu.sg/rpapers.html.

Jang, Hoyoon, and Wonsik Sul, 2002. The Asian Financial Crisis and the Co-Movement of Asian Stock Markets. *Journal of Asian Economics* 13, 94–104.

Johnson, Simon, and Todd Mitton, 2003. Cronyism and Capital Controls: Evidence from Malaysia. *Journal of Financial Economics* 67, 351–382.

Kaplan, Ethan, and Dani Rodrik, 2001. Did the Malaysian Capital Controls Work? National Bureau of Economic Research Working Paper 8142.

Kasa, Kenneth, 1992. Common Stochastic Trends in International Stock Markets. *Journal of Monetary Economics* 29, 95–124.

Kleimeier, Stefanie, and Harald Sander, 2000. Regionalisation versus Globalisation in European Financial Market Integration: Evidence from Co-integration Analyses. *Journal of Banking & Finance* 24, 1005–1043.

Ling, Hazel Yuen Phui, 2001. Optimum Currency Areas in East Asia. *ASEAN Economic Bulletin* 18, 206–217.

Madhur, Srinivasa, 2002. Costs and Benefits of a Common Currency for ASEAN. Asian Development Bank Working Paper. Available at http://www.adb.org/Documents/ERD/Working_Papers/wp012.pdf.

Manning, Neil, 2002. Common Trends and Convergence? South East Asian Equity Markets, 1988–1999. *Journal of International Money and Finance* 21, 183–202.

Masih, Abul M.M., and Rumi Masih, 1999. Are Asian Stock Market Fluctuations Due Mainly to Intra-regional Contagion Effects? Evidence Based on Asian Emerging Stock Markets. *Pacific-Basin Finance Journal* 7, 251–282.

Phylaktis, Kate, and Fabiola Ravazzolo, 2005. Stock Market Linkages in Emerging Markets: Implications for International Portfolio Diversification. *Journal of International Financial Markets, Institutions and Money* 15(2), 91–106.

Plummer, Michael G., 2003. Structural Change in Globalized Asia: Macro Trends and US Policy Changes. *Journal of Asian Economics* 14(2), 243–281.

Plummer, Michael G., and Reid W. Click, 2005. Bond Market Development and Integration in ASEAN. *International Journal of Finance and Economics* 10, 133–142.

Rangvid, Jesper, 2001. Increasing Convergence Among European Stock Markets? A Recursive Common Stochastic Trends Analysis. *Economics Letters* 71, 383–389.

Richards, Anthony J., 1995. Comovements in National Stock Market Returns: Evidence of Predictability, But Not Cointegration. *Journal of Monetary Economics* 36, 631–654.

Sharma, Subhash C., and Praphan Wongbangpo, 2002. Long-term Trends and Cycles in ASEAN Stock Markets. *Review of Financial Economics* 11, 299–315.

Standard & Poor's, 2001. *Emerging Stock Markets Factbook*. New York, Standard & Poor's.

Sun, Qian, Yuen–Kin Tang, and Wilson H.S. Tong, 2002. The Impacts of Mass Delisting: Evidence from Singapore and Malaysia. *Pacific-Basin Finance Journal* 10, 333–351.

Tan, K.B., and Y.K. Tse, 2002. The Integration of the East and South-East Asian Equity Markets. International Center for the Study of East Asian Development Working Paper No. 11. Available at http://www.icsead.or.jp/indexe.htm.

Wellons, Philip, 1997. Integration of Stock Exchanges in Regions in Europe, Asia, Canada, and the U.S. Consulting Assistance on Economic Reform II Discussion Paper No. 14, Harvard Institute for International Development. Available at http://www.cid.harvard.edu/caer2/htm/framsets/fr_auth.htm.

World Bank, 2002. *World Development Indicators*. Washington, DC, World Bank.

Zhang, Zhaoyong, Kiyotaka Sato, and Michael McAleer, 2001. Is East Asia an Optimum Currency Area? International Center for the Study of East Asian Development Working Paper No. 37. Available at http://www.icsead.or.jp/indexe.htm.

CHAPTER 5

THE INSTITUTION OF A SINGLE CURRENCY AREA: LESSONS FOR ASIA FROM THE EUROPEAN MONETARY UNION*

Sergio Rossi

The financial crises that hit Asia at the end of the last millennium have raised concern about the best way to avoid the recurrence of these crises, and the related costs, in the future. As a matter of fact, even with the financial aid provided by the International Monetary Fund (IMF) — which in the case of South Korea (1997) amounted to 1,939 percent of this country's quota — the socio-economic costs of the Asian crisis could not be avoided. These costs mostly occurred in terms of output losses (owing to misallocation and under-utilization of resources), which aggravated the rates of unemployment in the countries hit by the crisis. In the own words of an IMF official, '[the Fund was] surprised by the speed and virulence with which the crisis spread to many countries in the region. The experience revealed the IMF had not kept up with the rapid developments in international capital markets' (Dawson 2002 Internet). Failure of the IMF to foresee this crisis, and to deal with it effectively, has induced a number of calls for regional monetary and financial cooperation in (part of) the Asiatic continent. The suggested forms of cooperation are multifaceted. They range from financial liberalization in order to facilitate cross-border transactions as well as international

* The first draft of this chapter was presented at the SAIS/ICSEAD Workshop on 'EU–Asia Links and Lessons', Johns Hopkins University, Bologna, May 12, 2003. The author would like to thank Erik Jones, Michael G. Plummer, and workshop participants for helpful comments. Valuable research assistance by Dante Caprara is also gratefully acknowledged. The usual disclaimer applies.

settlements, to more intensive forms of cooperation, and collaboration, like exchange rate coordination (including regional basket pegs or a regionally–harmonized fluctuation band for the exchange rates) (Rajan 2005).

Today, in fact, there are many different exchange rate regimes in Asia, ranging from hard pegs to floating rates, all of which have the potential to lead to financial instability and turmoil. Fixed exchange rates, hard pegs, and currency boards entail the risk of inflexibility, and could elicit many socio-economic costs for the countries pursuing one of these strategies, when they face asymmetric shocks in respect of the currency area to which they are linked. Indeed, as Grieve Smith (1999: 231) observes, '[t]he Asian crisis highlighted the difficulties which arise when smaller countries peg or stabilise their currencies against a major national currency, such as the dollar. Such a tie may involve an unwanted and inappropriate appreciation when the major currency itself appreciates as the dollar did against the yen from mid–1995.' On the other hand, intermediate exchange rate regimes such as a crawling band or a managed float may provoke financial instability in those emerging or developing economies where capital movements vis–à–vis the rest of the world are already almost totally free. A free float, however, does not represent a valid alternative either, because this regime is affected by exchange rate volatility, which raises the exchange–rate risk premium and therefore decreases potential capital inflows (largely in the form of foreign direct investment) to the detriment of the country's economic development. In addition, 'flexible exchange rates cannot protect banks against panic by external creditors who hold short–term claims denominated in foreign currency. This was the case in Asia to a significant extent. Therefore, a flexible exchange rate system would have provided only limited protection' (Wagner 2001: 11). In a nutshell, the available exchange rate strategies are costly and can affect economic performance negatively, owing to the resulting instability of the financial system.

As a matter of fact, with the rising degree of interdependence among (South–East) Asian economies through trade, investment, and capital flows, exchange rate stability has become an issue of growing importance, and today a form of policy coordination is necessary. This chapter explores the most ambitious form of monetary and financial coordination in (South–East) Asia, that is, full monetary union with a single currency and a common monetary policy decided by an independent, supranational central bank like the monetary authority of the European Monetary Union (EMU). Indeed, the idea of an Asian Monetary Union (AMU) is in the air and has been discussed since the immediate aftermath of the 1997–8 financial crisis that hit this region (see Chung 1999, and Xie and Yam 1999). At the Asian Development Bank Annual Meetings in Jeju (South Korea) on May 15–17, 2004, Haruhiko Kuroda, then Special Advisor to the Japanese Cabinet and at the time of writing President of the Asian Development Bank (ADB), went as far as presenting a five–stage project for the adoption of a single Asian currency (Mallet 2004). The idea of the AMU has also been endorsed by the former president of the ADB, Todao Chino, in an interview with the *Wall Street Journal* (June 8, 2004). In this connection, the past and the present of the EMU can surely provide some lessons worth learning for (South–East) Asia, and the AMU, in order to avoid as far as possible some of the economic problems that affect today the euro area.

In fact, the reasons for Asian monetary integration are not only economic, but also political and institutional. Indeed, this kind of integration among countries is likely not only to prevent the recurrence of a financial crisis, and to better manage it should it occur, but also to pull together a number of countries and strengthen their political as well as institutional links, to avoid political conflicts and institutional disputes. As a matter of fact, the ultimate objective of the European Economic Community Treaty signed in Rome on March 25, 1957 was to avoid the occurrence of further conflicts between France and Germany, notably by making them sit at the same institutional table and thus leading them to collaborate on a number of economic, political, and institutional issues (see Angresano 2004: 911–12). Today, as Henning (2002: 9) points out, '[a]lthough the Cold War is over in Europe, many political conflicts in Asia remain unresolved. Regional cooperation can nonetheless limit the damage to economic relations when political conflict breaks out. By raising the economic cost of political disputes, moreover, such cooperation provides additional incentives for peaceful resolution of conflicts.'

This chapter explores the economic situation (and performance) of European Union (EU) countries right before their monetary integration into the single currency area named after the euro, and compares it to the situation of the same countries after some years of membership in the EMU. It notably argues that fulfilling the EMU criteria consistently over the years requires huge efforts by would-be member countries, and this could give rise to important costs in terms of output and employment losses. The possibility that present EMU countries would have to bear part of these costs — by increasing transfers to and diminishing subsidies from the EU budget — cannot be ruled out either, with the risk of provoking tensions within the whole EU, in particular as regards the 'one-size-fits-all' monetary policy decisions of the European Central Bank (ECB). These issues are certainly of interest for other projects of regional monetary and financial integration that are likely to be implemented in a not too distant future outside Europe, particularly in Asia (or even in Latin America). Despite their European setting, the problems we discuss in this chapter could indeed occur in any part of the world where monetary union is or will be a political goal that countries may want to reach along the EMU path accomplished so far. It is therefore important to study the lessons that can be drawn from the EMU, to take stock of this experience in order to avoid coming across the same problems elsewhere.

The structure of this chapter is as follows. The next section briefly recalls the criteria for EMU membership, and notes the economic performance of the current EMU countries at the time of their entry into the single–currency area as well as in the recent past. The second section discusses and elaborates on a number of critical issues in the operationalization of this area, in particular the loopholes and shortcomings of the EMU convergence criteria that have led a number of countries to adhere to Euroland even though their economies were not really converging as required by the spirit of the criteria enshrined in the EU Treaty. The third section addresses some economic problems that are likely to occur if the ten new member countries of the EU are to join the euro area in this decade or even in the next. After reviewing the current economic situation of these countries, this section asks whether the required nominal convergence to adopt the euro in these countries is likely to increase real divergence between the new and the old EU countries, which would put territorial cohesion at risk at the level of the EU as a whole. In this section we also consider the exchange rate arrangement that the EU–10 countries have to comply with, in order for them to respect the relevant convergence criterion, and we then discuss the risks for financial instability that this arrangement could elicit for the same set of countries. The last section concludes and offers some final remarks.

The Maastricht Criteria for EMU Membership and Economic Performance

The criteria ruling membership in the EMU were ratified by the European Council meeting in Maastricht on February 7, 1992, and concern macroeconomic convergence between participating countries assessed with respect to nominal magnitudes. These criteria, known as the Maastricht criteria, are laid down in Article 121.1 of the EU Treaty and specified in two annexed protocols (see European Commission 1999).

- The criterion on price stability stipulates that a country has a price performance that is sustainable and an average rate of inflation, measured by the Harmonized Index of Consumer Prices (HICP) and observed over a period of one year before the EMU entry test, that does not exceed by more than 1.5 percentage points that of, at most, the three best performing EU countries in terms of price stability.
- The twofold criteria on the government budgetary position stipulate that at the time of examination a country should not trespass the benchmark of 3 percent for the ratio of the planned or actual government deficit to GDP, and of 60 percent for the ratio of government debt to GDP.
- The criterion on participation in the Exchange Rate Mechanism (ERM) of the European Monetary System (EMS) means that a

country has respected the so–called normal fluctuation margins provided for by this mechanism without severe tensions for at least two years before the examination.

- The criterion on the convergence of interest rates stipulates that, observed over a period of one year before the examination, a country has had an average nominal long–term interest rate that does not exceed by more than 2 percentage points that of, at most, the three best performing EU countries in terms of price stability.

Today, it is widely acknowledged that in the 1990s the economic convergence among current euro–area member countries was nominal only, and also that it was not much better than the present situation of would–be EMU countries in this respect. As a matter of fact, in the second half of the 1990s the first–round EMU countries converged nominally on measured inflation rates, interest rates and the general government position in respect of GDP, but did not show the same progress towards real convergence, measured with respect to the annual growth rate of real GDP, per capita GDP, unemployment rates, and output gaps. 'This was the major omission of the Maastricht Treaty, which is preoccupied by "nominal" as opposed to "real" convergence' (Bayoumi et al., 2000: 144). This situation does not seem to have changed much since the euro changeover. As empirical evidence shows, within the euro area real variables did not converge over the last six years (Figures 1 and 2). In fact, if there is convergence, this is towards lower growth rates of real GDP, and a persistent high rate of unemployment.

We may thus ask if the nominal convergence observed during the process of European monetary union can be deemed sufficient to guarantee the orderly working of a single–currency area, and to integrate would–be member countries with no disturbances coming from the integration process. Let us consider this question more closely.

Figure 5.1. Real GDP Growth Rates in the EU-15 Countries (1999–2004)

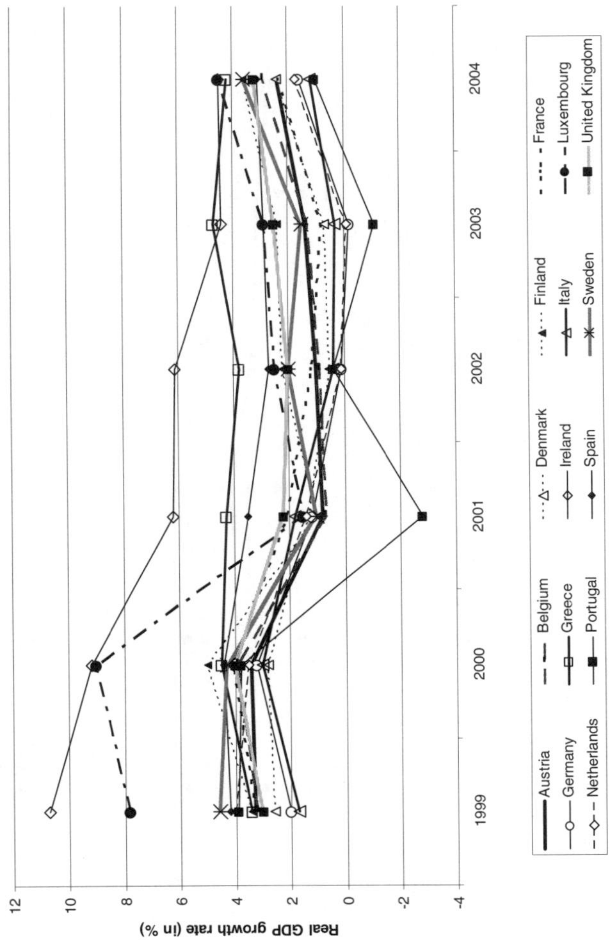

Source: Eurostat.

Figure 5.2. Unemployment Rates in the EU-15 Countries (1999–2004)

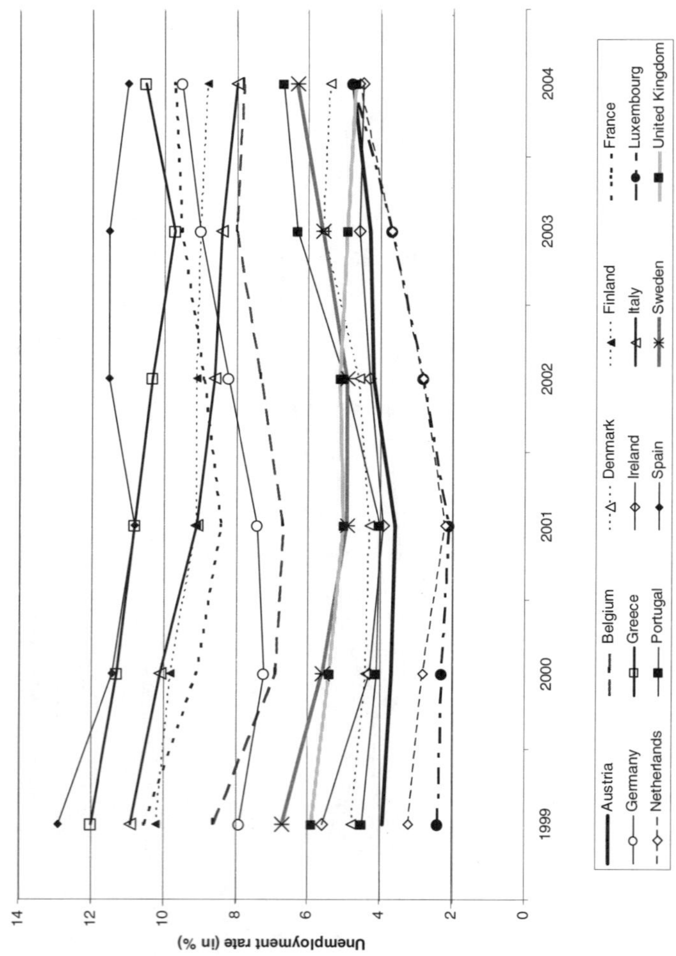

Source: Eurostat.

The Operationalization of the European Monetary Union

Both the institution and working of a single–currency area integrating a number of still heterogeneous countries such as those of the EU raise a number of issues in terms of choices, strategies, and risks for the whole political economy of monetary union. Let us consider first the criteria for EMU membership, before turning our attention to the issue of the lack of real convergence and its effects on monetary policy making by the ECB.

The Loopholes Embedded in the Convergence Criteria

The whole process of European monetary union has been characterized, first of all, by a 'measurement deficit' that does not help assess the observance of the Maastricht criteria. As a matter of fact, the data used for assessing the actual degree of nominal economic convergence between EU member countries are collected by the national statistical offices of the latter countries. Harmonization of these data by Eurostat is still under way but is not yet fully satisfactory, particularly as regards the so-called stock-flow adjustment (Eurostat 2005b). This is so much so that the relevant figures for evaluating, say, fiscal sustainability in line with the Maastricht parameters are not necessarily defined in a way consistent with the EU definitions laid down in the 1995 European System of Accounts (see Eurostat 1996). For example, in some of today's EMU member countries, privatization revenues — which Eurostat now excludes from the calculations to assess nominal economic convergence according to the Maastricht criteria — helped reduce the general government deficit below the 3 percent threshold with respect to GDP. These revenues might now accrue to the transition economies of the new EU member countries, which might be interested in privatizing a number of public enterprises in order to facilitate the respect of the convergence criteria for euro adoption.

Once all privatization programmes are over, however, a EU country's government will lose the corresponding revenues and might need to promote other initiatives in order to keep up with the convergence requirements. This could lead would-be EMU countries to behave strategically, namely, to implement a series of accounting fiddles in order for them to enter the euro area by cooking the books during the examination period. Indeed, this gimmick with official figures would be neither new nor unexpected. As shown by Dafflon and Rossi (1999), a number of the first-round EU countries entering the single-currency area on January 1, 1999 smoothed the Maastricht convergence process by cooking the books of the relevant year (1997) when their entry test was carried out. In fact, as Figure 5.3 clearly shows, since the euro replaced their national currencies (in 1999), several EMU countries have been experiencing a relative deterioration of their fiscal magnitudes with respect to GDP. Over the last six years, in a number of EMU countries fiscal deficits moved steadily towards the 3 percent ceiling, infringing it in many important cases. 'Presently, five out of 12 euro area Member States are subject to EDPs [excessive deficit procedures]' (European Central Bank 2005: 72). This is even more worrying for the future of the EMU since the revisions of and amendments to the Stability and Growth Pact (SGP) decided by the European Council meeting in Brussels on March 22–23, 2005 released the EMU straitjacket for the member countries' fiscal policy. In particular, the current interpretation of the SGP states that the EU, 'by taking account of the characteristics of the economy of each Member State, [...] should allow room for budgetary manoeuvre, in particular taking into account the needs for public investment' (ECOFIN 2005: 9).

Within the EU there seems therefore to exist a strong political will among current member States to support EMU despite the lack of fiscal discipline measured by the Maastricht parameters and required by the original SGP as well as by the ECB (see Eichengreen and Bayoumi 1999, and European Central Bank 2005). This is so much so that, 'as shown by recent experience, there are still weaknesses in the compilation, reporting and publication of budgetary statistics' (European Commission 2003: 2). As a result, loopholes that keep softening the fiscal constraints and therefore facilitate the respect of the relevant convergence criteria are still available to (would-be) euro-area countries.

Figure 5.3. Government Deficit (or Surplus) as a % of GDP in the EU-15 Countries (1994–2004)

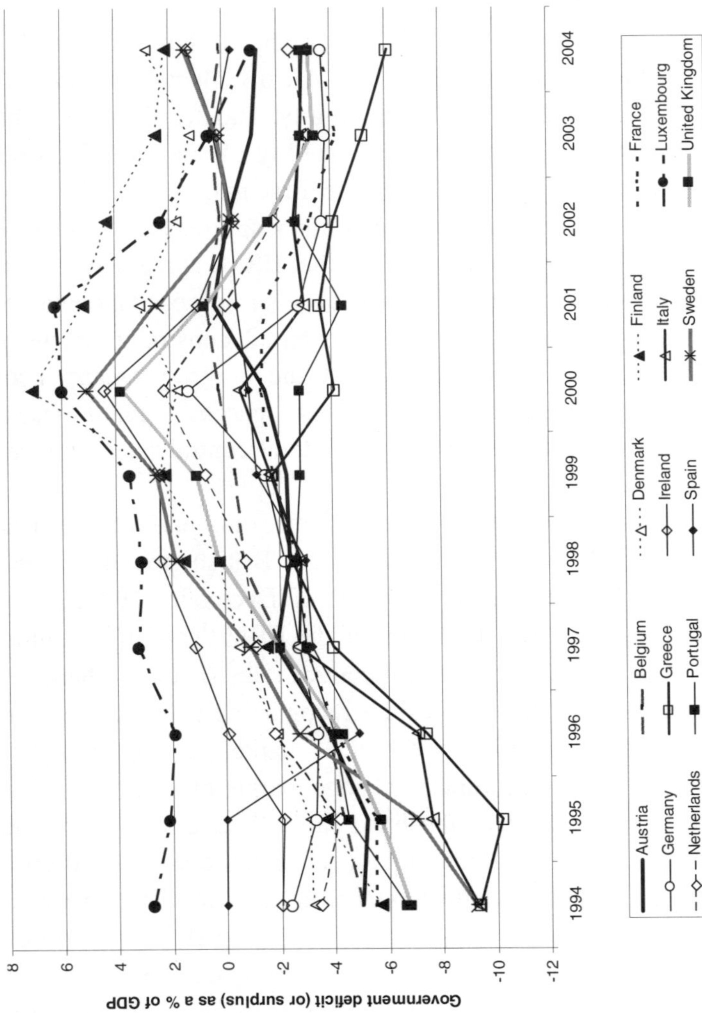

Sources: Eurostat and OECD.

A second example of this ad hoc operationalization of monetary union in Europe relates to the Maastricht criterion on exchange rate stability. Before the turmoil on foreign exchange markets in the 1990s, the so-called normal fluctuation margins of the ERM (I) were defined at ±2.25 percent around bilateral central rates. On account of the relative exchange rate stability that EMS currencies showed over the period 1987–92, the definition of such a narrow fluctuation band did not represent a real danger to the credibility, and feasibility, of the whole EMU project. In fact, despite the volatility of some EMS currencies in foreign exchange markets during the first half of the 1980s (when in some cases many bilateral exchange rates approached, or even reached, the upper or lower limits set by the ERM agreement), neither the European Commission nor EU officials ever proposed an enlargement of the fluctuation band to soften this external constraint on the member countries' economic policies — on the contrary, many economists emphasized the need to abide by these margins and, if necessary, to proceed with a realignment of the bilateral central rates with respect to the ECU.

Yet, after the currency crises of the first half of the 1990s that affected the EU economy (notably the British pound in 1992), and following the 'Lamfalussy proposal' of December 1994, in 1995 EU officials broadened the definition of the ERM 'normal' margins to ±15 percent, first around the bilateral central rates (ERM I) then around the euro central rate (ERM II). Besides recognizing a de facto breakdown of the ERM I and signalling to financial market speculators the intention not to intervene in the foreign exchange market in case of a new currency crisis, the enlargement of the band in 1995 also served to enlarge the first-round group of EU countries meeting the convergence criterion on exchange rate stability. Indeed, since the relevant data for assessing the respect of this criterion were those of the period 1995–7, the enlargement of the normal fluctuation band was instrumental in implementing the EMU on January 1, 1999 with a critical mass of EU countries. One therefore cannot deny that this wide, yet 'normal', fluctuation band might serve to facilitate the entry of new EU member countries in the euro area, even though their exchange rates might be rather volatile over the next years on account of the transition process still going on within their economies. This is an issue to which we shall return in the fourth section, in connection with financial liberalization.

A third example of the shortcomings of the nominal convergence criteria concerns the requirement of price stability. Eurostat has been working for many years on a proper measure of inflation in the single currency area, taking stock also of the measurement problems encountered by national consumer price indices (CPIs) all around the world (see Diewert 2002, and Wynne and Rodríguez–Palenzuela 2002). As a result, a so-called Harmonized Index of Consumer Prices has been developed and put to practical use for assessing this criterion, and serves today as a prominent monetary-policy indicator in the euro area. To be sure, Eurostat aims at 'harmonizing' the extent and weighting of the representative items that enter the bundle of consumer goods and services surveyed for evaluating the price of the HICP basket and its variations over time (see European Commission and Eurostat 2001). This objective, in fact, has been driven by the wish to reduce to a minimum, if not eliminate, the item categories (for instance homeownership) that either pose difficult analytical problems for the measurement of inflation or might jeopardize the ultimate target of the single monetary policy, i.e., price stability in the euro area. As Figure 5.4 shows, however, this practice has made it easier for a number of current EMU countries to fulfil the relevant convergence criterion when their entry test was carried out (in 1997). Time-series analysis and cross-country comparisons also show that HICP figures often indicate lower price increases than national CPIs do for the 15 old member countries of the EU (see Table 5.1a and Table 5.1b).

No one can deny that the same phenomenon may occur with respect to the ten new EU member countries, since the inflation convergence criterion is based on HICP figures, not on national CPIs. This phenomenon, however, does no justice to the economic philosophy behind the convergence criteria laid down in the EU Treaty. To be true, there is a considerable discrepancy between theory and practice of the whole EMU process. So far, in fact, it would seem that only nominal interest rate figures were not manipulated for EMU membership purposes, but on this point further research is needed.

Figure 5.4. Annual Inflation Rates in 1997 in the EU-15 Countries, CPIs and HICPs

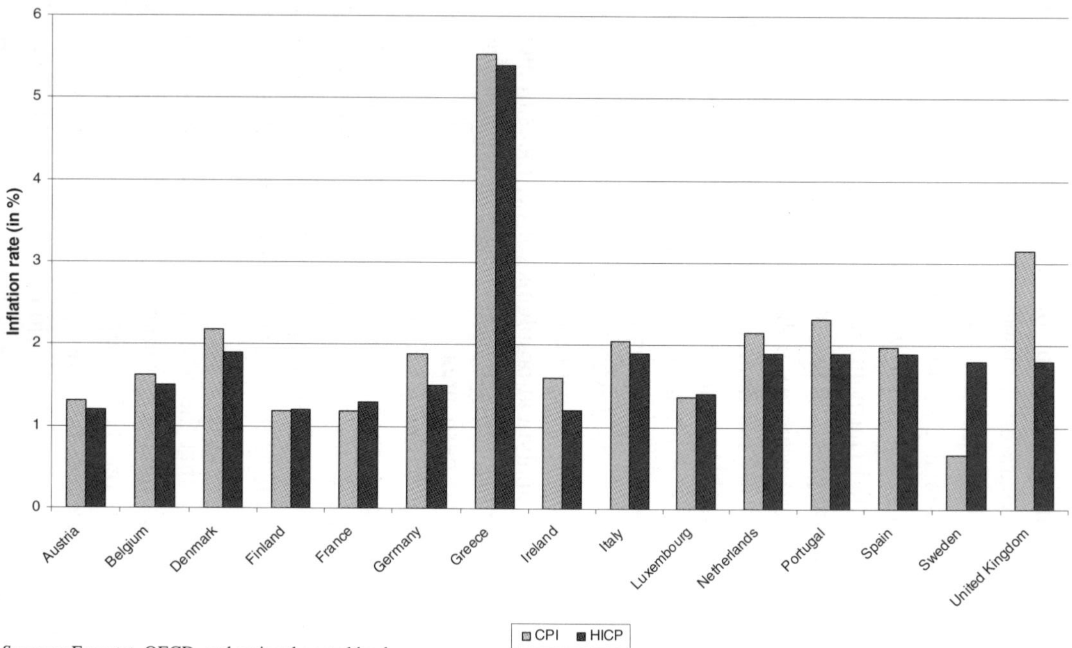

Sources: Eurostat, OECD, and national central banks.

Table 5.1a. Average Annual Inflation Rates in the EU-15 Countries as Measured by National CPIs and HICPs (1997–2000)

Country	1997 CPI	1997 HICP	1998 CPI	1998 HICP	1999 CPI	1999 HICP	2000 CPI	2000 HICP	1997–2000 CPI	1997–2000 HICP
Austria	1.3	1.2	0.9	0.8	0.6	0.5	2.3	2.0	1.3	1.1
Belgium	1.6	1.5	1.0	0.9	1.1	1.1	2.5	2.7	1.6	1.6
Denmark	2.2	1.9	1.8	1.3	2.5	2.1	2.9	2.7	2.4	2.0
Finland	1.2	1.2	1.4	1.4	1.2	1.3	3.0	3.0	1.7	1.7
France	1.2	1.3	0.6	0.7	0.5	0.6	1.7	1.8	1.0	1.1
Germany	1.9	1.5	0.9	0.6	0.6	0.6	1.5	1.4	1.2	1.0
Greece	5.5	5.4	4.8	4.5	2.6	2.1	3.2	2.9	4.0	3.7
Ireland	1.6	1.2	2.4	2.1	1.6	2.5	5.6	5.3	2.8	2.8
Italy	2.0	1.9	2.0	2.0	1.7	1.7	2.5	2.6	2.0	2.1
Luxembourg	1.4	1.4	1.0	1.0	1.0	1.0	3.2	3.8	1.6	1.8
Netherlands	2.2	1.9	2.0	1.8	2.2	2.0	2.4	2.3	2.2	2.0
Portugal	2.3	1.9	2.8	2.2	2.3	2.2	2.9	2.8	2.6	2.3
Spain	2.0	1.9	1.8	1.8	2.3	2.2	3.4	3.5	2.4	2.4
Sweden	0.7	1.8	–	1.0	0.5	0.6	0.9	1.3	0.4	1.2
United Kingdom	3.1	1.8	0.3	1.6	1.5	1.3	3.0	0.8	2.8	1.4
			3.4							
Benchmark	2.5	2.7	1.9	2.2	2.0	2.1	2.9	2.7	2.4	2.6
EU-12	2.0	1.7	1.8	1.2	1.5	1.1	2.8	2.1	2.0	1.5
EU-15	2.0	1.7	1.8	1.3	1.5	1.2	2.7	1.9	2.0	1.5

Sources: Eurostat and national central banks. The benchmark is calculated according to Article 1 of the Protocol on the convergence criteria referred to in Article 121 of the EU Treaty. RPIX figures are used for the United Kingdom's CPI. EU-12 covers the euro area. EU-12 and EU-15 CPI data are based on our own calculations.

Table 5.1b. Average Annual Inflation Rates in the EU-15 Countries as Measured by National CPIs and HICPs (2001–2004)

	2001		2002		2003		2004		2001–4		1997–2004	
Country	CPI	HICP	CPI	HICP	CPI	HICP	CPI	HICP	CPI	HICP	CPI	HICP
Austria	2.7	2.3	1.8	1.7	1.4	1.3	2.1	2.0	2.0	1.8	1.6	1.5
Belgium	2.5	2.4	1.6	1.6	1.6	1.5	2.1	1.9	2.0	1.9	1.8	1.7
Denmark	2.3	2.3	2.4	2.4	2.1	2.0	1.2	0.9	2.0	1.9	2.2	2.0
Finland	2.6	2.7	1.6	2.0	0.9	1.3	0.2	0.1	1.3	1.5	1.5	1.6
France	1.6	1.8	1.9	1.9	2.1	2.2	2.1	2.3	1.9	2.1	1.5	1.6
Germany	2.0	1.9	1.4	1.3	1.0	1.0	1.7	1.8	1.5	1.5	1.4	1.3
Greece	3.4	3.7	3.6	3.9	3.6	3.4	2.9	3.0	3.4	3.5	3.7	3.6
Ireland	4.9	4.0	4.7	4.7	3.5	4.0	2.2	2.3	3.8	3.8	3.3	3.3
Italy	2.8	2.3	2.5	2.6	2.7	2.8	2.2	2.3	2.5	2.5	2.3	2.3
Luxembourg	2.7	2.4	2.1	2.1	2.0	2.5	2.2	3.2	2.3	2.6	1.9	2.2
Netherlands	4.2	5.1	3.3	3.9	2.1	2.2	1.2	1.4	2.7	3.2	2.4	2.6
Portugal	4.4	4.4	3.6	3.7	3.3	3.3	2.4	2.5	3.4	3.5	3.0	2.9
Spain	3.6	2.8	3.5	3.6	3.0	3.1	3.0	3.1	3.3	3.2	2.8	2.8
Sweden	2.4	2.7	2.2	2.0	1.9	2.3	0.4	1.0	1.7	2.0	1.1	1.6
United Kingdom	1.8	1.2	1.7	1.3	2.9	1.4	3.0	1.3	2.3	1.3	2.5	1.3
Benchmark	3.3	3.1	3.0	3.0	2.6	2.7	2.1	2.2	3.0	2.9	2.8	3.0
EU-12	3.1	2.4	2.6	2.3	2.3	2.1	2.0	2.1	2.5	2.2	2.3	1.9
EU-15	2.9	2.2	2.5	2.1	2.3	2.0	1.9	2.0	2.4	2.1	2.2	1.8

Sources: Eurostat and national central banks. The benchmark is calculated according to Article 1 of the Protocol on the convergence criteria referred to in Article 121 of the EU Treaty. RPIX figures are used for the United Kingdom's CPI. EU-12 covers the euro area. EU-12 and EU-15 CPI data are based on our own calculations.

On the whole, the picture on the fulfilment of the nominal convergence criteria by the first-round EMU countries appears rather gloomy. One may wonder what would have been the actual extent of the euro area if these ad hoc alleviating interventions and loopholes had not occurred (or if they had occurred less systematically). Be that as it may, there is no reason to think of, or to allow for, the institution of (another) regional monetary union on the same grounds. Indeed, the enlargement of the euro area will not take place in the same vein. As a matter of fact, various calls within the EU–15 have made it clear that the EMU convergence process of the new EU member countries will be strictly monitored with respect to the convergence criteria for full EMU membership.[1] This limits, or even annihilates, the possibility of implementing accounting fudges, and raises a serious concern about the real chances for the new EU countries to enter the EMU by 2008–10, that is, after the two-year period enshrined in the EU Treaty before new EU member countries may adopt the euro has elapsed.

The Definition of Price Stability: Maastricht versus ECB

Assuming that the loopholes embedded in the Maastricht criteria are avoided, or at list limited to some extent, there are some other problems that have to be addressed by the EMU institutions. To illustrate one of these problems, let us focus here again on the criterion of price stability, which is also the primary (not to say unique) objective of the single monetary policy of the ECB.

In 2004, the three best-performing EU countries with respect to the Maastricht criterion on price stability were Denmark, Finland, and Sweden, with an unweighted average rate of inflation equal to 0.7 percent. This means a benchmark value of 2.2 percent for the relevant convergence criterion. In this respect, however, some remarks are in order. First, as Buiter and Grafe (2002) point out, one may wonder

---

[1] EU-15 denotes those countries that were members of the EU already before its May 2004 enlargement (Austria, Belgium, Denmark, Finland, France, Germany, Greece, Ireland, Italy, Luxembourg, the Netherlands, Portugal, Spain, Sweden, and the United Kingdom).

whether requiring inflation rates convergence before entering a single-currency area 'puts the cart before the horse', since monetary union is the means par excellence for reducing measured inflation-rate differentials among participating countries. Secondly, as the single monetary policy does not align national inflation rates absolutely, national differences remain in the HICP-measured inflation rates that may justify using the average inflation rate of the whole euro area — rather than the benchmark provided for in the EU Treaty — for assessing price stability in the ten new EU member countries as a precondition for them to adopt the euro. Thirdly, 'in the pursuit of price stability the ECB aims to maintain the inflation rate below, but close to, 2 percent over the medium term' (European Central Bank 2003a: 79). Indeed, the ECB does not consider the arithmetics of the price stability criterion enshrined in the EU Treaty, but aims at hitting the 2 percent targeted rate of inflation from below.

All these remarks point to the need to revise the price stability criterion for euro adoption, and to consider the average inflation rate of the whole euro area instead of referring to the three best-performing EU countries (Begg et al. 2003: 57; Kenen and Meade 2003: 4–5). Indeed, the European Commission made a first step in this direction in its *Convergence Report 2000*, when, in assessing the price stability performance of Greece, it acknowledged that '[it] seems desirable that the assessment of "a high degree of price stability" should also take into consideration the price stability performance of the euro area as well as the ECB's definition of price stability. This is all the more so since the euro and the euro area economy constitute the economically relevant benchmarks to which countries aiming to join the euro should orient their convergence efforts' (European Commission 2000: 53).

In April 2004, the month before the last EU enlargement took place, the euro-area average rate of inflation was 2.0 percent (Eurostat 2004). If this rate were used as the benchmark for the price stability criterion on which adoption of the euro is assessed, a country might abandon its currency if it has an inflation rate, as measured by the HICP, equal to or lower than 3.5 percent. In that same month, by contrast, the average inflation rate of the three best-performing EU countries (Austria,

Finland, and the Netherlands) was 0.9 percent: this means that the relevant convergence criterion would prevent a country from adopting the euro if it has a rate of inflation higher than 2.4 percent. This rate, in fact, is close to the price stability definition of the ECB, and is even lower than the year-to-year inflation rates that three euro-area member countries reported in April 2004 (namely, Greece, Luxembourg, and Spain). At the time of writing, the three best-performing EU countries in respect of the EMU price stability criterion are Cyprus, Finland, and Sweden, whose average rate of inflation is 1.0 percent. This means a benchmark value for fulfilling the price stability criterion equal to 2.5 percent. In fact, no less than one third of the present EMU countries are currently above this value, the highest being the inflation rate in Greece (3.9 percent in July 2005 on a year-to-year basis).

Some Further Problems for the Enlargement of the Euro Area

Consider first the situation in the ten new members of the EU (EU–10) with respect to nominal macroeconomic convergence according to the Maastricht criteria (Table 5.2a and Table 5.2b).

Over the last five years (2000–4), none of the ten new EU countries satisfied all EMU criteria, although a number of countries satisfied at least one criterion, and often more than that. The criteria most often satisfied concern the general government position in respect of GDP. Several EU–10 countries have a deficit-to-GDP ratio below the 3 percent ceiling required by the EU Treaty, and in most of these countries public debt is considerably lower than the 60 percent benchmark with respect to GDP. Indeed, in a number of would-be EMU countries the data on general government debt and deficits over the period 2000–4 are closer to the Maastricht thresholds than they were for a number of today's euro-area member countries in the years preceding their 1997 examination. Nevertheless, we should not forget that most EU–10 countries still need to modernize and develop their infrastructure to achieve full transition to a market-based economy. This is bound to require very high levels of public investment in these countries, which probably increase their public deficits and debt in the years to come.

Table 5.2a. Nominal Convergence in the EU-10 Countries (2000–2004)

Country	2000			2001			2002			2003			2004		
	1	2	3	1	2	3	1	2	3	1	2	3	1	2	3
Cyprus	4.9	–2.4	61.6	2.0	–2.3	61.9	2.8	–4.5	65.2	4.0	–6.3	69.8	1.9	–4.1	72.0
Czech Republic	3.9	–3.7	18.2	4.5	–5.9	26.3	1.4	–6.8	29.8	–0.1	–12.5	36.8	2.6	–3.0	36.8
Estonia	3.9	–0.6	4.7	5.6	0.3	4.7	3.6	1.5	5.8	1.4	2.6	6.0	3.0	1.7	5.0
Hungary	10.0	–3.0	55.4	9.1	–3.5	52.2	5.2	–8.5	55.5	4.7	–6.5	57.4	6.8	–5.4	57.4
Latvia	2.6	–2.8	12.9	2.5	–2.1	15.0	2.0	–2.3	14.2	2.9	–1.2	14.6	6.2	–1.0	14.7
Lithuania	0.9	–2.5	23.8	1.3	–2.0	22.9	0.4	–1.4	22.4	–1.1	–1.2	21.4	1.1	–1.4	19.6
Malta	3.0	–6.2	56.4	2.5	–6.6	63.5	2.6	–5.7	63.3	1.9	–10.4	72.8	2.7	–5.1	75.9
Poland	10.1	–0.7	36.8	5.3	–3.7	36.7	1.9	–3.3	41.2	0.7	–4.8	45.3	3.6	–3.9	43.6
Slovak Republic	12.2	–12.3	49.9	7.2	–6.6	49.2	3.5	–7.8	43.7	8.5	–3.8	43.1	7.4	–3.1	42.5
Slovenia	8.9	–3.5	27.4	8.6	–3.9	28.4	7.5	–2.7	29.8	5.7	–2.7	29.4	3.6	–2.1	29.8
Minimum	0.9	–12.3	4.7	1.3	–6.6	4.7	0.4	–8.5	5.8	–1.1	–12.5	6.0	1.1	–5.4	5.0
Average	6.0	–3.8	34.7	4.9	–3.6	36.1	3.1	–4.2	37.1	2.9	–4.7	39.7	3.9	–2.7	39.7
Maximum	12.2	–0.6	61.6	9.1	0.3	63.5	7.5	1.5	65.2	8.5	2.6	72.8	7.4	1.7	75.9

Sources: Eurostat and OECD. Criteria: (1) year-to-year variation of the HICP, (2) general government budget deficit (–) or surplus (+) as a % of GDP, (3) general government debt as a % of GDP.

Table 5.2b. Nominal Interest Rates in the EU-10 Countries (2000–2004, yearly averages)

Country	2000			2001			2002			2003			2004		
	1	2	3	1	2	3	1	2	3	1	2	3	1	2	3
Cyprus	7.6	6.4	6.1	7.7	5.9	5.2	5.4	4.4	3.5	4.7	3.9	3.5	6.1	4.7	4.2
Czech Republic	6.9	5.4	5.3	6.3	5.2	5.0	4.9	3.5	3.6	4.1	2.3	2.3	n/a	2.4	2.2
Estonia	n/a	5.7	4.6	n/a	5.3	3.9	n/a	3.9	3.0	n/a	2.9	2.3	n/a	2.5	2.0
Hungary	8.6	11.4	11.1	7.9	10.9	10.9	7.1	9.2	8.9	6.8	8.5	8.3	8.2	11.5	11.5
Latvia	n/a	5.4	3.4	7.6	6.9	5.8	5.4	4.4	3.4	4.9	3.8	3.2	4.9	4.2	3.7
Lithuania	n/a	8.6	4.8	8.2	5.9	4.1	6.0	3.7	2.6	5.2	2.8	2.1	4.4	2.7	1.9
Malta	5.8	4.9	4.7	6.1	4.9	4.4	5.7	4.0	3.9	5.0	3.3	3.3	4.7	2.9	2.9
Poland	11.8	18.8	17.6	10.7	16.1	17.1	7.3	9.0	9.5	5.8	5.7	5.7	6.9	6.2	5.7
Slovak Republic	8.3	8.6	8.0	8.1	7.8	7.4	6.9	7.8	7.2	5.0	6.2	6.0	5.0	4.7	4.5
Slovenia	n/a	10.9	n/a	n/a	10.9	n/a	8.7	8.0	4.9	6.4	6.8	5.5	n/a	4.7	4.4
Minimum	5.8	4.9	3.4	6.1	4.9	3.9	4.9	3.5	2.6	4.1	2.3	2.1	4.4	2.4	1.9
Average	8.2	8.6	7.3	7.8	8.0	7.1	6.4	5.8	5.0	5.3	4.6	4.2	5.7	4.7	4.3
Maximum	11.8	18.8	17.6	10.7	16.1	17.1	7.3	9.2	9.5	6.8	8.5	8.3	8.2	11.5	11.5

Source: Eurostat. (1) long-term interest rates (government bond with maturities of close to ten years), (2) 3-month interest rates (EURIBOR), (3) day-to-day money market interest rates. Unweighted averages.

As a result, the assessment of the respect of the public finance criteria (and in particular the deficit-to-GDP ratio) might shift for some EU–10 countries. Further, their enormous public investment needs could also lead to some price increases in the short run, owing to an upward pressure on real interest rates induced by an increased public sector borrowing requirement. This would indeed slow down the convergence path to price stability in some of the EU–10 countries, also on account of the transition process that many would-be EMU countries are still undergoing. Finally, although the data on long-term nominal rates of interest in the EU–10 countries are not yet fully comparable with those of present EMU countries, mainly because long-term capital markets are still insufficiently developed in the former group of countries, we can suppose that a certain degree of interest rate convergence has already taken place between the two groups of EU countries. This trend may be ascribed to the growing importance of the new EU countries' public sector debt traded in euro markets, with respect to debt securities issued in their local currencies. As the ECB indicates in its December 2004 survey of bond markets, in fact, government securities traded in euro markets have become an interesting option for new EU countries like Lithuania (62 percent of public debt issues in 2003), Slovenia (53 percent), Estonia (47 percent), and Latvia (40 percent), that is, those EU–10 countries that are more converging in the sense of the EU Treaty (see European Central Bank 2004).

Now, when one considers real economic convergence of the new EU countries with respect to the EMU, the picture looks worse than the scenario depicted by the state of nominal convergence (Table 5.3).

If we measure economic performance in terms of per capita GDP, only Cyprus and Slovenia have reached a degree of prosperity matching or slightly exceeding that of the economically weakest EMU member countries (Greece and Portugal). In 2004, in the former two countries per capita GDP was, respectively, 81.2 percent and 77.9 percent of the EU average when measured at PPP exchange rates, but these figures might even be lower when current exchange rates are taken into account. The majority of the new EU countries are at any rate far below this level, with approximately two thirds of the EU average GDP per head.[2] As many authors explain, this income gap is the result of an economic development differential between present and prospective EMU member countries (Berger 2002, European Central Bank 2003b, and Angeloni et al. 2005). For instance, in the new EU countries agricultural employment is on average three times larger than in current EMU countries (13.2 percent and 4.4 percent respectively in 2004), Poland with 18.0 percent having the highest rate of agricultural employment with respect to total employment (Eurostat 2005a). As Angeloni et al. (2005: 12) point out, 'a higher level of development tends to be associated with a smaller share of agriculture in aggregate output and a larger share of services'. Indeed, agriculture accounts for a significantly larger share in the EU–10, and services represent a much smaller share, than in the euro area. Another clear sign of the big differential in economic development between the EMU and the EU–10 is the higher share of food and non-alcoholic drinks in household expenditure as well as the lower level of infrastructure in the latter group of countries than in the EMU (Eurostat 2003). Unemployment rates, overall as well as for the young (aged 25 or less), are also a sign of the difficult situation experienced today by several new EU member countries. In 2004, the measured unemployment rate in the EU–10 countries was between 5.0 percent (Cyprus) and 18.8 percent (Poland): five new EU countries have unemployment rates below or just around the EU average rate (9.0 percent), while the other five new EU countries are largely above this rate, approaching the double in Poland and the Slovak Republic. The unemployment figures are even more worrying for the under–25s, because in some of the EU–10 countries one young out of five is unemployed (one young out of three in Poland and in the Slovak Republic).

By contrast, if we consider the growth rate of real GDP, many new EU countries have on average (2000–4) a better record than euro-area

---

[2] The poorest would-be EMU countries are Estonia, Latvia, Lithuania, and Poland, whose level of per capita GDP is considerably lower than the EU average and, in some cases, does not even reach half of that level.

member countries: in the former group of countries the growth rates of GDP at constant prices are higher than in the latter group by nearly 2 percentage points on average. We must not overlook the fact, however, that GDP figures are still very tiny in a number of highly-populated EU–10 countries (in Poland, for instance). In addition, their economic structure is not yet similar to that of present EMU countries, and in a number of areas (like competition policies, corporate governance, financial law, and banking supervision) the EU–10 countries still lack appropriate institutions. In this respect, as the European Central Bank (2002: 53–4) emphasizes, '[a]lthough different income levels as well as different economic structures can, in principle, be compatible with eventual participation in Monetary Union, advancing real macroeconomic convergence with the euro area — in terms of both per capita income levels and economic structures — is desirable. This will foster economic cohesion within EMU, promote integration among Member States, and help in reducing the risks and effects of asymmetric shocks' (see also Angeloni et al. 2005).

Nominal Convergence at the Expense of Real Divergence?

One cannot rule out that, by fudging and/or implementing drastic economic policies that call for enormous sacrifices (largely in terms of employment and output losses) for their population over the next years, some would-be EMU countries could be able to converge in nominal terms when their EMU entry test will be carried out. Even these nominally converging countries, however, will probably still diverge in real as well as structural terms from the EMU member countries, which could make their participation in the euro area problematic. For instance, those new EU countries that can meet all criteria for full EMU membership may still experience a rapid structural change of their economy as a result of their ongoing transition to a market-based system. This would make it difficult to assess the level at which their exchange rates are to be irrevocably fixed against the euro. This level, in fact, might soon prove to be inadequate. 'Also, a newcomer with an insufficient degree of structural convergence and economic and financial integration with the EU will be more likely to suffer asymmetric shocks with respect to the EMU area' (Temprano–Arroyo and Feldman 1998: 23). In fact, a country's premature accession to the single-currency area that was not supported by real as well as nominal macroeconomic convergence may pose substantial risks to all member countries, with the result of provoking tensions in economic policy making. As Schwartz (2001: 16) points out, '[r]elatively less-well-off members stand to lose a share of social and regional transfers to the new poorer countries. Farmers of the present member countries will have to sacrifice some of their subsidies from the Common Agricultural Policy to extend subsidies to farmers of the new member countries. Inflation may seem a cure-all for these tensions. Will the ECB stand firm?'

To be sure, if within the (enlarged) euro area real convergence is insufficient, it will be extremely difficult for the single monetary policy to do justice, at the same time, to the needs of both present and prospective EMU member countries. The different stages in economic development reached by these two groups of countries will indeed bring about tensions in monetary policy making at the ECB. Hence, the 'one-size-fits-all' interest rate policy oriented towards the needs of the euro area as a whole might be hampered on account of extensive country heterogeneity. Further, as has already been observed for present euro-area countries (Suardi 2001), with heterogeneous cross-country responses the single monetary policy itself could induce idiosyncratic business cycles across the EMU. As a result, the income gap between the two groups of EMU countries (that is, present and prospective euro-area member countries) might increase, slowing down the speed of the catching-up process rather than doing the opposite. Also, if the ECB felt obliged to intervene in an attempt to counteract a major shock in one euro-area country, it might in fact increase cyclical divergence between its members, and thus hinder the synchronization of the business cycle across the EMU. Indeed, 'most NMS [new EU member countries] are still significantly diverse as to the size and nature of the economic shocks to their business cycles. While for some countries the cycles and the underlying shocks seem to be strongly correlated with the euro area, in many other cases no stable co-movements can be detected. In addition, with few exceptions, most NMS exhibit a generally low speed of adjustment to shocks' (Angeloni et al. 2005: 18).

In order for would-be EMU countries to enter the single-currency area without creating unbearable economic (policy) disturbances within it, therefore, these countries have to make huge efforts during their 'pre-ins' period, to achieve a high degree of sustainable macroeconomic convergence, both as defined in Article 121 of the EU Treaty and with respect to real magnitudes. Moreover, these efforts are to be provided also after joining the EMU, as required by the SGP under the cover of so-called stability programmes. Let us consider therefore the likely scenarios for would-be EMU countries on their road to euro-area membership, before turning to the risks of financial instability with respect to the exchange rate arrangement at the disposal of these ('pre-ins') countries.

The first scenario is that a number of would-be EMU countries decide to make those efforts required to converge nominally, and succeed, in the reference year when the EU assesses their performance in relation to the criteria for full EMU membership. In this case, these new EU countries may accept, and be able, to undergo a process of sharp structural adjustment of their transition economies within the next few years, in order to meet the convergence criteria in (say) 2008 — assuming this is the reference year for the assessment of economic convergence in line with the EU Treaty. The EMU entry test having been passed in (say) 2008, these countries will still have to prove, and to make sure, that they can endure nominal as well as real convergence with the EMU economy — by then possibly embracing no less than 20 countries — if they want to avert tensions in monetary and economic policy making. This might prove to be much more difficult than the entry test, as the latter is merely based on a year or two of converging efforts and results. In fact, enduring nominal convergence may require from would-be EMU countries an abrupt reduction of government expenditures — with all the ensuing negative effects on infrastructures and institutions, for instance the ageing-related pension schemes — as well as a widespread restructuring of their corporate sector — with dramatic consequences on local labour markets, which in some new EU countries have already been suffering from a severe increase in unemployment rates during recent years (see Table 5.3). Alternatively, new EU countries may content themselves to have entered the euro area in the year when they converged nominally, and then, once in this area, begin to care more about their real and structural reforms, probably at the expense of nominal convergence. Yet, 'the Eurosystem has emphasised that advancing real convergence should be done in parallel with — and not at the expense of — nominal convergence, understood as the gradual lowering of inflation rates towards levels compatible with price stability' (European Central Bank 2002: 54). In fact, for the present EMU countries the process of real convergence has been rather slow before as well as after their entry in the single-currency area (see Figure 5.1). This conclusion might apply to the new EU countries as well. It would mean that the EMU process of nominal convergence can be undertaken with some success only at the expense of accepting (an increasing degree of) real divergence among the countries participating to the EMU.

The second scenario for prospective EMU countries, therefore, is that these countries are neither willing nor able to undertake the convergence process required by the EU Treaty to join the single-currency area in this decade or even in the next. To be sure, the EU-10 countries aim first and foremost at catching up the income gap between them and the EMU, in order to improve the well-being of their population through a higher per capita GDP. Now, as the European Central Bank (2002: 54) acknowledges, '[t]he sheer size of the income gap suggests that even with the wider growth differentials, the process of convergence in income levels may extend well beyond the date of EU accession or euro area membership'. If so, then what? The official position of the European Commission is inflexible: countries not fulfilling the criteria for full EMU membership will remain outside the euro area with the status of EMU member countries with a derogation ('pre-ins'), but will also be required to submit convergence programmes on a regular basis. So, in the very long run, when these countries are converging in the sense of the EU Treaty, they will become part of the single-currency area too, although this process may take decades to complete and may thus lose much of its significance for the further construction of Europe.

Table 5.3. Real Convergence in the EU-10 Countries (2000–2004)

Country	2000			2001			2002			2003			2004		
	1	2	3	1	2	3	1	2	3	1	2	3	1	2	3
Cyprus	85.5	5.0	5.2	88.5	4.1	4.4	83.0	2.1	3.9	81.6	2.0	4.5	81.2	3.8	5.0
Czech Republic	64.3	3.9	8.7	65.6	2.6	8.0	67.2	1.5	7.3	68.4	3.2	7.8	70.0	4.4	8.3
Estonia	43.2	7.9	12.5	44.4	6.5	11.8	46.3	7.2	9.5	48.7	6.7	10.2	50.7	7.8	9.2
Hungary	53.1	5.2	6.3	56.0	3.8	5.6	58.2	3.5	5.6	59.6	2.9	5.8	60.9	4.2	5.9
Latvia	35.2	6.9	13.7	37.1	8.0	12.9	38.7	6.4	12.6	40.7	7.5	10.4	43.2	8.5	9.8
Lithuania	38.2	3.9	16.4	40.4	6.4	16.4	42.1	6.8	13.5	45.5	9.7	12.7	47.8	6.7	10.8
Malta	77.1	6.4	6.8	72.7	–0.8	7.7	72.7	1.0	7.7	72.4	–1.9	8.0	71.2	1.0	7.3
Poland	45.9	4.0	16.4	45.5	1.0	18.5	45.4	1.4	19.8	45.6	3.8	19.2	46.7	5.3	18.8
Slovak Republic	47.5	2.0	18.7	48.5	3.8	19.4	51.1	4.6	18.7	52.0	4.5	17.5	52.1	5.5	18.0
Slovenia	72.7	3.9	6.6	74.1	2.7	5.8	74.8	3.3	6.1	76.2	2.5	6.5	77.9	4.6	6.0
Minimum	35.2	2.0	5.2	37.1	–0.4	4.4	38.7	1.0	3.9	40.7	–1.9	4.5	43.2	1.0	5.0
Average	56.3	4.9	11.1	57.3	3.9	11.1	58.0	3.8	10.5	59.1	4.1	10.3	60.2	5.2	9.9
Maximum	85.5	7.9	18.7	88.5	8.0	19.4	83.0	7.2	19.8	81.6	9.7	19.2	81.2	8.5	18.8

Sources: Eurostat and OECD. Real variables considered: (1) index of per capita GDP in PPS (EU-25 = 100), (2) real GDP growth rate, (3) unemployment rate.

It is in this connection that the choice of the exchange rate regime to help prospective EMU countries prevent financial instability in the presence of fully liberalized capital flows becomes relevant on their road to monetary integration with the euro area. Let us address this issue in the remainder of this chapter.

The ERM II and the Risks of Financial Instability

It cannot be denied that currency crises are a major source of disruption for the new EU countries on their road towards full EMU membership. In fact, exchange rate volatility (as measured by the standard deviation in the nominal exchange rate) tends to reduce trade growth and decreases the level of trade considerably (see Anderton and Skudelny 2001). The chances for the new EU countries to bridge the income gap with respect to the euro area are therefore smaller in case of exchange rate volatility, since in this case the existing commercial ties with the foreign sector cannot contribute to output growth and economic development as they should in order to catch up with present EMU countries. Further, as pointed out in the literature integrating analyses of banking and currency crises — the so-called 'twin crises' — there are important complementarities between bank insolvency and currency instability, so much so that causation may run in either direction (see Sbracia and Zaghini 2001). Indeed, the current reforms of domestic settlement systems in transition economies to implement a real-time gross settlement (RTGS) protocol for large-value transactions are an important step to reduce settlement and systemic risks within them and to limit output losses during a banking crisis (see Bank for International Settlements 2000, 2001, and Banca d'Italia 2002). This step in turn helps reduce the risks of a financial crisis that could eventually lead to a currency depreciation, or turmoil, such as the Mexican, Asian, and Russian crises of the second half of the 1990s and the more recent Argentinean crisis.

Now, being predominantly small open economies with strong commercial and financial ties with the euro area (in respect also of the currency denomination of the financial instruments used in a framework where capital account transactions have largely been liberalized), the EU-10 countries have a strong interest in stabilizing the exchange rates of their currencies against the euro. For these countries 'the choice of the exchange rate strategy is key, as it provides the framework within which monetary policy can continue to be geared towards price stability, while real convergence may proceed without being hampered by undue exchange rate movements' (European Central Bank 2003b: 120).

The new EU countries are currently debating over the most appropriate exchange rate arrangement in order for them to integrate eventually into the euro area, elaborating on the most convenient timing of entry in the ERM II, within which they have to remain for at least two years before they may adopt the euro — as far as the two-year qualifying period is applied strictly (Table 5.4).[3]

The ERM II is meant to help its member countries achieve exchange rate stability and foster macroeconomic convergence with the euro-area countries. In fact, most new EU countries 'regard ERM II as an institutional requirement for the adoption of the euro that cannot be avoided, but whose appropriateness as an exchange rate policy framework is questionable' (Backé and Thimann 2004: 6). Generally speaking, these countries consider that participation in the ERM II offers at best little value-added and is subject to risks of speculative attacks that can be disruptive to their economy as well as to their convergence efforts. They would cite in support of this argument the 1992–3 ERM-I crisis, which began with an attack on the Italian lira and quickly affected other EMS currencies such as the British pound and the French franc.

[3] Baldwin et al. (2000) note that this qualifying period for euro adoption may be skipped if the exchange rate criterion is interpreted loosely (as was done for Finland, Italy, and Greece; see Buiter and Grafe, 2002: 28–30) and if, by contrast with present euro-area countries, there is no changeover period.

Table 5.4. Exchange Rate Regimes, and Plans for ERM-II Entry and Euro Adoption by the EU-10 Countries

Country	Exchange rate regime (as of September 2005)	Entry into the ERM II	Planned adoption of the euro
Cyprus	ERM-II member	May 2005	as soon as possible after ERM-II entry
Czech Republic	managed float	not announced	2010
Estonia	ERM-II member	June 2004	2007
Hungary	peg to the euro with a ±15% band	not announced	2010
Latvia	ERM-II member	May 2005	2008
Lithuania	ERM-II member	June 2004	2007
Malta	ERM-II member	May 2005	as soon as economic convergence permits
Poland	free float	not announced	2008–2009
Slovak Republic	managed float	2006	2009
Slovenia	ERM-II member	June 2004	2007

Source: European Central Bank.

More recently, Hungary — which 'shadows' the ERM II by pegging the forint to the euro within a horizontal fluctuation band (±15 percent around central parity), but which also has an inflation target (between 3 and 5 percent by end-2005) — faced a policy dilemma between its inflation targeting strategy and its exchange rate strategy, owing to intense currency speculation and volatile capital flows during much of 2003–4, which showed the inconsistency between its exchange rate target and its inflation target. Indeed, this dilemma poses a real problem, since productivity in the tradable-goods sector has been growing faster in Central European countries like Hungary than in the EU-15, putting an upward pressure on the Hungarian price level via an increase in money wages (the Balassa–Samuelson effect).[4] A similar problem stems also from the obligation for the EMU member countries with a derogation (the so-called 'pre-ins') to satisfy both the convergence criterion on price stability and that on exchange rate stability before joining the euro area (Kenen and Meade 2003, and Eichengreen 2005).

In fact, participation of a 'pre-ins' country in the ERM II cannot be deemed enough to avoid exchange rate fluctuation and speculation. As pointed out by Wagner (2001: 14), '[s]ticking to the ERM-II may prove to be too costly for countries that are directly hit by a speculative attack as well as for neighbour countries hit by negative spillovers'. In particular, participation in the ERM II may expose a country to the risk of exchange rate crises that could be very damaging for its economy and further delay its adoption of the euro (Kenen and Meade 2003: 2). This is so much so that the ECB has no legal obligation to intervene in order to keep an ERM-II participating currency within the so-called normal fluctuation band, if this intervention might conflict with the objective of maintaining price stability in the euro area.[5] This could pose problems

---

[4] The Balassa–Samuelson effect reflects the rise in the relative price of non-tradable goods owing to lower productivity growth in this sector compared to that in the tradable-goods sector.

[5] Under the ERM I the obligation to stabilize exchange rates was borne jointly by the strong and weak currency member countries. Under the ERM II, by contrast, this obligation resides primarily with the government of the country concerned: the ECB has no legal obligation to intervene. This puts all the risks to ERM-II participating countries,

for those new EU member countries that participate in the ERM II: market speculators will be tracking the progress made by these countries in meeting the convergence criteria to adopt the euro. If they do not see satisfactory progress in this respect, they will bet against convergence by selling ERM-II currencies. Further, the Balassa–Samuelson effect and free capital inflows and outflows from the new EU countries are likely to affect the exchange rate stability of their currencies, and to increase tensions in the ERM II. As a matter of fact, the large current account deficits as a percentage of GDP that several new EU countries experience — which have been financed by large net capital inflows (mainly in the form of foreign direct investment) — point to the need of enough exchange rate flexibility. This is so much so that these countries have not yet observed comparable inflows of portfolio investment, which tend to be more volatile. Indeed, 'the volatility of portfolio flows and of other short-term capital flows has been a major cause of the currency and financial crises that have beset many emerging-market countries in recent years, and it is widely agreed that insufficient exchange rate flexibility has been a root cause of their vulnerability to that volatility' (Kenen and Meade 2003: 9).

As the new EU countries dismantle the few remaining restrictions on capital flows, as required by the *acquis communautaire*, they are very likely to attract large amounts of portfolio investment, especially if they (have to) adopt an exchange rate regime that stimulates costless one-way bets by market speculators. In fact, as Begg et al. (2003: 6–7) point out in their review of financial crises in the 1990s, the inception as well as the virulence of the 1992–3 ERM-I crisis was due to the narrow (±2.25 percent) fluctuation band combined with the lifting of capital controls and the related increase in the size and volatility of capital flows as a result of the 1986 European Single Act. In their own words, '[t]he

---

which have the onus of imposing the hardships required to have discipline and respect the ERM-II fluctuation margins. See Article 3.1 of the 'Agreement of 1 September 1998 between the European Central Bank and the national central banks of the Member States outside the euro area laying down the operating procedures for an exchange rate mechanism in stage three of economic and monetary union', *Official Journal of the European Communities*, C 345, 13.11.1998, pp. 6–12.

combination of full capital mobility and a requirement to participate in ERM-II may entail an interim period in which accession countries face enhanced vulnerability to capital flows before the eventual safety of monetary union is available' (Begg et al. 2003: vii). The challenge for the new member countries of the EU is thus to come to grips with the likelihood of large speculative capital inflows under the ERM-II regime, particularly in the period preceding their changeover to the European single currency.

All in all, the exchange rate question is still open and asks what kind of arrangement should the new EU countries implement if they really want to enter the EMU without increasing (the risks of) financial instability and breakdown. The answer might consist in a case-by-case assessment in light of both economic conditions and path of reform undertaken by each of the EU-10 countries. In fact, these countries need an exchange rate agreement that helps them accelerate the catching-up process in respect of the EU-15, both in nominal and real terms. 'On the one hand, a high degree of exchange rate flexibility may reduce the burden on policy-makers, freeing up room for manoeuvre that can be used to attain domestic policy targets. On the other hand, excessive exchange rate volatility may be a hindrance to the convergence process itself, by undermining the effort to stabilise market expectations. Striking the correct balance can be particularly complex' (Angeloni et al. 2005: 29).

Conclusion

This chapter has investigated a number of shortcomings of the monetary union process undertaken by present euro-area countries, as well as some open issues for the EMU, in order to point out what lessons we can learn for the institution of a single-currency area in some other parts of the world. These lessons can indeed be instructive for the setting up of other regional monetary unions around the world, particularly in Asia, which is still a very heterogeneous continent (more than Europe) as considered from an economic point of view.

This chapter has shown that the operationalization of European monetary union suffers from a number of pitfalls in both the definition and application of the relevant criteria, which allow for a considerable room for manoeuvre and accounting fiddles. Indeed, as recently pointed out by Eichengreen (2005), among the institutional requirements for monetary union one should distinguish preconditions from 'pseudo preconditions', the latter being either superfluous or counterproductive. Among the pseudo preconditions, Eichengreen (2005) includes nominal convergence criteria, public deficit ceilings, and sanctions and fines for those countries trespassing them. This chapter also pointed out that for the new EU countries the nominal criteria for full EMU membership may not be easy to satisfy, if these criteria are applied rigorously over time. This is so much so that the process of real convergence cannot be neglected at all, and should in fact go ahead together with the respect of the nominal convergence criteria. In this chapter we also pointed out that the EMU criteria may lead to pitfalls and dangers if the EU-10 countries try to fudge them by taking advantage of some 'measurement deficits' enshrined in EU legislation.

Indeed, the most worrying danger of applying the monetary union strategy laid down in Maastricht to the EU-10 countries would consist in output and employment losses for these countries — before as well as after their full integration in the euro area — if would-be EMU countries raise their policy rates of interest to abide by the Maastricht nominal convergence requirements (particularly as regards inflation rates and public deficits and debt) at the expense of employment and output growth. In fact, increasing unemployment in these countries would run counter to the interests of the EU as a whole, because it would imply more intra-EU transfers to pay for social security and reduce regional unemployment disparities across the euro area. Following the enlargement of this area, the economies of the EU-10 countries would surely have to bear part of these costs in order for them to integrate Euroland. This burden, however, ought to be avoided if the process of nominal as well as real macroeconomic convergence is to have any meaning at all, and in order not to completely jeopardize the single interest rate policy of the ECB when the euro area is eventually enlarged to include some, if not all, prospective EMU countries among the EU-10.

To be sure, among the new EU countries there are different levels of regional development, which makes the conduct of common macroeconomic policies (not only monetary policy) a very difficult and challenging task.

This last conclusion is particularly noteworthy for Asia, and even more so for South-East Asia, which 'features developed; "dynamic Asian economies"; middle-income developing countries; and least-developed countries' (Jones and Plummer 2004: 831). As Jones and Plummer (2004) point out, the coefficient of variation on income levels within the Association of South-East Asian Nations (ASEAN)[6] is higher than in the EU. Figures are farther apart if we consider all the geographic and institutional groupings that exist in Asia (Asian Development Bank, 2005). If we just consider 'emerging Asia' — comprising China, Hong Kong, India, Indonesia, Malaysia, Philippines, Singapore, South Korea, Taiwan, and Thailand — three very different groups of economies can be readily identified: Hong Kong and Singapore, with per capita incomes exceeding 20,000 US dollars in 2004, South Korea and Taiwan, with per capita incomes around 12,000 US dollars in 2004, and the remaining countries, with per capita incomes of 4,000 US dollars or less in the same year (among which India still has the lowest per capita income level despite its rapid economic growth in recent years).[7]

In fact, a monetary union of Asian countries, notably within the ASEAN, is neither possible nor advisable along the same path that led to the European single currency: political as well as economic divergences — more intensive in South-East Asia than within the European Union — point to the necessity to search for alternative strategies for Asian monetary integration. In particular, financial liberalization and international capital mobility in emerging market economies might prove to be incompatible with exchange rate stability, not to say with exchange rate fixity and adoption of a single currency.

---

[6] The ASEAN comprises Brunei Darussalam, Cambodia, Indonesia, Lao People's Democratic Republic, Malaysia, Myanmar, Philippines, Singapore, Thailand, and Vietnam.

[7] Data are from the World Bank (Development Indicators) and the ADB (Key Indicators).

References

Anderton, R., and Skudelny, F., 2001. Exchange rate volatility and euro area imports. *European Central Bank Working Paper*, no. 64.

Angeloni, I., Flad, M., and Mongelli, F.P., 2005. Economic and monetary integration of the new member states: helping to chart the route. *European Central Bank Occasional Paper*, no. 36.

Angresano, J., 2004. European Union integration lessons for ASEAN+3: the importance of contextual specificity. *Journal of Asian Economics* 14(6), 909–926.

Asian Development Bank, 2005. *Asian Development Outlook 2005: Promoting Competition for Long-Term Development*. Manila, Asian Development Bank.

Backé, P., and Thimann, C., 2004 (Eds.). The acceding countries' strategies towards ERM II and the adoption of the euro: an analytical review. *European Central Bank Occasional Paper*, no. 10.

Baldwin, R., Berglöf, E., Giavazzi, F., and Widgrén, M., 2000. EU reforms for tomorrow's Europe. *Centre for Economic Policy Research Discussion Paper*, no. 2623.

Banca d'Italia, 2002. *The Banking and Financial Sector in the Countries of South-Eastern Europe*. Rome, Banca d'Italia.

Bank for International Settlements, 2000. *Clearing and Settlement Arrangements for Retail Payments in Selected Countries*. Basle, Bank for International Settlements.

Bank for International Settlements, 2001. *Recommendations for Securities Settlement Systems*. Basle, Bank for International Settlements.

Bayoumi, T., Eichengreen, B., and Mauro, P., 2000. On regional monetary arrangements for ASEAN. *Journal of the Japanese and International Economies* 14(2), 121–148.

Begg, D., Eichengreen, B., Halpern, L., von Hagen, J., and Wyplosz, C., 2003. Sustainable regimes of capital movements in accession countries. *Centre for Economic Policy Research Policy Paper*, no. 10.

Berger, H., 2002. The ECB and euro-area enlargement. *International Monetary Fund Working Paper*, no. 02/175.

Buiter, W., and Grafe, C., 2002. Anchor, float or abandon ship: exchange rate regimes for the accession countries. *Banca Nazionale del Lavoro Quarterly Review* 56(221), 1–32.

Chung, A.S., 1999. Is the formation of Asian Monetary Union feasible? Hong Kong University, unpublished.

Dafflon, B., and Rossi, S., 1999. Public accounting fudges towards EMU: a first empirical survey and some public choice considerations. *Public Choice* 101(1–2), 59–84.

Dawson, T.C., 2002. The IMF's role in Asia: part of the problem or part of the solution? Paper prepared for remarks at the Institute of Policy Studies and Singapore Management University Forum, Singapore, 10 July. Available at http://www.imf.org/external/np/speeches/2002/071002.htm.

Diewert, E., 2002. Harmonized indexes of consumer prices: their conceptual foundations. *European Central Bank Working Paper*, no. 130.

ECOFIN, 2005. Improving the implementation of the Stability and Growth Pact. Report to the European Council, 22-23 March 2005. Brussels, 21 March.

Eichengreen, B., 2005. Real and pseudo preconditions for an Asian Monetary Union, in: Asian Development Bank (Ed.), *Asian Economic Cooperation and Integration: Progress, Prospects, and Challenges*. Manila, Asian Development Bank, 149–190.

Eichengreen, B., and Bayoumi, T., 1999. Is Asia an optimum currency area? Can it become one? Regional, global, and historical perspectives on Asian monetary relations, in: Collignon, S., Pisani-Ferry, J., and Park, Y.-C. (Eds.), *Exchange Rate Policies in Emerging Asian Countries*. London, Routledge, 347–366.

European Central Bank, 2002. The Eurosystem's dialogue with EU accession countries. *Monthly Bulletin* 4(7), 51–63.

European Central Bank, 2003a. The outcome of the ECB's evaluation of its monetary policy strategy. *Monthly Bulletin* 5(6), 79–92.

European Central Bank, 2003b. *Annual Report 2002*. Frankfurt, European Central Bank.

European Central Bank, 2004. *The Euro Bond Market Study, December 2004*. Frankfurt, European Central Bank.

European Central Bank, 2005. The reform of the Stability and Growth Pact. *Monthly Bulletin* 7(8), 59–73.

European Commission, 1999. *Economic and Monetary Union: Compilation of Community Legislation*. Luxembourg, Office for Official Publications of the European Communities.

European Commission, 2000. *Convergence Report 2000*. Brussels, European Commission, COM(2000) 277 final.

European Commission, 2003. Opinion on a Code of best practice on the compilation and reporting of data in the context of the Excessive Deficit Procedure. Council of the European Union, 6064/03.

European Commission and Eurostat, 2001. *Compendium of HICP Reference Documents*. Luxembourg, Office for Official Publications of the European Communities.

Eurostat, 1996. *European System of Accounts, ESA 1995*. Luxembourg, Office for Official Publications of the European Communities.

Eurostat, 2003. *Statistical Yearbook 2003 on Candidate Countries, Data 1997–2001*. Luxembourg, Office for Official Publications of the European Communities.

Eurostat, 2004. Euro-zone annual inflation up to 2.0percent in April 2004. *Euro-indicators News Release*, no. 65/2004.

Eurostat, 2005a. Labour force survey: principal results 2004. *Statistics in Focus: Population and Social Conditions*. Luxembourg, Office for Official Publications of the European Communities, September, KS-NK-05-009-EN-N.

Eurostat, 2005b. Stock–flow adjustment for the euro-zone and the EU 25 2001–2004 reported in the second 2005 EDP notification. Luxembourg, 26 September.

Grieve Smith, J., 1999. A new Bretton Woods: reforming the global financial system, in: Michie, J., and Grieve Smith, J. (Eds.), *Global Instability: The Political Economy of World Economic Governance*. London, Routledge, 227–250.

Henning, C.R., 2002. *East Asian Financial Cooperation*. Washington DC, Institute for International Economics.

Jones, E., and Plummer, M.G., 2004. EU–Asia: links and lessons. *Journal of Asian Economics* 14(6), 829–842.

Kenen, P.B., and Meade, E.E., 2003. EU accession and the euro: close together or far apart? *Institute for International Economics Policy Brief*, no. 03–9.

Mallet, V., 2004. Closer East Asia financial ties ahead. *Financial Times*, 17 May, 1.

Rajan, R.S., 2005. Sequence of financial, trade, and monetary regionalism, in: Asian Development Bank (Ed.), *Asian Economic Cooperation and Integration: Progress, Prospects, and Challenges*. Manila, Asian Development Bank, 77–92.

Sbracia, M., and Zaghini, A., 2001. The role of the banking system in the international transmission of shocks. *Bank of Italy Discussion Papers*, no. 409.

Schwartz, A.J., 2001. Assessing the euro three years after its launch. *The Region* 15(4), 14–16.

Suardi, M., 2001. EMU asymmetries in the monetary policy transmission. *European Commission Economic Papers*, no. 157.

Temprano-Arroyo, H., and Feldman, R.A., 1998. Selected transition and Mediterranean countries: an institutional primer on EMU and EU relations. *International Monetary Fund Working Paper*, no. 98/82.

Wagner, H., 2001. Pitfalls in the European enlargement process: challenges for monetary policy. Paper presented at the Bundesbank conference *How to pave the road to E(M)U: the monetary side of the enlargement process (and its fiscal support)*. Eltville, 26-27 October 2001.

Wynne, M.A., and Rodríguez-Palenzuela, D., 2002. Measurement bias in the HICP: what do we know, and what do we need to know? *European Central Bank Working Paper*, no. 131.

Xie, A., and Yam, D., 1999. East Asia: is Asian Monetary Union possible? *Global Economic Forum*, Morgan Stanley Dean Witter.

CHAPTER 6

DEEP INTEGRATION AND ITS IMPACTS ON NON-MEMBERS: EU ENLARGEMENT AND EAST ASIA*

Hiro Lee and Dominique van der Mensbrugghe

As the Iron Curtain fell in the early 1990s, it was clearly expected at the outset that many of the Central and Eastern European countries (CEECs) would join their Western counterparts in an enlarged EU, but the question was when. The moment arrived in 2004 with 8 CEECs — the Czech Republic, Estonia, Hungary, Latvia, Lithuania, Poland, Slovakia, and Slovenia — along with Cyprus and Malta joined the world's biggest customs union. It was the largest expansion of the EU in terms of the number of countries, jumping in a single bound from 15 to 25 countries, and also increasing dramatically the number of different customs and languages. The process of integration started well before actual accession, with all acceding countries transforming their domestic and external policies to align with the EU's so-called *acquis*. In a next phase, Romania and Bulgaria are scheduled to follow suit in January 2007. Croatia, Macedonia and Turkey have received the candidate status from the European Commission and are expected to become members at some future dates.

The 2004 enlargement of the EU was preceded by the establishment of the 'Single Market,' which called for removal of all intra-EU barriers to the movement of goods, services, people and capital by 1992 (Baldwin

* We are grateful to Eric Fisher, Erik Jones, Eric D. Ramstetter, and particularly Michael G. Plummer for helpful comments on earlier versions. The authors are solely responsible for any remaining errors. The usual disclaimer applies; i.e. the views expressed herein do not necessarily reflect the views of our respective institutions.

and Venables 1995). Although it has not been completely implemented, trade barriers on most goods and services within the EU have largely been eliminated, and establishments of EU firms, financial institutions and other service providers have proliferated — through mergers, acquisitions and cross-border investments — in the past 15 years. The past negotiations among the member countries have included harmonization of standards, coordinating regulatory requirements, and cooperation in migration policy matters. Of course, the foundation of the EU itself was based on EU-wide regulation of entire sectors — coal and steel initially — but even more importantly agriculture.

In 2004, the 10 new member states only represented 4.7 percent of the combined $12.8 trillion economy consisting of the 25 member states, though 16 percent of the combined population of 457 million. Thus, there is a 4 to 1 ratio in per capita incomes between EU-15 and the 10 new member states.[1] Bulgaria, Romania, Croatia, Macedonia and Turkey are somewhat smaller in economic importance, but contain a population of 108 million, compared with 74 million for the 10 new member states. Despite the relatively small economic size of the new member, acceding and candidate countries, this type of deep integration can have non-negligible effects on countries outside of the preferential zone as the reduction in barriers across partners leads to a re-orientation of trade.

Empirical evidence on benefits and costs of the EU and other regional integration agreements (RIAs) suggests that trade creation dominates trade diversion in almost all RIAs (Robinson and Thierfelder 1999). The positive effect on economic welfare resulting from eastern enlargement of the EU is supported by Baldwin et al. (1997), Keuschnigg and Kohler (2002), and Kohler (2004). Lejour, de Mooij and Nahuis (2004) evaluate the effects of EU enlargement by taking into consideration three policy aspects: the creation of a larger customs union, the enlargement of the internal market, and free movement of labor. When all three aspects are combined, GDP per capita of CEECs is predicted to increase by more than 8 percent in the long run. By contrast, GDP per capita of the present EU members is predicted to increase by only about 0.1 percent. Fuller et

[1] The average per capita GDPs of the EU-15 and the new member states were respectively $31,974 and $8,094 in 2004.

al. (2002) analyze the impact of accession of three CEECs (Czech Republic, Hungary and Poland) on agricultural markets and find that domestic prices of many agricultural commodities increase dramatically in the three CEECs while those in the EU decrease moderately. The CEECs' exports to third countries decline, but the impact on world agricultural markets is limited. Using a gravity equation, Nahuis (2004) estimates the impact of EU enlargement on the internal market for different industries and different countries. Not surprisingly, the impact of accession is highly asymmetric across industries and the accession countries would have to experience large adjustments, which necessitate a flexible labor market.

Based on empirical evidence, Deardorff and Stern (2004) suggest that the effect of European integration on long-run growth rates is minimal. Using a theoretical model of trade with increasing returns to scale, they show that the current members that are able to expand into the increasing-returns sector would realize gains in income from the enlargement of the EU. By contrast, the acceding countries' gains would be limited because they initially specialize in the constant-returns sector. While their theoretical model provides good insights into what might take place when increasing returns to scale play an important role in manufacturing, their model appears too simple to predict what might actually happen to economic welfare of the current and acceding countries resulting from EU enlargement.

For East Asian countries, the EU is an extremely important export market. Thus, whether the accession of CEECs to the EU would result in reductions of their exports to the EU is a great concern for them. Using a dynamic global computable general equilibrium (CGE) model, we evaluate the effects of EU enlargement on economic welfare, trade flows and sectoral output of the EU-15, the 10 new member states, the acceding and candidate countries, and East Asian countries, paying particularly close attention to the implications for East Asia.

The rest of the chapter is organized as follows. The next section provides an overview of the model, followed by a description of the baseline and policy scenarios in section 2. Section 3 presents the assessments of computational results and policy implications. The final section summarizes the main conclusions.

Overview of the Model

A CGE model is an empirical tool that is well suited to evaluating policies that have regional and sectoral ramifications. First, it captures extensive indirect effects, such as inter-industry linkages between sectors and trade linkages between countries and regions. Second, it can evaluate the effect of removing trade barriers on resource allocation and structural adjustment in each country. Third, it can detail the impacts on both member and nonmember countries and thereby better elucidate implications for the negotiating environment. Thus, a CGE model is an ideal tool to examine the impact of EU enlargement on the current members, the acceding countries, and the East Asian economies.

The model used in this study is based on the dynamic global CGE model developed by van der Mensbrugghe (2003). All sectors are assumed to be perfectly competitive and to operate under constant returns to scale.[2] Production in each sector is modeled by a series of nested constant elasticity of substitution (CES) production functions, which are intended to represent the different substitution and complementarity relations across the various inputs in each sector. Labor can have three different skill levels: unskilled, skilled, and highly skilled. The first two are substitutable and combined in a CES aggregation function as a single labor bundle. Highly skilled labor is combined with capital to form a physical plus human capital bundle.

In each period, the supply of primary factors — capital, labor, and land — is generally predetermined. The supply of land is assumed to be sensitive to the contemporaneous price of land, however. Land is assumed to be partially mobile across agricultural sectors. Thus rates of

[2] The assumption of constant returns to scale is a simplification and generally biases downwards the gains from trade reform because expansion of trade provides scale efficiencies. The introduction of scale economies raises a number of important issues, each of which could significantly modify the results, but we prefer to leave them out of the current study. They include the lack of data on the minimum efficient scale and the specification of market structure (e.g., Cournot versus Bertrand competition), the number of firms, conjectural variations, and whether there is free entry and exit.

return are sector-specific, but sectoral land supply reacts to changes in relative rates of return. Some of the natural resource sectors also have a sector-specific factor whose contemporaneous supply is price sensitive. The model includes adjustment rigidities. An important feature is the distinction between *old* and *new* capital goods. In addition, capital is assumed to be partially mobile, reflecting differences in the marketability of capital goods across sectors. Labor and population growth are exogenous. Labor within each skill category is perfectly mobile across sectors.

All income generated by economic activity is assumed to be distributed to consumers. A single representative consumer (or household) allocates optimally his/her disposable income among the consumer goods and saving. The consumption/saving decision is static: saving is treated as a good and its amount is determined simultaneously with the demands for the other goods. The price of saving is set arbitrarily equal to the average price of consumer goods. Investment is driven by aggregate saving, or the sum of household, government, and foreign savings. We assume that foreign saving is exogenous and that the ratio of government expenditures to GDP remains constant in each region over time.

Products are differentiated by region of origin and modeled as imperfect substitutes. On the import side, this is reflected by the implementation of the so-called Armington assumption, where a nested-CES specification is used to incorporate imperfect substitution of imported goods with respect to domestically produced goods. At the top level, agents choose the optimal combination of an aggregate import bundle and demand for the domestically produced good. At the second level, agents choose the optimal combination of imports across all trading partners. A symmetric specification is used to model export supply, the latter being implemented with nested constant elasticity of transformation (CET) functions.

Tariffs are fully bilateral and the model captures both direct and indirect trade and transportation costs. The CIF price of imports into region r' originating in region r, $WPM_{r,r',i}$, is given by

$$WPM_{r,r',i} = \left(1+\zeta_{r,r',i}\right)WPE_{r,r',i} \big/ \lambda_{r,r',i} \tag{1}$$

where $WPE_{r,r',i}$ is the FOB price of commodity i in region r for exporting to region r'. Between the originating port in region r and the destination port in region r', the price of the commodity is adjusted by a trade and transport margin represented by the ad valorem adjustment $\zeta_{r,r',i}$. The model also allows for non-monetary trade and transport cost, which is represented by the efficiency parameter $\lambda_{r,r',i}$.[3] In our model, an increase in $\lambda_{r,r',i}$ represents a reduction in trade-related risk, lower administrative barriers to trade (e.g., customs procedures) and/or a fall in technical barrier (e.g., mutual recognition of product standards). Most of the data used in the model come from the GTAP database, version 5.4, which provides 1997 data on input-output, value added, final demand, bilateral trade, tax and subsidy data for 78 regions and 57 sectors.[4]

For the purpose of the present study, the database is aggregated into 10 regions and 15 sectors as shown in Table 6.1. The present and prospective future EU member states are divided into three regions: (i) EU-15, (ii) the countries that became EU members in 2004 (CEEC-10 hereafter), and (iii) the acceding and candidate countries (Bulgaria, Romania, Croatia and Turkey: BRCT). Macedonia is excluded from the third region because it is aggregated into the rest of the world in the GTAP 5.4 database. In addition, we have chosen to aggregate the acceding countries (Bulgaria and Romania) and the two candidate countries (Croatia and Turkey) because each pair's trade with the present EU members is extremely small relative to the total EU trade.

---

[3] This type of cost is referred to as 'iceberg' transport cost. If $\lambda_{r,r',i}$ is equal to 0.9 for some transport node, it implies that if 100 units leave port r, the destination port, r', receives only 90 units. Iceberg transport costs were developed by Samuelson (1952) based on a concept developed earlier by von Thünen. More recently, these have been used in work by Helpman and Krugman (1985) and Fujita, Krugman and Venables (1999).

[4] Dimaranan and McDougall (2002) give detailed descriptions of the GTAP database, version 5.0. The number of regions is increased from 66 to 78 in Version 5.4, which disaggregates the Central and Eastern European regions into single countries (with some exceptions).

The Baseline and Policy Scenarios

To assess the implications of the enlargement of the EU, we first establish a baseline, which shows the path of each economy in the absence of enlargement over the period 1997–2015. In the baseline, several key variables, including GDP growth rates, population and labor supply, are predetermined by the exogenous assumptions. Projections of real GDP, population and labor supply are broadly consistent with the World Bank's long-term forecast.

Several assumptions underline the calibration of productivity. Agricultural productivity is fixed and is assumed uniform across factors of production. Sectoral productivity (outside of agriculture) is assumed to be labor-augmenting and is composed of three components: a uniform economy-wide factor that is calibrated to achieve the given GDP target, a sector-specific factor related to openness, and a constant shifter. The sector-specific factor intended to capture openness-sensitive changes in productivity, $\chi_{i,t}$, is given by

$$\chi_{i,t} = \phi_{i,t}\left(\frac{E_{i,t}}{X_{i,t}}\right)^{\eta_i} \tag{2}$$

where $E_{i,t}$ is exports of commodity i, $X_{i,t}$ is output of commodity i, $\phi_{i,t}$ is a shift parameter, and η_i is the elasticity of productivity with respect to openness. $\phi_{i,t}$ is calibrated in the baseline scenario so that the trade-sensitive portion of sectoral productivity is some share of total productivity.[5]

[5] Three main channels have been identified linking openness with productivity: imports of technology-laden intermediate inputs (for example fertilizers in agriculture), imports of capital goods, and export market penetration (with the requirement to produce to a higher standard than at home to be able to penetrate new markets; expanding foreign markets can also lead to scale economies). Much empirical work is ongoing trying to identify the extent to which each one of these channels operates. At a macro level, there are to some extent observationally equivalent to the extent that current account balances are more or less exogenous. de Melo and Robinson (1990) and Dessus, Fukasaku and Safadi (1999) take an approach similar to ours. Das, Roberts and Tybout (2001) have explored some firm-level characteristics of export supply response.

Table 6.1. Regional and Sectoral Aggregation

A. Regional Aggregation

Countries/Regions	*Corresponding economies/regions in the GTAP database*
EU-15	Austria, Belgium, Denmark, Finland, France, Germany, Great Britain, Greece, Ireland, Italy, Luxembourg, Netherlands, Portugal, Spain, Sweden
CEEC-10 (new members)	Cyprus, the Czech Republic, Estonia, Hungary, Latvia, Lithuania, Malta, Poland, Slovakia and Slovenia
Acceding and candidate countries (BRCT)[a)]	Bulgaria, Romania, Croatia and Turkey
Japan	Japan
China	China and Hong Kong
Asian NIEs	Korea, Taiwan and Singapore
ASEAN[b)]	Indonesia, Malaysia, Philippines, Thailand and Vietnam
United States	United States
Other developed countries	Australia, Canada, Iceland, Liechtenstein, New Zealand, Norway and Switzerland
Rest of world	All the other economies/regions

Table 6.1 (*Continued*)

B. Sectoral Aggregation

Sectors	*Corresponding commodities/sectors in the GTAP database*
Crops	Paddy rice, wheat, cereal grains n.e.s., vegetables and fruits, oil seeds, sugar cane and sugar beet, plant-based fibers, crops n.e.s.
Other agriculture	Bovine cattle, sheep and goats, animal products n.e.s., raw milk, wool, silk-worm cocoons, fishing
Natural resources	Forestry, minerals
Energy	Coal, oil, gas, petroleum and coal products, electricity, gas manufacture and Distribution
Processed food	Food products, beverages and tobacco products
Textiles	Textiles
Apparel	Wearing apparel, leather products
Chemical products	Chemical, rubber and plastic products
Metals and products	Iron and steel, nonferrous metals, metal products
Machinery	Machinery
Electronic equip.	Electronic equipment
Transport equip.	Motor vehicles and parts, other transport equipment
Other manufactures	Wood products, paper products, publishing, non-metallic mineral products, other manufactures
Construction	Construction, water distribution
Services	Trade, transport, communication, financial services, other services

[a)] Excludes Macedonia because it is aggregated into the rest of the world in the GTAP database.

[b)] Excludes Brunei, Cambodia, Laos and Myanmar because they are aggregated into the rest of the world. Singapore is also excluded because it is included in Asian NIEs.

Source: GTAP database, Version 5.4.

Ideally, the baseline should include policies that are already agreed upon, such as Uruguay Round commitments and China's WTO accession. Because our baseline does not include these policy commitments, we need to be cautious when interpreting policy results. However, with the exception of the textile and apparel sectors, the incorporation of post–Uruguay Round tariff rates and China's post–WTO accession tariff rates in the baseline is likely to change our results only slightly for several reasons. First, because the EU's tariff rates on industrial products were already quite low in 1997, additional reductions in the tariff rates committed under the Uruguay Round are relatively small.[6] Second, given that the main reference period used (1986–88) for tariffication of nontariff measures corresponds to peak farm protection in the EU, it makes effective agricultural liberalization minimal for the Union (Messerlin 2001). Third, post–Uruguay Round average tariff rates are only slightly lower than the average tariff rates in 1995 for CEECs (Francois and Strutt 1999).[7] Fourth, the omission of China's WTO accession from the baseline is likely to have only a minimal effect on the consequences of EU enlargement because China's trade policy remains unchanged in our policy scenarios.

Table 6.2 provides the export shares by product category for the 10 regions of the model for the year 1997. With the exception of crops in the acceding and candidate countries (BRCT), agricultural products and natural resources constitute small export shares of the EU-15, CEEC-10 and BRCT.

---

[6] Although the EU maintains significant tariff peaks in some so-called sensitive sectors, their impacts are hard to assess at the level of aggregation of our model. However, not incorporating the Uruguay Round's Agreement on Textiles and Clothing (ATC), which gradually phased out import quotas on textiles and apparel between January 1995 and December 2004, in the baseline scenario is likely to overestimate the effects of EU enlargement, particularly for the textile and apparel sectors.

[7] Francois and Strutt (1999) provide post-Uruguay Round average tariff rates for 45 regions and 50 product categories for the GTAP version 4 database.

Table 6.2. Export Shares by Product Category, 1997 (percent)

	Region									
Sector	EU-15	CEEC-10	BRCT	Japan	China	Asian NIEs	ASEAN	United States	Other developed	ROW
Crops	1.5	1.1	4.5	0.0	1.3	0.2	1.6	3.5	2.6	5.5
Other agriculture	0.5	0.7	0.5	0.0	0.8	0.2	0.5	0.4	1.6	0.5
Natural resources	0.3	0.7	0.8	0.0	0.3	0.1	1.2	0.4	1.9	2.5
Energy	2.4	5.9	2.1	0.3	1.9	2.9	6.9	1.4	12.2	29.5
Processed food	6.1	5.6	4.4	0.6	2.9	1.4	7.0	3.6	5.9	5.8
Textiles	2.9	3.2	9.2	1.5	8.2	6.4	3.3	1.3	1.3	3.2
Apparel	2.7	6.0	13.3	0.3	18.0	2.5	6.4	1.1	0.7	4.7
Chemical products	12.6	8.7	5.7	8.4	6.1	8.5	6.4	9.9	9.3	5.1
Metals and products	6.9	10.2	9.5	5.9	5.0	6.5	2.6	4.0	9.9	8.7
Machinery	17.7	13.1	5.7	25.8	12.3	12.8	7.0	18.8	13.5	5.9
Electronic equipment	7.5	5.2	1.2	21.7	12.8	34.6	29.6	12.8	3.8	3.0
Transport equipment	12.0	8.4	2.5	18.8	1.6	5.9	1.0	12.0	11.2	4.1
Other manufactures	8.9	11.4	6.2	3.6	12.5	4.5	8.7	6.2	11.6	6.2
Construction	0.8	1.1	3.4	1.4	0.3	0.1	0.1	0.5	0.1	0.2
Services	17.3	18.5	30.9	11.7	16.0	13.2	17.7	24.1	14.4	15.2
All sectors	100.0	100.0	100.0	100.0	100.0	100.0	100.0	100.0	100.0	100.0

Source: GTAP database, version 5.4.

The products with relatively high export shares are machinery (17.7 percent), chemical products (12.6 percent) and transport equipment (12.0 percent) for the EU-15, machinery (13.1 percent), other manufactures (11.4 percent) and metals and products (10.2 percent) for the CEEC-10, and apparel (13.3 percent), metals and products (9.5 percent) and textiles (9.2 percent) for BRCT.[8]

The most striking difference in the export patterns between the three (present and prospective future) EU regions and four East Asian regions is the export orientation of electronic equipment. The export shares of this product are 34.6 percent in Asian NIEs, 29.6 percent in ASEAN, 21.7 percent in Japan and 12.8 percent in China, which are significantly greater than 7.5 percent in the EU-15, 5.2 percent in the CEEC-10 and 1.2 percent in BRCT. For the rest of the products in which the export shares are relatively high in at least one of the East Asian regions, they are also relatively high in at least one of the EU regions — e.g., apparel in China (18.0 percent), machinery in Japan (25.8 percent), Asian NIEs (12.8 percent) and China (12.8 percent), transport equipment in Japan (18.8 percent), and other manufactures in China (12.5 percent).

Although not shown in the table, 56.1 percent of the EU-15's exports in 1997 went to the other EU-15 countries, 3.9 percent of its exports went to the CEEC-10, 1.7 percent to BRCT, and 10.9 percent to the four East Asian regions. In the same year, 55.6 percent of the CEEC-10's exports and 50.0 percent of BRCT's exports were destined to the EU-15 market. While 19.2 percent of East Asia's exports were shipped to the EU-15, its exports to the CEEC-10 and BRCT were, respectively, only 0.8 and 0.5 percent of total exports. Hence, changes in East Asia's exports to the new member states and the acceding and candidate countries resulting from EU enlargement would have an extremely small impact. By contrast, if East Asia's exports to the EU-15 were to be reduced substantially, it might lead to significant trade adjustments.

To assess the consequences of EU enlargement, we consider four policy scenarios. In scenario 1, we assume that the EU-15 and the CEEC-

[8] The export shares of the aggregated services are large in all regions mainly because the services sector includes the trade sector.

10 will remove bilateral tariffs and the latter will adopt the EU's common external tariffs (CET) with respect to third countries over the 1998–2005 period.[9] This is followed by the elimination of bilateral tariffs between the EU-25 and the acceding and candidate countries (BRCT) and the adoption of CET by BRCT over the 2005–2015 period. In this scenario, we assume that the sector-specific productivity factors related to openness ($\chi_{i,t}$) are fixed at the baseline levels. In scenario 2, we extend scenario 1 by reducing iceberg or non-monetary trade costs (e.g., administrative and technical barriers) between the EU-15 and the CEEC-10 by 5 percent over the 1998–2005 period, followed by the same rate of reduction in these costs between the EU-25 and BRCT over the 2005–2015 period.[10] Again, we fix $\chi_{i,t}$ at the baseline levels. Scenario 3 is the same as scenario 2 except that $\chi_{i,t}$ are now endogenous and determined by equation (2). We set $\eta_i = 0.75$ in agricultural sectors and $\eta_i = 1.0$ in all other sectors.

With respect to adoption of the Common Agricultural Policy (CAP), there will eventually be full integration of the enlarged EU within a transition period. We assume that the CEEC-10 and subsequently BRCT will adopt the EU's external tariffs on agricultural products as they do on all other products. After the adoption of CET, these regions' tariff rates of agricultural products to third countries would increase. The controversial part is whether direct payments would be extended to agricultural producers in these regions. In addition, the new member states are required to implement supply controls. Because the issues of

---

[9] The bilateral tariffs on most manufacturing products between the EU-15 and CEECs were largely removed before the CEEC-10 became new members in 2004. In addition, the CEEC-10 started changing their tariff structures to conform to the EU's CET before 2004. To the extent that the process had already been initiated, the estimated effects of EU enlargement reported in this study include those resulting from the changes in the tariff structures between 1997 and 2004.

[10] Smith and Venables (1988) use a 2.5 percent reduction in intra-EU trade cost in their study of the Single Market program's possible pro-competitive effects. Keuschnigg and Kohler (2002) and Madsen and Sorensen (2002) use a 5 percent reduction in real trade cost between EU-15 and CEECs, whereas Baldwin et al. (1997) assume a 10 percent reduction in real trade cost. We use a 5 percent reduction in scenarios 2 and 3, but report the welfare results with three different values of the trade efficiency parameter (2.5, 5 and 10 percent) in Table 6.7.

direct payments and supply controls have been investigated elsewhere (e.g., Fuller et al. 2002), we do not incorporate them in this study. It should be reminded, however, that the omission of the production quotas is likely to overestimate the new member countries' exports of agricultural products and processed food to the present EU members. In its recent proposed changes to the CAP, the EU continues to move away from a system of direct price support towards income support through so-called decoupled payments. Part of the motivation of these changes is to make the CAP more WTO–friendly, though the extent of decoupling is still widely debated both within and outside of the EU. It would be perhaps logical that over the longer term, the EU may consider devolving agricultural income support back towards national governments if it truly becomes direct income support.

It is also beyond the scope of this study to model the movement of labor between the EU-15 and CEECs, which is incorporated in the study by Lejour, de Mooij and Nahuis (2004). They find that GDP per capita increases in CEECs by 0.6–1.1 percent and decreases slightly in the EU-15, whereas GDP decreases in CEECs (because of the labor outflow) and increases in the EU-15.[11]

Results

Aggregate income gains and/or losses summarize the extent to which trade distortions are hindering growth prospects and the ability of economies to use the gains to help those whose income could potentially decline. We compared the EU enlargement scenario with the baseline situation in the terminal year, 2015, using Hicksian equivalent variation (EV) as the welfare measure. This represents the income consumers would be willing to forego to achieve post-EU enlargement well-being compared to baseline well-being at baseline prices. The model uses the extended linear expenditure system (ELES), which incorporates savings

[11] World Bank (2006) is largely devoted to the movement of workers from developing to developed countries and the development impacts of remittances. While the aggregate gains from labor movements are relatively small, the migrants themselves gain significantly because of the huge wage differentials, and the sending countries can benefit substantially from remittances. The gains increase with the level of remittances because migrant households can benefit from the lower prices in their home countries.

in the consumer's utility function (Lluch 1973; Howe 1975). The ELES expenditure function is easy to evaluate at each point in time.

Table 6.3 presents the welfare results for the four policy scenarios as deviations in equivalent variations (EVs) from the baseline in 2015. In scenario 1, EVs of the CEEC-10 and the acceding and candidate countries (BRCT) increase by $9.8 billion (2.15 percent) and $2.4 billion (0.59 percent), respectively, whereas EV of the EU-15 increases only very slightly in percentage terms (0.04 percent). These estimates include the effects of the removal of bilateral tariffs between the EU-15 and CEECs that has already taken place since 1997. In many products CEEC-10 and BRCT's exports to the EU-15 increase significantly, replacing some of the East Asian exports and causing trade diversion in products in which East Asian countries have a competitive advantage. All four regions in East Asia (Japan, China, Asian NIEs and ASEAN) incur losses in welfare, but they are extremely small. China's loss is larger than the other three regions because of a relatively large fall in the exports of wearing apparel and leather products, where 15 percent of its exports were shipped to the EU in 1997. When a 5 percent reduction in trade costs between the EU-15 and CEECs is added (scenario 2), the magnitudes of welfare gains for the EU-15, CEEC-10 and BRCT increase by a factor of 4.4, 3.7 and 4.3, respectively. A greater access of the internal market resulting from a reduction in trade-related risk and lower administrative and technical barriers would further facilitate trade among the three regions. While it would increase welfare losses of East Asian regions slightly, the world welfare gain increases five-fold in scenario 2 compared with scenario 1 ($53.6 billion versus $10.9 billion). Thus, trade creation resulting from a reduction in trade costs between the EU-15 and CEECs is likely to be far greater than trade diversion.[12]

[12] It should be noted that while trade creation always raises welfare, trade diversion may or may not reduce welfare.

Table 6.3. Effects on Welfare (deviations in equivalent variations from the baseline in 2015)

A. Absolute Deviations (US$ billion in 1997 prices)

Region	*Scenario 1*	*Scenario 2*	*Scenario 3*
EU-15	4.50	19.86	26.47
CEEC-10	9.75	35.97	31.30
Acceding and candidate countries (BRCT)	2.35	10.19	11.87
Japan	-0.48	-1.15	1.12
China	-2.04	-3.19	0.35
Asian NIEs	-0.32	-1.20	-0.24
ASEAN	-0.87	-1.26	-1.13
United States	-0.45	-1.56	7.46
Other developed countries	-0.20	-0.83	-0.08
Rest of world	-1.33	-3.19	-1.51
Enlarged EU	16.61	66.02	69.64
East Asia	-3.72	-6.80	0.10
Other regions	-1.98	-5.59	5.88
World	10.91	53.63	75.61

Table 6.3 (*Continued*)

B. Percent Deviations

Region	*Scenario 1*	*Scenario 2*	*Scenario 3*
EU-15	0.04	0.19	0.25
CEEC-10	2.15	7.93	6.90
Acceding and candidate countries (BRCT)	0.59	2.54	2.95
Japan	-0.01	-0.02	0.02
China	-0.07	-0.11	0.01
Asian NIEs	-0.02	-0.07	-0.01
ASEAN	-0.09	-0.12	-0.11
United States	0.00	-0.01	0.06
Other developed countries	-0.01	-0.04	0.00
Rest of world	-0.02	-0.05	-0.02
Enlarged EU	0.14	0.57	0.60
East Asia	-0.03	-0.06	0.00
Other regions	-0.01	-0.03	0.03
World	0.02	0.12	0.17

Definitions of scenarios:

Scenario 1: the removal of bilateral tariffs between the EU-15 and the CEEC-10 and the adoption of the EU's CET by CEEC-10 over the 1998-2005 period. This is followed by the elimination of bilateral tariffs between the EU-25 and the acceding and candidate countries (BRCT) and the adoption of CET by BRCT over the 2005-2015 period. The sector-specific productivity factors related to openness ($\chi_{i,t}$) are fixed at the baseline levels.

Scenario 2: Scenario 1 plus a 5 percent reduction in non-monetary trade costs between the EU-15 and the CEEC-10 over the 1998-2005 period, followed by the same reduction in these costs between the EU-25 and BRCT over the 2005-2015 period. $\chi_{i,t}$ are fixed at the baseline levels.

Scenario 3: Same as scenario 2 except that $\chi_{i,t}$ are endogenous and determined by equation (2).

In the next scenario, we allow the sector-specific productivity factors to change in response to changes in sectoral export-output ratios. A comparison of the results in scenario 3 with those in scenario 2 shows that endogenizing $\chi_{i,t}$ leads to an increase in welfare gains for the EU-15 and BRCT, but not for the CEEC-10. It should be noted that the CEEC-10's welfare and real GDP gains are larger under scenario 3 in earlier years (e.g., before 2005). Its export growth in some of the products becomes smaller after the latecomers (BRCT) accede to the EU and their exports to the Union increase significantly. In 2015, the CEEC-10's export-output ratios become smaller in scenario 3 than in scenario 2 in a number of sectors, including natural resources, energy, chemical products, metals and products, machinery, electronic equipment, other manufactures and services, which altogether account for a large share of GDP.[13]

The East Asian region as a whole no longer suffers from a welfare loss under scenario 3 because the export-output ratios increase slightly in some of the key sectors, particularly in Japan and China. For example, Japan's export-output ratios in machinery, electronic equipment and services are slightly larger in scenario 3 than in scenario 2. This is primarily caused by an increase in exports to the EU-15, whose welfare and real GDP gains are larger when productivity is endogenous. The world welfare gain also increases when productivity becomes endogenous ($75.6 billion versus $53.6 billion).

Table 6.7 presents the sensitivity of a change in the trade efficiency parameter $\lambda_{r,r',i}$ on economic welfare. A change in trade efficiency between the EU-15 and CEECs has a large impact on their welfare gains. For example, the CEEC-10's welfare gains increase from 6.9 percent to 12.4 percent when a trade cost reduction is increased from 5 percent to 10 percent. By contrast, economic welfare of the four East Asian regions is barely affected by the change in the value of $\lambda_{r,r',i}$.

[13] The relative decline in productivity is a possible consequence of our specification. Its plausibility depends on whether productivity changes are derived from scale economies — in which case a decline is possible if output declines, or whether one believes productivity is more driven from learning by doing, R&D, and imitating best practice. In the case of the latter, productivity — once achieved — is less likely to decline.

Table 6.4 summarizes world trade flow adjustments resulting from EU accession in scenario 3, which combines an enlargement of the customs union and a 5 percent reduction in trade costs among the EU-15, CEEC-10 and BRCT assuming endogenous productivity. The adjustments are expressed as percent deviations from the baseline for the year 2015. Not surprisingly, intraregional trade within the enlarged EU would increase drastically. For example, the EU-15's exports to the CEEC-10 and BRCT would be 52.4 and 42.3 percent higher, whereas the CEEC-10 and BRCT's exports to the EU-15 would be 74.8 and 53.9 percent higher, under this scenario compared with the baseline in 2015. The reductions in East Asian countries' exports to the EU-15 appear to be relatively small in percentage terms. In order to determine whether the accession of CEECs to the EU would induce substantial trade diversion in some products, however, it is necessary to examine the results on trade flows by product category.

Table 6.5 provides trade flow adjustments for eight selected products under scenario 3 in 2015. The results are reported for three aggregate regions (enlarged EU, East Asia, and other regions) as well as for the world. In four of the eight products (i.e., processed food, textiles, apparel and transport equipment), East Asia's exports to the enlarged EU region decline substantially.[14] The most notable sector is apparel, where its exports to the EU-29 (the EU-15, CEEC-10 and BRCT) would decline by 25.3 percent. Among East Asian countries, China would be particularly hit hard by a drastic fall in apparel exports because of its relatively large export share of this product (Table 6.2).

In many products, East Asia's exports to the EU-29 are affected very little. For example, its exports of metals and products and electronic equipment to an enlarged EU would decline by only 0.2 and 1.0 percent, respectively. Other products with small reductions in East Asia's exports to the EU-29 include chemical products and machinery.

[14] Although not included in Table 6.5, EU enlargement would also lead to significant trade diversion in 'other agriculture.'

Table 6.4. World Trade Flow Adjustments under Scenario 3 (percent deviations from the baseline for the year 2015)

	Importing region										
Exporting region	EU-15	CEEC-10	BRCT	Japan	China	Asian NIEs	ASEAN	United States	Other developed	ROW	World
EU-15	-3.2	52.4	42.3	-0.3	-0.8	-0.7	-0.6	-0.4	-0.4	-0.6	1.2
CEEC-10	74.8	23.9	19.2	-24.3	-22.1	-20.5	-22.6	-19.6	-15.6	-7.6	39.0
Acceding and candidate countries (BRCT)	53.9	54.7	49.3	-10.1	-8.7	-10.0	-10.2	-4.4	-8.6	-2.5	24.9
Japan	-1.4	2.8	-18.7		-0.1	-0.1	-0.1	0.1	0.3	0.0	-0.3
China	-4.6	6.5	-3.8	0.4	-0.1	0.3	0.4	0.6	0.6	0.7	-0.5
Asian NIEs	-1.4	-1.0	-10.3	0.0	-0.3	-0.1	-0.2	0.0	0.2	0.0	-0.4
ASEAN	-2.2	6.3	-11.4	0.1	-0.2	0.0	0.0	0.1	0.4	0.0	-0.4
United States	-1.1	7.4	-2.2	0.1	-0.2	-0.1	0.0		0.0	0.0	-0.3
Other developed countries	-0.8	7.0	-2.9	0.0	-0.5	-0.2	-0.2	-0.2	0.1	-0.1	-0.3
Rest of world	-1.8	0.6	-1.2	0.3	-0.2	0.1	0.1	0.1	0.4	0.1	-0.4
Enlarged EU	3.4	48.0	40.8	-1.9	-1.5	-1.8	-1.8	-1.4	-1.1	-1.2	4.2
East Asia	-2.6	3.2	-10.2	0.2	-0.2	0.0	0.0	0.3	0.4	0.3	-0.4
Other regions	-1.3	3.3	-1.7	0.1	-0.3	-0.1	0.0	0.0	0.1	0.0	-0.3
World	1.2	33.8	21.1	-0.3	-0.4	-0.3	-0.4	-0.2	-0.2	-0.3	1.3

Table 6.5. Trade Flow Adjustments for Selected Products under Scenario 3 (percent deviations from the baseline for the year 2015)

Panel A

	Importing region and sector							
	Natural resources				Processed Food			
Exporting region	Enlarged EU	East Asia	Other regions	World	Enlarged EU	East Asia	Other regions	World
Enlarged EU	1.9	-3.8	-5.5	-0.1	15.2	-0.7	2.5	10.3
East Asia	2.3	0.1	0.6	0.5	-9.0	0.0	-0.5	-1.1
Other regions	2.7	-0.2	0.3	0.9	-5.5	-0.3	-1.0	-1.8
World	2.4	-0.2	-0.3	0.7	9.2	-0.3	0.3	3.6

Panel B

	Importing region and sector							
	Textiles				Apparel			
Exporting region	Enlarged EU	East Asia	Other regions	World	Enlarged EU	East Asia	Other regions	World
Enlarged EU	14.9	-0.6	0.6	10.7	54.1	3.3	4.6	39.6
East Asia	-8.6	-1.5	-1.0	-2.1	-25.3	-0.3	0.1	-5.8
Other regions	-8.8	-1.7	-1.3	-3.3	-30.5	-2.1	-1.6	-11.1
World	7.8	-1.5	-0.7	1.9	13.8	-0.1	0.2	5.3

Table 6.5 (*Continued*)

Panel C

	Importing region and sector							
	Metals and products				Electronic equipment			
Exporting region	Enlarged EU	East Asia	Other regions	World	Enlarged EU	East Asia	Other regions	World
Enlarged EU	6.4	-3.1	-2.3	3.5	4.7	-1.2	-1.2	2.6
East Asia	-0.2	0.2	0.4	0.2	-1.0	0.0	0.0	-0.2
Other regions	-1.1	0.0	0.2	-0.2	-1.4	-0.1	0.0	-0.3
World	4.2	-0.3	-0.4	1.3	1.8	-0.2	-0.1	0.4

Panel D

	Importing region and sector							
	Transport equipment				Other manufactures			
Exporting region	Enlarged EU	East Asia	Other regions	World	Enlarged EU	East Asia	Other regions	World
Enlarged EU	15.1	0.0	1.0	10.8	5.2	-1.5	-1.7	2.5
East Asia	-11.7	-0.2	-0.3	-2.6	0.7	0.1	0.6	0.4
Other regions	-13.7	-0.8	-0.5	-2.6	0.0	-0.2	0.2	0.1
World	8.2	-0.4	-0.1	3.2	3.5	-0.2	-0.3	1.2

In natural resources and other manufactures, its exports to an enlarged EU are predicted to increase by 2.3 and 0.7 percent, respectively.[15] Although not shown in Table 6.5, East Asia's exports to the EU-29 are predicted to increase somewhat in three other product groups: crops, energy and services. Thus, the impact of EU enlargement on East Asia's trade adjustments is quite small for a large number of products.

Effects on Sectoral Output

While the aggregate welfare and trade results are of interest in themselves, the most useful results are at the industry level, where structural adjustments and resource reallocations occur in response to policy changes. Because sectoral interests can exert significant influence on policy negotiations, the sectoral results would be most important for political economy considerations. In this section we examine the effects of EU enlargement on sectoral output.

Table 6.6 summarizes output adjustments for the 15 sectors under scenario 3 in 2015. Before examining the results, it should be noted that the effects on textiles and apparel might be overstated because we did not incorporate the Uruguay Round's Agreement on Textiles and Clothing in the baseline scenario. Overall, sectoral output adjustments are very large for the CEEC-10 and BRCT mainly because these regions depend very heavily upon trade with the EU-15, which increases drastically as they accede to the Union. By contrast, sectoral adjustments are substantially smaller for the EU-15 because its trade with the CEEC-10 and BRCT constitutes only 5–6 percent of its total trade.

The magnitude and direction of changes in sectoral output depend upon a number of factors, including pre-accession tariff rates and *ad valorem* equivalents of nontariff barriers, the export-output ratios, the import-demand ratios, and the elasticities of substitution between domestic and imported products. The trade barriers in 1997 were relatively high in crops, other agriculture, processed food, textiles and apparel. In the CEEC-10, the export-output ratios in the same year were

[15] As shown in Table 6.2, the export shares of natural resources are extremely small in all EU and East Asian regions. Thus, a 2.3 percent increase in East Asia's exports to the EU-29 is negligible.

relatively high in electronic equipment (57 percent), apparel (53 percent), machinery (52 percent), textiles (43 percent) and transport equipment (43 percent), whereas the import-demand ratios for the same year were relatively high in electronic equipment (64 percent), machinery (63 percent), textiles (55 percent), transport equipment (50 percent) and chemical products (48 percent). In BRCT, the export-output ratios were highest in apparel (56 percent), followed by textiles (36 percent), machinery (24 percent) and metals and products (21 percent), whereas the import-demand ratios were highest in machinery (57 percent), followed by electronic equipment (36 percent), transport equipment (36 percent) and textiles (29 percent).

In both the CEEC-10 and BRCT, the apparel sector would expand substantially largely because the EU-15, CEEC-10 and BRCT all had relatively high pre-accession protection rates and both regions have a comparative advantage in this sector *vis-à-vis* the EU-15. Output of textiles in BRCT would increase significantly for the same reasons, but that in the CEEC-10 would also increase despite the fact that it does not appear to have comparative advantage in textiles. A relatively large increase in output of textiles in the CEEC-10 may be explained by a relatively large reduction in the price of imported textile materials (intermediate inputs) resulting from the removal of trade barriers on imports from the EU-15 and BRCT, leading to substantial domestic cost reductions and increased competitiveness.

The sectors that would experience contractions in output usually result from large import penetrations within the enlarged EU. For example, output of transport equipment in BRCT would decrease substantially mainly because its imports, which are more than four times its exports, are predicted to increase drastically following the accession. Another important factor is that an increase in demand for capital and labor in the expanding sectors would bid up factor prices. The services sector in the CEEC-10 and BRCT would contract primarily because of increases in factor prices.

Table 6.6. Sectoral Output Adjustments under Scenario 3 (percent deviations from the baseline for the year 2015)

Sector	Region									
	EU-15	CEEC-10	BRCT	Japan	China	Asian NIEs	ASEAN	United States	Other developed	ROW
Crops	0.0	0.2	2.7	0.0	0.0	0.0	-0.1	-0.1	-0.6	-0.2
Other agriculture	-0.6	7.4	1.2	0.0	0.0	-0.2	-0.1	0.0	-0.8	-0.3
Natural resources	0.4	-8.3	-2.0	0.0	0.3	0.0	0.1	0.0	0.0	0.3
Energy	0.5	-6.1	-0.7	0.0	0.1	0.0	0.1	0.0	0.2	0.4
Processed food	-0.7	15.1	0.2	0.0	0.0	0.0	-0.3	0.0	-0.7	-0.4
Textiles	1.3	18.0	33.8	-0.9	-1.1	-1.8	-3.0	-0.8	-1.6	-1.3
Apparel	-7.2	61.9	74.4	-0.5	-2.7	-1.9	-5.2	-1.0	-2.7	-2.7
Chemical products	0.5	-3.5	-0.4	0.0	0.1	-0.2	-0.1	0.0	0.0	-0.1
Metals and products	0.4	-0.9	-3.1	0.0	0.3	0.0	0.1	-0.1	-0.2	0.0
Machinery	0.5	12.5	-2.8	-0.1	0.2	-0.2	-0.1	-0.1	-0.3	0.1
Electronic equipment	0.0	16.9	5.2	0.0	0.2	-0.1	-0.1	-0.1	-0.3	0.0
Transport equipment	-1.9	98.3	-11.0	-0.8	-0.2	-1.3	-0.6	-0.9	-0.7	-0.7
Other manufactures	0.5	-7.1	-1.0	0.0	0.3	0.0	0.1	0.1	0.0	0.1
Construction	0.3	3.3	2.4	0.0	0.0	0.0	-0.1	0.0	0.0	0.0
Services	0.1	-2.8	-0.6	0.1	0.3	0.2	0.3	0.1	0.1	0.1

Turning to sectoral output adjustments in the four East Asian regions, we find that percentage changes in output exceed 1 percent only in the textiles and apparel sectors in China, Asian NIEs and ASEAN. In all other sectors, output adjustments are less than 1 percent. Because the effects of EU enlargement on sectoral output in East Asian countries are extremely small, industry lobbies from these countries are likely to sit quietly.

Concluding Remarks

In this chapter, we have used a dynamic CGE model to examine the consequences of EU enlargement on economic welfare, trade flows and sectoral output of the EU-15, the new member states, the acceding and candidate countries, and East Asian countries. A standard result in this class of analysis is that the poorer and smaller region in the formation of a free trade area or customs union tends to gain significantly more in overall welfare than the larger and richer region. The impact on the existing EU-15 yields at best an increase of 0.3 percent of real income, whereas the impact on the CEEC-10 varies from 2.2 to 7.9 percent gains, and on the BRCT countries from 0.6 to 3.0 percent gains. Our policy scenarios exclude the impact of increased capital mobility, which — as in the case of Mexico's joining NAFTA, or Spain and Portugal joining the EU — may have much greater effects than the removal of tariffs. However, it will be difficult to identify this impact precisely because much of the capital movement into Eastern Europe can also be attributed to the region's transition to a market economy. The welfare effects on non-member economies are small, though ASEAN and possibly China — perhaps the greatest direct competitors with East European producers — will be harmed the most.

The results also show that the reduction in frictional trade barriers could be more important at the macro-level than tariffs themselves. For the CEEC-10 and BRCT, the welfare gains increase by a factor of 3.7 and 4.3 respectively when a 5 percent reduction in frictional trade costs are incorporated in the policy-reform scenario, and even greater impacts occur with a more significant reduction in these costs. The incorporation of a linkage between productivity and openness has a more modest impact and is an area that would require more detailed sectoral and firm-level analysis.

The results clearly indicate that East Asia will lose export revenues — particularly in the enlarged EU-29, but also globally. The sectors facing the greatest threat are those where Central and Eastern Europe is likely to be very competitive with East Asian producers — processed food, textiles, apparel and transport equipment. This will mostly affect the low- and lower middle-income countries of ASEAN and China. East Asian exporters will hold up well in metals and metal products and electronic equipment — the latter, of course, is the high-growth sector globally, with linkages to high productivity growth.

* * *

Table 6.7. Appendix — Sensitivity of Changes in the Trade Efficiency Parameter to the Welfare Results for Scenario 3 (percent deviations from the baseline in 2015)

	Trade cost reduction		
Region	2.5%	5%	10%
EU-15	0.16	0.25	0.44
CEEC-10	4.33	6.90	12.36
Acceding and candidate countries (BRCT)	1.91	2.95	5.16
Japan	0.02	0.02	0.03
China	0.01	0.01	0.02
Asian NIEs	0.00	-0.01	-0.03
ASEAN	-0.10	-0.11	-0.14
United States	0.05	0.06	0.08
Other developed countries	0.00	0.00	-0.01
Rest of world	-0.01	-0.02	-0.04
Enlarged EU	0.38	0.60	1.07
East Asia	0.00	0.00	0.00
Other regions	0.02	0.03	0.03
World	0.11	0.17	0.29

References

Baldwin, R.E., J.F. Francois, and R. Portes (1997). The costs and benefits of eastern enlargement: The impact on the EU and Central Europe. *Economic Policy*, 12: 125-176.

Baldwin, R.E. and A.J. Venables (1995). Regional economic integration. In G.M. Grossman and K. Rogoff, eds., *Handbook of International Economics*, Vol. 3. Amsterdam: North-Holland.

Das, S., M.J. Roberts, and J.R. Tybout (2001). Market entry costs, producer heterogeneity, and export dynamics. NBER Working Paper No. 8629, Cambridge, MA: National Bureau of Economic Research.

de Melo, J. and S. Robinson (1990). Productivity and externalities: Models of export-led growth. Policy Research Working Paper No. 387, Washington, DC: World Bank.

Deardorff, A.V. and R.M. Stern (2004). EU expansion and EU growth. In A.V. Deardorff, ed., *Past, Present and Future of the European Union*. Basingstoke: Palgrave Macmillan.

Dessus, S., K. Fukasaku, and R. Safadi (1999). Multilateral tariff liberalization and the developing countries. *OECD Development Centre Policy Brief*, No. 18, Paris: OECD.

Dimaranan, B.V. and R.A. McDougall, eds. (2002). *Global Trade, Assistance, and Production: The GTAP 5 Data Base*. West Lafayette: Center for Global Trade Analysis, Purdue University (http://www.gtap.agecon.purdue.edu/databases/v5/v5_doco.asp).

Francois, J.F. and A. Strutt (1999). Post Uruguay Round tariff vectors for GTAP version 4. Mimeo, Erasmus University, June.

Fujita, M., P. Krugman, and A.J. Venables (1999). *The Spatial Economy: Cities, Regions, and International Trade*. Cambridge, MA: MIT Press.

Fuller, F., J.C. Beghin, J. Fabiosa, S. Mohanty, C. Fang, and P. Kaus (2002). Accession of the Czech Republic, Hungary and Poland to the European Union: Impacts on agricultural markets. *World Economy*, 25: 407-428.

Harrison, G.W., T.F. Rutherford, and D.G. Tarr (1996). Increased competition and completion of the market in the European Union. *Journal of Economic Integration*, 11: 332-365.

Helpman, E. and P.R. Krugman (1985). *Market Structure and Foreign Trade: Increasing Returns, Imperfect Competition, and the International Economy*. Cambridge, MA: MIT Press.

Howe, H. (1975). Development of the extended linear expenditure system from simple savings assumptions. *European Economic Review*, 6: 305-310.

Keuschnigg, C. and W. Kohler (2002). Eastern enlargement of the EU: How much is it worth for Austria? *Review of International Economics*, 10: 324-342.

Kohler, W. (2004). Eastern enlargement of the EU: A comprehensive welfare assessment. *Journal of Policy Modeling*, 26: 865-888.

Lejour, A.M., R.A. de Mooij, and R. Nahuis (2004). EU enlargement: Economic implications for countries and industries. In H. Berger and T. Moutos, eds., *Managing European Union Enlargement.* Cambridge, MA: MIT Press.

Lluch, C. (1973). The extended linear expenditure system. *European Economic Review*, 4: 21-32.

Madsen, A.D. and M.L. Sorensen (2002). Economic consequences for Denmark of EU enlargement. Paper presented at the International Conference on Policy Modeling, Brussels, 4-6 July (http://www.ecomod.net/conferences/ecomod2002/papers/due.pdf).

Messerlin, P.A. (2001). *Measuring the Costs of Protection in Europe: European Commercial Policy in the 2000s.* Washington, DC: Institute of International Economics.

Nahuis, R. (2004). One size fits all? Accession to the internal market; an industry-level assessment of EU enlargement. *Journal of Policy Modeling*, 26: 571-586.

Robinson, S. and K. Thierfelder (1999). Trade liberalization and regional integration: The search for large numbers. Discussion Paper No. 34, Washington, DC: International Food Policy Research Institute.

Samuelson, P.A. (1952). The transfer problem and transport costs: The terms of trade when impediments are absent. *Economic Journal*, 62: 278-304.

Smith, A. and A.J. Venables (1988). Completing the internal market in the European Community: Some industry simulations. *European Economic Review*, 32: 1501-1525.

van der Mensbrugghe, D. (2003). LINKAGE technical reference document: Version 5.3. Washington, DC: The World Bank, March.

World Bank (2006). Global Economic Prospects 2006: Economic Implications of Remittances and Migration. Washington, DC: The World Bank.

CHAPTER 7

SMALL CHANGE: A CRITICAL EXAMINATION OF THE ECONOMIC RELATIONSHIP BETWEEN SOUTH ASIA AND THE EUROPEAN UNION

Jonathon W. Moses and Maggi Brigham*

South Asia constitutes one of the world's poorest regions. By contrast, the European Union (EU) is one of the richest. This chapter examines the nature of the economic relationship between these two different regions from the perspective of South Asia. In other words, we examine how South Asia's economic relationship with the EU contributes to economic growth and the alleviation of widespread poverty.

National policies for economic growth and development in South Asia today rest, in large part, on three pillars: trade, investment and migration. This has not always been the case, as South Asian markets were relatively protected before the mid 1980s. While individual countries could liberalize even more, South Asia as a whole has strived to develop export platforms that can better exploit their comparative advantages; they have liberalized domestic capital markets with an eye at encouraging foreign investors; and they have actively encouraged short-term labor emigration. All in all, countries in South Asia rely increasingly on foreign labor-, capital- and goods markets as a means for reducing domestic poverty and high unemployment levels while encouraging economic growth and development. As one of the richest regions of the world, we might expect the EU to figure prominently in the development designs of South Asian policy-makers. Although it is unreasonable to expect the EU to bear responsibility for South Asian poverty and underdevelopment, we

---

* We acknowledge the helpful comments of Indra de Soysa. Obviously, any errors or shortcomings that remain herein are our own doing.

assume that it has a moral commitment to open its markets, in order that South Asia might pull itself out of its poverty. This commitment should be especially strong, given the colonial ties that once bound South Asia to Europe's individual member states. Unfortunately, our study reveals a remarkably modest role played by EU-markets in accommodating South Asia's exports.

This study proceeds in five steps. We begin with some theoretical reflection. While policy-makers in South Asia recognize that migration complements trade and investment as important tools in each country's development basket, economic theoreticians — true to form — cannot agree whether migration complements (or substitutes for) trade and financial flows. This section discusses how we might conceptualize the relationship between different types of economic integration and their effect on development.

The main body of the paper is empirical and is itself divided into four parts. The first part describes South Asia with a brief overview of economic conditions in the individual countries that make up the region: Bangladesh, Bhutan, India, the Maldives, Nepal, Pakistan and Sri Lanka. As the quality of data varies substantially across countries, the remaining sections will mostly discuss developments with reference to the first four countries. This discussion is separated into three distinct categories: trade, investment and migration.

Theoretical Backdrop

Trade-based approaches to economic development are increasingly common, so we see little point in describing the posited mechanisms that link international trade to national economic development.[1] Our more immediate concern is to sketch the ways in which economists perceive of the role played by migration in this process, as migration has become increasingly important in recent years. Despite this increased importance, migration's role in international factor price equalization and/or for the process of development is under theorized and studied.

[1] For a review, see McCulloch, Winter and Cetera (2001).

In this light, there are two theoretical perspectives from which we might survey the nature of South Asia's economic relationship to the European Union. The first is more common and is already familiar to most students of economics: neo-Ricardian trade theory associated with Eli Heckscher, Bertil Ohlin and Paul Samuelson. We call this a trade-based approach to economic development, and it arguably dominates today's development agenda. The second approach is less familiar and more radical: a migration-based approach to development.

Due to the general nature of this project (comparing two diverse regions), the lack of systematic data across countries, and the remarkable dearth of economic exchange between the two regions, these theoretical approaches will not be tested in any rigorous fashion in the pages that follow. Rather, we use these approaches to guide an empirical description of the relationship between these two regions and to help us better understand why policy-makers in South Asia today, if often implicitly, employ both approaches in their drive to economic development.

Trade-Based Frameworks

In a now classic paper, Mundell (1957) used a Heckscher–Ohlin framework to show how trade and international factor mobility could substitute for one another. While this neo-Ricardian framework has proved ineffective at explaining the bulk of world trade (among industrialized countries), it does an adequate job of explaining North-South trade. This, in itself, has provided great comfort to academics and policy-makers in the developed world, as it has legitimized the erection of substantial barriers to immigration from the developing world. In short, international trade is seen as a tide that can lift all boats (both rich and poor) on the basis of comparative advantage. Because of this, international migration is unnecessary: trade itself can reduce the rich-poor wage differentials that are often assumed to drive international migration. Similar substitution effects are seen to exist between trade and capital flows.

On the other hand, several authors have shown that by changing some of the underlying assumptions in the Heckscher–Ohlin framework, migration, trade and capital flows (including foreign aid) could complement one another.[2] While some of these assumed conditions would seem more relevant to understanding North-North trade (e.g., economies of scale and sector-specific technological differences), others are directly relevant to understanding North-South relations (e.g., the potential costs of migration and constraints on credit). For example, under the conditions described by Markusen (1983), free trade without factor mobility does not bring about factor-price equalization, as the relatively high-priced factor in each country is the one used intensively in the goods being exported. Hence, factor mobility is seen to increase the supply of the factor that is used intensively in the goods being exported, which results in an increase in the volume of trade.[3]

Indeed, the Heckscher–Ohlin framework (with migration costs and financing constraints) does seem to explain the sort of trade flows, migration flows and wage convergence that occurred in the Atlantic economy prior to World War I. The recent work by a handful of economic historians has documented the remarkable convergence of European and American wages that resulted from economic integration across all three fronts (trade, investment and migration).[4]

To conclude, trade-based approaches assume that economic integration will benefit both rich and poor countries and each recognizes that different groups will benefit (and suffer) from increased integration. These approaches differ in terms of the role played by factor mobility as a complement to trade. For some, trade by itself may be insufficient for economic development.

Migration-Based Frameworks

Another, more radical, approach focuses squarely on the role of migration for alleviating economic and political ailments in the developing world. As this approach is largely inspired by the historical accounts of

[2] This issue is examined in Markusen (1983) and Wong (1983). See also Jones and Neary (1994), Razin and Sadka (1995), Markusen and Melvin (1981), and Markusen and Svensson (1985).

[3] Alternatively, factor mobility is seen to decrease the supply of the factor that is used intensively in the goods being imported into a country.

[4] E.g., Hatton and Williamson (1992) and O'Rourke and Williamson (1995); Williamson (1995); and O'Rourke, Taylor and Williamson (1996).

economic convergence prior to WWI (described above), it tends to assume (implicitly) that migration complements trade and investment. Its focus, however, is on the relative lack of international migration in the postwar period, and how this may have stifled the potential development benefits from trade.

Generally, migration can influence international development in four inter-related ways. First, international migration allows for a more efficient matching of international supplies and demand for labor. This generates enormous efficiency gains internationally, as described in the paragraph that follows. Second, emigration tightens the sending country labor markets (albeit often at the regional, not national, level), strengthening the bargaining position of the labor that remains.[5] Third, immigrant labor provides a large and dependable source of development capital in the form of remittances. Finally, returning migrants bring capital, skills and market access that benefit the sending economy.[6]

One wing of this approach is highly stylized and draws from the influential (and provocative) work by Hamilton and Whalley (1984) to show the potential economic gains from a more liberal international migration system. Using computable general equilibrium models, recent work has suggested that the efficiency gains from free migration could absolutely dwarf the gains from other, more traditional, development approaches.[7] For example, Moses and Letnes (2004) find that even a small liberalization of international migration restrictions can yield sub-

---

[5] The logic here is akin to that of the Nobel laureate, Arthur Lewis' (1954) two-sector approach, but backwards. Lewis was interested in how to attract labor from the agricultural to the industrial sector (and how high industrial wages had to be in order to do this). In this context we are interested in how much wages in the sending country need to increase in order to stave off potential emigration.

[6] The traditional argument for countering international migration builds on posited 'brain drain' effects. However, recent work suggests that these concerns may be exaggerated. Either way, most migration from South Asia is in the form of unskilled labor, where concerns about brain drain are not particularly relevant. Conversely, the recent hyperbole about 'outsourcing' to India in the 2004 US presidential elections suggest that South Asian concerns about brain drain may be overblown. For more on development and migration, see Massey (1988) and Skeldon (1997). For a brief introduction to the new revisionist work on brain drain, see Faini (2005).

[7] E.g., Winters (2002); Iregui (2005); and Moses and Letnes (2004, 2005).

stantial gains: they estimate that a 10 percent increase in international migration corresponds to an efficiency gain of about 774 billion (1998) dollars!

This section is meant to show how migration can be seen as an integral part of South Asia's development strategy, and to illustrate how some theoretical frameworks have managed to ignore the subject for so long. Recently, policy-makers and academics alike have come to recognize the significant and stabilizing role played by migration remittances (see, e.g., Kapur and McHale 2003 and World Bank 2003) and international organizations have come to embrace the potential of temporary migration (e.g., the WTO has introduced temporary migration to the international trade agenda — so-called Mode 4 trade).

South Asia and its Relationship to the EU

The Asian Development Bank describes South Asia in terms of eight states: Afghanistan, Bangladesh, Bhutan, India, Maldives, Nepal, Pakistan and Sri Lanka. With the exception of Afghanistan, these states are the signatories of the South Asian Association for Regional Cooperation (SAARC), which was formed in 1985 to promote economic, social and cultural development across the region.

Poverty is the most common (and obvious) defining characteristic of the countries of South Asia. In addition, the region's sheer demographic size draws attention. The countries of South Asia constitute 22.5 percent of the world's population, totaling 1,395 million people (see Table 7.1). However, among this group there are important differences separating the most populous (India) from the least populous (the Maldives) states. Worst, the region's population is growing at almost twice the rate of the world's annual average. Indeed, only Sri Lanka seems to have turned the demographic corner, while Bangladesh and India have only recently entered the fertility-declining phase of the demographic transition.

Table 7.1. General Economic Features

	Population, 2002			*GDP growth rates, annual averages*		
	Millions	% world	Annual growth rate, 2001-2	1994-97	1997-01	2001-03
Afghanistan	21.8	0.35	1.7	-	-	-
Bangladesh	131.2	2.12	1.5	4.6	5.4	4.9
Bhutan	0.7	0.01	2.4	6.3	6.6	7.2
India	1,055.0	17.02	1.8	7.7	5.5	5.0
Maldives	0.3	0.00	1.6	7.6	8.1	4.7
Nepal	23.7	0.38	2.0	5.6	4.7	2.1
Pakistan	143.7	2.32	2.2	5.3	3.3	2.8
Sri Lanka	19.0	0.31	1.5	4.8	5.2	4.6
South Asia	1,395.4	22.51	1.8	7.1	5.2	4.6
WORLD	6,198.3	100.00	1.0			

Sources: Asian Development Bank (2004b); and RIS (2004: 21).

Over the past decade or so, the South Asian economies have embarked upon major reforms aimed at liberalizing their external (and, increasingly, their domestic) sectors. While the relationship between these reforms and economic growth is complicated and unclear,[8] what is clear is that the annual GDP growth rate in South Asia has declined over the same period: averaging 7.1 percent annually in the period 1994–97, falling to 5.2 percent in the 1997–2001 period, and falling further to 4.6 percent in most recent years.[9] In 2001, the aggregate GDP for the SAARC region was €711 billion, or €538/capita (DG TRADE 2002).

Consequently, the region suffers from a dismal human development profile, as exhibited in Table 7.2: about 41 percent of the region's population finds itself below the income poverty line, as defined by 1 US$/day (1993 PPP US$). About one third of the populations of Bangladesh, Pakistan and India are estimated to live below the poverty level, as defined in each country. Indeed, on average, South Asian countries rank relatively low on the UNDP's Human Development Index (HDI): only the Maldives, Sri Lanka and India are defined as Medium Human Development countries, the others find themselves toward the bottom of the UNDP's HDI country ranking (i.e., in the category 'Low Human Development').

The result is a regional population mired in poverty and facing a number of intimidating challenges. These include an enormous population (of 1.4 billion people, 60 percent of whom are working-age); a labor force participation rate that is only about 60 percent of the working age group; employment growth rates across the region that are lower than both GDP and labor force growth rates (and a labor market that is characterized by pervasive unemployment, especially among the young and educated); and the region continues to be swamped by poverty and illiteracy (Mahbub Ul Haq Human Development Centre 2004).

---

[8] See Round and Whalley (2002) for a discussion of the potential linkage mechanisms between trade liberalization and poverty reduction in South Asia.

[9] Recent projections by the World Bank suggest that this trend will change in the near future, because — in part — of the influence of massive remittance inflows (World Bank 2003).

Table 7.2. Human Development Profiles

	India	*Pakistan*	*Bangladesh*	*Nepal*	*Sri Lanka*	*Bhutan*	*Maldives*	*South Asia, weighted average*	*Developing countries*
Population below income poverty line (%)									
• $1 a day (1993 PPP US$) 1983-2000	44.2	31	29.1	37.7	6.6	-	-	41	-
• national poverty line 1997-2000	26.1	34	35.6	42	25	-	-	-	-
Population without access to health service, 1995									
• number (millions)	143	63	68	-	1.3	0.6	0.1	276T	910T
• % of total population	15	45	55	-	7	35	25	22	20
Population without access to safe water, 2000									
• number (millions)	122	17	4	5	3	0.8	-	151T	-
• % of total population	12	12	3	19	17	38	-	11	22
Population without access to sanitation, 2000									
• number (millions)	700	54	61	18	3.2	0.7	0.13	835T	2439T
• % of total population	69	39	47	73	17	31	44	63	48
Illiterate adults, 2000									
• number (millions)	434	78	76	14	1.6	-	0.01	604T	-
• % of total adult population	42.8	56.8	58.7	58.2	8.4	-	3.3	45.5	26.3
Illiterate female adults, 2000									
• number (millions)	270	48	44	9	1	-	-	372T	-
• % of total adult female population	55	72	70	76	11	-	-	58	31
Child malnutrition (weight for age), 2000									
• % of children under 5	47	38	61	47	33	-	-	47	-
Under 5 mortality rate (per 1000 live births), 2000	96	110	82	100	19	100	80	95	59
People living with HIV/AIDS, 2001									
• Adult (% age 1-49)	0.79	0.11	<0.1	0.49	<0.1	<0.1	0.06	-	1.32
UNDP Human Development Index, 2002									
• Score	.577	.499	.478	.49	.741	.494	.743		
• Ranking	124	138	145	142	89	140	84		

Source: RIS (2004: 94); UNDP (2002).

Notes: See original sources for further clarification and detail.

The Relationship Defined

This paper addresses the nature of the economic relationship between South Asia and the European Union. To be perfectly honest, it is an exaggeration (or perhaps premature) to speak of a relationship here. There are remarkably few formal links at the level of regional organizations (although nation-state links, steeped in history, continue to be important for individual member states in both regions). As we shall discuss in the empirical section that follows, the level of economic integration between these two regions is surprisingly small.[10] Having said this, the EU has made official offers of assistance and cooperation,[11] and SAARC countries depend increasingly on the export markets of the world, including (but not confined to) those of EU-member states.

Indeed, Europe's institutional attention seems to be placed elsewhere in Asia. In the early 1990s, as the Asian tiger economies began to experience double-digit economic growth, Europe's interest in Asia increased phenomenally. Within the EU, at a number of levels, one could find a growing awareness of the need to intensify and deepen Europe's relationship with Asia on a number of fronts (economic, political, strategic, etc.). Toward that end, the European Commission submitted a communication to the Council of Ministers on the need for a new Asian strategy in

---

[10] On the other hand, this level of integration is not too surprising when we consider that the SAARC countries themselves have not come very far in their own internal economic integration.

[11] Of course, the European Union has maintained cooperation agreements with SAARC member countries before the formation of SAARC. At the formation of SAARC, the European Parliament (EP) expressed its intention for economic cooperation. In October 1988, the EP adopted a resolution in which it called the Commission to contact the SAARC institution and the member countries in order to examine possibilities of cooperation and completing a cooperation agreement with SAARC. SAARC countries, however, showed little interest at the time, arguing that they needed to establish better links within the region before establishing them with third parties (Quddus 2001: 66). As a consequence, the EU's relationship to SAARC is limited to signing a 1996 Memorandum of Understanding with the SAARC Secretariat, offering them technical assistance. There were two main results of this otherwise limited co-operation: the inclusion of SAARC in the General System of Preferences (GSP) Cumulative Clause of the Rules of Origin and an exploratory mission in the autumn of 1999 to launch an assistance program ('Assisting SAARCs Integration Process').

order to maintain Europe's leading role in the world economy (European Commission 1994).

These concerns were heightened when the Asia Pacific Economic Council (APEC) held its first summit in Seattle, in 1993. When it was launched in 1989, APEC had been largely ignored by Europe. Now that world leaders were gathering to discuss Asia's economic potential, Europe saw itself increasingly isolated from developments in Asia. Indeed, the European Commission sought, but did not receive, formal representation at the Seattle summit.

Europe's response to this institutional lacuna was the 1996 launching of the Asia Europe Meeting (ASEM), which brought together 26 European and Asian partners in a dialogue that covers political, economic and cultural affairs.[12] For us, the most noteworthy aspect of the ASEM is the absence of representation from any South Asian countries. Although the ASEM is meant to capture and strengthen Europe's relationship to Asia, South Asia is not included amongst its members.

This paper describes the nature of the economic relationship between the European Union and the states of South Asia, all of whom find themselves outside of the ASEM framework. Unfortunately, the neglect of this relationship is not confined to regional agreements such as the ASEM. There is surprisingly little work done, and data collected, on the nature of the economic relationship between South Asia and Europe. As a result, the remainder of the paper is largely descriptive and exploratory.

Trade

Since the mid 1980s, the liberalization of foreign trade has become a fundamental part of South Asia's economic development strategy; each country in the region undertook unprecedented reforms. This new emphasis is clearly shown in the reduction of tariff rates across South Asia

[12] On the European side the membership includes the European Commission and the (then) 15 Member States of the European Union — Austria, Belgium, Denmark, Finland, France, Germany, Greece, Ireland, Italy, Luxembourg, Netherlands, Portugal, Spain, Sweden and the United Kingdom. The Asian side has ten partners, seven from South East Asia - Brunei, Indonesia, Malaysia, the Philippines, Singapore, Thailand and Vietnam and three from East Asia — China, Japan and the Republic of Korea. See O'Brien (2001) for a description and overview.

during the 1990s (RIS 2004: 19), as well as in the region's growing trade shares. While trade represented just 41.2 percent of South Asia's GDP in the mid 1980s, it rose to over 71.4 percent in the new millennium. Of course, these aggregate figures conceal large differences across the region: differences that we should expect to see with country size (i.e., smaller countries such as the Maldives and Bhutan rely much more heavily on trade than does the largest country, India). The general picture, however, is one of a region that has become increasingly integrated in the world's trading economy.

These rising trade shares resulted from an unprecedented growth in the value of both exports and imports across South Asia since 1992 (combined with a drop in GDP as shown in Table 7.3, below). Over the past twenty years, SAARC member countries have managed to increase their level of both imports (from 17,509 million ECU/euros in 1980 to 83,940 million in 2001) and exports (from 9,046 million ECU/euros in 1980 to 72,268 million in 2001). In doing so, the region's share of world trade has improved (while its share of world imports has dropped from 1.7 percent to 1.5 percent, the region's share of world exports has actually increased from 0.9 percent to 1.4 percent) (DG TRADE 2002). While the growth is encouraging, it totals to a pittance: a world export share of 1.4 percent is not very encouraging for a region that is home to about 23 percent of the world's population![13]

Unfortunately, the European share of South Asia's exports is only a little bit larger. According to the EU's statistical yearbook of external EU trade (European Communities 2002), only four countries from South Asia have any measurable trading relationship with EU member states: India, Pakistan, Bangladesh and Sri Lanka, and the extent of these relationships are shown in Table 7.4.

[13] Given the enormous size of India's domestic market, and the region's traditional emphasis on inward-looking development strategies, it is somewhat misleading to use world per capita trade shares. Having said this, however, the region's world trade share is still remarkably small.

Table 7.3. South Asian Trade Shares (as % of GDP)

	1985-87	*1990-92*	*1996-98*	*2000-2001*
Bangladesh	24.7	19.8	30.5	35.5
Bhutan	61.5	75.1	76.2	89.5
India	14.1	18.8	25.5	29.8
Maldives	60.3	88.5	167.1	168.9
Nepal	31.9	36.3	59.6	55.1
Pakistan	34.0	37.5	36.4	35.8
Sri Lanka	61.9	68.4	79.2	85.4
SAARC average	41.2	49.2	67.8	71.4

Source: RIS (2004).

Table 7.4. EU Trade with South Asia (million ECU/Euros, and % share in parentheses)

	Exports			*Imports*		
	1980	1990	2000	1980	1990	2000
India	2,432	6,408	13,384	1,840	4,765	12,372
	(1.10)	(1.60)	(1.40)	(0.60)	(1.00)	(1.10)
Pakistan	929	1,528	1,918	465	1,555	2,621
	(0.40)	(0.30)	(0.20)	(0.10)	(0.30)	(0.20)
Bangladesh	349	416	701	157	523	3,091
	(0.10)	(0.10)	(0.00)	(0.00)	(0.10)	(0.20)
Sri Lanka	298	368	1,580	234	479	1,907
	(0.10)	(0.00)	(0.10)	(0.00)	(0.10)	(0.10)
S Asian total	3,918	8,720	17,583	2,696	7,322	19,991
	(1.86)	(2.23)	(1.87)	(1.01)	(1.67)	(1.93)
Total EU	211,124	390,555	942,044	268,036	439,411	1,033,436

Source: European Communities (2002: Table 2B).

The largest European trade partner, India, captured just 1.1 percent of Europe's imports in the year 2000. Indeed, together, South Asian states delivered just under 2.0 percent of Europe's imports in the year 2000 (and imported about the same amount from Europe!). In 2003, when we can measure the European market in terms of 25 member states (EU25), the SAARC share has remained about the same: 2.5 percent of EU25's imports and 2.2 percent of EU25's exports (DG TRADE 2004).

Table 7.5 provides a glimpse of how European markets play an important, but not the sole, destination for South Asian exports. As a whole, in the year 2002, European markets captured just 25.3 percent of South Asian exports to the world. However, this share has dropped from where it was a decade earlier in 1990 (29.9 percent). The US share of South Asian exports, by contrast, have grown significantly over the same period, from 16.3 percent to 24.7 percent, with sizeable increases across all countries (the exception being Bangladesh, where the US share actually fell).[14]

When we break down this trade into product groups, we see that European countries tend to import mostly textiles and clothing from South Asia (worth €10,598 million in 2001), followed by agricultural products (worth €2,134 million in 2001), chemical products, machinery, transportation material and energy. Even in the sector where South Asian imports to Europe are strongest (textiles and clothing), SAARC imports constituted only 14.5 percent of the EU's total import of these products (DG TRADE 2002). Two years later, with the European market extended to include 25 member states, SAARC's share has, if anything, gotten worse. While the regional balance of trade in transport, energy and chemical products has stayed about the same, the trade deficits in South Asia's most important export sectors (textiles and clothing, machinery and agricultural products) has gotten worse (DG TRADE 2004).

[14] To give the reader a rough indicator of the relative size of these two important markets, the US GDP in 2001 was US$11.2 trillion (in current prices), while the comparative figure for the EU15 was $8.7 trillion. See http://www.eurunion.org/profile/EUUSStats.htm.

Table 7.5. Direction of South Asian Exports (% of total)

To:	*DMCs*		*China*		*Japan*		*US*		*EU*		*Others*	
From:	1990	2002	1990	2002	1990	2002	1990	2002	1990	2002	1990	2002
Afghanistan	14.3	57.6	0.4	0.1	1.5	1.6	3.4	4.3	61.7	19.0	18.7	17.3
Bangladesh	8.6	4.7	1.5	0.2	3.9	1.0	30.5	27.6	31.5	42.9	24.0	23.5
Bhutan	-	-	-	-	-	-	-	-	-	-	-	-
India	11.3	16.4	0.1	4.2	9.3	3.8	15.1	22.9	27.7	22.9	36.5	29.8
Maldives	38.5	28.9	0.0	0.0	8.5	7.5	24.2	50.7	26.2	9.1	2.6	3.7
Nepal	11.6	49.7	2.3	0.9	0.8	1.1	23.4	28.0	53.3	15.4	8.6	5.0
Pakistan	17.2	15.6	1.2	2.4	8.2	1.4	12.4	24.5	36.0	27.2	25.0	28.9
Sri Lanka	9.1	7.5	0.2	0.2	5.4	3.5	25.9	40.8	26.3	29.7	33.2	18.3
South Asia	12.3	15.2	0.4	3.3	8.4	3.2	16.3	24.7	29.9	25.3	32.8	28.2

Source: Asian Development Bank (2004a: 287, Table A11).

Note: DMC stands for "Developing Member Country" of the Asian Development Bank.

For its part, the EU exports a variety of goods to SAARC countries, including machinery (€4,733 million in 2001) and chemical products (€2,039 million in 2001), followed by transportation material, agricultural products, textiles and clothing, and energy (DG TRADE 2002). As we saw on the import side of the equation, the South Asian market is not very important for European exporters: it constitutes less than 2 percent of the total export share in any one of these product groups. Still, in the area of machinery, transport and chemical products, the EU exports more than it imports from South Asia.

To get a better picture of the character of South Asian export trade to the EU, we can briefly trace developments in the textile and garments sector — the fastest growing export sector in South Asia. This development has been encouraged by changing domestic policies (often in response to international pressure for liberalization) as well as international agreements (such as the Multi-Fibre Arrangement [MFA]) that provide some limited access to developed country markets. In addition, South Asia was able to move upstream to fill a niche left vacant by the first generation of garment exporters who had lost their labor-cost advantage when they developed into Newly Industrialized Countries.

As a result of this happy coincidence of events, South Asian export earnings from textiles and garments have been growing faster than the region's total export growth since the mid 1980s. For most South Asian economies, the textile and garment sector emerged as the mainstay of industrial growth and employment creation. This development shows the importance of market access for South Asian exports as a potential development tool. It also shows how South Asian countries have been able to exploit their comparative advantage in cheap labor when provided with that market access. While the EU (along with the US) are the main export markets for most of these readymade garment products, this section has shown how South Asia's access to these markets remains remarkably limited.

Capital Flows and Investments

For many years, South Asia was the poster child for foreign aid from the industrialized world (Sobhan 2004). Between 1980 and 2001, $17 billion worth of Official Development Assistance (ODA) flowed into South Asia, as shown in Table 7.6. In recent years, however, these flows — in both per capita and percent of GDP terms — have declined significantly, as has South Asia's share of the world's ODA. As is common elsewhere, these developments reflect the changing perspectives of aid donors, and a new emphasis on the role of private capital to meet developing country needs.

Until quite recently, international investors were not particularly interested in investing in South Asia — neither were they particularly welcome. Before the 1990s, Foreign Direct Investment (FDI) flows were miniscule, and the level of portfolio investment was even smaller because of the region's capital account restrictions and relatively underdeveloped capital markets. As the countries of South Asia began to pursue more liberal and open economic policies in the mid 1990s, many of which were driven by international donors and their institutional agents (see appendix to IPSSL 2000), more FDI began to flow into these countries.

Under these new conditions, where developing countries compete over world FDI flows, South Asia has managed to increase its level of FDI substantially. Still, its level and share of world (and even developing world) FDI remains quite small. As evidenced in Table 7.7, South Asia attracted about 4.58 billion dollars worth of FDI in 2002, but this was just 0.7 percent of total global flows (and most of this went to India). This table also reveals that South Asia relies much less than the world (or developing country) average on FDI as a share of its gross fixed capital supplies. Indeed, only Pakistan seemed capable of attracting as much as 10 percent (the developing world's average) of its investment needs from foreign suppliers in 2002.

While the conditions for FDI appear to be improving in South Asia, none of these countries scored well on the UNCTAD's Inward FDI Performance Index ranking (1999–2001), which ranks countries by the FDI they receive relative to their economic size (see UNCTAD 2003). In this ranking of 140 countries, Belgium and Luxembourg tops the list (1), while countries such as Surinam (140) and Gabon (139) find themselves at the bottom.

Table 7.6. Official Development Assistance (ODA)

	Total ODA (millions USD)			*Per capita ODA ($)*		*ODA as % of GDP*	
	1980	1990	2001	1990	2001	1990	2001
Bangladesh	1,282	210	1,023.9	19.7	7.3	7.0	2.2
Bhutan	8	47	59.2	32.7	27.9	16.5	11.1
India	2,147	1,586	1,705.4	1.9	1.7	0.4	0.4
Maldives	-	-	25	-	83.2	9.8	4.3
Nepal	163	429	388.1	22.7	16.1	11.7	7.0
Pakistan	1,130	1,152	1,938.2	10.3	13.2	2.8	3.3
Sri Lanka	390	665	330.2	39.1	17.6	9.1	2.1
Total S. Asia	5,120	6,174	6,032.1	5.4	4.2	1.1	0.8
S. Asia as % of world total ODA	18.50	12.58	11.73	-	-	-	-

Source: Sobhan (2004).

Table 7.7. Foreign Direct Investment (FDI) Inflows

	Annual average 1991-96		*2002*		
	Millions USD	% Gross fixed capital formation	Millions USD	% Gross fixed capital formation	% world total
Bangladesh	8	0.1	45	0.4	0.0
Bhutan	1	0.6	-	0.2	-
India	1,085	1.3	3,449	3.2	0.5
Maldives	8	8.5	12	6.5	0.0
Nepal	8	0.9	10	0.9	0.1
Pakistan	501	5.3	823	10.7	0.1
Sri Lanka	125	4.6	242	6.6	0.0
South Asia	1,736	3.04	4,581	4.07	0.7
Developing countries	91,502	6.5	162,415	10.5	24.9
World	254,326	4.4	651,188	12.2	100

Source: RIS (2004: 40, Tables 5.1 and 5.2).

It is closer to this end of the ranking that the countries of South Asia find themselves: Sri Lanka ranks best (111), while Nepal does worst (with 130), with the other countries placed somewhere in between.

As with the trade figures, we find that Europe does play a role in supplying FDI to South Asia (along with the US). In Table 7.8 we have ranked the most important investors in five South Asian countries. In this ranking we see the predominant role played by the United States (except in the cases of Nepal and Sri Lanka): the US delivered about a third of all FDI to Pakistan and Bangladesh, and a fifth of India's FDI supply. The measure of the EU share is illustrative of the EU's larger relationship to South Asia, as it is a composite indicator of member state activity in this area (i.e., it is based on investments originating in Germany, the UK, France, the Netherlands, Italy, Denmark, Sweden, Belgium and Luxembourg). The EU presence is strongest in Pakistan (delivering 32.8 percent of all FDI) and Bangladesh (25.8 percent), with the United Kingdom supplying the lion's share of this investment in both countries.

We began this paper by suggesting that it was reasonable to depict the European Union as a world region that was relatively rich in capital, and that South Asia could be characterized as a region rich in labor (but poor in capital). Given this depiction, it is rather disappointing to see such a small share of FDI coming from EU-member states (or, for that matter, from the richer countries altogether). It is unreasonable to place the sole blame for this rather dismal showing on European or American markets. Obviously, the South Asian economies could improve their attractiveness to international investors. Still, this section shows how difficult and problematic it is for countries in South Asia to rely on FDI as an engine for economic growth and development — just as the previous section showed with regard to trade.

Table 7.8. Leading Investors in South Asia

Source	*Bangladesh*	*India*	*Nepal*	*Pakistan*	*Sri Lanka*
USA	*29.5*	*22.1*	*4.4*	*41.6*	
EU	*25.8*	*16.1*	*9.3*	*32.8*	*11.9*
Japan	*7.6*	*4.4*	*6.1*	*15*	*11.6*
Korea, Rep.	2.8	4.5		1.6	32.7
Hong Kong	7.5		2.1		11.9
Singapore	5.9				6.4
Malaysia	-	2.75			
Australia	-	*3.0*			*15.0*
China PR	1.3		7.5		
Mauritius	-	10.4			
Bermuda	-		14.6		
Philippines	-		9.6		
New Zealand	-		*2.1*		
UAE	-			1.6	
Intra-SAARC	3.9	.04	37.6	Na	2.1
Others	15.7	36.71	6.7	7.4	8.4
Non-industrial, total	37.1	54.4	78.1	10.6	61.5

Source: IPSSL (2000: 15-16, Table 7).

Note: Investment amounts are in terms of percentages, based on the top ten investors in each country as reported by different national authorities. See the original source for details. For the EU-share, we combined the 9 EU states that were represented in the top ten categories (Germany, UK, France, Netherlands, Italy, Denmark, Sweden, Belgium and Luxembourg). Of course, the EU-share may be larger, as other EU-member states may have contributed. Non-industrial totals are the total percentage, minus investment shares from the US, EU, Japan, Australia and New Zealand.

Migration

Despite significant attempts at reform and a push to exploit international markets, trade and investments have proven insufficient for meeting the region's development needs. As a result, the region has been drawn, increasingly, to the potential offered by international migration. Thus far, we have seen that the EU's share of South Asian trade and investment needs is remarkably small. Given the possibility that labor flows may actually complement trade and capital flows, the European Union could provide an outlet for some of South Asia's migrant workers. This could also benefit Europe: its total population is only growing because of the net inflow of international migrants (in the year 2000, these totaled 680,000) (Eurostat 2002: 1), and there are growing concerns in Europe about the shortage of young workers to pay for future pension schemes.

On the South Asian side of the equation there is also a realization of the role that emigration can play in national development strategies. Indicative of this realization is the recent claim by the (then) Bangladeshi Prime Minister, Sheikh Hasina, that the solution to the country's problems of poverty lay in migration: 'We'll send them to America...Globalization will take that problem away, as you free up all factors of production, also labour. There'll be free movement, country to country. Globalization in its purest form should not have any boundaries, so small countries with big populations should be able to send population to countries with big boundaries and small populations. Already, we have nearly two million working abroad' (*Migration News* [June 2001], cited in Watkins and Nurick 2002: 68). Indeed, Islam (1995: 360) holds that, 'The export of manpower and the resultant in-flow of remittances have largely been acclaimed as the crucial factors in keeping the Bangladeshi economy afloat in recent years'.

And South Asians are definitely on the move. Emigration is pervasive to the region, and the remittances it generates are one of the most important sources of foreign exchange for each South Asian economy. Across the region, countries have benefited considerably from migration and they are positioning themselves to exploit these markets all the more in the near future. Only India seems to have seen a serious decline in its number of registered emigrants recently, as witnessed in Figure 7.1 below.

Sri Lanka and Bangladesh have the region's most explicit and active emigration policies.[15] Sri Lanka has introduced a range of policies and institutions that encourage and actively support migrants leaving to look for work. The result has been a rapid growth in the number of migrants (especially female migrants)[16] and a growth in the importance of remittances to the Sri Lankan economy. Bangladesh also encourages emigration actively, but here we find a large number of people who are choosing to (or are forced to) migrate illegally as well. On the other hand, India and Pakistan employ a more 'hands-off' policy stance with respect to emigration: they have largely removed restrictions to emigration and do relatively little to support and protect migrants once they leave the country.

Figure 7.1 draws on data collected largely by Wickramasekera (2002: 15) to show the size and trends of recent emigration from the largest states in South Asia: Bangladesh, India, Pakistan and Sri Lanka. Here we see that the annual outflow of migrants has been increasing phenomenally over the past three decades, although it has appeared to drop off in India and Bangladesh in the most recent years (recent data for the other countries was more difficult to obtain). As we shall see below, events in the Gulf region have a significant impact on these trends.

This outflow in people corresponds to a rise in annual remittances, as shown in the Table 7.9. Because of the patchy nature of this data, cross-national and temporal comparisons are tricky. Still, we see a phenomenal rise in the amount of remittances that are returning home to each South Asian country from their emigrant workers abroad. This trend is clearly

---

[15] See IOM (2003) and Watkins and Nurick (2002) for useful descriptions of national sending country policies.

[16] Countries in South Asia have responded in different ways to the demand for women migrants. USAID in Bangladesh has estimated that between 10-20,000 women and children are trafficked from the country to India, Pakistan and the Middle East each year to work in the sex trade, as domestic labor, or as camel jockeys and beggars (USAID/Bangladesh website, cited in Watkins and Nurick 2002: 76). As a result, Bangladesh has actually banned the travel of unskilled women workers overseas. Sri Lanka, on the other hand, has actively nurtured (and monitored) the market for female labor overseas in countries such as the Philippines and Indonesia.

evident in Figure 7.2, which provides a longer time series of Indian remittances since the mid 1980s.

In fact, a recent World Bank report, *Global Development Finance 2003*, noted that home remittances are a hugely important source of development capital and foreign reserves across South Asia: in Sri Lanka, remittances account for over ten percent of GDP; in Nepal, it would be appear, the economy would be in dire straits but for remittances; India was the world's second-largest recipient of remittances worldwide; in Pakistan, remittances tripled between 2001 and 2003; and in Bangladesh, remittance flows increased by nearly 50 percent during the same time period. In 2001, Indian workers abroad sent home a remarkable US$10 billion in remittances!

Indeed, as a region, the size of workers' remittances dwarfs other sources of external financing, as shown in Table 7.10. In 2002, the region of South Asia received $16 billion in remittances. This is the second highest among developing country regions and equals 2.5 percent of the region's GDP. More significantly, this injection of capital dwarfed more traditional sources of foreign investment (and touched different lives): cf., the 5 billion dollars that entered the region (net) in terms of foreign direct investments, and/or the 0.8 billion dollars of portfolio equity inflows.

But this bonanza of foreign exchange is not coming mostly from Europe. Indeed, it would seem that Europe has little room for South Asian migrants. In 2000, the European stock of foreign population from these countries was almost non existent, except for in the UK, Italy and Denmark. In the UK, because of its colonial ties, there was a fairly significant stock of Indians (132,000), Pakistanis (82,000), Bangladeshis (70,000) and Sri Lankans (50,000), representing several years of previous immigration. Indeed, these four nationalities captured about 13 percent of the foreign population in the UK (SOPEMI 2003: B.1.5). Yet recent flows are relatively small: in 2001, only 33,700 Indians and 13,800 Pakistanis immigrated to the UK, representing 10 percent and 4 percent of the total immigrant inflows that year (flows from the other countries were not large enough to score in the top ten) (SOPEMI 2003: 39, chart 1.3).

Figure 7.1. Officially Reported Outflows of Migrant Workers

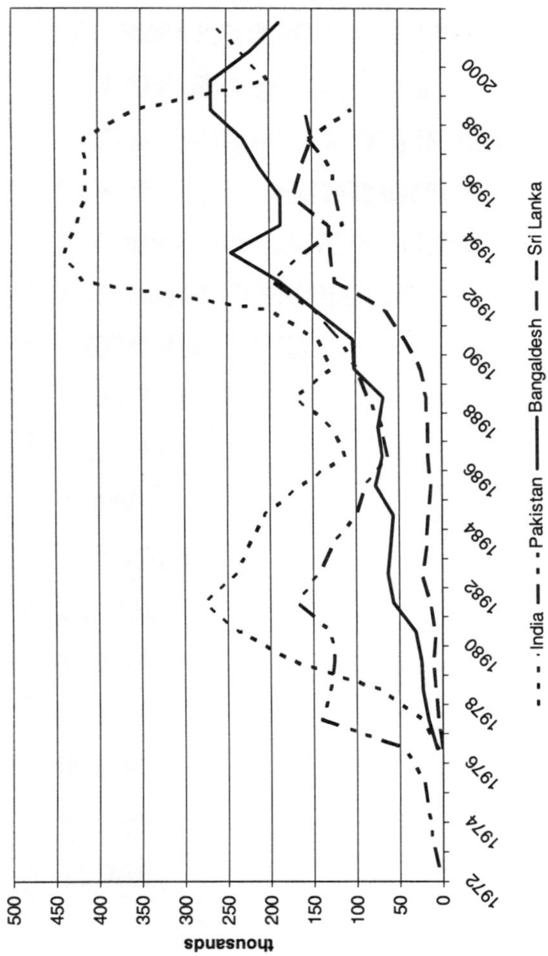

Sources: Wickramasekera (2002: 15); Skeldon (2003: 5).

Figure 7.2. India's Remittances, 1985-2001

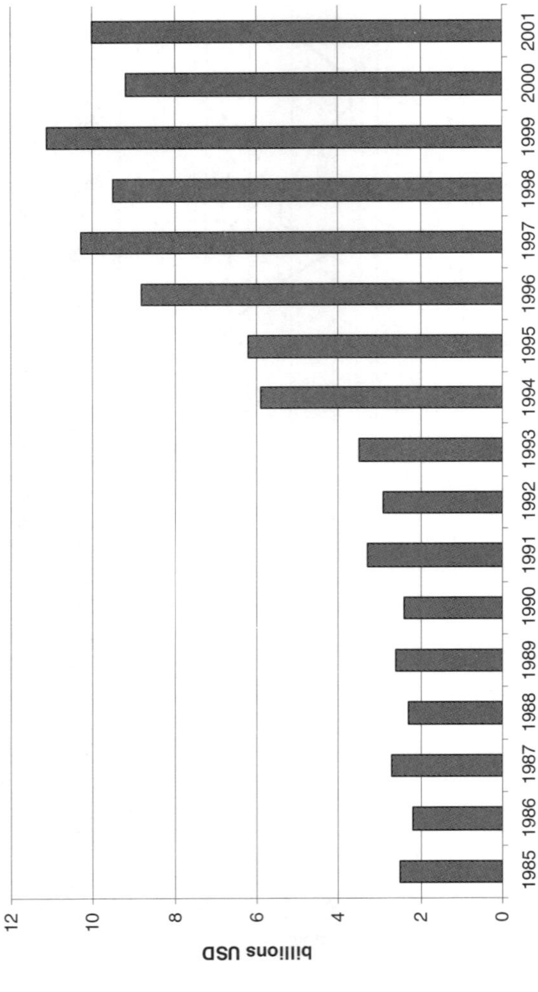

Source: IMF *Balance of Payments* Yearbook.

Table 7.9. Average Annual Remittances (US$ billions), Selected Years and Countries

	1977	*1980*	*1986*	*1990*	*1995*	*1999*	*2000*	*2001*	*2002*
Bangladesh	.079	.339	.502	.779	1.202	1.807	1.949	1.882	2.501
India	.934	2.757	2.469	2.384	6.223	11.124	9.2	10	
Nepal	-	-	-	-	.057	.443	-	-	-
Pakistan	.868	2.038	2.525	1.997	1.712	1.06	.984	1.087	2.389
Sri Lanka	.018	.152	.292	.401	.801	1.068	1.16	1.155	1.287

Sources: Watkins and Nurick (2002: 11-12) for 1977-1999, respective central banks for most recent years.

Table 7.10. South Asian External Financing Sources (US$ billions)

	1997	*1998*	*1999*	*2000*	*2001*	*2002*
Worker remittances	14.6	13.3	15.1	13.5	14.9	16.0
Net inward FDI	4.9	3.5	3.1	3.1	4.1	5.0
Net inward portfolio equity flows	2.9	-0.6	2.4	1.7	1.6	0.8

Source: World Bank (2003: 185, Table a6).

Table 7.11. Average Annual Number of Migrant Workers and Share by Region of Destination

	1980-84	*1980-89*	*1990-94*	*1995-99*
Bangladesh				
• Number of clearances (land)	53,000	78,000	174,000	262,000[a]
• % Gulf (western Asia)	92.0	95.9	83.5	
• % Other Asia	1.0	0.5	15.6	
• % Outside Asia	7.0	3.6	0.9	
India				
• Number of clearances	223,500	139,800	297,225	400,275[a]
• % Gulf (western Asia)	92.4	95.8	96.0	
• % Other countries	7.6	4.2	4.0	
Pakistan				
• Number of clearances	124,500	76,800	143,000	127,075[a]
• % Gulf (Western Asia)	97.2	99.9	99.6	
• % Other Asia	0.0	0.0	0.2	
• % Outside Asia	2.7	0.1	0.2	
Sri Lanka				
• Number of clearances	31,300	18900	52,300	164,312
• % Gulf (Western Asia)	-	94.5	95.4	94.0
• % Other Asia	-	4.3	3.3	4.0
• % Outside Asia	-	1.2	1.3	2.0

Source: IOM (2003: 16).

Note: Average annual number of migrant workers originating in each country; [a]1995-98.

In Italy, the South Asian immigration figures were much smaller and confined to Sri Lanka (33,700) and India (30,300), totaling just 5 percent of the stock of foreign population in 2000. In Denmark, 7,100 Pakistanis made up less than 3 percent of the total stock of foreigners in the year 2000. In neither country did South Asians make a noticeable dent on the immigration inflow statistics for that year (SOPEMI 2003).

As evidenced in Table 7.11 (above), the vast majority of emigrants from these countries are going to the Gulf region, with only very small shares going to regions 'outside Asia'. Saudi Arabia hosts (by far) the greatest number of migrants from Bangladesh, India, Pakistan and Sri Lanka, while Kuwait, the UAE and Oman struggle over second, third and fourth positions. The majority of Nepalis are still going to traditional destinations such as India, but increasing numbers of Nepalese migrants are heading for the Gulf. Most early emigration from Pakistan went to the UK, but this began to dry up in the mid 1970s. Since that time, Pakistan has relied almost entirely on migration to Western Asia or the Middle East. The figures for Bangladesh, India and Sri Lanka from the 1980s also show the growing importance of other destinations in Asia (e.g., Malaysia), though these are still relatively small.

What these emigration figures reveal is a remarkable, mostly untapped, development potential. South Asian labor markets are swamped, and a significant number of their workers are willing to work abroad to improve their circumstances. Indeed, worker remittances have become the most stable and significant source of investment and aid in these countries, and yet most of these remittances are coming from non-European and non-American markets. It is in these markets that we find the greatest potential for South Asia to exploit its comparative advantage in cheap labor.[17] Obviously, this will require a significant change of attitude in the developed world.

---

[17] By pointing to the economic potential of emigration and remittances, we do not mean to belittle the social and human costs associated with migration, in both sender and receiver countries. These can be considerable. Our point-of-departure is the improved welfare of the poor in developing countries, and we assume that it is better for the poor, themselves, to decide which is worse: to live in an area mired in poverty and with little economic recourse, or to escape to a labor market that can put food on the family's table.

Conclusion

This empirical overview of South Asia's economic relationship to the European Union has revealed a remarkably small web of interconnections. Despite strong historical ties that have linked individual countries in both regions, today's economic ties are hardly sufficient to pull South Asia from the poverty in which it is mired. There is simply not enough economic exchange between the two regions to make any noticeable difference in South Asia.

Still, two cautious conclusions might be drawn from this review. First, there is much room for improvement across all three fronts of economic integration. South Asian exporters have shown themselves competitive in exporting labor-intensive manufactured goods, when provided with market access. They have also — increasingly — managed to attract more foreign capital to the region. Finally, emigrant remittances are providing a much needed injection of foreign capital. If continued, these trends are encouraging. By providing greater market access and information about market opportunities in South Asia, the European Union can offer continued opportunities for South Asian economic development.

Second, more attention might be paid to the role of migration in helping poor countries escape from their poverty. Policy-makers in South Asia seem to recognize the importance of migration as one arm of a three pronged strategy for development and poverty reduction. Increased trade and foreign direct investment are the others. Recent developments in economic theory and a growing realization among international policymakers (and their host institutions) provide hope that migration may one day join trade and FDI as an equal partner in the triumvirate of development policy options.

References

Asian Development Bank (2004a) *Asian Development Outlook 2004* (ADB and Oxford).

Asian Development Bank (2004b) 'Statistics'. Available at http://www.adb.org/statistics. Accessed 20 August 2004.

DG TRADE (2002) 'SAARC' DG TRADE A2/CG/SG/WB. October. Brussels.

DG TRADE (2004) 'SAARC' DG TRADE A2/CG/SG/WB. May. Brussels. Available at http://trade-info.cec.eu.int/doclib/docs/2004/june/tradoc_113489.pdf. Accessed 19 August 2004.

European Commission (1994) *Towards a New Asia Strategy* (Luxembourg: Office for Official Publications).

European Communities (2002) *External and intra-European Union Trade. Statistical Yearbook. Detailed Tables*. Catalogue No. KS-CV-02-001-EN-N.

Eurostat (2002) 'Migration keeps the EU population growing'. *Statistics in Focus* Theme 3–7/2002. Catalogue No. KS-NK-02-007-EN-N.

Faini, Riccardo (2005) 'Migration, Remittances, and Growth'. In George J. Borjas and Jeffery Crisp (eds.), *Poverty, International Migration and Asylum* (Houndmills, Basingstoke, Hamsphire: Palgrave): 171–187.

Hamilton, B. and J. Whalley (1984) 'Efficiency and Distributional Implications of Global Restrictions on Labour Mobility'. *Journal of Development Economics* 14: 61–75.

Hatton, T. and J. Williamson (1992) 'What Drove the Mass Migration from Europe in the Late Nineteenth Century?' *Population and Development Review* 20: 533–559.

Hirschman, A.O. (1970) *Exit, Voice and Loyalty. Responses to Decline in Firms, Organizations, and States* (Cambridge, Mass: Harvard University Press).

IOM [International Organization for Migration] (2003) *Labour Migration in Asia. Trends, challenges and policy responses in countries of origin* (Geneva: IOM).

[IPSSL] Institute of Policy Studies of Sri Lanka (2000) 'Foreign direct investment and economic integration in the SAARC region'. Paper presented at the Second Conference of the South Asia Network of Economic Research Institutes (SANEI). Kathmandu, 28–29 August.

Iregui, Ana María (2005) 'Efficiency Gains from the Elimination of Global Restrictions on Labour Mobility: An Analysis using a Multiregional CGE Model'. In George J. Borjas and Jeffery Crisp (eds.), *Poverty, International Migration and Asylum* (Houndmills, Basingstoke, Hamsphire: Palgrave): 211–240.

Islam, M. (1995) 'Bangladeshi Migration: An Impact Study'. In R. Cohen (ed.), *The Cambridge Survey of World Migration* (Cambridge: Cambridge University Press).

Jones, R.W. and J.P. Neary (1994) 'The Positive Theory of International Trade'. In R.W. Jones and P.B. Kenen (eds.), *Handbook of International Economics*, Vol. 1 (New York: North Holland).

Kapur, Devesh and John McHale (2003) 'Migration's New Payoff — Globalization at Work'. *Foreign Policy* (November–December): 49–57.

Lewis, W. Arthur (1954) 'Economic Development with Unlimited Supplies of Labour'. *The Manchester School* 22(2): 139–191.

Mahbub Ul Haq Human Development Centre (2001) *Human Development in South Asia 2001* (Dhaka: University Press and Oxford: Oxford University Press).

Mahbub Ul Haq Human Development Centre (2004) *Human Development in South Asia 2003– The Employment Challenge* (Oxford: Oxford University Press).

Markusen, J.R. (1983) 'Factor Movements and Commodity Trade as Complements'. *Journal of International Economics* 14: 341–356.

Markusen, J.R. and J.R. Melvin (1981) 'Trade, Factor Prices and Gains from Trade with Increasing Returns to Scale'. *Canadian Journal of Economics* 14: 450–469.

Markusen, J.R. and L.E.O. Svensson (1985) 'Trade in Goods and Factors with International Differences in Technology'. *International Economic Review* 26(1): 175–192.

Massey, Douglas S. (1988) 'Economic Development and International Migration in Comparative Perspective'. *Population and Development Review* 14(3): 383–413.

McKay, A., L.A. Winters and A.M. Kedir (2000) 'A Review of the Empirical Evidence on Trade, Trade Policy and Poverty'. A DFID report prepared as a background document for the Second Development White Paper.

Moses, Jonathon W. and Bjørn Letnes (2004) 'The Economic Costs to International Labor Restrictions: Revisiting the Empirical Discussion'. *World Development* 32(10): 1609–1626.

Moses, Jonathon W. and Bjørn Letnes (2005) 'If People were Money: Estimating the Gains and Scope of Free Migration'. In George J. Borjas and Jeffery Crisp (eds.), *Poverty, International Migration and Asylum* (Houndmills, Basingstoke, Hamsphire: Palgrave): 188–210.

Mundell, R. (1957) 'International Trade and Factor Mobility'. *American Economic Review* XLVII (June): 321–335.

OECD (2001) *Trends in International Migration*, SOPEMI Annual Report (Paris: OECD).

O'Brien, Nicholas (2001) 'ASEM: Moving from an economic to a political dialogue?' Briefing Paper, European Institute for Asian Studies.
Available at http://www.eias.org/publications/briefing/2001/aseammoving.pdf

O'Rourke, K.H., A.M. Taylor and J. Williamson (1996) 'Factor Price Convergence in the Late Nineteenth Century'. *International Economic Review* 37(3): 499–530.

O'Rourke, K.H. and J. Williamson (1995) 'Around the European Periphery 1870–1913: Globalization, Schooling and Growth'. NBER Working Paper No. 5392. Cambridge, Mass., December.

Quddus, Abdul (2001) *European Union's Emerging Relations with Asia. Politico-Economic Perspectives* (Dhaka: Gatidhara).

Razin A. and E. Sadka (1995) *Population Economics* (Cambridge, Mass: MIT Press).

RIS [Research and Information System for the Non-Aligned and Other Developing Countries] (2004) *South Asia Development and Cooperation Report 2004* (New Delhi: RIS).

Round, Jeffery and John Whalley (2002) 'Globalization and Poverty: the Implications of South Asian Experience for the Wider Debate'. Paper prepared for the ESCOR project 'Exploring the links between Globalization and Poverty in South Asia'. Available at http://www.gapresearch.org/production/JJoverview.pdf. Accessed 18 August 2004.

Schiff, Maurice (1996) 'South-North Migration and Trade. A Survey'. Policy Research Working Paper No. 1696. World Bank, December.

Skeldon, Ronald (1997) *Migration and Development* (Essex: Addison Wesley Longman).

Skeldon, Ronald (2003) 'Migration and migration policy in Asia: A synthesis of selected cases'. Paper presented to the Regional Conference on Migration, Development and Pro-Poor Policy Choices in Asia. Dhaka, Bangladesh, 22–24 June. Available at www.livelihoods.org/hot_topics/docs/Dhaka_CP_1.pdf

Sobhan, Rehman (2004) 'Aid, Governance and Ownership'. *South Asian Journal* 4. Available at http://www.southasianmedia.net/Magazine/Journal/aid_ownership.htm. Accessed 18 August 2004.

SOPEMI (2003) *Trends in International Migration* (Paris: OECD).

UNCTAD (2003) *World Investment Report 2003.* Available at http://www.unctad.org/Templates/Page.asp?intItemID=2441&lang=1 Accessed 10 August 2004.

UNDP (2002) 'Human Development Report 2002'. Available at http://hdr.undp.org/reports/global/2002/en/pdf/HDR percent20PR_HDI.pdf

Watkins, Francis and Robert Nurick (2002) 'Migration in South Asia in Policy and Practice: A Regional Overview'. Unpublished manuscript obtained from author. Available at http://www.eldis.org/cf/search/disp/docdisplay.cfm?doc=ADOC363&resource=f1

Wickramasekera, Piyasiri (2002) 'Asian Labour Migration: Issues and Challenges in an Era of Globalization'. International Migration Papers No. 57 (Geneva: ILO).

Williamson, J. (1995) 'The Evolution of Global Labor Markets since 1830: Background Evidence and Hypotheses'. *Explorations in Economic History* 32(2): 141–196.

Winters, L.A. (2002) 'The Economic Implications of Liberalising Mode 4 Trade'. Paper prepared for the Joint WTO-World Bank Symposium on 'The Movement of Natural Persons (Mode 4) under the GATS'. Geneva, 11–12 April.

Wong, K-Y. (1983) 'On Choosing Among Trade in Goods and International Capital and Labor Mobility: A Theoretical Analysis'. *Journal of International Economics* 14: 223–250.

World Bank (2003) 'Statistical Annex' Global Development Finance. Available at http://www.worldbank.org/prospects/gdf2003/statappendix/stattoc.htm

CHAPTER 8

THE EFFECTS OF NORTH–SOUTH REGIONAL TRADE POLICIES: A COMPARISON OF MEDITERRANEAN COUNTRIES WITH ASEAN*

Nicolas Péridy

Mediterranean countries have been enjoying a long standing economic integration experience with Northern countries, namely the European Union. This experience started in the 70s with a EU preferential tariff treatment for a selection of Mediterranean exports. Thereafter, the EU-Mediterranean integration process was progressively extended by additional trade preferences. More recently, the Barcelona conference (1995) gave rise to the Euro-Mediterranean agreement (Euromed), which provides for greater cooperation and the completion of a free trade area (FTA) between the EU and these countries. Finally, the 2003 European Neighborhood policy reinforces this North–South cooperation: it aims at providing the four freedoms (goods, services, capital and people) within the Euro-Mediterranean area.

This far-reaching integration process strengthened the political, economic, cultural and human links between Europe and its Mediterranean partners. As an example, the EU share with regards to Mediterranean countries' exports reached 43 percent in 2002. This share remained remarkably stable during the past three decades.

Asian countries generally have not implemented such regional arrangements with Northern countries. They rather tended to liberalize their trade and economic structure within the multilateral trading system. In recent years however, as multilateral negotiations seemed to stall, they started negotiating free trade arrangements as a means of fostering trade

* We are grateful to Michael Plummer for helpful comments and suggestions.

and economic development. In particular, the ASEAN FTA (AFTA) was established in 1992 to eliminate tariff barriers among Southeast Asian countries. As a first step, the agreement on the Common Effective Preferential Tariff (CEPT) required that tariff rates levied on a wide range of products traded within the region be reduced to no more than five percent. In addition, quantitative restrictions and other non tariff barriers (NTBs) were to be eliminated. In 2003, ASEAN countries went further by initiating the ASEAN economic community process (AEC), which provides for the completion of a single market within the region by 2020.[1] In addition, a free trade agreement was signed between Singapore and Japan, and similar arrangements are expected to be completed between the ASEAN and developed countries, namely the USA, Australia, New Zealand, in addition to Japan.

This paper compares the North–South regional policy experienced by Mediterranean countries with the on-going ASEAN integration process. One major question relates to the lessons ASEAN countries may draw from the EU-Mediterranean integration process. Such an issue is motivated by the fact that ASEAN and Mediterranean countries present some similarities, in terms of size, economic development, trade and trade policies. These similarities are investigated in the first section. The second section is devoted to the assessment of the EU-Mediterranean regional agreements. In particular, one major issue consists in appraising whether Mediterranean countries have actually gained from the EU trade preferences since the 70s. This issue will be dealt with through the estimation of a trade model, which combines the new trade theory, initiated by Helpman and Krugman (1985), and recent theoretical developments related to trade costs (Anderson and van Wincoop 2003, 2005; Deardorff 2004). Several model specifications will be estimated, including a generalized fixed effect model (with exporter, importer, time and bilateral specific effects), a Hausman and Taylor Random effect model, as well as a dynamic Arellano, Bond and Bover's GMM model.

---

[1] Although it is not clear exactly what the AEC will ultimately look like, it will be more modest than the Single Market Program (SMP). As an example, the AEC provides for the free movement of business persons and skilled labour only, as stated during the 9th ASEAN summit.

The main result indicates that Mediterranean countries' exports to the EU have significantly increased thanks to the successive preferential agreements: the gross trade creation is estimated to be about 20–26 percent of actual exports, depending on the model specification.

The concluding section focuses on the implications of the EU-Mediterranean regional integration experience for the ASEAN on-going integration process with Northern countries.

ASEAN and Mediterranean Countries: Similarities and Differences in the Regional Integration Process

This section intends to compare ASEAN and Mediterranean countries in terms of trade policy. The selected Mediterranean countries are all the non-EU Mediterranean partners which have concluded a preferential regional agreement with the EU, namely: Algeria, Morocco, Tunisia, Egypt, Israel, Turkey, Lebanon, Jordan and Syria.[2]

As a first comparison, it is striking to observe that Mediterranean and ASEAN countries present some similarities in terms of economic size, development and macroeconomic performance. For example, the overall GDP is estimated to be equal to 613 and 882 billion US$ for Mediterranean and ASEAN countries respectively (Table 8.1). Similarly, the annual real GDP growth is also very close in these two economic areas: +3.4 percent for the Mediterranean and +3.0 percent for the ASEAN countries (during the 1996–2004 period). GDP per capita is also similar ($2423 and $1611 respectively), as well as variations in per capita incomes within each area (1.41 and 1.63 respectively for the coefficient of variation).

---

[2] Although Palestinian autonomous territories have also concluded a regional agreement with the EU, there is a lack of data concerning these territories. For this reason, they are not included in the present analysis. In addition, Middle-East countries are also excluded, since they are not concerned by the preferential trade schemes with the EU, except in the Generalized System of Preferences (GSP) framework.

Table 8.1. Basic Indicators for Mediterranean and ASEAN Countries

	Population	GDP (billion US$)	GDP per cap. (US$)		Annual GDP growth
Export zone:	million	constant price	constant price	coefficient of var.	(average 1996-2002)
Mediterranean countries, of which:	**246.1**	**547.2**	**2223.8**	**1.42**	**2.8%**
Turkey	67.3	204.2	3034.0	-	2.2%
Israel	6.0	104.4	17317.5	-	2.0%
Egypt	73.3	82.3	1122.3	-	4.5%
Algeria	32.3	51.4	1592.1	-	2.8%
Morocco	31.2	43.8	1404.1	-	2.9%
Tunisia	9.8	25.3	2578.8	-	4.6%
Syria	17.2	14.3	835.6	-	2.7%
Lebanon	3.7	12.9	3514.6	-	1.9%
Jordan	5.3	8.5	1607.9	-	3.7%
				-	
ASEAN, of which:	**547.0**	**794.0**	**1451.7**	**1.61**	**2.2%**
Indonesia	231.3	224.4	970.1	-	0.7%
Thailand	63.6	182.4	2866.2	-	0.6%
Malaysia	22.7	116.8	5152.2	-	3.2%
Singapore	4.5	113.6	25501.4	-	4.1%
The Philippines	83.0	95.4	1149.8	-	3.3%
Viet Nam	80.6	31.6	391.8	-	6.1%
Myanmar	42.3	17.2	405.7	-	7.2%
Brunei Darussalam	0.4	6.1	17403.4	-	2.1%
Cambodia	12.9	4.0	307.2	-	3.9%
Laos	5.8	2.7	459.4	-	5.9%

Sources:
- International Monetary Fund : International Financial Statistics (2004).
- CEPII : CHELEM (Harmonized Accounts on the World Economy), vol. 5.2 (2003).

In this connection, it must be stressed that Mediterranean and ASEAN countries are, together with SPARTECA,[3] the preferential trading areas in the world with the highest GDP per capita's coefficient of variation across members.[4] For instance, some countries display more than $15000 per capita (Israel, Singapore, Brunei), whereas some other are below $1500 (Syria, Morocco, Egypt, Indonesia, the Philippines, Vietnam, Myanmar, Laos and Cambodia).

Other similarities may be found in these countries' multilateral trade policies. Indeed, most of them progressively liberalized their economies over the past three decades, and joined the WTO (Table 8.2). The Mediterranean and ASEAN countries which have not yet joined the WTO are Algeria, Syria, Lebanon, as well as Laos and Vietnam. In the same way, ASEAN and Mediterranean countries enjoy a similar export/head ratio ($476 and $738 per head respectively), with again some differences within each area.

Finally, some aspects of the recent ASEAN and Mediterranean regional policies are also similar. A first aspect is the move towards further economic integration within each of these two areas: for example, the progressive implementation of the AFTA and the move towards a single market (through the AEC) are striking examples of recent economic integration within the ASEAN area. In the same way, on 25 February 2004, a free trade agreement was concluded between Jordan, Egypt, Morocco and Tunisia. This agreement, known as the Agadir declaration, is the first step towards economic and social integration in the Arab Mediterranean world.[5] Further integration is expected with the implementation of GAFTA (Greater Arab Free Trade Area), which now include 16 Arab countries. It is mainly aimed at removing tariff and non tariff barriers to trade within the Arab area.

---

[3] South Pacific Regional Trade and Economic Cooperation Agreement.

[4] Coefficients of variation are for example equal to 0.6 for MERCOSUR, 0.7 for the Andean Pact and NAFTA, 1.2 for APEC and 0.3 for the EU (Asian Development Bank, 2002).

[5] In fact, there have been some unsuccessful attempts in the past. In particular, the Arab Maghreb Union (AMU) agreement, concluded in 1988 between Algeria, Morocco, Tunisia, Lybia and Mauritania, has never been applied.

Table 8.2. Key Trade Figures for Mediterranean and ASEAN Countries

	Year of GATT accession	Total exports (mio US$)	Exports/head US$	Export share by country		
				EU	USA	Japan
TOTAL Medit. Countries, of which:		**117018.9**	**475.6**	**43.1%**	**14.8%**	**2.4%**
Turkey	1951	35761.9	531.3	48.5%	8.2%	1.1%
Israel	1962	29511.4	4894.1	22.6%	35.1%	0.4%
Algeria	-	22031.3	682.5	48.2%	8.9%	2.1%
Morocco	1987	7850.3	251.9	62.5%	4.2%	0.2%
Tunisia	1990	6874.2	700.3	69.0%	1.1%	3.4%
Syria	-	6230.1	363.1	51.5%	2.0%	0.3%
Egypt	1970	5100.4	69.6	49.7%	22.1%	0.3%
Jordan	2000	2770.0	522.0	8.3%	12.4%	1.1%
Lebanon	-	889.3	241.8	16.1%	5.8%	0.5%
TOTAL ASEAN, of which:		**400742.1**	**738.4**	**12.1%**	**16.2%**	**10.7%**
Singapore	1973	125177.0	28110.7	8.2%	9.8%	3.3%
Malaysia	1957	93281.2	4116.2	12.1%	21.4%	10.0%
Thailand	1982	65113.2	1023.1	13.5%	18.9%	13.4%
Indonesia	1950	57158.7	247.1	14.1%	14.1%	20.7%
The Philippines	1979	35208.1	424.2	17.0%	26.0%	15.4%
Brunei	1993	3719.8	10597.7	1.7%	6.4%	34.0%
Vietnam	-	16706.0	207.3	20.7%	11.9%	12.6%
Myanmar	1948	2316.9	54.8	14.9%	12.8%	4.0%
Cambodia	2004	1750.1	135.8	22.9%	51.0%	3.6%
Laos	-	311.1	53.8	35.7%	0.7%	1.8%

Sources:
- United Nations Statistics Division: COMTRADE.
- OECD : Monthly Statistics of International Trade, vol. 1 (2004).
- CEPII : CHELEM (Harmonized Accounts on the World Economy), vol. 5.2 (2003).

A second common aspect is the recent extension of regional integration to new partners: in the ASEAN case, we find many examples, amongst which the ASEAN–China Free Trade Initiative,[6] the ASEAN–Japan Comprehensive Economic Partnership, the ASEAN+3 (China, Japan and Korea) Framework, the ASEAN–Australia–New Zealand move towards a FTA, as well as the Comprehensive Economic Cooperation with India. Additional economic cooperation agreements have also been concluded with Russia and Korea (2005).[7] ASEA countries also concluded the Enterprise for ASEAN Initiative (EAI) with the USA in 2002. The latter offers the prospect of bilateral FTAs with the USA to be in force within a decade, after several steps have been concluded, namely: The WTO's accession for the remaining non signatory countries; the conclusion of Trade and Investment Framework Agreements (TIFAs), which intend to progressively reduce discriminating trade and FDI barriers.[8] The final step is the implementation of bilateral FTAs, as was the case with Singapore.[9]

In the same way, Mediterranean countries extended their regional arrangements: Indeed, some of them concluded a free trade agreement with the USA, such as Jordan (2002) and Morocco (2004). These agreements are all part of the MEFTA (Middle-East Free Trade Area) program with the USA, which has more recently included Bahrain (2006), Oman (2005) as well as the United Arab Emirates (negotiations launched in March 2005). At the same time, Egypt, Tunisia and Algeria signed the U.S.–Middle-East free trade initiative,[10] which provides for the implementation of TIFAs as a first step towards the completion of a FTA with the USA. Hence, the economic integration process with the USA is very similar for Mediterranean and ASEAN countries.

---

[6] The agreement, concluded in 2002, provides for the completion of a FTA between ASEAN countries and China by 2012.

[7] Consult the ASEAN website (http://www.aseansec.org) for more details regarding ongoing integration projects.

[8] TIFAs have recently been concluded with Indonesia, Philippines, and Thailand.

[9] Consult http://www.ustr.gov/new/fta for a detailed description of these agreements.

[10] Together with Kuwait, Qatar, Saudi Arabia and Yemen.

These new regional arrangements are motivated by the present impasse and missed deadlines in the multilateral negotiations (especially Cancun). In particular, the lack of multilateral trade liberalization regarding agriculture greatly restricts these countries' market access. This is a rationale for regional negotiations, as a means of opening more successfully Northern agricultural markets. Although the '2004 July Package' and the 2005 Hong-Kong agreement provide some improvements regarding the Doha Agenda Work Programme,[11] negotiations at a regional level still remain an alternative for further trade liberalization.

Another specific rationale for Mediterranean countries is the enlargement of the EU to Cyprus, Malta as well as Eastern European countries. These countries, which are competing with non-EU Mediterranean countries, now represent a more important economic threat. For example, as they are now protected by the common agricultural policy (CAP), the non-EU Mediterranean preferential margin is eroded. This further motivates these countries to diversify their market access towards other Northern countries, in particular the USA. In addition, the prospect of the opening negotiations for Turkey's accession into the EU reinforces this motivation.

Despite these similarities in terms of economic performance and trade policy, ASEAN and Mediterranean countries very much differ in their regional policy experience regarding Northern countries: Indeed, ASEAN countries have not had any regional agreement for decades. On the contrary, Mediterranean countries have been enjoying a long time preferential trade policy experience with the EU. Indeed, the first arrangements, known as the Association Agreements, were concluded in the late 60s with selected Mediterranean countries, including Morocco and Tunisia (in addition to Greece and Spain). These agreements provided a free access for these countries' manufactured goods in the Euro-

[11] The main trade provisions of the 'July package', concern agriculture, especially cotton, as well as improving market access for industrial products (refer to the decision adopted by the General Council on 31 July 2004, WT/L/579). In the same way, the 2005 Hong-Kong summit provided an agreement concerning the removal of agricultural export subsidies by 2013. However, no concrete agreement was achieved regarding services as well as tariffs for industrial products.

pean Economic Community (EEC).[12] In addition, half agricultural exports were granted reductions in the EEC common external tariff (CET), provided the observance of a reference price.

In 1972, the EEC implemented the Global Mediterranean Policy (GMP). It was aimed at extending non discriminating tariff concessions across all Mediterranean countries. A second objective was to extend the scope of the existing agreements to non trading aspects, including financial aid and technical cooperation. As a consequence, the EEC concluded 'Cooperation Agreements' with all Mediterranean countries from 1973 to 1980. From a trade point of view, the main improvement concerned agricultural products: new products were granted tariff concessions, including wine, fruit and vegetables. Thus, 80 percent of agricultural exports were covered by this new agreement. However, these exports were also subject to protectionist measures imposed by the CAP (minimum prices, countervailing taxes, restricted export calendars, etc.).

An additional step was reached after the accession of Spain and Portugal into the EC. These countries' exports, which very much competed with non European Mediterranean countries, were all granted an unrestricted access into the EC, including the most sensitive agricultural products. In order to reduce the tariff discrimination within the Mediterranean region, the EC concluded a new wave of arrangements, known as 'Adaptation Agreements'. They provided for removal of all tariffs' for non EC Mediterranean countries. Thus, in 1993, at the end of the transition period, no tariff was charged any longer on Mediterranean exports. However, the non tariff barriers (NTBs) related to the CAP were not removed for these countries. In particular, the persistence of countervailing taxes, import calendars, minima prices and the other CAP regulations continued to restrict these exports' access into the EC.

The last agreement was reached in 1995, at the Barcelona conference. This Euro-Mediterranean (Euromed) scheme initiated the implementation of a FTA between the EU and Mediterranean countries (to be completed by 2010). In addition to political and security aspects, further

[12] Except cork, which was still subject to the Common External Tariff (CET), and refined petroleum products, which enjoyed duty-free access within the limit of a quota.

cooperation was also carried out between these two economic areas, including financial, technical, and education fields. However, the scope of this agreement was reduced because the EU still refused to remove the NTBs concerning agricultural products. Future negotiations are expected in order to solve this problem.

The Euromed agreement progressively came into effect in Tunisia (1998), Israel (2000), Morocco (2000), Jordan (2002), Lebanon (2003) and Egypt (2004). The European Parliament ratified the agreement with Algeria in 2002. Negotiations were also recently concluded with Syria (2004). For these two countries however, the agreements concluded are still not in force.

In addition, special agreements were signed with European Mediterranean candidates, namely Cyprus, Malta and Turkey. All these countries completed a customs union with the EU before their accession. In May 2004, Cyprus and Malta joined the EU, whereas the customs union agreement with Turkey is still in force. However, the latter does not fully include agricultural products, as in the Euromed agreement.

To sum up, the long standing regional integration experience between the EU and its Mediterranean partners contrasts with the ASEAN traditional lack of regional policy with Northern countries. This may explain the sharp difference in the Northern countries' export shares between these two economic areas: for example, we calculate from Table 8.2 that the EU, the USA and Japan account together for more than 60 percent of Mediterranean countries exports, whereas they only represent 38 percent of ASEAN countries' exports. This difference is greatly due to the EU share regarding Mediterranean exports (43 percent), against only 12 percent with regards to ASEAN. Of course, part of this difference may be explained by the geographic proximity between Mediterranean countries and Europe, as well as by the large size of the EU market. However, we suspect that these factors alone cannot explain such a big difference in the EU share between Mediterranean and ASEAN countries. In fact, the EU-Mediterranean countries' regional integration experience may have played a major role. As a comparison, Japan's share regarding ASEAN exports is only equal to 10.7 percent. Given a comparable geographical proximity, this share is much less important than the EU market share with regards to Mediterranean countries.

The next section explores further this issue, by proposing a model which intends to quantify the trade effects of the EU-Mediterranean integration.

The Mediterranean Regional Integration Experience with the European Union: An Econometric Assessment

Although there is an extensive literature concerning this issue,[13] the model proposed here is the first attempt to apply some new trade theory aspects to Mediterranean countries: Indeed, the model used here combines the new trade theory (NTT), initiated by Helpman and Krugman (1985), and recent theoretical developments related to trade costs, as described in Anderson and van Wincoop (2003, 2004), as well as Deardorff (2004). Therefore, the equation proposed here is the following:

$$\ln EXP_{ijt} = \alpha_0 + \alpha_1 \ln SGDP_{ijt} + \alpha_2 \ln DGDP_{ijt} + \alpha_3 \ln SIMI_{ijt}$$

$$+ \alpha_4 \ln DIST_{ij} + \alpha_5 \ln BORD_{ij} + \alpha_6 \ln REG_{ijt} + \alpha_7 \ln LANG_{ij} + \lambda_{ij}$$

$$+ \beta_i + \gamma_j + \delta_t + \varepsilon_{jt} \qquad (1)$$

The first line of Equation (1) corresponds to the basic NTT formulation: The exports from country i to country j in year t depend on several variables. The first is country size (SGDP), which reflects the sum of country i's and country j's GDP. α_1 is expected to be positive whatever the nature of trade (inter or intra-industrial). Bilateral exports also depend on the difference in factor endowment (DGDP), which is measured by the difference in GDP per capita between country i and j in absolute value. A positive sign for α_2 fits a standard HOS framework, whereas a negative sign rather supports the Linder hypothesis. Finally, exports may be determined by the similarity in country size (SIMI), with a positive

[13] See for instance Martinez-Zarzoso (2003), Dessus, Devlin and Safadi (2001) as well as Fontagné and Péridy (1997).

parameter value expected from the NTT.[14] This first line equation thus corresponds to a generalized gravity equation, which may be used to test most trade theories, including Ricardian, Hecksher–Ohlin and monopolistic competition frameworks (Evenett and Keller 2002, Haveman and Hummels 2004) or the reciprocal dumping model (Feenstra, Markusen and Rose 2001).

The second line in equation (1) includes bilateral trade costs (or benefits): The first cost is the standard geographical distance between country i and country j (DIST). It is measured by the great circle distance between capitals. BORD is another bilateral trade cost, which reflects border effects. It accounts for the trade resistance across countries as compared to trade within countries. It is measured by a dummy variable, which is equal to 1 for trade within a country and e for trade across countries.[15] REG denotes the regional arrangements between the EU and Mediterranean countries and LANG the common language between two countries. These two variables are measured with dummies. The last bilateral trade cost is λ_{ij}: It reflects any time-invariant bilateral specific effect (cultural, political), which leads to a deviation of normal propensity to trade for any bilateral flow. It may be considered as fixed or random, depending on the econometric specification.

The third line essentially accounts for multilateral trade costs, as theoretically justified by Feenstra (2002) and Anderson and Van Wincoop (2003, 2004): β_i measures any specific exporter effects regarding all

---

[14] Following Helpman (1987), it may be measured as follows:

$$SIMI_{ijt} = \ln\left[1-\left(\frac{GDP_{it}}{GDP_{it}+GDP_{jt}}\right)^2-\left(\frac{GDP_{jt}}{GDP_{it}+GDP_{jt}}\right)^2\right]$$

with 0<SIMI<0.5.

[15] Taking internal trade flows into account requires the calculation of internal export flows (X_{ii}) and internal distance (D_{ii}). The former is calculated by using the difference between country i' GDP and its overall exports. In the same way, the latter has been measured following Head and Mayer (2002):

$$d_{ii} = \frac{2}{3\Pi^{1/2}} S_i^{1/2}$$

assuming that economic activity is evenly distributed within a country (S_i denotes the size of country i).

import destinations, whereas γ_j denotes specific importer effects, whatever the export origin.[16] Finally, δ_t reflects specific time effects, which account for business cycles as well as changes in openness across all countries. As for λ_{ij}, the multilateral specific effects may be considered as fixed or random. It must be pointed out that the inclusion of all these specific effects (bilateral, multilateral and time) is not only justified from a theoretical point of view, but also from an econometric point of view, as shown in Egger and Pfaffermayr (2003) as well as Baltagi, Egger and Pfaffermayr (2003).

Equation (1) has been estimated for the Mediterranean countries described in section 1,[17] with 42 selected partner countries. The latter include OECD countries (except Eastern European countries), South Africa, Brazil, Argentina, Chile, India, Hong Kong, Singapore, Taiwan, Malaysia, Philippines, Thailand, China, as well as Mediterranean countries. Together, they account for more than 90 percent of the Mediterranean countries' exports. For the time period 1975–2003, the dataset contains 8526 observations, including 294 bilateral trade flows.

The main data sources are as follows: OECD Monthly Statistics of International Trade (Trade by Country, annual, vol.1, 2006); OECD International Direct Investment Yearbook (2003), United Nations (COMTRADE), as well as CEPII (CHELEM: Harmonized Accounts on the World Economy 2004).

Several specifications are presented in Table 8.3. For all of them, the heteroskedasticity corrected variance-covariance matrix has been applied. The LM test clearly rejects the standard OLS specification, whereas the Hausman test tends to reject the random effects model (REM) in favour of the fixed effects model (FEM).

[16] It may also be shown that these country-specific effects also reflect prices, as shown in Feenstra (2002), as well as Anderson and van Wincoop (2004).

[17] Except Lebanon and Syria due to the delays in the conclusion of the Euromed agreement, and the small amount of trade with the EU.

Table 8.3. Estimation Results

	Static				Dynamic	
	(1) OLS	(2) FEM	(3) REM	(4) HTM	(5) GMM	long run par.
SGDP	1.711***	1.865***	2.945***	2.988***	0.562***	2.161
DGDP	0.065***	1.366***	1.410****	1.435***	0.096***	0.369
SIMI	-0.194*	0.365*	0.134*	0.328***	-0.034	-0.131
LDIST	-1.285***	-	-1.574***	-0.601***	-0.379***	-1.457
BORD	-5.051***	-	-4.311***	-4.039***	-1.208***	-4.646
REG	1.641***	0.308***	0.222***	0.227***	0.111***	0.427
LANG2	0.375***	-	0.333*	0.347***	0.066*	0.253
ONE	-3.569***	"-19.411***	"-15.299****"	-19.01***	-1.878***	-7.223
lagged exports	-	-	-	-	0.740***	-
specific effects (F-tests):						
exporter	-	*101.27****	-	-	-	-
importer	-	*109.88****	-	-	-	-
time	-	*89.56****	-	-	-	-
bilateral	-	*96.25****	-	-	-	-
Gross trade creation (%)	-	***26.5***	***20.0***	***20.3***	-	***34.7***
r-squared	0.54	0.85	0.85			
AIC	1.77	0.75	0.75			
Log Likelihood	-18201	-13855	-13903			
LM-Test	-	54120***	37862***			
Hausman	-	89.95***	-			
autocorr (Rho coeff)	0.83	0.58	0.59			
Eigenvalue	54.5	-	-			

*** significant at a 1% level ; ** significant at a 5% level ; * significant at a 10% level

In the first column, the F-tests for fixed effects are presented. They include the importer, exporter, time and bilateral effects. All of them are highly significant. This strongly justifies their inclusion in the model, as suggested by Egger and Pfaffermayr (2003).

However, since this model cannot take into account time-invariant variables (distance, border, and language), REMs are also estimated, with both uncorrelated and correlated error structures (column 3 and 4).[18] In the latter case, a Hausman and Taylor model (HTM) is estimated in three steps: we first selected the variables potentially correlated with the random effects. Secondly, we used deviations from group means to consistently estimate parameters of the time-varying independent variables. This has been carried out through LSDV. From this estimation, we used group means residuals as the dependent variable, regressed on the time-invariant variables, in order to provide a consistent estimator of the parameters of the latter. This has been implemented through 2SLS. We finally used the residual variance in this regression to calculate the Hausman and Taylor estimators, through Weighted Instrumental Variable regression.

All the static specifications generally provide significant and similar parameter estimates. For example, the country size parameter is always positive and significant at a 1 percent level. In the same way, differences in GDP per capita are significant and positive. This unsurprisingly supports the HOS theoretical framework, since our dataset mainly includes South–North bilateral trade flows. The similarity in country size is also generally positive and significant, in line with the new trade theory. With regards to bilateral trade resistance variables, they also present the expected sign. In particular, with a border parameter coefficient which is equal to -4 or -5, it seems that Mediterranean countries face large border effects. This suggests rather high trade costs in these countries, as compared with OECD countries.[19] Finally, the common language and regional dummies are also significant and present the expected sign.

---

[18] As suggested by Egger (2004).

[19] As a matter of fact, Feenstra (2002), Anderson and Wincoop (2003), Chen (2004) and Péridy (2005) find border coefficients which are generally close to -2 for the main OECD countries.

Looking at the specific effects estimated in the FEM (Table 8.4) most Mediterranean countries show overall exporter effects (β_i) which are close to zero. This indicates that these countries do not present any specific export performance as compared with the other exporting countries. The two exceptions are Algeria (with a much below average exporter effect), and Israel, which enjoy on the contrary an above average export performance. The bilateral effects (λ_{ij}) are generally high with EU countries, and much lower with the USA, Canada and Japan.[20] This indicates the strong time-invariant cultural and historical ties between the EU and Mediterranean countries, independently of the trade agreement, which may have varied over time.[21]

The final specification corresponds to the dynamic estimation, which is presented in column (5) of Table 8.3. The lagged dependent variable accounts for habit persistence in trade flows. However, the introduction of this variable may introduce a bias due to the correlation with the composite disturbance terms. Due to the likely existence of a simultaneity bias, the most appropriate method of estimation appears to be GMM. We thus applied the corresponding Arellano, Bond and Bover's (ABB) estimator (Arellano and Bond 1998; Arellano and Bover 1995). In order to compare the dynamic parameter's magnitude with their static counterpart, long run parameters have been calculated (last column). These parameters are generally close to those observed in the static specifications, especially the REM.

We now turn to the effects of the EU regional policy regarding Mediterranean countries. These effects are clearly significant, whatever the specification. Moreover, there are only minor differences in the magnitude of the regional dummy coefficient: for instance, in the static versions of the model, the minimum regional dummy parameter is equal to 0.222 (REM) and the maximum value is 0.308 (FEM).

---

[20] The only exception is Israel, which also has high bilateral effects with these countries.

[21] This is especially due to the various enlargements of the EU during the considered time period. Indeed, all the new members adopted the preferential EU tariff policy regarding Mediterranean countries as they joined the EU. This was the case of Greece in 1981, then Portugal and Spain in 1986, and finally Austria, Sweden and Finland in 1995.

Table 8.4. The Bilateral Fixed Effects between Mediterranean Countries and Selected Partners

bilateral effects (λij)	Algeria	Morocco	Tunisia	Egypt	Jordan	Turkey	Israel
France	0,86	2,36	2,96	3,14	3,41	0,92	4,70
Belgium-Lux	1,28	3,48	2,20	2,32	2,85	0,97	4,38
Germany	1,90	2,52	2,37	1,80	2,79	0,77	5,12
Italy	1,12	2,10	2,93	1,62	3,25	2,51	5,65
The Netherlands	1,36	3,13	2,65	1,78	2,21	0,79	2,27
The UK	0,97	2,86	1,14	1,46	0,92	1,36	6,23
Ireland	0,68	2,24	-2,45	1,26	1,24	-0,60	2,50
Denmark	0,65	1,48	-1,06	0,46	0,22	-0,45	1,76
Spain	0,06	2,07	0,00	0,49	2,19	1,97	5,14
Greece	0,57	1,58	0,77	1,28	-0,09	1,03	0,31
Portugal	0,57	1,28	0,00	0,88	1,36	-0,34	6,53
USA	*-0,12*	*0,04*	*2,30*	*-0,46*	*-0,28*	0,08	4,00
Canada	*-1,31*	*0,51*	*0,54*	*-0,21*	*-1,96*	-1,36	1,09
Japan	*-1,40*	*1,83*	*-0,50*	*0,62*	*-1,78*	-0,42	5,64
All countries (βi)	***-1,15***	***0,85***	***-0,62***	***0,18***	***-0,36***	***-0,56***	***2,93***

The only exception is the OLS specification, which gives a parameter value equal to 1.641. However, the OLS does not take into account any specific effect referred to above, and notably the bilateral effects. Consequently, it seems reasonable to think that part of these effects are captured in the regional parameter, which is thus overestimated.

To go further in this analysis, we can calculate the gross trade creation due to the EU preferential agreements regarding Mediterranean countries. To that end, we rewrite equation (1) as:

$$\ln EXP_{ijt} = \ln HEXP_{ijt} + \alpha_6 \ln REG_{ijt} \tag{2}$$

where $\ln HEXP_{ijt}$ reflects the hypothetical exports from Mediterranean countries to the EU, assuming no regional agreement:

$$\begin{aligned} \ln HEXP_{ijt} = \alpha_0 + \alpha_1 \ln SGDP_{ijt} + \alpha_2 \ln DGDP_{ijt} + \alpha_3 \ln SIMI_{ijt} \\ + \alpha_4 \ln DIST_{ij} + \alpha_5 \ln BORD_{ij} + \alpha_7 \ln LANG_{ij} + \lambda_{ij} \\ + \beta_i + \gamma_j + \delta_t + \varepsilon_{jt} \end{aligned} \tag{3}$$

We then define the gross trade creation as the difference between actual and hypothetical exports from Mediterranean countries to the EU:

$$G = EXP_{ijt} - HEXP_{ijt} \tag{4}$$

Replacing $HEXP_{ijt}$ from equation (4) into equation (2) and giving REG_{ijt} the value corresponding to the preferential case (REG_{ijt}=e), we find:

$$\ln EXP_{ijt} = \ln(EXP_{ijt} - G) + \alpha_6 \ln e \tag{5}$$

This allows us to derive G:

$$G = EXP_{ijt}\left(1 - \frac{1}{e^{\alpha_6}}\right) \tag{6}$$

From this equation and the parameters α_6 estimated previously, we can calculate that over the period 1975–2003, the EU trade preferences granted to Mediterranean countries increased these countries' exports by about 20 percent–26 percent in the static versions, and by 35 percent in the dynamic one (Table 8.3). These results highlight that the gross trade creation due to the EU-Mediterranean partnership has been significant.

Additional insight may be provided by the calculation of the gross trade creation at various periods of time. This has been implemented through the estimation of the various models for any successive 5-year period. All the estimations indicate that the trade preference impact has become progressively lower. For example, Figure 8.1 describes the calculations for the HTM model. From 1980 to 2000, the gross trade creation decreased from 27.4 percent to 8.3 percent. This decrease may be due to several factors: the first is the restrictive EU trade policy regarding Mediterranean agricultural exports. A second reason may be found in the removal of the multi-fibre agreement (MFA). This agreement, which discriminated textile imports from most countries, except the Mediterranean area, provided a positive relative preference margin for the latter.[22] Finally, the conclusion of free trade agreements with Eastern European countries in the early 90s also eroded Mediterranean countries' trade preferences.

However, the trade impact of the EU policy remains significant, even recently. In addition, the conclusion of the Euromed agreement should stop the preference erosion in the future, unless the market access of Mediterranean agricultural products remains restricted for a long time.

[22] Although MENA countries' textile exports were in fact restricted by Voluntary Export Restraints (VERs), the latter instrument was less restrictive than the MFA. This is why MENA countries traditionally enjoyed a positive relative preferential margin for textile products.

Figure 8.1. The Effects of the EU-Mediterranean Countries' Preferential Agreements: A Calculation of the Gross Trade Creation (percent of actual exports)

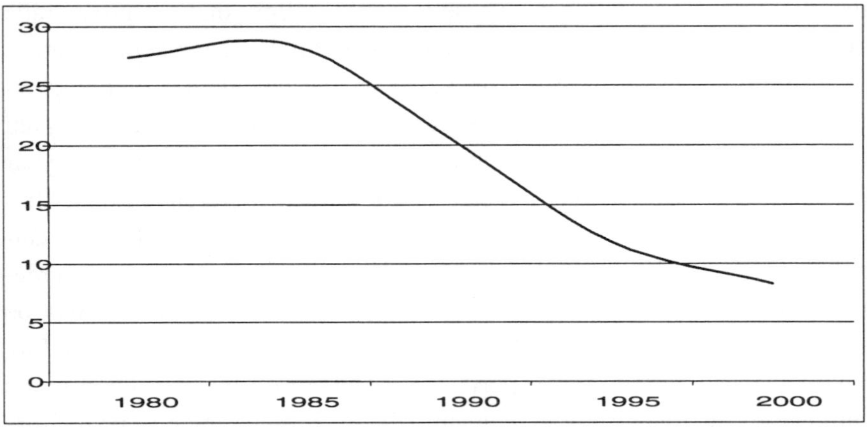

Concluding Remarks

This paper investigated the trade effects of the EU-Mediterranean agreements. It has been shown that these agreements have significantly increased Mediterranean countries' exports to the EU: The gross trade creation is estimated to be equal to 20–26 percent of actual exports, depending on the model specification. As a consequence, the observed high EU share regarding Mediterranean exports, which is equal to 43.1 percent, is greatly influenced by these agreements. Substracting the gross trade creation (in value) from actual exports, allows to recalculate the EU share assuming no agreement between the EU and Mediterranean countries. This share is estimated to be in the middle range between 31.0 percent to 34.1 percent, which is significantly below the current EU share.

The ASEAN countries do not enjoy such a regional integration experience with Northern countries. However, the recent regional initiatives with Japan, the USA, Australia and New-Zealand may also offer significant trade prospects, given the similarities between ASEAN and Mediterranean countries. These similarities primarily concern the trade agreements' contents with their Northern partners, i.e. the progressive implementation of a free trade area. But they also concern the size, the economic development and their recent macroeconomic performance, as shown in section 2. Finally, the geographic proximity between ASEAN countries and Japan, Australia and New-Zealand is not very different from that between Mediterranean countries and the EU.

In these conditions, the conclusion of free trade agreement between ASEAN countries and their most developed partners may also increase these partners' market share with regards to ASEAN countries. Further investigation would however be needed in order to assess more accurately the potential impact of these new trade agreements with ASEAN countries.

References

Anderson, J. and E. van Wincoop (2003) 'Gravity with Gravitas: A Solution to the Border Puzzle', *American Economic Review* 93(1): 170–192.

Anderson, J. and E. van Wincoop (2004) 'Trade Costs', *Journal of Economic Literature* 42(3): 691–751.

Arellano, M. and S. Bond (1998) *Dynamic Panel Data Estimation Using DPD98 for Gauss: A Guide for Users*, Madrid: CEMFI.

Arellano, M. and O. Bover (1995) 'Another Look at the Instrumental Variable Estimation of Error Component-Models', *Journal of Econometrics* 68: 29–51.

Asian Development Bank (2002) *Asian Development Outlook 2002*, Oxford: Oxford University Press.

Baltagi, B., P. Egger and M. Pfaffermayr (2003) 'A Generalized Design for Bilateral Trade Flow Models', *Economics Letters* 80: 391–397.

Chen, N. (2004) 'Intra-National versus International Trade in the European Union: Why do National Borders Matter?' *Journal of International Economics* 63: 93–118.

Deardorff, A. (2004) 'Local Comparative Advantage: Trade Costs and the Pattern of Trade', Research Seminar in International Economics, Discussion Paper No. 500, University of Michigan.

Dessus, S., J. Devlin and R. Safadi (eds.) (2001) *Towards Arab and Euro-Med Regional Integration*, Paris and Washington, D.C.: Organisation for Economic Co-operation and Development.

Egger, P. (2004) 'On the Problem of Endogenous Unobserved Effects in the Estimation of Gravity Models', *Journal of Economic Integration* 19(1): 182–191.

Egger, P. and M. Pfaffermayr (2003) 'The Proper Panel Econometric Specification of the Gravity Equation: A Three-Way Model with Bilateral Interaction Effects', *Empirical Economics* 28(3): 571–580.

Evenett, S. and W. Keller (2002) 'On Theories Explaining the Success of the Gravity Equation', *Journal of Political Economy* 110(2): 281–316.

Feenstra, R. (2002) 'Border Effects and the Gravity Equation: Consistent Methods for Estimation', *Scottish Journal of Political Economy* 49(5): 491–506.

Feenstra, R., J. Markusen and A. Rose (2001) 'Using the Gravity Equation to Differentiate among Alternative Theories of Trade', *Canadian Journal of Economics* 34(2): 430–447.

Fontagné, L. and N. Péridy (1997) *The EU and the Maghreb*, Paris and Washington, D.C.: Organisation for Economic Co-operation and Development.

Haveman, J. and D. Hummels (2004) 'Alternative Hypotheses and the Volume of Trade: The Gravity Equation and the Extent of Specialization', *Canadian Journal of Economics* 37(1): 199–218.

Head, K. and T. Mayer (2002) 'Effet Frontière, intégration économique et Forteresse Europe', *Economie et Prévision* 152–153: 71–92.

Helpman, E. (1987) 'Imperfect Competition and International Trade: Evidence from Fourteen Industrialized Countries', *Journal of the Japanese and International Economies* 92(3): 451–471.

Helpman, E. and P.R. Krugman (1985) *Market Structure and Foreign Trade: Increasing Returns, Imperfect Competition and the International Economy*, Cambridge, Mass.: MIT Press.

Martinez–Zarzoso, I. (2003) 'Gravity Model: An Application to Trade between Regional Blocs', *Atlantic Economic Journal* 31(2): 174–187.

Péridy, N. (2005) 'Towards a New Trade Policy Between the USA and Middle-East Countries: Estimating Trade Resistance and Export Potential', *The World Economy* 28(4): 491–518.

CHAPTER 9

RECONCILING THE TENSIONS BETWEEN REGIONAL INTEGRATION AND COHESION

Mary Farrell

Within the European Union, the member states have long accepted the possibility that uneven development can be a feature of the process of integration. It is almost inevitable that in dismantling the barriers to trade and competition, so as to create an integrated area, competitive forces will be unleashed that result in an uneven distribution of the costs and benefits. For one thing, an enlarged economic space means that some industries and firms can compete while others lose out once there is greater competition. The resulting inequality can shape the overall features of the regional arena, as much as that of specific firms and sectors. In other words, regions as well as firms and industrial sectors must be able to compete in the enlarged market. In the case of lagging regions, the lower levels of economic development may act as a draw upon the ability to compete and to attract resources for development.

If regions with lower levels of growth and per capita income cannot also share in the benefits of integration, then a strong case can be made for effective redistributive mechanisms that compensate for losing out to more competitive regions. In the context of regional integration, there is also a convincing political argument for a regional (redistributive) policy, to harness the support of political actors and thereby facilitate the process of regional integration. It is easy to lose sight of the fact that regional economic integration depends to a fundamental level on the continued political commitment of governments, political authorities and other societal actors.

This chapter examines the impact of the European Union's Structural Funds on regional cohesion in two of the member states — Spain and Ireland. The choice of countries may seem somewhat odd, since they appear to be quite dissimilar in many respects. Irish accession to the then European Community in 1973 (alongside Britain and Denmark) preceded that of Spain by more than a decade. Spain is a country of some 40 million people, and the second largest country of the EU. By contrast, Ireland, with a population of 3.7 million, is significantly smaller in terms of both population and also physical size.

On accession, Ireland had a large agricultural sector with a small and poorly developed manufacturing and services sector. Since the country was heavily dependent on trade with Britain, with over 80 percent of exports destined for the British market, Ireland had little choice but to join the European Community along with its major trading partner. Prior to 1973 Britain and Ireland shared a Free Trade Area, and this meant that Anglo–Irish commercial transactions were subject to duty-free status. Post–1973, any future trade with Britain would be subject to the imposition of the common external tariff, unless Ireland also joined the EC.

Both Spain and Ireland joined the European Union with low levels of economic development, and disparities in regional development. Inflation and high unemployment levels were persistent features of both economies, as was high emigration. Regional disparities in both income and output levels meant that the national per capita income in each country was well below the average for the EU as a whole. It was this gap between the national level and the EU, together with the persistent regional disparities that provided the basis for eligibility under the Structural Funds, the EU's principal instrument for regional redistribution.

This chapter offers an account of the impact of the Structural Funds on economic and social cohesion, and looks at the re-distributive effect of the EU's regional policy examination in the two countries. The following section offers a brief review of the theoretical contribution from regional integration theory, and considers the extent to which the empirical evidence supports the predictions of the classical integration theory. This is followed by a description of the principles and mode of operation of the Structural Funds in Section 2. Sections 3 and 4 set out the national context and the nature of regional development in the two countries. In

Section 5, the chapter reviews the convergence and cohesion in the two countries, and assesses the reasons why divergence remained for long a feature of the Spanish experience with European integration despite the country being the principal recipient of European Union financial transfers. The concluding section refers to the contemporary debate on the future of the EU's regional policy, and considers the implications for the Structural Funds and the potential for cohesion in the context of European enlargement. The chapter ends with a consideration of the broader lessons and challenges for integration between small and large countries in the context of Asian regional integration.

Regional Integration — What the Theory Says

The literature on regional integration offers a fairly clear-cut analysis of the costs and benefits that result from the decision by a group of countries to remove all obstacles to trade among themselves, and to establish certain elements of cooperation and coordination. However, there is less agreement over the precise impact on individual countries, and how this might vary over time.

The creation of a single (integrated) economic space, spanning and over-lapping the national political boundaries of the member countries, is expected to give rise to economies of scale, greater efficiency and larger output. Increased levels of competition in the integrated market create pressures on national firms and national economic sectors to be more competitive, to offer lower prices and better quality products. Technology also plays a decisive role, in helping firms to become more competitive through the incorporation of new processes and methods. Technology can also be a driver of further integration.

In addition to these advantages of regional integration, further benefits are predicted for deeper levels of integration — the common market and economic union bring positive gains as a result of co-ordinating economic policies. It should be possible for participating countries to achieve economies of scale from policy co-ordination, and by combining their efforts to deal with economic problems of inflation, unemployment and growth. Traditional theory also predicts that factor mobility across national borders leads to higher national incomes — and hence greater prosperity.

With all of these possible advantages that accrue to economic sectors and to political units it may seem surprising that after many years of integration such positive outcomes are not always to be observed. Is integration theory wrong, or at least failing to live up to its predictive capability? Like neo-classical economics of the market, the predictions of integration theory rests on several assumptions and these determine the likelihood of the predicted outcomes. In the first instance, the possible gains from integration relate to the resource reallocation that follows on from the integration process, and are therefore of a short-term static nature. What the theory fails to take sufficient account of is the long-term or dynamic effects that result from the new environment — investment decisions, new technologies, the effects on output and employment, as well as the long-term growth effects.

The other aspect of integration theory relates to the fact that what it promises is *possible* economic gains. But there is no guarantee that these can ever be realised in full. Regional integration can result in losses rather than gains, and the losses (measured in terms of output, employment, income, social inequality) can be unevenly spread across different regions.

The EU cohesion policy is aimed at reducing regional inequalities and promoting the development of the lagging regions (European Commission 2001). From the evidence to date, there is no indication that regional disparities are being eliminated. On the contrary, many member states have experienced an increase in the disparities between regions within states (European Commission 2003). Recently, the Structural Funds have come under criticism from a number of quarters (Economist 2003; Midelfart–Knarvik and Overman 2002). However, there are good reasons for a cohesion policy as part of a regional integration arrangement. These reasons can be located in the economic and political spheres, and have general validity in any regional integration arrangement between states with different levels of economic development.

The economic case for cohesion policy rests with the nature of markets and the allocation of resources under integration (El–Agraa 2001). The literature tends to support either a convergence or a divergence thesis, and much of the debate around the Structural Funds is similarly divided. Classical Ricardian trade theory, for instance, supports the convergence thesis, and assumes that factor mobility will operate to bring about equilibrium, acting as a correcting mechanism with regard to regional inequalities. The theory suggests that factor endowment is not so important, and that integration will lead to a rearrangement of economic activity, with investment and innovation going to the low-cost areas while labour flows to the high-cost areas. In the process, regional disparities will even out and therefore intervention is not needed. Similarly, neo-classical growth theories support the notion of convergence, based upon the market as a mechanism of reallocation. In this viewpoint also, there is no need for development policies. However, neo-classical markets are ideal types that behave according to the theory only when certain key assumptions hold — which is frequently not the case in real world situations.

On the other hand, regional disparities are evident in regional integration arrangements around the world. The reasons may vary, and it is important to consider each case in order to understand and identify the appropriate policy implications. However, there are some general causal factors likely to be found in any region: an inherited economic situation, manifested in lower than average per capita GDP; the quality and quantity of human capital, where the aim must be to ensure skilled labour, and to match the skills with the demand for labour; the quality and accessibility of the infrastructure endowment; the capacity for generating and assimilating innovation; the nature of the sectoral structure, including the mix of industries and the number of leading-edge sectors.

Contemporary endogenous growth theory and new economic geography reflect the view that greater accessibility, higher skills, and a greater capacity to generate and assimilate innovation will lead to the concentration of economic activity (Barro and Sala–i–Martin 1995; Krugman 1991). So, it is not desirable to rely on the market to effect a reallocation of resources in order to eliminate regional disparities. The implication of these theoretical perspectives is that some public intervention in the form of a regional policy is needed — and all the more so in the context of regional integration where geography, history, and politics combine together in an area likely to be characterised by significant spatial inequalities (Cheshire and Magrini 2001; Boldrin and Canova 2001).

The political argument in support of cohesion policy can be considered as part of the criteria for judging what makes regional integration work. Cooperation between sovereign states, and involving non-state actors, will be most sustainable where there is a political commitment towards cooperation even when this involves costs and burdens in adjusting to the new arrangements. This holds true even more for those states that may be less able to bear the costs. A sound regional integration process emerges only slowly; it is effectively a long-term strategy. Furthermore, the benefits may only be realised over the long-term while the costs can all too be apparent in the early stages of integration. Therefore, states and non-state actors are more likely to bear the costs in the knowledge that cooperation will produce results, and not just for the more prosperous or more powerful in the group.

EU Structural Funds

The origins of the EU Structural Funds are to be found in the Treaty of Rome. The preamble of the founding treaty set out the commitment of the states to 'ensure their harmonious development by reducing the differences existing between the various regions and the backwardness of the less favoured regions'. Although this statement was subsequently regarded as a commitment to regional policy, the Treaty did not contain any substantive provision for regional policy. Rather, the core common policies foreseen then were confined to the areas of competition, agriculture, and trade.

However, in the mid–1970s, the European Regional Development Fund was established as an embryonic regional policy, with a limited budget. A decade later, the Single European Act provided the impetus for a more substantive regional policy, introducing the concept of 'economic and social cohesion'. The SEA took the lead from the original clause in the Treaty of Rome, declaring 'in order to promote its overall harmonious development, the Community shall develop and pursue its actions leading to a strengthening of its economic and social cohesion. In particular the community shall aim at reducing the disparities between the various regions and the backwardness of the least favoured regions, including rural areas' (Art. 158 — revised Treaty).

The system for regional support received a further boost with the decision in 1989 to double the amount of funding allocated to regional policy and to amalgamate the different initiatives under the one umbrella of the Structural Funds. In 1992, the EU agreed to the creation of a Cohesion Fund to support the four poorest member states (Spain, Portugal, Greece and Ireland) in their efforts towards economic convergence as part of the preparation for economic and monetary union. Together, the Structural and Cohesion Funds represent the EU's regional policy. Commonly known as cohesion policy, it entails the funding of infrastructure and employment projects in lagging regions of the EU member states. In financial terms, cohesion policy involves the distribution of more than 35 billion euro annually, making it the second most important EU policy in budgetary terms, after the Common Agricultural Policy.

The Structural Funds are allocated according to three 'objectives':

- Objective 1 is aimed at regions whose development is lagging behind, with a per capita GDP of less than 75 percent of the EU average.
- Objective 2 is aimed at the economic and social restructuring of regions dependent on industries in decline, agriculture, fishery, or areas suffering from problems related to urbanis action. In order to qualify for Objective 2 funding industrial regions must have an unemployment rate above the EU average, a higher percentage of jobs in the industrial sector than the EU average, and a decline in industrial employment. In addition, regions must not be eligible for Objective 1 support.
- Objective 3 is aimed at modernising education and increasing employment. Any region can qualify for Objective 3 funding, provided it does not receive Objective 1 funding.

Most of the Structural Funds expenditure has been concentrated in the Objective 1 Regions. In effect, the targeting of financial resources (under the combined Structural and Cohesion Funds) in the less advantaged regions of the EU has meant that European development support throughout the 1990s represented an addition to the national GDP of around 3.5 percent for Portugal, between 2.5 percent and 3 percent in Greece and Ireland, and around 3 percent for Spain.

The overall aim of regional policy was to promote cohesion and convergence. A crucial role was played by the European Commission in fostering a particular model of partnership between the supranational European Commission, the national governments and the sub-national authorities in the member states. The multi-level partnership involved different actors in regional policy — its formulation and implementation — by encouraging the national governments and their regional authorities to work together in preparing regional development plans. The Commission held the view that only projects forming part of a coherent regional development plan would be financed under the Structural Funds. In effect, the European authorities sought to influence the member states so as to effect closer collaboration among the different levels of government, and a more effective coordination of initiatives for regional development.

The European Commission's role was enhanced by the introduction of the concept of cohesion in the Single European Act, and the increased expenditure allocated to the Structural Funds. In the actual implementation of cohesion policy, the Commission adopted four key principles as part of the strategic programme: the concentration of measures around certain priority objectives; partnership, involving cooperation between the Commission and the most appropriate authority at national, regional, and local level in each member state; additionally, such that EU funds would supplement, rather than replace, national funding; and, programming, whereby multi-annual and multi-activity programmes were funded, rather than discrete, individual projects (Allen 2000).

The Treaty of Rome had recognised in the preamble the importance of even development, and regional growth based upon equality rather than disparities for certain regions. Two decades later, the idea that all countries and regions should share in the growth associated with the Single European Market was linked to the recognition that this could only happen with targeted intervention.

Ireland — Experience in the EU

For Ireland, membership of the European Union brought modernisation in both the economic and social spheres (O'Donnell 2002). Though the EC was less important as a large market for domestic firms, the European market proved an attraction for the large number of foreign firms that decided to locate in Ireland. Domestic firms were less interested, initially, in the European market since indigenous industry was characterised by small and medium-sized firms with a preference for the national and local markets. By the 1990s, however, a substantial number of 'new economy' enterprises were also targeting the European market.

More generally, the experience of participation in EU decision-making had a positive effect on the political system and especially the quality of government decisions and strategies. Public policy was increasingly framed in the context of the shifting priorities of the European Union — but without abandoning the sense of what constituted the national priorities and strategies for development. In addition, European Union accession gave a strong impetus to more clear-cut strategic direction across the policy spectrum.

Ireland joined the European Community in 1973, together with Britain and Denmark. But it did not begin to exhibit any signs of significant economic growth for almost twenty years after its accession. The 1980s was a decade of severe economic and political crisis, and there was a growing disquiet over the inability of the government to find lasting solutions to continued high unemployment, low growth and persistent emigration. The economy was characterised by a dual nature, with a mix of indigenous industry and a growing presence of foreign-owned firms. Significant differences existed between the two economic groups.

Indigenous industry was dominated by the small firms in traditional manufacturing and service activities, oriented to the domestic market and with low technological intensity. The foreign-owned sector was characterised by multi-nationals in the high-tech sectors (notably pharmaceuticals and informatics-technology), oriented to the export market. Between 1987 and 1997, the foreign-owned sector continued to increase their share of manufacturing output, employment, and exports as against the share of indigenous industry. Foreign investment, in the form of mainly US multinational corporations, was attracted to Ireland by a combination of the attractive low-taxation policy of the government, and the prospects of being able to supply the large European market from a low-cost location within the EU, where there was a ready supply of low-wage and high-skilled workers.

It is perhaps not surprising that the European Commission initiative to launch the Single Market programme was so well received by the political and economic community. The Single Market was expected to bring opportunities and benefits — but the economy would have to maintain competitiveness, and the government believed to achieve this it was essential to have a strong wage bargaining system, with restrictions on the public spending. In large measure, the combination of the European internal market, the Structural Funds, and the move to European monetary integration all exerted positive effects on the economic system.

The positive effects did not come all at once. Rather, there was a significant time lag between accession (1973), the EU decision to implement the Single Market (1986), the reform of the Structural Funds (1988) and the declaration of the EU's intention to go ahead with monetary union (1992). The Irish economy was showing slow growth in the early 1990s, just as the other European economies were sharing a period of recession. The real take-off in economic growth occurred from the end of 1995, and the next seven years exhibited growth rates far in excess of the European average.

A key question is what role did European integration, and particularly the Structural Funds play in the remarkable economic progress since the mid-1990s. A second, and related question is to what extent have the economic benefits been evenly distributed across regions and groups. There was general agreement among the political and economic interest groups that the European internal market could bring benefits and opportunities for Irish economic interests. Ireland, like Spain, was optimistic regarding the positive benefits that could accrue to the domestic economy as a result of this newest phase of integration.

A study published in 1992 suggested that Irish GNP would grow by as much as four percent (Bradley et al. 1992). Later studies were more cautious in their assessment of the impact on small, open economies in the European periphery (ESRI 1997). It was suggested that the impact could vary, with certain sectors benefiting in terms of employment and output while other sectors were threatened with decline. However, even with the downward revisions made in the light of ex–post estimates, it was still expected that the Single Market could add 3.5 percent to the country's economic growth (Barry et al. 2001).

Despite these positive expectations about the impact of the Single Market, Ireland was the recipient of large allocations under the Structural Funds. From 1989 to 2000 the annual receipts from the structural funds averaged around 2.6 percent of GDP. The majority of the financial support was intended for three main target areas: physical infrastructure; human resource development; and private sector development, especially investment and innovation activities. A little over one-third of the total Structural Funds receipts were allocated to physical infrastructure investment, followed by around 28 percent going to human resource development. Ultimately, the anticipated effect of these expenditures on the physical and human capital resource is the longer-term increase in productivity and profitability.

The question is whether the national output would have increased in any event, due to the overall positive effects of the Single Market Programme, even without the Structural Funds. However, research suggests that the long-run impact from the EU–funded programmes contributed to an increase of the national output, estimated at between 1 percent (ESRI) and 2 percent (Honohan 1997). By the end of the 1990s, Ireland was widely considered the success story of the EU, while Spain still had many difficulties in catching up to its neighbouring member states.

Spain — Experience in the EU

Spain was, like Ireland, a peripheral state within the European Union. Both countries placed a strong emphasis on the export sector; although in neither country did the domestic sectors enjoy a competitive advantage. Historically, both countries shared poor employment performance, high emigration, and a tendency towards inflationary pressures in the macroeconomy. However, Spain differed from the smaller country in a number of respects. It had a larger domestic economy, dominated by small and medium sized firms, with low technological intensity and a high dependence on foreign technology. Ireland's economy was significantly smaller, with a mix of manufacturing and services, and a heavy reliance on foreign investment

Research has shown that peripheral economies may experience negative effects in certain sectors, in the context of regional integration and the trade liberalisation that comes with it (Krugman and Venables 1990). In the Spanish case, there was a further claim to back up the national entitlement for funding under the EU programme. This was based on the significant regional disparities that existed within the country, and the gap in output and income levels in comparison with the EU average.

In the decade before its accession to the European Community, Spain had experienced both national and regional (ie. sub-national) economic growth rate, and a closing of the gap between the prosperous and less well-off regions in the country. However, this process of catch-up slowed in the 1980s, so that in the second half of the decade the disparities between regions widened. Even the high growth rates in the early years of membership, supported by an influx of foreign direct investment and high consumer spending, were unable to exert an appreciable impact in terms of regional convergence.

The inter-regional gap can be explained in part by the quite distinct differences in economic structures, in the levels of technological development, and in the quality of each region's stock of physical and technological infrastructure (Cuadrado Roura 1998). The less-developed regions faced a vicious circle, whereby inadequate levels of technological capability and of research and development spending were reflected in an industrial base of low technological intensity. This low-tech industrial structure combined with limited investment in human capital to produce growth rates below those achieved by the more advanced regions.

Spain's regional autonomous communities were established under the Constitution signed in 1978, giving rise to the new democratic state. The model of decentralisation was created in the recognition of the distinctive regional identities that existed and, to make it work, provision was made for a system of inter-regional transfers under the control of the central government. In Ireland, geographical and historical factors had resulted in a centralised model of government. And, for the purposes of the Structural Funds the country was treated as one region. Spain, on the other hand, had seventeen regions with diverse (and diverging) levels of development, measured in terms of both the national and the European average.

When it joined the European Community in 1986, per capita income in Spain was just under 70 percent of the European average. By 2003, the national per capita income had reached 83 percent of the EU average — and still well below that of its neighbour, France. In the intervening period, regional growth rates also continued to diverge and there was very little upward movement of the regions classified with Objective 1 status. During the programming period 1994–99, Spain received a little more than half of the Cohesion Fund, and altogether about one quarter of the structural funds allocation — making it the largest beneficiary in absolute terms.

What was the impact upon cohesion? The assessment of the outcome inevitably depends upon how it is measured, and also upon the perspective of the assessor. The optimist will highlight the slow but steady rise in the national per capita income. But by the end of the 1990s, ten of the Spanish regions remained below the 75 percent threshold — thereby retaining their classification as lagging regions. Regional unemployment rates were also diverging, varying from 10.5 percent (Navarra) to 29 percent in Andalucia and Extremadura — a difference of twenty percentage points between the highest and the lowest rates.

There was no clear link between the proportion of Structural Funds received and the level of unemployment. Andalucia consistently received over twenty percent of the funds, four times as much as Extremadura, yet both held the worst rates of unemployment in 1998. In absolute terms, four regions that received substantial shares of the Structural Funds throughout the period 1986–95 (Castille and Leon, Galicia, Castilla–La Mancha, and Canary islands) continued to have high unemployment rates up to the time of Spain's entry into European monetary union.

The Spanish government undertook its own assessment of the macro–economic effects of the Structural Funds (reported in Fernández Martínez 1997), which suggested that the gross domestic product would have been 0.7 percent less on average over the period 1989–93, and 0.97 percent less between 1994–96 in the absence of the Structural Funds. Private investment and employment would have been lower, and unemployment higher, without the Structural Funds. The strongest effects were, according to the government's estimates, on total national investment, national demand, exports, and imports. However, unemployment was one of the variables least affected by the Structural Funds, despite the stated objective of the programme to reduce unemployment in those regions most adversely affected by joblessness. The results of the government's assessment suggested, moreover, that though the Structural Funds contributed to aggregate demand, raised income, and increased the demand for imports, there was a limited effect on unemployment.

What were the funds used for? In the Spanish case, the priorities were infrastructure, transport, and the environment. A second priority was business and tourism support, with human capital ranked third. In placing more emphasis upon the allocation of structural fund support on infrastructure development rather than upgrading the quality of its human capital resource base, it may be that the national and regional authorities side-stepped an opportunity to create the conditions for sustained employment growth.

Comparing the Outcomes

Both Spain and Ireland were major beneficiaries of the financial transfers under the Structural Funds, with Spain receiving the largest amount in absolute terms, while on a per capita basis Ireland benefited the most. However, by the second half of the 1990s the Irish economic growth rates far exceeded those in the EU as a whole with an average annual growth rate of 8.7 percent for the period 1993–1998. Between 1987 and 2000, Irish GNP grew by 140 percent, compared to 40 percent in the US and 35 percent in the EU 15 (Barry et al. 2001). By 1997, the Irish per capita GDP had exceeded the EU average. So, growth rates produced a notable degree of convergence in income levels during the 1990s. The same degree of convergence was not evident in the Spanish case. Despite steady growth after accession, the Spanish per capita income was just under 84 percent of the EU average in 2003.

Does this mean that cohesion did not take place, and that the EU's principal policy instrument, the Structural Funds, failed to deliver the main objective? The answer is not so clear-cut, despite the evidence produced by the European Commission for the most recent progress report on cohesion. In the Irish case, there were improvements in growth, and also in income and employment levels. Until 2000, the country was treated as one single region for the purposes of the Structural Funds programme. After that date, the Irish government opted to create two regions in an effort to preserve the entitlement to future funding, though only one of those regions was eligible for financial support.

In Spain, regional disparities in income, output, and employment actually increased. Although some regions, notably Madrid and Navarre, succeeded in attaining growth and income levels above the European average, the majority of the regions failed to improve their position *vis–à–vis* either the fast-growing regions elsewhere in Spain or in the European Union as a whole.

To what should we attribute the difference in the impact and experience of the two countries? Part of the explanation lies in the institutional differences and policy decisions taken in each country. Spain is a large country, with a great diversity in climate, topography, and regional development levels that reflect the historical pattern of industrialisation. Much of the traditional manufacturing industry has been subjected to intense pressures for reform in the face of increased international competition. Even with the structural shifts over the past three decades, and a services sector that accounts for a greater share of output and employment than agriculture or manufacturing combined, these structural changes have not made any impact in reducing the regional disparities across the country. Instead, the fastest-growing regions (including Madrid, Canary Islands, the north–east, and the Balearic islands) actually added to regional divergence.

Like Ireland, Spain was a magnet for foreign direct investment (FDI) in the years immediately following its accession to the EU. But these increased investment levels failed to generate improved competitiveness and a sustained capacity for higher productivity. And, in the first half of the 1990s the inward investment slowed as the EU economy entered recession. From the mid–1990s outflows of investment increased in volume, particularly to Latin America — mainly targeting the telecommunications and banking sectors.

Recent literature has emphasised the importance of endogenous factors such as the accumulation of skills and technological innovation, as well as physical infrastructure, together with localised collective learning, in contributing to economic growth (Lucas 1988; Rivera–Batiz and Romer 1991; Romer 1986, 1990). However, models of localised endogenous growth indicate that market integration favours the growing regions that are already in the forefront of the development process, and thus integration can foster regional disparities and divergence. Capital and labour tend to move to existing prosperous and competitive regions, reinforcing increasing returns and cumulative growth in those areas (Bertola 1993; Martin 2001).

Between 1986 and 1996, the policy of the Spanish Socialist-led government was directed at a number of objectives — price stability, economic growth, and the reduction of unemployment — with regional development and growth predicated on continued growth of the national economy, supplemented by the financial transfers from the European Structural Funds. From 1996 onwards, the Partido Popular government of José María Aznar supported economic liberalisation both at home and in the European Union. It also followed a restrictive fiscal policy in line with the conditions imposed on all countries in the euro zone. Under the Partido Popular government, the privatisation programme was intensified while public spending was increasingly restricted.

The conditions of monetary integration challenged the commitment of both the central and regional governments in the seventeen autonomous communities. The receipts under the Structural Funds were therefore an important resource for the policy of regional development, particularly since national public spending was being curtailed. Indeed, throughout the 1990s regional income levels exceeded output largely due to those transfers. Receipts under the Structural Funds were mainly used to finance major infrastructure projects, particularly road and railway investments, as well as investments directed at urban renewal and cultural and civic centres. One result of these investments was the stimulation of a boom in the construction industry.

Nonetheless, productivity was not improved since Spanish industry invested little in research and development. Most companies were either small or medium-sized and had little capital at their disposal to invest in research. A second reason for low productivity may be found in the educational attainment of the workforce. Although the quality of the Spanish university system is comparable to international standards, there remains a deficit in education and training. This is reflected in the fact that Spanish investment in educational measures is 40 percent below the EU average. Many people are either highly qualified or very poorly qualified, but remarkably few people have attained an intermediate level of education. Geographical and sectoral mobility of labour is low and, added to the wide-ranging skills deficit, the result is high unemployment at regional levels.

The broader picture as far as Spain is concerned suggests a reliance on the Structural Funds for investment in physical infrastructure. But, as the literature on endogenous growth suggests, there is an important role for other factors, notably human capital and technology. These have either been neglected or regarded as of secondary importance in Spanish government policy since the 1980s.

The Irish government also invested heavily in physical infrastructure, and particularly in new highways. Similar to Spain, the construction industry boomed and house price inflation became a matter of concern in the second half of the 1990s. However, the economic boom of the 1990s cannot be attributed solely to the multiplier effect of the Structural Funds expenditure. The Irish state played a key role through the particular policy choices made in the areas of education and industrial policy, maintained consistently by the different governments from the 1980s (Kirby 2002).

The Irish state had devised a long-term strategy to attract multinational corporations, selecting those enterprises in leading-edge sectors such as information and communications technologies, and pharmaceuticals — high-tech enterprises producing high value-added output for export markets. Multinational corporations were attracted to Ireland by a large range of government incentives, including a low corporation tax rate (12 percent, compared to the European average of around 32 percent), a generally favourable (liberal) environment for business, and a low-cost, high-skilled workforce.

The Irish education system was instrumental in producing graduates with the skills that were in demand from the sectors targeted by the government. Hence, education policy complemented the industrial policy as part of the long-term strategy for development. By the 1990s, the multinational corporations (predominantly of US origin), and mainly in the IT and pharmaceuticals sectors) employed over 40 percent of the total workforce, and accounted for almost 90 percent of exports. This combination of government policy and the EU Structural Funds produced favourable conditions to stimulate economic growth — and an effective set of conditions for endogenous growth based upon investment, human capital, technology, and physical infrastructure.

However, this is not to suggest that each country is permanently locked into its particular model of cohesion and development. The Irish economy began to slow down with a growth rate of 4 percent in 2003. The exceptional and rapid growth rates in recent years have produced new social inequalities and an increase in the level of poverty. Although there has been an increase in the absolute standard of living, many people are relatively (and absolutely) worse off, and the effect is to reduce the cohesion levels.

The slowdown in the global (and US) economy since 2000, and the reversal in the information technology sector adversely affected the Irish economic situation. A growing number of plant closures were announced in the half decade of the new millennium, with a fall in the number of jobs being created in the sectors involved. Indeed, recent experience highlights the risks of the Irish strategy with its heavy reliance on foreign investment in a limited number of sectors and an almost total dominance of investors from one country, the United States. Also, as a small, open economy, Ireland is exposed to the vagaries of the international economic system, and a slowdown in global output and demand will exert a negative impact upon the economic well-being of the country. In this regard, it may be observed that the capacity for endogenous growth is ultimately limited by an exogenous factor — namely, the strength of international demand.

The challenge facing the Irish government is how to ensure sustained (if lower) growth rates in the future, given that the country will no longer receive significant contributions from the Structural Funds. With the extremely difficult negotiations for the next round of the EU budget (covering the period 2006–2013) highlighting the tensions among the now–enlarged European Union, Ireland will most likely become a net contributor to the budget. The country will also face keen competition from the Eastern European states as low-cost locations for foreign direct investment, so national policy must remain focused upon preserving competitiveness on several fronts at the same time. The current low rate of corporation tax set by the Irish government gives the country a competitive advantage in attracting foreign investment, but it also invites criticism from the European Commission as a distortion of the Single Market. For the moment, the Irish corporation tax remains, but so do the pressures from the EU authorities to raise it to EU levels on order to avoid distorting competition.

The Irish government clearly foresees the continuation of its role in managing regional economic development. The National Development Plan 2000–2006 provided for a total of 51 billion euro (made up of private, public and EU funds) for investment in services, social housing, education, roads and public transport, and rural development). The EU contribution to this will amount to €6 billion, with much of the investment to be undertaken by public–private partnership arrangements. In an era of slower growth and the increased uncertainties in the wake of the EU enlargement and in the international economy generally, the Irish government will be obliged to use the National Development Plan as a means towards social inclusion, combining solidarity with equality to a degree that did not occur during the height of the economic boom.

Spanish progress towards the European level as measured by the principal economic indicator of per capita GDP was slow (Farrell 2001). In 2004, the country came close to the European average, with a per capita income at 98 percent of that in the EU–25. Taking other indicators into consideration, however, the process of convergence has some way to go yet. Within the country, growth rates continue to show divergence between the regions. Employment levels remain below those of the other leading member states, and regional employment growth varies significantly as does the quality of labour. There is a need for more public investment in education, research and technological innovation, as well as in more active labour market policies. Yet, Spain must also comply with the requirements on public spending levels within the context of monetary integration. For now, the government is relying upon market-led growth to deliver regional cohesion when in fact growth may be dependent upon certain prerequisites that can only be put in place through increased public spending.

European enlargement has affected how the Structural Funds will be distributed over the coming period, and the Spanish share of these funds will decline. Although Ireland will receive less in the future due to the fact that the country's growth rate has placed it outside the eligibility band, in the Spanish case eligibility is likely to be affected more by default (and a statistical convergence). EU enlargement meant the accession of eastern European states with lower levels of economic development, and this produces the effect of reducing the average per capita income in the EU–25.

In addition, enlargement will produce a geographical shift in the pattern of disparities, with a quarter of the total EU population (116 million people) living in regions with per capita GDP below 75 percent of the EU average, as against 18 percent in the former EU–15. If current eligibility criteria for Objective 1 Structural Funds are maintained, only 3 of the 10 Spanish Objective 1 regions that currently receive support will continue to do so in 2007. Spain would also lose the assistance which it receives under the Cohesion Funds (Martín, Herce, Sosvilla–Rivero, and Velasquez 2002).

More generally, EU cohesion policy can be judged a success in political terms. It emerged in the context of demands for redistributive measures to counter the pressures anticipated from the deepening of integration, such as the Single Market programme, and the subsequent agreement to create a monetary union. Both these decisions were expected to create pressures for individual countries, from the greater competition likely to arise with the implementation of the Single Market programme to the restrictions on the public finances with the introduction of the euro. European cohesion policy (embodied in the Structural and Cohesion Funds) provided a means to alleviate the pressures on the poorer and weaker countries associated with the deepening of integration. It was also an instrument for securing the political support of those countries and groups less likely to see the immediate benefits of further integration. And, for the European Commission it was a way to extend its influence to interest groups at the sub-national level and in the process to widen and consolidate the political community around European integration.

Lessons for Regional Cohesion Elsewhere?

Regional integration develops on the basis of cooperation between sovereign states that pursue common interests through collective action. On this basis, regional integration need not preclude the continued pursuit of individual national interests or impinge upon national sovereignty. Essentially, such cooperation evolves over time, propelled by the political commitment of diverse actors to extend the scope of joint decision-making into new areas and policies. However, while the logic of cooperation may be accepted to a greater or lesser degree by all participants, the willingness to cooperate is tempered by the recognition that there are costs as well as benefits. The asymmetrical impact of integration often reflects the asymmetrical nature of the regional cooperation arrangement itself.

The Association of South East Asian Nations (ASEAN) is one such asymmetrical form of regionalism. There are significant differences in economic and political structures, population, levels of development, and degree of integration with the rest of the world, among the ASEAN members. Such differences affect not only the potential to cooperate, but also the capacity to absorb the integrative outcomes. For smaller and less-developed countries, a key question is how to ensure that liberalisation and openness, consequent upon regional economic integration, does not prejudice national and regional development. For ASEAN, the shift from regional security community towards the ASEAN Free Trade Area, and perhaps ultimately some form of monetary cooperation, prompts a serious consideration of how to deepen regional integration while avoiding the imposition of serious adjustment costs on weaker regions and economic sectors in what would become a more open and competitive environment.

The question is important because it raises issues that extend beyond the implementation of regional agreements to include more political considerations regarding the nature of regional institutional arrangements, and the effect that these might have upon national political structures.

Nonetheless, the next step in ASEAN's regional integration is conditional upon maintaining the political commitment of each member country, and in large measure such commitment is more likely if all countries/regions can benefit (even if some benefit more than others) while the weaker countries (and the weaker regions within those countries) can access redistributive mechanisms to compensate for adjustment costs.

Would an ASEAN Structural Fund facilitate adjustment and promote convergence among the member countries? What lessons, if any, can be derived from the study of the EU's Structural Funds? And, can we infer any useful guide for the ASEAN context? The European Structural Funds has both proponents and critics. The critics argue that the funds have failed to correct regional imbalances, and instead merely serve to distort the allocation of resources as firms and regional (sub-national) authorities make decisions in order to obtain financial transfers from the European Commission, instead of being guided by efficiency and other market-led criteria. Proponents stress the need for a long-term strategy in the pursuit of convergence and cohesion, and argue that already there are signs of such convergence. Moreover, the policy has already created a greater awareness of the need for strategic and coordinated regional planning, bringing together sub-national, national, and European authorities to address regional inequalities in a comprehensive manner.

However, as the cases examined in this chapter have shown, financial transfers alone will not reduce regional disparities, and certainly not in the short-term. These funds were important as supplementary financing mechanisms to fund infrastructural investments in the countries concerned. But other factors also played a crucial role in regional development. In particular, the quality of the productive resources and the nature of the national government policy, within a broader strategic framework for development and growth, were critical success factors. Somewhat ironically, the European Commission itself has stressed the importance of national policies in the task of promoting cohesion — but this is not so surprising in the light of the fact that public expenditure by the member states amounts to on average 47 percent of the GDP of the European Union, while the budget allocated to cohesion policy is less than 0.4 percent (European Commission 2004).

The particular combination of policy measures adopted by the Irish government, extending back to the 1980s, was central to setting the conditions for growth — a policy mix that combined interventionism with liberalisation, strategically–oriented industrial and education policies, together with policies that fostered a favourable climate for business, and especially for foreign direct investment. Moreover, this mix blended well with the institutional arrangements and locally–specific factors. The size of the economy, the nature of the economic system, and other variables such as population, the place of technology and the role of education all affect the capacity for convergence and cohesion.

Research suggests that domestic institutions have an important role to play in development, and that governments are not helpless in the face of globalisation or increasing international interdependence (Weiss 2003). But we must also be careful about assuming that models can be exported, or indeed that there is a one–size–fits–all solution to regional growth and development. The Irish model may only be appropriate for a particular set of circumstances, political context, or a particular time frame. Similarly, the European model may work well in the context of the institutional arrangements of the EU–15, but not an EU–25.

A Structural Fund for ASEAN to support the processes of regional integration in the weaker countries would require complementary measures on the part of the ASEAN member states. On its own, a Structural Fund does not constitute a panacea for regional inequalities, nor will it necessarily promote convergence and cohesion under regional integration. Its success depends upon the effective co-ordination with national programmes that carefully reflect the developmental needs and the institutional arrangements in each member state.

Significantly, a Structural Fund can play a crucial role at the political level in fostering and maintaining the support for regional integration, and to facilitate deeper integration. National politicians can lend support more readily to programmes that provide financial support for local initiatives that have high visibility. These kinds of programmes represent little challenge to concerns over national sovereignty, whether in Europe, Asia, or other parts of the world. Ultimately, this may be the most important contribution of a Structural Fund in any regional arrangement characterised by asymmetrical relations among the participating countries.

References

Allen, D. (2000) Cohesion and the structural funds, in H. Wallace and W. Wallace (eds.), *Policy-making in the European Union*. Oxford: Oxford University Press.

Barro, R.J., and Sala–I–Martin, X. (1995) *Economic Growth*. New York: McGraw–Hill.

Barry, F., Bradley, J., and Hannan, A. (2001) The Single Market and Ireland's Recent Economic Growth. *Journal of Common Market Studies*, 39(3), 537–552.

Bertola, G. (1993) Models of economic integration and localised growth, in F. Torres and F. Giavazzi (eds.), *Adjustment and Growth in the European Monetary Union*. Cambridge: Cambridge University Press.

Boldrin, M., and Canova, F. (2001) Inequality and convergence in Europe's regions: Reconsidering European 681 regional policies. *Economic Policy*, 32, 207–253.

Bradley, J., Fitzgerald, J., and Kearney, I. (1992) The role of the structural funds: Analysis of the consequences for Ireland in the context of 1992. *Policy Research Series No. 13*. Dublin: ESRI.

Cheshire, P.C., and Magrini, S. (2001) Endogenous processes in European regional growth: Convergence and policy. *Growth and Change*, 31, 455–479.

Cuadrado Roura, J., Mancha Navarro, T., and Garrido Tserte, R. (1997) *Convergencia regional en España. Hechos, tendencias y perspectivas*. Madrid: Fundacion Argentina–Visor Dis.

Economist. (2003) Drowning in a sea of structural funds? 29 March, London.

El–Agraa, A. (2001) *The European Union. Economics and Policies*. Harlow: Pearson.

ESRI. (1997) *The single market review: Aggregate and regional impact — The case of Greece, Spain, Ireland, and Portugal*. London: Kogan Page in association with the Commission of the European Communities.

European Commission. (2001) *Unity, solidarity, diversity for Europe, its people and its territory: Second report on economic and social cohesion*. Luxembourg.

European Commission. (2003) *Second Progress Report on Economic and Social Cohesion*. COM (2003) 34 final.

European Commission. (2004) *Third Report on Economic and Social Cohesion*. COM (2004) 107 final.

Farrell, M. (2001) *Spain in the EU. The road to economic convergence*. London: Palgrave.

Fernández Martínez, P. (1997) Los Fondos Estructurales Europeos y el Desarollo Regional: Balance de una Decada Desde la Perspectiva Española. *Informacion Comercial Española*, 766. Madrid: Ministerio de Economía y Hacienda.

Honohan, P. (1997) EU structural funds in Ireland: A mid–term evaluation of the CSF 1994–1999. *Policy Research Series No. 31*. Dublin: ESRI.

Kirby, P. (2002) *The Celtic Tiger in distress. Growth with inequality in Ireland*. London: Palgrave.

Krugman, P. (1991) Increasing returns and economic geography. *Journal of Political Economy*, 99, 483–499.

Krugman, P., and Venables, A. (1990) Integration and competitiveness of peripheral industry, in C. Bliss and J. Braga de Macedo (eds.), *Unity with diversity in the European Economy*. Cambridge: Cambridge University Press.

Lucas, R.E. (1988) On the mechanisms of economic development. *Journal of Monetary Economics*, 22, 3–42.

Martin, R. (2001) EMU versus the regions? Regional convergence and divergence in Euroland. *Journal of Economic Geography*, 1, 51–80.

Martín, C., Herce, J.A., Sosvilla–Rivero, S., and Velasquez, F.J. (2002) European Union enlargement. Effects on the Spanish economy. *La Caixa Economic Series, 27*, Madrid.

Midelfart–Knarvik, K., and Overman, H. (2002) Delocation and European Integration — Is structural spending justified? *Economic Policy*, 35, 322–359.

O'Donnell, R. (2002) *Ireland and Europe. The economic dimension*. Dublin: Dublin Institute of European Affairs.

Rivera–Batiz, L.A., and Romer, P.M. (1991) Economic integration and endogenous growth. *Quarterly Journal of Economics*, 106, 531–555.

Romer, P.M. (1986) Increasing returns and long–run growth. *Journal of Political Economy*, 94, 1002–1037.

Romer, P.M. (1990) Endogenous technological change. *Journal of Political Economy*, 98, 71–102.

Weiss, L. (2003) *States in the global economy: Bringing domestic institutions back in*. Cambridge: Cambridge University Press.

CHAPTER 10

LESSONS FOR ASIA? LEGITIMACY AND QUASI-DEMOCRATIC MECHANISMS IN EUROPEAN AND AMERICAN MARKET INTEGRATION

Craig Parsons and J. David Richardson[1]

No regions anywhere in the world today come as close as the 'United' States and the European Union to a 'single market' within their territory. Most border-based measures restricting commercial activities have shrunk to a minimum or disappeared altogether, unleashing unparalleled prosperity on both continents. Asian nations, especially East Asian nations,[2] are consciously being drawn in the same single-market direction, both in internal nation-building (especially China and Indonesia) and in regional market integration.[3]

Yet the most striking success of US and EU history is not actually commercial! It is the legitimacy and public support for the single-market experiment that is firmly grounded in the United States and evolving fitfully in Europe. Even if the recent failure of the EU constitution opens a

[1] The authors appreciate greatly Michael Plummer's critical comments on an earlier draft.

[2] For recent treatments, see Bergsten and Park (2002), Lloyd and Lee (2001), Scollay and Gilbert (2001), Yusuf et al. (2003), and World Bank (2005). We will conceive of East Asia as China, Japan, the Koreas, and the members of the Association of Southeast Asian Nations (ASEAN).

[3] It is already clear that we are initially blurring two distinct types of market integration for nation-states — within-border and across-border. The two are not unrelated. The thinking of current Chinese leaders, for example, is that external integration can encourage domestic reform that includes breaking down barriers to internal integration. We think ultimately that such a combined analysis will not blur, but rather clarify the feasible and necessary regulatory, political, and social supports for market integration to be legitimate.

more troubled chapter in the EU story, there is little question that it will remain a regional integration project of unique scope, depth, and solidity.

Legitimacy is the key to sustained market integration. We have argued elsewhere[4] that there is a *necessary* nexus between social stability, political participation, and legitimacy on the one hand and the growth of a single market on the other. A mixture of treaties, institutions, and symbols serve as mediators of the legitimacy nexus.

We have also argued that the *content* of the nexus includes certain necessary and ubiquitous elements (like courts that implement commercial law), whereas the historical *mechanisms* by which legitimacy is attained are far more varied (and often only quasi-democratic).

In this paper we will argue that East Asia still lacks some important content that is necessary for broadly legitimate market integration, but that certain views of European and American experience suggest that political-diplomatic mechanisms are indeed available for Asians to pursue this goal. We make the somewhat ironic observation that quasi-democratic accounts of EU and US history — that portray the legitimization of their integration as historically difficult and surprising — make it more plausible to extrapolate optimistic lessons for Asia's future.

Asian market integration is, of course, not yet very well developed, though it is deepening rapidly. The administrative and diplomatic practices that might help to legitimize such integration are even less extant. Broad popular assent to growing regional intra-dependence is hardly articulated anywhere, and completely absent in the least democratic Asian polities. Popular anxiety, protest, and resistance more than occasionally punctuate the rapidly shifting economic trends.[5]

Government and business elites who have initiated deepening East Asian integration have two design challenges: designing the ancillary thresholds for business regulation that are the necessary props to making an Asian single market sustainable, and steering the political-diplomatic mechanisms that help Asia transition from a traditional development re-

---

[4] Frost et al. (2002).

[5] Chinese and Indonesian workers and farmers have mounted well-publicized protests, meanwhile other Asian media are full of fears that Chinese competition will 'hollow out' key export-oriented sectors.

gime of national economic polities and priorities to a regime of regionally well-managed economic interdependence.

This paper draw lessons from recent EU experiences, in the light of more distant US experiences, and applies them to Asian internal and regional integration. Though widely separated in time, shape, and culture, the US and EU undertook many similar initiatives, in roughly similar sequences, to reach regional market integration. These initiatives sketch a common content in the construction of regulatory and administrative structures that Asians might take as a guide to their similar aspirations. Another more complex set of lessons concern the mechanisms by which the US and the EU legitimized market integration. East Asia might or might not legitimize in the same ways.

After a relatively brief overview of the historical contents lessons, we focus most of our attention on the issue of mechanisms.[6] But we need to begin with more precision in our terms.

Background Clarifications and Distinctions

In suggesting that market integration depends on a range of social and political supports, we stake out ground between two old and active scholarly literatures on 'embeddedness' and 'exceptionalism.'

We borrow from, yet confront, a large literature that sees market integration as a 'natural,' spontaneous evolution that propels itself forward despite (and to the detriment of) social, political, or cultural constructs. Such views are most visible today in the widespread notion that global market integration is an unstoppable process that is sweeping aside states, national cultures, and other barriers. We side with Karl Polanyi in rejecting this view in favor of a more 'embedded' view of economic integration.[7] Enduringly successful market integration in the past has proceeded only with the help of social and political supports; future regional or global market integration will depend on finding such extra-economic supports as well.

---

[6] For a more complete treatment of the 'contents' lessons especially, see Frost et al (2002).

[7] Polanyi (1944).

We also confront a large literature that portrays either the American or the European experiences as special, so special as to be fundamentally unique, in suggesting that there are historical parallels and potentially generalizable lessons in these socio-political formulae for market integration. We accept many of this literature's insights on 'American exceptionalism' and on the idiosyncratic geopolitical and ideological foundations of postwar 'Europeanism.' But we believe that these cases are far from *fully* unique. Many of their background conditions may arise elsewhere, and variations on some of their socio-political responses may be reproducible as well.

Three terms are crucial to our discussion: legitimacy, market integration, and mechanisms.

- *Legitimacy*, as we conceive it, does not simply mean broad popularity. The legitimacy of policies or institutions matters most precisely when they do not enjoy much immediate popularity — and yet people still choose to respect them. We try hard to avoid falling into the kind of tautology that has bedeviled political theorists (and particularly liberal theorists) at least since Locke, who saw 'tacit consent' simplistically wherever there was no active revolt.[8] Our more selective definition encompasses the relative freedom and capacities of most citizens to formulate and express their views to begin with, as individuals and as social groups. The more citizens have the legal freedom and organizational resources to compose and express informed views, and the less sustained challenges arise to the fundamental frameworks of particular institutions or policies, the more confidently we can call those institutions or policies 'legitimate.'[9] We add importantly that legitimacy can arise either through active assent (where actors with input into a decision give conscious

---

[8] Our criticism here is largely at the level of definitions. Locke and many other liberals have often been accused of overlooking the variety of factors other than real approval that may produce apparent consent (collective action problems that block mobilization, subtle repression, hegemonic ideology, etc.), but we expect most liberal thinkers would readily accept our extended definition.

[9] Our conception of legitimacy is close to that adopted by Nicolaidis and Howse (2001), p.4, in their comparative EU-US treatment of federalism.

endorsement) or through attenuated assent (where actors without an immediate voice in a decision rationalize it as necessary or even desirable as time goes by). These active and attenuated mechanisms can reach similar endpoints — creating policies or institutions which go unchallenged despite later opportunities to question them — but do so through very different legitimizing means.

- *Market integration*, as we conceive it, does not mean simply price arbitrage. Our more sophisticated definition encompasses the convergence across regions of: production technologies[10] (around 'best-practice'); menus of diverse varieties of goods and services; the prices and costs of each variety; and basic contestability conditions for those pioneering new or cheaper techniques and varieties. In services our conception includes corporate, financial, and labor services — market integration for these implies cross-border mergers and other direct investment, lending and borrowing, and migration. By convergence of varieties we mean increased region-wide availability of comparable qualities of goods and services,[11] as well as a rationalization of the array of qualities available, including regularization of technical standards for the differentiated goods and services available.

- *Mechanisms*, as we conceive them, describe the socio-political processes by which the legitimacy of market integration is achieved. We distinguish three, which we label pluralism, commercialism, and developmentalism. Pluralistic mechanisms are funda-

[10] Production technologies are *menus* of production and management methods, not a single-method-to-fit-all. The specific methods chosen in various regions reflect weather, environment, culture, availability of types of labor and other inputs, and other local conditions. By including management methods, we are subsuming corporate governance under technologies; convergence of varieties of corporate governance is then one of the markers of integration, too.

[11] This increased availability of comparable varieties would be presumably reflected in increased shares of so-called two-way 'intra-industry trade' as a share of total trade (which would itself rise relative to output). See Venables and Winters (2002), Table 4.1, for the growth of intra-industry trade within the EU. See Plummer (2003) and Yusuf et al. (2003) for evidence on the growth of this kind of trade within East Asia.

mentally bottom-up processes of bargains between market 'winners' and 'losers.' Winners and losers negotiate consent that involves compensatory payoffs to attract broad support and legitimacy. The frameworks that bolster market integration are thus viewed as legitimate by majority coalitions, and remain stably in place over time for the same reason. Under commercialist mechanisms, market integration is an aggressive agenda allying business and the state. In a version of Polanyi's 'double movement,'[12] top-down pressure provokes bottom-up resistance from the rest of society, which objects broadly to the social dislocations of the market. The state and business concede some market-mitigating palliatives to these opponents, but also baldly impose much of their agenda. Developmentalism describes even more top-down mechanisms in which market integration is a vehicle for state-building. Politicians or government officials lead these accounts; even big business is lukewarm about market integration. State-builders extract support for single markets from most societal actors, including business, but the impetus and broad form of those projects aim for political integration and centralization of power, not for economic incentives.

Pluralistic mechanisms, of course, lead to negotiated legitimacy (active assent); the others have elements of forced assent and attenuated resignation. Under the other mechanisms, to the extent that the resultant partly-embedded market appears eventually to achieve broad societal assent, this reflects a *fait accompli* that gains 'taken for granted' status over time more than genuine approval. Current legitimacy is thus to some degree a product of resignation or reluctant concession.

Our paper will address a key historical issue — whether historical EU (and US) legitimizing transitions were mostly consistent with the first

---

[12] Polanyi argued that human societies tended to embed markets deeply in social norms and institutions. When an attempt was made to create a 'modern market society' in 19th century Europe — organizing society by market rules rather than the reverse — this brought an accelerating destruction of the basic social fabric, provoking widespread social reactions. Polanyi thus saw a 'double movement' in the creation of any modern market: steps to free markets from social impediments would be countered by reactions from society. Polanyi (1944).

view or rather with the second or third. To pose our issue more provocatively using modern caricatures: Does EU (and US) history 'feel' more like its own mythology (often view 1) or more like post–Meiji Japanese history (a stereotype of view 2) or modern Malaysian history (a stereotype of view 3)?

We will answer that EU and US history is relevant for Asian regional integration in revealing that at least some elements of 'coerced legitimization' at some stage is familiar if not necessary.

It is also worth noting that there are other forms of regional economic integration than the market integration that we have just defined and on which we focus. Each alternative has distinctive legitimacy questions attached to it: imperial or colonial integration;[13] planned, often scale-based integration such as that practiced within the Soviet Union; early 20th-century cartelized integration in which corporate national champions are left free to divide global market territories; and 'ethnic network integration' in which family and keiretsu/chaebol networks and diasporas link economies in informal ways.[14] We ignore the first three alternative forms of economic integration because they seem not to have delivered the significant benefits that market integration has delivered to the EU and the US, making moot the issues of sustaining or legitimating them.

Ethnic network integration is a more serious alternative, as argued in a growing literature on postwar Asian growth.[15] But this sort of integration seems much less amenable to policy manipulation than the market form. Either a region has ethnic networks or it does not. And our reading of modern Asian single-market initiatives is that they are increasingly premised on the belief that ethnic market integration has gone as far as it can go, and more formal, organized initiatives are the next step.[16] If so, then US and European histories may be all the more relevant to Asia.

---

[13] Examples of each are, respectively, 19th-century colonial integration and the 20th-century Council for Mutual Economic Assistance (CEMA) centered on the Soviet Union;

[14] Katzenstein (1997).

[15] Rauch and Trindade (2002), Bergsten and Choi (2003).

[16] Thus ASEAN formalized a commitment to trade liberalization in its mid-1990s, AFTA Agreement, and is extending it with China. The Chiang Mai was a formalization of official-reserve lines of credit among central banks. Within China, the next mid-decade Five-

In that spirit, we review EU history below, with US history as a backdrop. We emphasize the various mechanisms by which growing market integration was legitimized, and highlight contrasting historical accounts that debate their relative importance. We then discuss our putative historical 'lessons' and in the last section of the paper apply them to growing Asian market integration.

Capsule Histories: Content and Mechanisms

We see significant parallels between the substantive arrangements that gradually legitimized 'single markets' in the US and the EU. Europe has used the US in part as a model. But historical parallels in legitimizing *content* do not necessarily mean that these frameworks arose by identical legitimizing *mechanisms* on both sides of the Atlantic, nor that Asia will copy the mechanisms of either case. To the extent that the US and the EU arrived at much the same structures to legitimize market integration, different routes may have brought them to that place. Even if Asia were to end up reproducing market-supporting arrangements similar to those in the US or Europe, it might arrive at that outcome by a new set of mechanisms. And the ultimate legitimacy of Asian market integration may correspondingly differ in character and intensity.

To set out our backdrop, we begin by sketching the relatively uncontroversial record of the legitimizing content of US market integration over time, and then point to debates over its driving mechanisms. Then we discuss the content and contested mechanisms of European market integration in considerably more detail.

Backdrop: Content and Mechanisms of US Market Integration[17]

A thumbnail sketch of the content of US market integration begins with a fragmented economy and the promising but ambiguous institutional framework of the Constitution. It starts to change as falling transaction costs facilitate greater integration on the ground, which engender politi-

Year Plan formalizes banking and company law, competition and bankruptcy policy. See Kahler (2000) for explanations of the move toward formalization.

[17] See Frost et al. (2002) for a more detailed treatment.

cal battles over regulation and jurisdiction. The early resolutions tend to favor big business and an untrammeled free market, but in the face of broad political pressure a variety of market-mitigating measures are constructed in the late 19th and early 20th centuries.

To be more specific, for much of the first half of the 19th century the US economy was poorly integrated. Rather than displaying broad and diffuse patterns of domestic exchange, economic activity was mostly either localized in fairly distinct regions or flowed through parallel networks to ports for export. Mountains, settlement gaps (empty geographical spaces bounded by 'the frontier'), and a lack of navigable rivers kept markets quite separate from each other.

Variation in state-level regulation further encouraged economic fragmentation. As a reaction to the pervasive trade disputes under the Articles of Confederation, the US Constitution had given the federal government broad power to regulate commerce. But it also authorized states to maintain distinct regulation for health, safety, or welfare reasons. Combined with a decentralized monetary system — the federal government had the sole legal authority to coin and regulate money, but no mandate for a single currency — the early American regulatory framework provided openings for an agenda of national market integration, but did not immediately challenge the fragmented status quo.

As the mid-century approached, however, slow change in economic and regulatory patterns began to accelerate. First the canals and then, even more strongly, the telecommunications and railroad booms, followed by internal migration, merged markets that had been local and regional. With improved technology and infrastructure came the growth of cross-frontier trade and 'national'[18] corporations now able to contemplate profitable sales and division of labor across a wider geographical scope. Firms began consolidating and 'competing in one another's back yards' with similar ('best-practice') production techniques and product arrays, whose prices gradually converged from region to region. Vertical integration, facilitated by refinements in best-practice corporate governance

---

[18] One could provocatively call them 'trans-national' with only a tiny rhetorical spin. The corporate form of governance blossomed during this era, for example, displacing less formal family ownership and partnerships.

made regions increasingly inter-dependent, as did the rationalization of national finance and insurance.

The basic facts about the regulatory and institutional responses to these American integration trends are familiar.[19] The chartering of national banks and banknotes after 1863 began to reduce monetary chaos — replacing the 8,000 or so state-chartered banks that had been issuing different notes as of 1860. Business actors mobilized to seek favorable regulation (or the lack of it) at the national level. In parallel, a growing 'social reform' movement emerged to seek national fixes for 'robber-baron' capitalism and corrupt machine politics. They were amply catalyzed by 'muckraking' journalists, pamphleteers ('mugwumps'), and novelists of the era.[20] Regulatory experiments at the state and local levels were quickly superseded by federal government counterparts, including the Interstate Commerce Act, the Sherman and Clayton antitrust acts, the Interstate Commerce Commission, and the Federal Trade Commission. Though initially symbolic because the Supreme Court limited their application and because American political institutions lacked any tradition of rational public administration,[21] the eventual result was a broad framework of regulatory laws and institutions. Waiting in the wings were ensuing re-distributive innovations in fiscal and social policies provoked by growing inequality of wealth, rural-urban dislocation, and immigration.

The broader political agenda attached to these economic regulations included pressure for direct primaries and election of Senators, women's suffrage, civil-service reform, and procedures for initiative, referendum and recall. There is little disagreement over the basic sequence of American market growth and reform in this period. There is considerable disagreement over the mechanisms that generated the story and their respective emphases and causal links.

One account emphasizes pluralism. American market integration generated broad resistance from elements of society that benefited only

---

[19] Civic and political institutions also were revolutionized in response to market integration. See Frost et al. (2002).

[20] Hofstadter (1955) and Wiebe (1967) are two classic and complementary accounts.

[21] See Bensel (2000) on the first, Skowronek (1982) on the second, and our further discussion of both in the 'mechanisms' sub-section below.

marginally or who actually seemed to lose — for example, farmers, squeezed between the late-1800s decline in agricultural prices and the rise in the price of credit and manufactured inputs. Open, flexible democracy enabled bargaining and policy responses that re-distributed these gains adequately enough to enlist the legitimate consent of most of the populace. Fogel (2000) and McGerr (2003), for examples, emphasize pluralistic mechanisms and the catalytic role of a radically-crusading, progressive-Christian middle class.

Bensel (2000), however, in treating the same historical content, emphasizes the primal importance of the post-Civil-War 'national' project — the construction of an economically prosperous yet legitimately democratic nation state. In Bensel's view, which combines our commercialist and developmentalist mechanisms, national market integration was first and foremost a *political* construction. The US Supreme Court and the business-backed Republican Party (that maintained the Court) were the political agents (the Presidency and the whole Executive Branch were still weak). Pro-business, pro-development internal transportation systems were enabled by land grants, sympathetic regulatory policies, and the hard-fought battle for a single, gold-based 'hard' currency. The Supreme Court was 'packed' with justices who vigilantly defended the rights of commercial firms to be treated the same as persons with respect to property rights and who struck down state regulatory challenges to unfettered markets on the constitutional grounds that the Federal Government controls inter-state commerce. Yet legitimacy could not be neglected in American democracy — parties (especially the Republicans) 'purchased' popular acquiescence (however fitfully) by raising tariffs against foreign manufactures, then irregularly re-distributing the tariff revenues as needed to win grudging acceptance. The tariffs maintained Northern support, and their re-distribution placated the South and West. In Bensel's account, the legitimacy of the national project to develop prosperous internal market integration was essentially bought from above, not born from below.[22]

[22] Skowronek (1982) and Cohen (2002), in treating the same history, emphasize the roles of other elites as well as business. Skowronek focuses on elite 'reformers' of the army, civil service, and early federal regulatory bureaucracy. Cohen (2002) focuses especially

The Content and Mechanisms of EU Market Integration

Market integration happened faster in some American sectors than in others (transportation, finance). The same has been true of Europe. The European Coal and Steel Community (ECSC), set up in 1952, amounted to a sectoral experiment in more institutionally centralized and substantively deeper market integration. The goal of full sectoral liberalization was supported by a social fund for payoffs to losers and a variety of other conditional safeguards, and embedded in an autonomous market regulator (the High Authority), a court, a political assembly, and an intergovernmental organ (the Council of Ministers). Competition (antitrust) law was the High Authority's key policy tool to integrate and rationalize these sectors.

As is familiar, the ECSC birthed an institutionally centralized, *multi*-sectoral experiment, also with well-developed mechanisms for adjudication and side-payments to losers. The largest continental economies extended the ECSC institutional framework into a general Common Market in the European Economic Community (EEC) in 1958. A court, assembly, and intergovernmental body again flanked an autonomous market regulator (now the European Commission) for which competition policy remained a key integrative tool.

To the social fund was added a promise, realized in the 1960s, for a much larger set of compensatory payoffs to farmers[23] (the Common Agricultural Policy, CAP). The other major development of the 1960s (though little recognized at the time) was judicial: the EEC's European Court of Justice declared itself supreme to national law, resolving (by unchallenged fiat) ambiguities in the EEC treaty. Within this framework the EEC achieved full customs union in the early 1970s. British accession encouraged still another set of payoffs to losers; since it received few CAP subsidies: EEC 'structural funds' would go largely to British deindustrialized areas. These funds were then greatly expanded with the

---

on elite liberal intellectuals who mediated the reconciliation of 'economic consolidation' and an 'active liberal state' – in our language 'who articulated the legitimization of national economic integration.' This way of describing late-19th and early 20th-century American history will have a close likeness to the 'institutional' account of European Union development, described below.

[23] Farmers were also the key societal group needing compensation in the 19th-century US.

accession of Greece, Spain, and Portugal in the 1980s, all of which insisted on adjustment money before opening themselves to single-market EEC competition.

The 1980s and 1990s brought the addition of monetary cooperation and later monetary union, much deeper market integration (now inclusive of many services), further extension of payoff mechanisms, and a strengthening of institutional rules and democratic accountability. Long-running attempts to mitigate intra-EEC exchange-rate fluctuation finally resulted in enduring cooperation after the European Monetary System (EMS) deal of 1979.[24] In the mid–1980s the EEC added an ambitious new 'Single Market 1992' agenda of elimination of non-tariff barriers, harmonization of standards, and capital liberalization — again to be policed by an aggressive competition policy. More majority voting in the Council of Ministers decreased the political obstacles to this push. A few short years later the member-states agreed on a schedule for monetary union (though with an 'opt-out' clause for the less enthusiastic members). With these massive integrative commitments the poorer members successfully demanded hugely increased payoffs in the Structural Funds, which doubled in 1988 and again in 1992. Richer actors insisted that monetary union be accompanied by significantly greater powers for the EEC assembly — now known as the European Parliament — a new 'social protocol' on working conditions, and stronger environmental standards.[25]

This basic 'content' changed little in the later 1990s. Negotiations over the accession of twelve mostly post-communist states seemed to threaten the EU payoff systems — the cost of extending the CAP and Structural Funds to the east looked prohibitive — but clever formulae were found to preserve the benefits to current members while offering

---

[24] Although it was not until 1983 that it was clear that the EMS would endure.

[25] Support for these additional elements varied across the larger, richer EU countries, however. The German government championed a stronger European Parliament and environmental policies as the key accompaniment to economic integration; the French government saw social-policy coordination as the most important flanking element; and the British saw neither monetary union itself nor any of these additional policies as necessary for market integration.

more modest subsidies to new members.[26] Mechanisms of majority voting among member-states and Parliamentary influence were slightly strengthened in the treaty modifications of 1997 and 2000 that readied the institutions for larger membership. Further-reaching reforms were envisioned in the 'constitution' proposal of 2003-2005, but they foundered in what have been widely interpreted as 'protest votes' by French and Dutch citizens who were as much disillusioned with their own national leaders and problems as with any aspect of the EU.

That today's deeply-integrated EU developed this content in this basic sequence of events is a matter of widely accepted historical record.

Why and how this framework appeared, however, is much more contested — and is critical to how we interpret the lessons of this story for legitimizing market integration, and to whether we find them relevant for Asia.

Just how did the EU's socio-political scaffolding around its single market appear?

The dominant view — what we call the pluralistic mechanism, and what its proponents call a 'liberal' account — is that this legitimizing scaffolding emerged from a set of pluralistic deals between those who stood to profit from market integration and those who stood to lose. Elaborate institutions were required to pay off the losers and to make credible such long-term commitments to openness and cooperation.[27] The most competitive farmers mobilized in similar ways to European business, but the preponderance of small, uncompetitive farming in Europe focused agricultural arrangements on protection at the EU's border and internal subsidies more than on true liberalization. The choice of the formally institutionalized, legally elaborate EEC framework, while important to signal the binding nature of its economic deals, was also partly dictated by the leverage of the least competitive actors — notably

[26] Structural Funds, for example, had previously been distributed according to a region's level of poverty relative to EU averages. This had resulted in Greece, Spain, Portugal, and Ireland receiving as much as 4 percent of their GDP annually from the EU. To cut down subsidies to the East while preserving the appearance of fairness, the Commission proposed that Structural Fund benefits be capped at 4 percent of any member's GDP — which in the much poorer East meant much smaller payments than the original formula.

[27] Moravcsik (1998); Milward (1992).

the French — who accepted liberalization only given multilateral mechanisms to craft strong and elaborate regulation, safeguards, and payoffs. The same pluralistic logic in a context of still-greater interdependence explains the concomitant moves to the deeper 'Single Market 1992' program in the 1980s and to the strengthening of institutional rules and payoffs.

At each step of this pluralistic account, deeper market integration acquired broad legitimacy by striking a balance between liberalization and measures mitigating its social effects. EU market integration derived its main legitimacy from the support of interest groups who cared about its policies. Of course, as Moravcsik argues (2002), this legitimacy depends to a certain degree on citizen disinterest in the EU's main technical responsibilities — but citizens are generally uninterested in detailed regulatory and monetary policy-making in all modern polities. If we factor in the disinterest of most citizens in many of the EU's main tasks, the overall pattern of the creation of the EU and its current workings look quite democratic.

This first view sees the EU institutional framework as the series of ancillary bargains that were politically necessary to satisfy interest-group demands, some for market integration, some to be better insulated from its effects — delivering side-payments and enhancing the credibility of policy cooperation.

A second, more commercialist, view sees the European institutional framework itself as a calculated mechanism to foment 'ever deeper' regional market integration, a mechanism propelled by Euro-societal interest groups, especially business. According to 'institutionalist' scholars in the tradition of Ernst Haas, these societal interests in regional integration were encouraged to develop by the channeling effects of early institutional innovations.[28] The choice for strongly institutionalized, legalized international frameworks in the ECSC and EEC treaties created a governance arena in which pro-integration business and other societal actors could step beyond their national-government guardians, connecting transnationally with like-minded actors to press for change in restrictive national rules. Even more important, the treaties created potentially pow-

[28] Haas (1958); Sandholtz and Stone-Sweet (1998).

erful 'supranational' allies for pro-integration actors: the executive European Commission and the European Court of Justice (ECJ). The Commission built coalitions of pro-integration groups to pressure national governments to facilitate integration and delegate more power to the European level; the ECJ asserted its own supremacy over national law and moved systematically to strike down national impediments to transnational exchange.

The effective result was an expanding alliance between supranational entrepreneurs and business actors to advance a fairly revolutionary agenda of national deregulation with some EU-wide 'reregulation.'[29] The Commission also allied strategically with certain market 'losers' where their demands could also result in transfers of power to the European level — most notably in agriculture.[30] Big business found it easier than other kinds of domestic actors to organize in effective transnational groups, such as the European Roundtable of Industrialists (ERT). In the episode that epitomizes this second, commercialist view of the mechanisms of EU integration, the ERT allied with Commission President Jacques Delors to champion the deregulatory '1992' agenda.[31]

This account emphasizes the lopsided shape of the EU project with respect to broad domestic interests and national democratic representation. In a new international arena about which grass-roots publics and even national governments were ill-informed, European political economy was commandeered by a coalition of business actors who championed 'Europe' out of genuine interest in free markets and supranational actors who championed free markets instrumentally — in the interest of increasing their own cosmopolitan authority.[32] Workers and their unions in particular were left out of what became a largely neo-liberal commercial project.[33]

In terms of legitimacy, this second view is more problematic than the first. While it too sees the EU project as founded on interest-group demands, the unintended consequences of institutional evolutions at its

---

[29] Majone (1994).
[30] Lindberg (1963); Lindberg and Scheingold (1970).
[31] Cowles (1994).
[32] Jabko (1999).
[33] Schmitter and Streeck (1993); Fligstein and McNichol (1998).

heart have advantaged certain domestic interests over others. To the extent that national leaders represent broadly the interests of domestic majorities, this emphasis on dynamics that increasingly escape national control suggests an impaired democratic process. Institutionalist analysts of the EU have thus tended to see a growing 'democratic deficit' in the integration process.[34] Much of the European population has participated little in the supranational-subnational project that ensued, outside of periodic ratification votes on new EU treaties.

This does not necessarily mean the EU is in danger of serious mobilization against its legitimacy. These scholars also see institution-building as so difficult to reverse that grass-roots populations and narrowly national actors tend to resign themselves to an institutional *fait accompli*, reorienting their strategies within the new framework. Furthermore, this school offers a deeper normative justification for the legitimacy of this integrative process. It claims (or implies) that many European citizens and national leaders did not fully learn the 20th-century lesson that narrowly national sovereignty leads to war, and so blocked a more direct and democratic-pluralistic route to integration. Only a more surreptitious, incremental, enlightened-elite process could carry Europeans to peace and prosperity in a regional union.[35]

In the second view, business and other elites were important as enablers and mediators, but not necessarily as catalysts (the metaphor of the third view of mechanisms). A third view of EU history goes much further in challenging the bottom-up portrayal of the EU as the product of pluralistic mechanisms for legitimizing market integration. In this view, the construction of the EU was led by a minority of national political elites who were ideologically committed to the development of supranational European institution-building.[36] Market integration was even more a by-product of a top-down political agenda than in the commercialist-institutionalist account. If growing structural interdependence oriented many postwar Europeans toward wider *market* integration, it did not spontaneously orient them toward the unusually strong European *institu-*

[34] Schmitter (2000); (Hix 1998).
[35] Monnet (1976).
[36] Parsons (2002, 2003).

tions that made unusually deep market integration possible. Only a top-down ideological crusade for the development of European institutions carried Europe to such profound integration.

The early 1950s saw a new debate over the appropriate institutional format for European cooperation. Elites' positions in this debate did not initially correspond to their positions in markets or their preferences for other policies. Scattered voices from right, left, and center called for a wide range of cooperative projects in a quasi-federal supranational format; others preferred to address the same policy problems through more standard multilateral cooperation without major delegations of national power. Still others in the same political groups insisted the cooperation was best pursued without any major European forum at all, through traditional bilateral relationships. Elections and coalition-building, however, continued to operate along other cleavages (largely right-left issues). Thus on the occasions when pro-supranational leaders gained national power, this was due to their support on other, cross-cutting issues. Though they were never elected with a mandate for supranational initiatives, their support on other issues gave them the autonomy to pursue that agenda.

This agenda of supranational institutional development then sometimes led these leaders to endorse deeper market integration as a vehicle to supranationality. Left-wing leaders like Guy Mollet (the French premier who championed the EEC treaty of 1957) or François Mitterrand (the French president who led the push to the SEA and EMU in the 1980s and 1990s) stood out from their socialist allies not in favoring freer markets, but in favoring more supranational institutions. They reluctantly accepted freer trade, deregulation, and eventually a monetarist single currency because these policies connected strongly to a federal-style institutional format. Institutional agendas also trumped substantive policy preferences in the other direction: many actors who championed free markets and monetarism ultimately argued for less substantive integration because they opposed supranationality (Margaret Thatcher, for example).[37]

[37] Thatcher led the shift to deregulation in the 1980s but strongly opposed any new treaty commitments in the Single European Act. Despite a strong commitment to monetarism,

This compromise was also forced on European business throughout the postwar period. Many business actors preferred freer trade and deregulation, but they generally opposed the creation of supranational institutions to manage that economic agenda. Yet to get the market prizes they really wanted, they were willing to learn to live with the unwelcome institutional costs that the supranational enthusiasts pressed on them.[38]

On this Euro-developmentalist view, then, the remarkable extent of market integration in the EU resulted from an elite project of political integration and centralization of authority. Economic integration was merely a convenient instrument for a Europe-wide state-building enterprise. Increasingly interdependent economies focused debates around economic integration, but even some of the most interdependent business actors did not see deep economic 'union' as the necessary response to simple interdependence (which was, after all, concurrently happening at the global level). Ultimately the debate was resolved in favor of a single market and currency only due to an institutional agenda that gained the support of key national leaders in addition to cosmopolitan elites.

This account connects even more poorly to norms of democratic legitimacy. European publics have never understood the major alternatives within these debates, making the EU 'the pure product of a modern form of enlightened despotism.'[39] At best, European publics granted certain leaders the autonomy — never the mandate — to push for supranational projects. The apparent legitimacy of today's EU thus reflects ex post consent to a *fait accompli* rather than genuine achievment of consensus, much less approval. Neither voters nor business really knew what choices were being made, and generally were not asked. Among the contrarian elites who opposed this construction of a massive new legal and institutional framework (Jacques Chirac being the most prominent to-

---

she rejected European monetary cooperation to the point of ending her career over internal British fights on joining the EMS. Thatcher (1993).

[38] Business also tended to be agnostic about the benefits of monetary cooperation and union. In France, though the French government led the push to EMU, business expressed no clear preference for or against a single currency . See De Boissieu and Pisani-Ferry (1998); Coutu (1993).

[39] Védrine (1996), 298.

day), most have today concluded that the costs of dismantling it would be prohibitive.

Lessons

The skeptical reader may still say that the American and postwar European histories are mostly context-specific, unsuitable for comparison with each other, without lessons beyond themselves, certainly not beyond 'the West,' and so on.[40] And the wise man might say that particularly with reference to the *mechanisms* of market integration, there is so much debate that lessons can hardly be drawn about either of these cases, let alone both of them.

We are not so skeptical or fatalistic. We grant the challenges of empirical complexity and academic disagreement, and they certainly encourage us to tread carefully. Yet in the *content* and basic sequence of integration-legitimizing we see substantial similarities. Even within *mechanisms*, we believe that an inclusive-middle-ground view that incorporates insights from each strand of scholarly argument can produce valuable observations.

We develop these contentions below. In the next section we discuss their implications for legitimizing internal and regional East Asian market integration.

Content Lessons

We see important principles, institutions, and regulatory protocols in the EU's history (and the US's also) that suggest the core content of an agenda for socially-embedded, legitimate market integration.

Relative political centralization. At the broadest level, both the US and the EU created substantial union-level institutions with mandates and some resources independent from the constituent units. This may seem a thin parallel — the considerable differences between the two institutional frameworks are noted below — but it is a fundamental one: among large

---

[40] Wallace (1994), Ch. 2 passim, for example, who emphasizes the 'particularities' of EU experience.

regional markets, the US and EU stand out for the early creation of relatively substantial administrative *centers*.

Hierarchies of law, with central judicial jurisdiction. Early in their market-building process both created formally independent union-level courts with the power of final adjudication. This observation too needs qualification, since both in the US and the EU the final supremacy of union-level courts was actually ambiguous in the original institutional arrangements. The courts themselves had to make rulings that clarified their own power, and other actors had to accept those rulings. But relative to other regions, the US and the EU stand out for the early establishment of powerful federal courts that then defended (and sometimes aggressively pushed) market integration.

Centralized market facilitation institutions. From the outset, both the US and the EU made central competition (antitrust) institutions foundational to union-level pressure for rationalization of unit-level policies. Rather than disputing the merits of unit-level policies, centralized representatives and courts simply addressed whether or not they formed a barrier to cross-border competition within and among members. Likewise both adopted increasingly strong union-wide standards-setting institutions — explicit procedures for setting threshold standards for products, production standards, intellectual (and other) property, and labor relations. Both applied mutual recognition principles for threshold product standards across members. Regulatory centralization was, however, softened by leaving services and professional standards to unit-level differentiation.

Subsidiarity. Both elaborated principles of 'subsidiarity' between union-wide and local regulation (and politics), with responsibilities left to the unit level that were not explicitly given to the union. This was formal in the US constitution; the foundation of the EU in diplomatic treaties arguably made such a formal statement unnecessary (since it was obvious that anything not delegated to the EU remained with the member-states), but the Maastricht Treaty formalized this rule to eliminate all doubt.

Border non-discrimination. Both the US and the EU made clear and formal commitments to internal single markets in their founding documents, and located ultimate authority over single-market issues at the union level. Single markets imply that all policies apply even-handedly to unit-level suppliers and demanders from any member unit. In both cases this original commitment was softened by the retention of unit-level rights in health, safety, culture, welfare, and some services, leaving it to courts to adjudicate between these 'exceptions' and market-building at the union level.

Explicit membership. Both formalized membership in the union through explicit accession procedures at the unit level and internal and external migration law at the level of individuals.

Common external commercial policy. Both made commercial policy toward non-members a union-level responsibility early on. This is particularly striking because it would seem to limit either the legitimacy or the integration momentum of currently popular regional free trade agreements (i.e., those without common external policies). As the histories suggest, such common external border policies helped redistribute the gains from market integration *within* the members in a legitimacy-enhancing way.

Symbolic fiscal redistribution? Both the EU and the US adopted systems of geographically-redistributive transfers relatively early in the single-market process, but achieved major market integration without large-scale fiscal redistribution (in excess of 0.5 percent of GDP). Substantial redistributive policies only developed well after most of US market integration was accomplished, and have yet to develop in the EU.

Single Currency? Both only adopted a single currency only after their earliest push towards market integration and after market-facilitation and judicial-centralization devices were in place. Still, more centralized monetary systems clearly consolidated and extended market integration in both cases. Much market integration can occur without a single currency, but it seems to contribute strongly to later-phase deepening and stability.

We appreciate that there are also enormous differences in the principles and institutions by which the EU and US 'embedded' their single markets; indeed we discuss them in some detail elsewhere (Frost et al. 2002). These 'instructive differences' nevertheless imply the 'lesson' that even when the final destination is similar, there are multiple *routes* to legitimate market integration, routes that depend on the challenges and pressures faced by the integrating units. The US case proceeded from much more promising pre-conditions (stronger initial central institutions, stronger cultural affinities and shared identity, a Zeitgeist of classical liberalism, and primitive pre-existing unit-level institutional and regulatory barriers), and built a market without much pressure from global forces to do so. The EU single-market project confronted much more significant obstacles on all these scores, but was encouraged to tackle them by much stronger global pressures and by the imitative power of the American example. It also circumvented some important obstacles with the innovation of a 'regulatory state' model that allowed for minimal organizational change in elaborate national administrations.

Overall, despite differences, we think the US and EU cases sketch a fairly robust common profile for the regulatory-institutional frameworks in which successful market integration can be politically sustained.[41]

Mechanisms Lessons

Drawing lessons about the *mechanisms* by which market integration became legitimized is considerably more complex than pointing out parallels in the content of the ultimate legitimizing scaffold. But if we take a very pragmatic, middle-ground position — converging on a view that accepts basic insights from all three prominent accounts of historical mechanisms — we find that lessons begin to emerge. Given the incentives to hyperbole in academic debates, such a middle-ground view has the additional virtue of probably being correct.

To the extent that we do attribute some plausibility to the more top-down, non-pluralistic mechanisms to legitimate integration, however, our lessons should not simply focus on what 'worked' in the long run. These top-down mechanisms generate at least some conflict between our basic normative stance in favor of market integration and our distinct prefer-

[41] Other comparisons of US and EU histories ask different and broader questions, e.g., about how the US and EU developed as *polities* overall. In these comparisons, there may be fewer commonalities. Alberta Sbragia, for example, goes so far as to suggest that the EU formed in a 'mirror image' process from the US or other federations, with the latter centralizing sovereignty in foreign affairs and then gradually developing internal authority. See Sbragia (2002); Egan (forthcoming).

ence for democratic processes. No matter what the long-term economic and political success of a market integration project, it is problematic to endorse as a 'lesson' a mechanism that reaches that outcome through undemocratic processes, or that only develops legitimacy through manipulated consensus and widespread resignation to fait accompli. We would not want to advise other regions to ignore or minimally placate their populations.

That said, our belief in the positive benefits of market integration (when properly embedded) justifies in some cases the partial insulation of policy processes from broad democratic input. Thus our 'inclusive middle ground' view of the mechanisms tries to emphasize first those steps that look most likely to attract broad democratic support, but we also note that certain aspects of market-building seem to proceed best (and can justifiably proceed) with some top-down leadership and insulation.

One thing that makes this task slightly easier is that we think EU and US historical experience reduces the uncertainties of future single-market legitimization. Pursuing market integration in a world where the US and EU have already succeeded is different from doing so prior to these pioneering cases. Much of the historical opposition to market arrangements derived from their uncertainties, or from exaggerated claims about their likely negative consequences. Now that the US and the EU markets have been largely successful, they have solidified their own support internally, and other regions that have them as models may face less uncertainty (or may at least believe that they face less uncertainty). In other words, even if certain elements of market integration emerged in partly undemocratic (or a-democratic) ways in the US and/or the EU, similar arrangements may be feasible democratically today. In our view some commentaries have exaggerated how much the failure of the EU constitution changes this situation.[42] The existing EU architecture is not in danger of major revision, and especially in international perspective it is still perceived as a remarkable success story.

---

[42] For example, see 'EU Lessons for East Asian Regionalism,' *Japan Times*, June 25, 2005.

We present these lessons in two groups, corresponding to our most democratic and less democratic legitimizing mechanisms.

Lessons from the pluralistic/bottom-up view of legitimizing mechanisms
Sectoral experimentation is often an acceptable beginning. When market integration on the ground begins in piecemeal, sectoral ways, it is often more palatable to broad publics. The most natural candidate sectors are those with relatively high and rising intrasectoral interdependence because market integration projects in those sectors are most visibly promising.[43]

Some strategic protectionism may bind special interests together in democratic coalitions that in turn advance liberalization overall. Advancing market integration across many sectors may require effectively anti-market regional arrangements in other sectors. That seems to be the core of the argument for the EU's historical agricultural protectionism and for the high American manufactures tariffs in the 19th century.

Integration proceeds best in sectors or economies with relatively evenly-distributed bargaining power. Where one central actor is much more powerful than others — or sometimes much weaker, as French business was perceived in the 1950s — it can dictate the terms. Sometimes such asymmetries deter less powerful actors from agreeing to integrative deals at all; this risk was apparent in small-state/large-state debates over early US federalism, and in consistent European fears of a German-dominated EU. Asymmetrical situations are likely to reach successful bargaining outcomes only when extended to multiple issues that allow for trade-offs across arenas with different power dynamics.

---

[43] Sub-national experimentation through the sequential identification of 'Special Economic Zones' for integration has many of the same advantages as sectoral experimentation, though it was not a part of either the American or European experience.

Lessons from the commercialist-developmentalist and institutional-elitist views of legitimizing mechanisms
Institutional isolation can help. The creation of union-level institutional actors with some independent resources and decision-making ability can lead to the generation of integrative ideas, entrepreneurial leadership, and potentially new coalitions in favor of integration down the line.

Independent courts are key. Union-level courts are probably the single most important institutional feature of a market-integration project. They create an arena which attracts and privileges the interests of actors who prefer more market integration, and mechanisms by which these actors can move forward without a great deal of political attention. To the extent that they do attract political attention, they can often make bold decisions that are protected from opposition by the legitimacy of law (which has separate bases from the legitimacy of public participation and endorsement).[44]

Support for market integration depends on *embeddedness and vision.* Market projects advance best with ideological justifications that can appeal to many causes. Both US and EU leaders effectively hooked technical steps of market integration to larger (and less redistributively-divisive) debates or projects about identity, security, effectiveness in the world, and moral righteousness.

Support for market integration can also be built *indirectly*. Market projects are likely to work best where market-building leaders build solid support on other issues. Leaders who can be maintained in office due to coalitional support for *other* agendas are best able to make the redistributively-difficult commitments market-building may require. Taken together with the preceding point, this amounts to the advice that leaders make market integration part of a much broader political program.

Applying the Lessons to Asia?

In the large and growing literature on Asian regionalism and integration, the notion of potential lessons from the EU experience (if not from the American one) is a common refrain. Many economists have also argued

[44] Burley and Mattli (1993).

that at least some of the foundations for strong regional integration are present in East Asia. Michael Plummer and Jeffrey Frankel have documented the rapid growth in intraregional Asian trade in the past several decades, as well as a trade bias toward an increasing intraregional orientation.[45] John Williamson argues that China, Hong Kong, Indonesia, Korea, Malaysia, the Philippines, Singapore, Taiwan, and Thailand are 'a natural monetary grouping like the EMS countries are widely agreed to be.'[46] In terms of broader social foundations, Manoranjan Dutta suggests 'The pan-Asian culture and civilization is as real as the concept of pan-European culture and civilization.'[47] Several recent articles offer well-elaborated calls for further development of ASEAN, APEC, SAARC, or other groupings toward a longer-term 'Asian Economic Community' or 'Asian Union,' replete with references to the EU model.[48] Many observers also note the Japanese shift in recent years from regional skepticism to leadership in ASEAN and other regional formats. Coupled with increasing openness from Beijing, some experts hint, leadership for more substantial Asian integration might materialize in coming decades.

But we argue here that Asian market integration will be quite ordinary without more formal, institutionalized judicial and regulatory supports — the main theme of this article. Others seem to agree.[49] For example, Henning observes that though the Chiang Mai Initiative (CMI) of May 2000 for currency swaps and other financial cooperation in the 'ASEAN +3' format is a promising step, it only brings cooperation to a level that was 'a common feature of international financial relations in the last half of the twentieth century' more broadly.[50] Eichengreen and Bayoumi observe that relative to Western Europe, Asian economies are

---

[45] Plummer (2003); Frankel (1997).

[46] Williamson (1996).

[47] Dutta (2002).

[48] Khan and Khan (2003); Dutta (2002).

[49] Plummer points out, 'Asian regional integration over this [recent] period is unique in a global context as it is driven almost exclusively through informal, market-led initiatives, rather than policy initiatives through preferential-trading arrangements,' but goes on to note that 'While intra-regional *trade* has been increasing, there is no evidence that intra-regional *financial* transactions have risen, at a time when finance has been shown to be the Achilles' Heel of regional development.' Plummer (2003), 267.

[50] See Henning (2002).

more heterogeneous in basic structural conditions, vary considerably in levels of openness and regulation, and follow potentially divergent exchange-rate strategies.[51]

Some commentators are even more pessimistic about the prospects for Asian regionalism, and for the applicability of EU lessons to it. Peter Katzenstein is representative in noting that, '[T]he history of formal regional institutions in Asia is a history of failures so conspicuous, in comparison to Europe, that they beg for explanation.'[52] He argues that while World War II oriented some Europeans toward 'supranational' integration projects, 'National liberation struggles, the heady experience of a new-found sovereignty, and the overwhelming domestic pressures that poor, nonindustrialized societies and economies put on weak state institutions made international integration an implausible political option in Asia,'[53] and led Asian nations to favor looser, more ethnically-based ties and to dislike formal institutions. American alliance and economic policies in Asia, unlike those in Europe, further oriented the region toward bilateralism rather than multilateralism.[54] Even without American meddling, the existence of two radically different powers in Asia (Japan and China) seems a particularly unfavorable constellation for regional projects.[55] Katzenstein sums up the pessimists' case: 'International power and norms as well as domestic state structures mitigate against the creation of a closed form of Asian regionalism under either Japanese or Chinese leadership. Conditions favor instead an open Asian regionalism. Its economic form will be network-like. Its political shape will be multicephalic. And its political definition will remain contested.'[56]

Such a conclusion is probably inevitable if we ask what kind or degree of economic integration is most *likely* in Asia. To this question we

[51] Eichengreen and Bayoumi (1996); Robert Mundell (2003, 5) suggests that monetary cooperation in Asia will be more difficult than in Europe in the 1970s because 'the institutional, economic, and political groundwork had already been laid in Europe, whereas very little exists at the present time in Asia.'
[52] Katzenstein (1997), 3. See also Rozman (2004).
[53] Katzenstein (1997), 21.
[54] For an implicit contrast see Weber (1992).
[55] For largely negative assessments see Cowhey (1995); Higgott (1995); Dent and Huang (2002).
[56] Katzenstein (1997), 41; see also Katzenstein (forthcoming).

would give the same basic answer offered in most of the literature: the most likely kind of integration in Asia is 'open' or 'soft' integration that relies largely on informal interaction and ethnic networks.

But in contrast to some who endorse an informal path to intensive co-operation and integration, we claim that such integration would be undistinguished in its economic benefits and limited in its momentum.[57] It would reach a mild plateau and stagnate. Looking at the array of European and American supports that appear to have given broad legitimacy to deep market integration in the long run (whatever the immediate mechanisms that set them up), we fear that 'open' or 'soft' Asian regionalism is *not* truly an alternative path to the same beneficial outcomes. Informal, ethnic-network integration may be able to create wealth — the record of Japanese production networks and the Greater Chinese diaspora is hard to deny — but is likely to do so in the most politically and socially conservative of ways, without explicit political decision-making that can be accountable, without many cohesive market-mitigating policies, and with a tendency to inequality unlimited by any potential for redistribution. This in turn will limit the substantive degree of economic integration in the long run, both because central institutions *facilitate* deep market-building in functional terms and because the lack of such institutions leaves socio-political tensions unresolved.

But our aspiration is not to evaluate the likelihood of Asian reproduction of US or EU models of market integration. We want to consider whether lessons from those Atlantic models may be relevant to an alternative Asia. Asking that looser question — *might* Asia be able to imitate substantial elements of the US or EU experiences? — admits the possibility of some positive lessons.

We would not want to call Asian imitation of the EU likely, but in 1950 it would not have been very reasonable to call today's EU a likely outcome. The potential for meaningful parallels is strengthened notably by the 'commercialist' and 'developmentalist' mechanisms that we have highlighted in EU and US history, acknowledgement of which is the major novelty of this article relative to the rest of the literature on comparative regionalism. These more top-down accounts have more than a little

[57] For carefully optimistic claims about informal regionalization, see Pempel (2005).

Asian resonance. They suggest to varying degrees that neither western Europe nor the United States initially had much spontaneous, 'bottom-up' pressure for a major continental market-building project. Elite initiative and institutional insulation from politics circumvented or overcame broad resistance and major obstacles. We do not contest the basic gist of the literature on comparative regionalism — that by most measures, obstacles are larger and more numerous in Asia than we can see in any reasonable interpretation of American or European history. We simply claim that institutional projects can start small and have major effects, and that committed leadership can push through remarkable changes.

Learning and diffusion from varied regional cases further encourages this qualified optimism. One of the instructive *differences* between the US and EU cases is that the US pioneered new ground, while the EU had the immensely successful US model as an inspiration (and as an actor giving substantive encouragement and support). We suggested that this is one reason why the EU reached deep regional market integration despite confronting more substantial obstacles than did the US. This special issue itself shows why it is reasonable to think that the same logic will apply even more strongly to Asia: many Asian actors today are explicitly looking to the EU as a model. The EU is also reaching out as an actor to advance this process, as is the US in some ways.[58]

Our ironic conclusion, then, is that by paying attention to accounts that see EU and US market integration as more contested and difficult, we arrive at somewhat greater optimism about the long-term potential for broadly-supported, legitimate market integration in Asia. The path to such an outcome seems unlikely to follow from an open, inclusive, bottom-up set of bargains; nor will it be the spontaneous instinct of most actors in Asia today (or tomorrow). Yet we see good reasons to think that it was neither as inclusive nor as spontaneous in the EU and US as the common wisdom on these cases suggests. Strangely enough, strong leadership informed by the *real* EU and US models, rather than their myths, could eventually have the *effect* of installing an Asian facsimile of pluralistic, rule-bound, democratic-capitalist polities.

---

[58] Yeo (2003); Gilson (2002).

References

Bensel, Richard F. 2000. *The Political Economy of American Industrialization, 1877–1900.* New York: Cambridge University Press.

Bergsten, C. Fred and Inbom Choi. 2003. *The Korean Diaspora in the World Economy.* Washington, D.C.: Institute for International Economics.

Bergsten, C. Fred and Yung Chul Park. 2002. 'Toward Creating a Regional Monetary Agreement in East Asia.' Asian Development Bank Institute Research Paper No. 50, December.

Burley, Anne–Marie and Walter Mattli. 1993. 'Europe Before the Court: A Political Theory of Legal Integration,' *International Organization* 47:1, 41–76.

Cohen, Nancy. 2002. *The Reconstruction of American Liberalism, 1865–1914.* Chapel Hill, North Carolina: University of North Carolina Press.

Coutu, Diane. 1993. 'Views of the Business Community on Post–1992 Integration in Europe,' in Alexis Jacquemin and David Wright, eds., *The European Challenge Post–1992.* New York: Cambridge University Press, 47–80.

Cowhey, Peter. 1995. 'Pacific Trade Relations after the Cold War: GATT, NAFTA, ASEAN and APEC,' in Peter Gourevitch, Takashi Inoguchi, and Courtney Purrington, eds., *United States–Japan Relations and International Institutions after the Cold War.* San Diego: UCSD, 184–220.

Cowles, Maria Green. 1994. *The Politics of Big Business in the European Community.* Unpublished dissertation, Government, American University.

De Boissieu, Christian and Jean Pisani–Ferry. 1998. 'The Political Economy of French Economic Policy in the Perspective of EMU,' in Barry Eichengreen and Jeffry Frieden, eds., *Forging an Integrated Europe.* Ann Arbor: University of Michigan Press, 49–90.

Dent, Christopher and David Huang, eds. 2002. *Northeast Asian Regionalism: Learning from the European Experience.* New York: Routledge.

Dutta, Manoranjan. 2002. 'Asian Economic Community: Intra-community Macro and Microeconomic Parameters,' *Journal of Asian Economics* 13:4, 447–491.

Egan, Michelle. Forthcoming. *Single Markets: Economic Integration in Europe and America.* Manuscript. Incomplete draft.

Eichengreen, Barry and Tamim Bayoumi. 1996. 'Is Asia an Optimum Currency Area? Can It Become One? Regional, Global, and Historical Perspectives on Asian Monetary Relations.' Paper presented to a conference on 'Exchange Rate Policies in Emerging Asian Countries: Domestic and International Aspect,' 15–16 November.

Fligstein, Neil and Jason McNichol. 1998. 'The Institutional Terrain of the European Union,' in Wayne Sandholtz and Alec Stone–Sweet, eds., *European Integration and Supranational Governance.* New York: Oxford University Press, 59–91.

Fogel, Robert. 2000. *The Fourth Great Awakening & The Future of Egalitarianism.* Chicago: University of Chicago Press.

Frankel, Jeffrey. 1997. *Regional Trading Agreements in the World Economic System.* Washington, DC: Institute for International Economics.

Frost, Ellen L., Craig Parsons, J. David Richardson, and Michael Schneider. 2002. 'Lessons for a Globalizing World: European and U.S. Experiences in Market Integration,' Manuscript, December.

Gilson, Julie, ed. 2002. *Asia Meets Europe.* London: Edward Elgar.

Haas, Ernst. 1958. *The Uniting of Europe: Political, Social, and Economic Forces, 1950–1957.* Stanford: Stanford University Press.

Henning, C. Randall. 2002. *East Asian Financial Cooperation Policy*, Analyses in International Economics No. 68. Washington D.C.: Institute for International Economics.

Higgott, Richard. 1995. 'Economic cooperation in the Asia–Pacific: a theoretical comparison with the European Union,' *Journal of European Public Policy* 2:3, 361–383.

Hix, Simon. 1998. 'Elections, Parties, and Institutional Design: A Comparative Perspective on European Union Democracy,' *West European Politics* 21:3, 19–52.

Hofstadter, Richard. 1955. *The Age of Reform: From Bryan to F.D.R.* New York: Random House (Vintage Books).

Jabko, Nicolas. 1999. 'In the Name of the Market: How the European Commission Paved the Way for Monetary Union,' *Journal of European Public Policy* 6:3, 475–498.

Kahler, Miles. 2000. 'Legalization as Strategy: The Asia–Pacific Case,' *International Organization* 54: Summer, 549–571.

Katzenstein, Peter. 1997. 'Introduction: Asian Regionalism in Comparative Perspective,' in Peter Katzenstein and Takashi Shiraishi, eds., *Network Power: Japan and Asia.* Ithaca: Cornell University Press, 1–46.

Katzenstein, Peter and Takashi Shiraishi, eds. Forthcoming. *Beyond Japan: East Asian Regionalism.* Ithaca, NY: Cornell University Press.

Khan, Saleem and Zahira Khan. 2003. 'Asian Economic Integration: A Perspective on South Asia,' *Journal of Asian Economics* 13:6, 767–785.

Lindberg, Leon. 1963. *The Political Dynamics of European Economic Integration.* Stanford, CA: Stanford University Press.

Lindberg, Leon and Stuart Scheingold. 1970. *Europe's Would-Be Polity.* Englewood Cliffs, NJ: Prentice–Hall.

Lloyd, Peter J. and Hyun–Hoon Lee. 2001. 'Subregionalism in East Asia and Its Relationship With APEC,' *The Journal of the Korean Economy* 2: Fall, 211–227.

Majone, Gianomenico. 1994. 'The rise of the regulatory state in Europe,' *West European Politics* 17:3, 77–102.

McGerr, Michael. 2003. *A Fierce Discontent: The Rise and Fall of the Progressive Movement in America, 1870–1920.* New York: Free Press.

Milward, Alan. 1992. *The European Rescue of the Nation–State.* Berkeley: University of California Press.

Monnet, Jean. 1976. *Mémoires.* Paris: Fayard.

Moravcsik, Andrew. 1998. *The Choice for Europe: Social Purpose and State Power from Messina to Maastricht*. Ithaca, NY: Cornell University Press.

Mundell, Robert. 2003. 'Prospects for an Asian Currency Area,' *Journal of Asian Economics* 14, 1–10.

Nicolaidis, Kalypso and Robert Howse. 2001. *The Federal Vision: Legitimacy and Levels of Governance in the US and the EU*. Oxford: Oxford University Press.

Parsons, Craig. 2002. 'Showing Ideas as Causes: The Origins of the European Union,' *International Organization* 56:1, 47–84.

Parsons, Craig. 2003. *A Certain Idea of Europe*. Ithaca, NY: Cornell University Press.

Pempel, T.J., ed. 2005. *Remapping East Asia: The Construction of a Region*. Ithaca, NY: Cornell University Press.

Plummer, Michael. 2003. 'Structural Change in a Globalized Asia: Macro Trends and US Policy Challenges,' *Journal of Asian Economics* 14, 243–281.

Polanyi, Karl. 1944. *The Great Transformation*. Boston: Beacon.

Rauch, James E. and Vitor Trindade. 2002. 'Ethnic Chinese Networks in International Trade,' *Review of Economics and Statistics* 84:1, 116–130.

Rozman, Gilbert. 2004. *Northeast Asia's Stunted Regionalism*. New York: Cambridge University Press.

Sandholtz, Wayne and Alec Stone–Sweet, eds. 1998. *European Integration and Supranational Governance*. New York: Oxford University Press.

Schmitter, Philippe. 2000. *How to Democratize the European Union...And Why Bother?* Lanham, MD: Rowan & Littlefield.

Schmitter, Philippe and Wolfgang Streeck. 1991. 'From national corporatism to transnational pluralism: organized interests in the single European,' *Politics and Society* 19:2, 133–164.

Scollay, Robert and John P. Gilbert. 2001. *New Regional Trading Arrangements in the Asia Pacific?* Washington, D.C.: Institute for International Economics.

Skowronek, Stephen. 1982. *Building a New American State*. New York: Cambridge University Press.

Spragia, Alberta M. 2002. 'The European Union, Federations, and Sovreignty: The EU as a 'Mirror Image' of Traditional Federations,' Manuscript.

Thatcher, Margaret. 1993. *Downing Street Years*. New York: Harper Collins.

Védrine, Hubert. 1996. *Les mondes de François Mitterrand*. Paris: Seuil.

Venables, Anthony J. and L. Alan Winters. 2002. 'Economic Integration in the Americas: European Perspectives,' Manuscript, 27 May.

Wallace, William. 1994. *Regional Integration: The West European Experience*. Washington, D.C.: The Brookings Institution.

Weber, Steven. 1992. 'Shaping the Postwar Balance of Power: Multilateralism in NATO,' *International Organization* 46:3, 633–681.

Wiebe, Robert H. 1967. *The Search for Order: 1877–1920*. New York: Farrar, Strauss, and Giroux (Hill and Wang).

Williamson, John. 1996. 'The Case for a Common Basket Peg for East Asian Currencies.' Paper presented to a conference on 'Exchange Rate Policies in Emerging Asian Countries: Domestic and International Aspects,' Association for the Monetary Union of Europe and the Korea Institute of Finance, 15–16 November.

World Bank. 2005. *Global Economic Prospects 2005: Trade, Regionalism, and Development.* Washington, D.C.

Yeo, Lay Hwee. 2003. *Asia and Europe: The Development and Different Dimensions of ASEM.* New York: Routledge.

Yusuf, Shahid, *et al.* 2003. *Innovative East Asia: The Future of Growth.* Washington, D.C. and New York: World Bank and Oxford University Press.

INDEX